A VISION FOR EUROPE

A VISION
FOR EUROPE
2020
NOTHING BUT AN ALTERNATIVE

Foreword by Yanis Varoufakis
Edited by David Adler & Rosemary Bechler

ERIS

An imprint of Urtext
Unit 1 53 Beacon Road
London SE13 6ED

First published in paperback by Eris 2019
The collection © Eris 2019
Individual contributions © the contributors 2019
This second edition published in paperback by Eris 2020
The collection © Eris 2020
Individual contributions © the contributors 2020

Printed and bound in Great Britain
Typeset by Hewer Text UK Ltd, Edinburgh

ISBN 978-1912475-285

British Library Cataloguing in Publication Data
A catalogue record for this book is available from the British Library

eris.press

Contents

Foreword

Yanis Varoufakis

A year is a long time in politics but would, ordinarily, be too short a time to make a difference to our vision for the future. Alas, last year was no ordinary year. By ensuring that the future no longer is what it used to be, the last twelve months made necessary a revised *Vision for Europe*. You are now, dear reader, holding the result.

In the May 2019 European Parliament elections, our *Green New Deal for Europe*, the Manifesto based on our *Vision for Europe*, was comprehensively trounced. Even though DiEM25 and our *European Spring* allies managed to gather one and a half million votes, we failed to elect a single MEP. Judging by that sorry result, some might plausibly say that our *Vision for Europe* sank like a lead balloon, at least electorally.

One explanation for our electoral failure is, indeed, this: our analysis and policies were poor or at odds with Europe's electorates. However, there is a second explanation. Even though many Europeans are ready to adopt DiEM25's analysis and to support our policy agenda, Europe's politics reproduce the dominance of unpopular institutions and the power of their functionaries. Judging by the evolution of conventional wisdom, especially among younger Europeans, this second explanation seems quite plausible. Indeed, since our electoral defeat in Germany, France etc., both the analysis in the first *Vision for Europe* and the policies in DiEM25's *Green New Deal for Europe* have gained incredible traction.

This paradox lies at the heart of Europe's disintegration—a process that began in 2010 with the euro crisis, accelerated in 2015 with the crushing of the Greek Spring, gathered pace with Brexit's triumphs in 2016 and 2019, and was turbocharged in 2020 by Covid-19 and the European Union's pathetic response to the pandemic. The structure of the paradox is easy to dissect.

On the one hand, there is the widespread consensus that the European Union's monetary and economic union is not merely flawed but the source of unnecessary recessions, environmental degradation, and avoidable pain for a majority of Europeans. On the other hand, Europe's politics guarantee that this consensus is paid lip service by the dominant political forces while being kept brutally and ruthlessly away from Europe's decision-making centres.

DiEM25's Manifesto, our *Green New Deal for Europe* and, yes, the first edition of *A Vision for Europe* acknowledged this paradox, as well as its capacity to undermine the European Union and progressive, radical Europeanism more broadly. However, I believe now that our language, our texts and the way we phrased our campaign speeches were far too timid. It was simply not enough to say "Europe will either be democratised or it will disintegrate". Although correct as a prediction, our political campaign needed something more powerful than a prediction: it needed a more radical statement of what was happening and what we should be about.

What we are *really* up against

Re-reading *A Vision for Europe*, I realised that it was missing something crucial: a class analysis of the true reasons why Europe's establishment is turning down sensible, moderate policies and institutional changes that would be mutually advantageous across Europe.

If I am right that DiEM25's *Green New Deal for Europe*, including its smart public debt and investment-financing technical proposals, would lift all boats at once (German and Italian, Dutch and Greek), why were the German and Dutch governments so hostile to the idea?

A Vision for Europe did not answer the question, leaving it to the reader mistakenly to think that either we are wrong or that the political agents of the northern establishment are inane. Neither is true. Our analysis is correct *and* the northern establishment is pursuing its self-interest smartly. Can it be so? How?

The events of 2020 settled this question. It is clear now that even the most hard-nosed fiscal conservative living in Northern Europe can see that, in the face of a gigantic recession caused by the pandemic, leaving each member state to fend for itself will lead, sooner or later, to the euro's disintegration. They are certainly smart enough to recognise that, given Italy's state of affairs, forcing Rome to borrow billions at a time of collapsing national incomes will lead to default and exit from the eurozone with a very high probability. Or, that it will, alternatively, cause such a depression that a neofascist government will rise up to do what the recession failed to: bring on a fatal clash between Rome and Brussels.

But, if I am right, why has the EU establishment killed off the only alternative to crippling increases in national debt, i.e. Eurobonds? Why has it ignored DiEM25's technically astute proposal for a European Central Bank bond issue, an ECB-bond, of thirty-years maturity by which to raise €1 trillion in order to absorb the catastrophic rise in national debt that will, inevitably, cause Italy's default, then Spain's, eventually France's, etc.?

Given that the establishment running the EU knows full well that Italy and the rest of Europe's South are great contributors to the surpluses of the North (by keeping down their exchange rate and the interest rates of their Treasuries below zero), why are they taking great risks with the euro's disintegration? Why are they not using the pandemic as an opportunity to solidify the North's advantages from

Europe's monetary union by embracing DiEM25's proposals both for an ECB-bond and a large pan-European investment drive financed by an alliance of the European Investment Bank (EIB) and the ECB? Who would benefit more from such an investment program than, say, Siemens and Volkswagen?

The answer that the first edition of *A Vision for Europe* lacked begins with a realisation. Yes, the politicians representing the oligarchy-without-frontiers recognise all of the above as well as you and I, dear reader. But they also see something that most progressives don't: that the architecture of the eurozone is unique in the history of capitalism in the way it has empowered the oligarchy that those politicians represent.

Having created a gargantuan central bank without a state to control or to support it, nineteen states (those using the euro) have been left without a central bank to support them directly. Once bereft of the power to control money and interest rates, soon these states hit the limits of their spending. Once on the fiscal ropes, no government, regardless of its political and ideological colours, can do much in the sphere of income and wealth redistribution.

Having removed control of money and interest rates from the states, the designers of the eurozone did something that had never been accomplished before: they robbed every democratically elected Prime Minister or President of the instruments with which to transfer significant amounts of wealth from the rich to the poor who constitute the majority—or, in Aristotle's definition, the demos. In short, they surreptitiously took the demos out of European Democracy. Whether they did this intentionally or not is irrelevant.

The fact that matters is that, with the creation of the euro, democratically elected governments could no longer shift large quantities of value from the oligarchy to the majority. Future economic historians will surely mark this as a momentous development.

Compare and contrast the German Chancellor with the Prime Minister of the UK. Even though Germany is far richer, its trade surplus is enormous, and the country is better run than the UK, the German Chancellor, even if she wanted to, could not shift large amounts of income and wealth from rich to poor Germans. Why? Because she is constrained not to run large deficits and has no control of the central bank. In contrast, the UK's Prime Minister, backed by the Bank of England, can run large deficits in pursuit of public investment or even simply transfer large amounts of wealth to poorer residents, e.g. in Northern England.

We are now ready to see what we are up against. Yes, the EU oligarchy can see that the implementation of our *Green New Deal for Europe* would do wonders to end the euro crisis that began in 2009 and which turned ballistic, courtesy of Covid-19, in 2020. It can see as well as you and I that its profits would rise, not fall, as a result. However, it also realises that DiEM25's policy proposals usher in new instruments, like ECB-bonds and a Green Investment Fund empowered by an EIB-ECB alliance.

These new instruments will, surreptitiously, re-enable elected politicians in Germany, in France, in Italy, etc. to re-distribute large chunks of income and wealth from the European oligarchy to poorer people living both in Europe's North and

South. Is it not understandable that this is not something the oligarchy will consent to lightly?

In summary, *A Vision for Europe* erred in not explaining to the reader two key points: First, that our proposed policies for transforming Europe are policies that even the oligarchs see as mutually beneficial for Europeans in Central, Northern, Southern and Eastern Europe. Secondly, they don't care. Understandably!

Indeed, the oligarchy-without-borders fears European disintegration far less than it fears the instruments of public finance that we propose because of their potential to redistribute some of its ill-gotten wealth. It is thus prepared to push Europe to the brink rather than allow these instruments to be forged.

Why not just accept that this EU must end?

We are faced by an EU oligarchy willing and able to push the EU to the brink rather than acquiesce to financial instruments that democratically elected governments can use against it and in the interests of a majority of Europeans in every EU member state. *A Vision for Europe* failed sufficiently to stress this reality, letting readers surrender to the mistaken belief that our task was one of persuasion. How can you persuade all-powerful people already convinced by, but wholly uninterested in, your argument?

No, our task was never to persuade the powers-that-be. It was to confront them. Our task was never to reform the EU by winning arguments in the Eurogroup or the European Council. It was to transform the EU through fierce confrontation taking the form of, what at DiEM25 we refer to as, Constructive Disobedience: constructive proposals like our *Green New Deal for Europe* coupled with a readiness to say NO, to disobey until the cows come home.

Lexiteer friends, leftists who have given up on the EU long ago and campaigned in favour of exiting the EU, have been admonishing us for the 'constructive' part of our Constructive Disobedience and our refusal to campaign for exiting. "Why make pie-in-the-sky proposals that the EU establishment will never consider?", they ask us. "Why maintain the false hope that this EU can be transformed?", they continue. "Why not do the honest thing and campaign to bring our countries out of this toxic EU?", they conclude. Our answers were, and remain, solid for at least three reasons:

1. Any campaign to exit the EU, even if it is meant for good progressive reasons, will alienate middle-of-the-road, relatively apolitical, Europeans that progressives must attract. They will ask: "Won't the dissolution of the EU, however terrible the EU might be, come at a huge cost for common people?" "Won't the end of the EU boost nationalism, thus jeopardising peaceful coexistence on our Continent?" The only honest answers to both questions are affirmative.
2. Any campaign to exit the EU will devastate activists in Germany and other surplus countries where the conservative establishment is unassailable. I recall

happily the excited faces of audiences of young activists in Hanover or Hamburg every time I recite DiEM25's call to unity across the continent, not as Germans or as Greeks, but as progressive Europeans forming a transnational movement aiming at a transnational European demos that will eventually construct a genuine European democracy. Do you know, dear reader, what these same young Germans would feel if the message was "To hell with the EU, let's all go back to our nation-states and collaborate via our governments"? They would feel devastated! They would immediately think to themselves: "We are alone. Us and the ironclad German oligarchy!" No, this is not something I would ever do. The call for a transnational movement to build a transnational European Democracy was right and, given the existence of this EU, uniquely consistent with progressive politics.

3. Any campaign to exit the EU, even if motivated by a left-wing agenda, will only be appended by the Nationalist International which will lose no time weaponising the tumult caused by the EU's rupture to build tall walls, to demonise foreigners, to turn European peoples and communities against one another, and to reinforce the alliance between an increasingly authoritarian state and an unfettered oligarchic corporate cartel.

DiEM25 was, for the three reasons above, right to reject the Lexiteers' strategy of calling for a campaign to disintegrate the EU via Brexit, Grexit, Italexit, Fraxit, etc.

Moreover, DiEM25 was not at all naïve to put forward a *Vision for Europe* that begins with specific policy recommendations for the short and medium term—our *Green New Deal for Europe* which provides a sensible, moderate blueprint that could, tomorrow morning, and under the current EU rules, cure all sorts of ills: the public and private debt crisis, how to fund the Green Transition, a jobs guarantee scheme to end precarity, a Universal Basic Dividend to deal with inequality and automation, etc.

No, DiEM25 did not naïvely think that the EU establishment would be so impressed by our *Green New Deal for Europe* that they would begin to implement it under the pressure of its logic. We knew full well that they would rather blow up the continent than allow its implementation. So why promote it as an EU-healer when we knew that those in control of the EU would prefer the EU's disintegration to our policies' implementation? The answer is simple: because it is the only way to win the hearts and minds of a majority of Europeans.

Let's be clear on this: there are two types of Europeans. A large minority ready to be convinced that this EU must end, people we are bound to lose to the Matteo Salvinis and Boris Johnsons of Europe. And a majority comprised of people who know that there is something rotten in the EU but who, also, roll their eyes when hearing progressives repeat empty slogans such as "Another Europe is Possible", especially when we tell them that this 'other Europe' will come only if we end the existing EU. If we tell them "this EU must end" all we achieve is to make them feel oddly sympathetic to the EU functionaries. To abandon their apathy and to withdraw their tacit consent to the EU establishment's ways, they need first to experience *rational rage* against the EU establishment.

How do we instil rational rage in the majority's souls and minds against the EU establishment? First, we need to answer their legitimate question: "Precisely how could things be done differently within the existing institutional framework?" If we do not provide them with a definitive, convincing answer, we shall lose them either to the racist Nationalist International or to the illiberal establishment. In particular, telling them that nothing good can happen within this EU is the death knell of every progressive political force. Euro-TINA (the doctrine that There Is No Alternative within this EU) is a right-wing, reactionary mantra that DiEM25 sensibly rejected from day one—that is, on the 9th of February 2016 when we founded in Berlin the first ever transnational movement.

DiEM25's analysis was right. The only way to generate rational rage amongst Europeans is to demonstrate to them how easy it is to end every single crisis destroying the life prospects of most Europeans. To show them how much good could be done to so many, even within the awful rules and treaties of the EU. Once they see that, they will automatically ask the pertinent question: "If all that good could be done today, why are those in power not doing it?" Since the only answer is that the authorities are in the pockets of an oligarchy ready and willing to destroy not only their lives, but the EU as well, helping them ask this question is the first step to making possible generalised civil disobedience to the EU's rulers. That's the essence of DiEM25's Constructive Disobedience: demonstrate what could be done and let even the politically apathetic feel rational rage that it is not being done.

In conclusion, DiEM25 rejected, and continues to reject, Lexit because there is no point in campaigning for the end of the EU. Progressives, we believe, must take a page out of the EU oligarchy's manual. Look at the oligarchy's political agents. They wrap themselves up in the EU flag pretending to be Europeanists so as to exploit the gut feeling of most Europeans that the EU's disintegration will cost common folk dearly and, also, help hatch the serpent's egg in every country. But, at the same time, they are ready and willing to destroy the EU to serve their interests. We should do something very similar on behalf of the suffering many.

What should we do? Like the oligarchy, we must remain tuned to the prescient intuition of most Europeans that ending the EU will inflict most costs upon the weakest while, at the same time, strengthening only the neofascists. This rules out a Lexit campaign. However, like the oligarchy, we must be prepared to take the EU to the brink, in pursuit of the minimum policies that are necessary to serve the interests of the many against those of the oligarchy. To put it bluntly, just like the Dutch and German finance ministers, we must be prepared to blow up the EU in order to protect the interests of *our* people; i.e. the vast majority of Europeans.

Re-reading *A Vision for Europe*, my self-criticism is that we put too much emphasis on the 'constructive' part of Constructive Disobedience and not enough on the 'disobedience' part, and the necessity of contemplating, and even planning for, the EU's ending.

The obvious case-study: Brexit

Covid-19 hit hardest people living in countries, like Italy and Spain, with the least capacity to spend the monies necessary to save lives and jobs. Faced with the EU's determination to insist on lending the victims money—with interest—instead of accepting the logic of fiscal union as a prerequisite for a stable and civilised monetary union, I wrote in *The Guardian* the following:

> The message today to Italians, Spaniards and Greeks is: your government can borrow large amounts from Europe's bailout fund. No conditions. You will also receive help to pay for unemployment benefits from countries where employment holds up better. But, within a year or two, as your economies are recovering, huge new austerity measures will be demanded to bring your government's finances back into line, including the repayment of the monies spent on your unemployment benefits. This is equivalent to helping the fallen get up but striking them over the head as they begin to rise.

On 25th March 2020, Ambrose Evans-Pritchard reported in *The Telegraph* on a conversation we had:

> The Greek socialist said he had always tried to keep the European faith—even in his worst clashes with Brussels—but has finally given up. "I don't think the EU is capable of doing anything to us other than harm. I opposed Brexit but I have now reached the conclusion that the British did the right thing, even if they did it for the wrong reason," he said.

Those were, I can confirm, my words. Interestingly, they impressed immensely many Brexiteers who welcomed my 'conversion'. Some Lexiteers went further by mixing approval of my 'new' stance with scorn that it took me too long, that when I was finance minister I had not enacted Grexit, that DiEM25 had wasted energy by sticking to a Remain-and-Reform agenda.

Did I have a road-to-Damascus moment after the EU's Covid-19 moment? No, I did not. For decades I have admonished the EU with strong arguments exposing its vicious misanthropy. Since the euro crisis began, I have spoken of its 'fiscal waterboarding' practices (which were recently referred to as 'torture devices' even by Heiko Maas, the current German foreign minister). I even referred to Brussels as a democracy-free zone. So, telling Evans-Pritchard that the EU is only capable of dishing out pain to our people was nothing new.

What was new was my assessment that, in the end, by opting for Brexit, Britons made the right choice for the wrong reasons. This is a statement that requires some unpacking if only because it has an important bearing on—at least my—vision for Europe.

First, let me explain why I said that Britons were, in the end, right to get out of the EU. The eurozone is often described as a union within a union, or a club within a club. While this description is formally correct, it fails to capture the centrifugal forces that the euro's creation unleashed. Once the single currency was created, in the designed absence of common debt instruments and a common banking system, the EU train was put on a track leading inexorably to a junction. There, it could turn sharply toward unification or continue on the same route until, running out of track, it disintegrated. That junction was reached with the euro crisis but the EU establishment, for reasons explained earlier, is resisting unification—thus forcing the EU off its rails. Under these circumstances, it is not wrong for the people of Britain to bail out of this slow-motion train wreck.

Secondly, why did I say, seemingly condescendingly, that the British got out for the wrong reasons? This should be obvious to progressives. The lies about the billions of pounds that would be saved and rechannelled to the National Health Service; the demonisation of EU migrants as having been the cause of stressed social services (when it was all down to Tory austerity); the jingoistic projections of a liberated free-market Britain sailing the oceans of enterprise and reconstituting its Empire; the role of dark networks of disinformation targeting those vulnerable to hate speech.

Thirdly, and most importantly, have I regretted that DiEM25, and I personally, campaigned against Brexit? No, I have not. Anyone who witnessed our 2016 campaign will realise that it was two-pronged: Against Brexiteers who were blowing, willingly or unwillingly, fresh wind into the sails of nationalism. And, with equal ferocity, against Remainers who were portraying the EU as the best thing since sliced bread.

As for the charge of my British Lexiteer friends that, when I was Greece's finance minister, I was not prepared to pull the trigger and exit the eurozone, this is simply a lie. I *was* prepared and I would have done it, if my own government had not buckled. Indeed, the reason I was so hated by the EU establishment was that I was *not* a Lexiteer but this would not have (and the troika knew this well) stopped me from pulling the trigger and issuing a new drachma. Had I been a Lexiteer, they would have not minded me, since the majority of Greeks would not have followed me. What made 2015 a moment when the EU establishment feared for its dominance, even only for a few short months, was that they were facing a Europeanist foe ready and willing to do as they did: to take matters to the brink by being ready even to blow up the euro, the EU itself, rather than betray the interests of his people (i.e. the majority of Europeans, not just of Greeks).

Our *Vision for Europe* demands new radicalism, new alliances, new ruptures

Our constantly evolving *Green New Deal for Europe* is crucial. But it is not enough. Covid-19 has created new facts on the ground. The sums our *Green New Deal* proposed for funding the Green Transition (€500 billion annually) were ridiculed in 2019 but, today, appear utterly understated.

Capitalism has been, temporarily, suspended. Our *Vision for Europe* can no longer rely only on the constructive proposals that are the 'constructive' part of our

Constructive Disobedience strategy. This is the time to envision a post-capitalist Europe. In this context, the *Green New Deal* must be recognised as the first stepping stone to a vastly different future. We must now inspire people with a vision of what follows both capitalism and our *Green New Deal*. What should that vision be? Here are some ideas: an economic democracy where companies are run on a one-person-one-non-tradeable-share-one-vote principle; where there are no private banks but, instead, the central bank provides free digital accounts to every citizen; a society that grants a trust fund to every baby born.

Turning to alliances, the original *Vision for Europe* got it right when warning xenophobes and crypto-fascists that we shall fight them everywhere. But it was remiss when it failed to warn the remnants of what was once social democracy that we shall treat them too as toxic agents of a recalcitrant establishment. Let's be clear on this: the social democratic establishment forces have done the most damage to the progressive cause in Europe.

Who gave the EU's oligarchy the greatest effective support and legitimacy over the past decade? No, it was not the conservative parties. It was the German and Austrian SPDs, the Socialists in France, the Democratic Party in Italy, Greece's PASOK and Syriza parties that signed up to every piece of troika nastiness, the new socialist Eurogroup President from Portugal, etc. While many progressive people are still entangled in the poisonous web of those parties, and need to be rescued, our vision for Europe will only stand a chance if DiEM25 has nothing to do with their leadership.

In contrast, the rift between us, DiEM25, and Lexiteers must now end. We must agree to disagree on whether the right tactic is to demand an exit from the EU or, as DiEM25 believes, to continue to envision a democratic union. But we must move beyond this disagreement and plan ahead for an internationalist, post-capitalist Europe. DiEM25 is about bringing European progressives together independently of the EU. Europe, we must scream from the rooftops, is <u>not</u> the EU. As bankers and fascists unite across EU and non-EU borders, so should we.

Finally, to make our vision for Europe consistent with our internationalism, we need to embed it within the vision for the world—exactly as DiEM25 is currently struggling to do by building the Progressive International together with wonderful progressives from all over the planet.

There is no doubt that to make any of this remotely feasible there is a lot of work to be done. Work that is physically exhausting, mentally gruelling, emotionally destructive. But work that, nevertheless, we can't even imagine giving up on. The best way to carry on is to take breaks during which to develop further our *Vision for Europe*, our *Vision for the World*.

DIEM25 has opened a Pandora's box.
Great ideas regarding economics and social policy are provided
by Yanis Varoufakis and by the other luminaries.
Still, there's infinite space for the rest of us…
Where do we start?
I say from drawing.
But also writing: we should be putting things down
on paper and also on our computers and on social media.

How should we write?
Writing should be an opportunity for research and experimentation.
New ideas should be imprinted in new ways.
Looking at my daughter Alpha while she was learning how to write,
I saw that society is programming our uniform thinking
also by driving us to write fast:
once you know the letters, put them down on paper
or type them on some keyboard.

But what if we slow down?

DIEMVOICE
People say stuff… they are asking questions…
Writing down, the slow way, their questions,
supplies me with a kind of urgent challenge.
I suggest you copy people's questions or sayings from this book,
try doing it the way I am teaching you here,
by drawing the alphabet first and a circle with the 10 numbers contained within it.

Then drag the letters and numbers down to spell out your phrases.
It is a slow process and will give you time to think and to elaborate on
whatever it is you are writing about.

At some point, the phrases will start stepping out of the paper,
and you will find yourself listening to Diem's Voice.

Miltos Manetas, Bogotá , 01/03/2019

SLOW

PROCESS

SLOW

PROCESS

SLOW

#@?
ABCD
EFGH
IJKLM
NOPQR
STUVW
XYZ

PART ONE

Manifesto

Which Idea of Europe Is Worth Saving?

Slavoj Žižek

In January 2019, a group of thirty writers, historians, and Nobel laureates (Bernard-Henri Lévy, Milan Kundera, Salman Rushdie, Orhan Pamuk, Mario Vargas Llosa, Adam Michnik, and others) published a manifesto in newspapers across Europe, including the *Guardian* in the UK.[1] They claimed that Europe as an idea is coming apart before our eyes: "We must now fight for the idea of Europe or see it perish beneath the waves of populism", they wrote. "We must rediscover the spirit of activism or accept that resentment and hatred and their cortege of sad passions will surround and submerge us."

This manifesto is deeply flawed and shows why populists are thriving: its signatories—the cream of European liberal intelligence—ignore the unpleasant fact that the populists also present themselves as the saviours of Europe.

In an interview just after attending a stormy meeting with leaders of the European Union, Donald Trump called the EU the first in the line of 'foes' of the US, ahead of both Russia and China. Instead of condemning this claim outright, we should ask some simple questions. What bothers him so much about the EU? Which Europe is he talking about? When asked by journalists about immigrants flowing into Europe, he answered like the anti-immigrant populist he is, saying immigrants are tearing apart the fabric of European culture and endangering its spiritual identity. In short, he answered as if Orbán or Salvini were talking through him. One should never forget that they also want to defend Europe—but which Europe is it that bothers them?

It is the Europe of transnational unity; the Europe aware that, to cope with the challenges of our time we must move beyond the constraints of nation states; the Europe which desperately strives to stay faithful to the old Enlightenment motto of solidarity with victims; the Europe conscious that humanity is One, that we are all in the same boat, and that the misery of others is our problem to solve.

Peter Sloterdijk notes that the primary struggle today is securing the survival of Europe's greatest economico-political achievement: the social-democratic welfare state. According to him, our current reality is 'objective social democracy', as opposed to 'subjective social democracy'. One should distinguish between social democracy as the panoply of political parties, and social democracy as the "formula of a system" which "precisely describes the political-economic order of things, which is defined by the modern state as the state of taxes, as infrastructure-state, as the state of the rule of law and, not last, as the social state and the therapy state."

> We encounter everywhere a phenomenal and a structural Social Democracy, a manifest and a latent one, one which appears as a party and another one which is more or less irreversibly built into the very definitions, functions, and procedures of modern statehood as such.[2]

This idea that underlies united Europe has been neglected, corrupted, and it is only in a time of crisis that we are compelled to return to this essential dimension of Europe and its hidden potential.

Europe lies vulnerable in the great pincers of America on one side and Russia on the other, both desperate to dismember it. Trump and Putin support Brexit and Eurosceptics in every corner. But what is it that bothers them about Europe, when the EU fails at every test, from its inability to enact consistent immigration policies to its miserable reaction to Trump's tariff war? It is obviously not this present Europe, then, but *the idea* of Europe, an idea that becomes palpable in moments of danger. The problem Europe faces now is how to remain faithful to its emancipatory legacy when threatened by this conservative-populist onslaught.

In his *Notes Towards a Definition of Culture*, the great conservative T. S. Eliot remarked that there are moments when the only choice is the one between heresy and non-belief, when the only way to keep a religion alive is to perform a sectarian split from its main corpse: this is what must be done. The only way to defeat populism and redeem what is worth saving in liberal democracy, is to perform a sectarian split from liberal democracy's main corpse. Sometimes, the only way to resolve a conflict is not to search for a compromise, but to radicalise one's position.

Ernesto Laclau insisted that the need to construct an enemy image immanent to populism was not a weakness, but its strength. Left populism, of course, should construct a different enemy image: not the threatening racial Other (immigrant, Jew, Muslim) but the financial elites, the fundamentalists, and other 'usual suspects' of the progressives. This urge to construct the enemy, however, is a fatal limitation of populism, because today the ultimate enemy is not a concrete social agent but the system itself, a certain functioning. Alain Badiou wrote that one doesn't fight capitalism but its concrete agents, and therein resides the problem, since the true target is capitalism itself.

Because of their focus on concrete enemies, left populists privilege national sovereignty as a defence against global capital. Aufstehen in Germany essentially follows this same path. In this way, most of them not only endorse populism but nationalism, presenting their struggle as a defence against international financial capital. Some leftist populists in the US have already deployed the term 'national socialism'.[3] While it would be stupid and unfair to claim that they are closet Nazis, one should nonetheless insist that internationalism is key to any project of radical emancipation.

DiEM25 sees that resistance against global capital has to be global itself, to become a new form of universalism. There definitely are enemies, and the topic of conspiracies is not one to dismiss. Years ago, Fred Jameson perspicuously noted that in today's global capitalism things happen which cannot be explained by blaming some anonymous 'logic of capital'. For example, now we know that the financial meltdown of 2008 was the result of a well-planned conspiracy by certain financial circles.

The true task of social analysis remains to explain how contemporary capitalism opened up the space for such 'conspiratorial' interventions. This is also why references to 'greed' and appeals for capitalists to show social solidarity and responsibility are misplaced: 'greed' (understood as the pursuit of profit) *is* what motivates capitalist expansion; the wager of capitalism *is* that the acting out of individual greed will contribute to the common good. So, again, the task is to change the system so it will no longer permit, let alone solicit, this 'greedy' behaviour.

Nowadays, it seems easy to agree that the enemy is neo-fascist, anti-immigrant nationalism, or Trump in the US. But the fact remains that the rise of Trump is the result of a failed liberal-democratic consensus, not its cause. So, although one should not exclude from the repertoire new forms of 'anti-fascist' alliance with the latter, it is this very consensus that needs to change.

Back to the letter of the thirty liberal luminaries. What they refuse to admit is that the Europe whose disappearance they lament is already irretrievably lost. The threat does not come from populism. Populism is merely a reaction to the failure of the European liberal establishment to remain faithful to the continent's emancipatory potentials, offering a false way out of ordinary people's troubles. The only way to really defeat populism is to submit the liberal establishment itself, its actual politics, to a ruthless critique.

Which political orientation promises to do this today in Europe? Which orientation enables us to break the vicious cycle of liberal establishment and the rise of populism? What remains of the radical left strangely reproduces the opposition between populism and liberalism: it is caught in the tension between left populism which openly flirts with nationalism, seeking the solution in a strong nation state, and abstract liberal tolerance which plays on Europe's guilt and preaches opening up to others (refugees, immigrants) without addressing the roots of the problem.

Only DiEM25 does what needs to be done. In its opposition to global capitalism, it remains staunchly internationalist. Its programme is devoid of moralistic dreams: it offers precise economic and political measures. Instead of opposing our reality on behalf of abstract dreams, it locates in this very reality the potential of a just future. DiEM25 is the voice of reason in our political landscape—not a cynical, opportunist reason, but a reason which addresses the irrationality of our predicament. If we ignore DiEM25's call, we are foresaking our future.

Notes

1   Bernard-Henri Lévy et al, "Fight for Europe—or the Wreckers Will Destroy It," *The Guardian*, 25 January 2019, www.theguardian.com/commentisfree/2019/jan/25/fight-europe-wreckers-patriots-nationalist.
2   Peter Sloterdijk, "Aufbruch der Leistungstraeger" Cicero, November 2009.
3   This happened at the conference of the Union for Radical Economics at Amherst, Massachusetts, in September 2018.

A Manifesto for Democratising Europe

For all their concerns with global competitiveness, migration, and terrorism, only one prospect truly terrifies the Powers of Europe: democracy! They speak in democracy's name but deny, exorcise, and suppress it in practice. They co-opt, evade, corrupt, mystify, usurp, and manipulate democracy to break its energy and arrest its possibilities. A Europe ruled by Europe's people, government by the demos, is the shared nightmare of:

- The Brussels bureaucracy (and its more than 10,000 lobbyists)
- Its hit-squad inspectorates and the troika they formed with unelected 'technocrats'
- The powerful Eurogroup that has no standing in law or treaty
- Bailed-out bankers, fund managers, and resurgent oligarchies contemptuous of the multitudes and their organised expression
- Political parties appealing to liberalism, democracy, freedom, and solidarity only to betray their principles in government
- Governments that fuel cruel inequality by implementing self-defeating austerity
- Media moguls who have turned fear-mongering into an art, for power and profit
- Corporations in cahoots with secretive public agencies, investing in that fear to promote secrecy and a culture of surveillance that bends public opinion to their will.

The European Union was an exceptional achievement, bringing together in peace European peoples speaking different languages, submersed in different cultures, proving that it was possible to create a shared framework of human rights across a continent that was, not long ago, home to murderous chauvinism, racism, and barbarity. The European Union could have been the proverbial Beacon on the Hill, showing the world how peace and solidarity may be snatched from the jaws of centuries-long conflict and bigotry.

Alas, today, a common bureaucracy and a common currency divide European peoples that were beginning to unite despite our different languages and cultures. A confederacy of myopic politicians, economically naïve officials, and financially incompetent 'experts' submit slavishly to the edicts of financial and industrial conglomerates, alienating Europeans and stirring up a dangerous anti-European backlash. Proud peoples are being turned against each other. Nationalism, extremism, and racism are being reawakened.

At the heart of our disintegrating EU there lies a guilty deceit: A highly political, top-down, opaque decision-making process is presented as 'apolitical', 'technical', 'procedural', and 'neutral'. Its purpose is to prevent Europeans from exercising democratic control over their money, finance, working conditions, and environment. The price of this deceit is not merely the end of democracy but also poor economic policies:

- The Eurozone economies are being marched off the cliff of competitive austerity, resulting in permanent recession in the weaker countries and low investment in the core countries
- EU member states outside the Eurozone are alienated, seeking inspiration and partners in suspect quarters where they are most likely to be greeted with opaque, coercive free trade deals that undermine their sovereignty
- Unprecedented inequality, declining hope, and misanthropy flourish throughout Europe

Two dreadful options dominate: retreat into the cocoon of our nation states, or surrender to the Brussels democracy-free zone. There must be another course.

And there is. It is the course that 'official Europe' resists with every sinew of its authoritarian mindset: a surge of democracy! Our movement, DiEM25, seeks to call forth just such a surge. One simple, radical idea is the motivating force behind DiEM25: Democratise Europe! For the EU will either be democratised or it will disintegrate!

Our goal to democratise Europe is realistic. It is no more utopian than the initial construction of the European Union. Indeed, it is less utopian than the attempt to keep alive the current, anti-democratic, fragmenting European Union. Our goal to democratise Europe is also terribly urgent, for without a swift start it may be impossible to chisel away at the institutionalised resistance in good time, before Europe goes past the point of no return. Our goal is 2025.

If we fail to democratise Europe within a decade, if Europe's autocratic powers succeed in stifling democratisation, the EU will crumble under its hubris. It will splinter, and its fall will cause untold hardship across Europe and beyond.

Why is Europe losing its integrity and its soul?

In the postwar decades during which the EU was initially constructed, national cultures were revitalised in a spirit of internationalism, disappearing borders, shared prosperity and raised standards that brought Europeans together. However, a serpent's egg lay at the heart of the integration process.

From an economic viewpoint, the EU began life as a cartel of heavy industry (later co-opting farm owners) determined to fix prices and to redistribute oligopoly profits through its Brussels bureaucracy. The emergent cartel, and its Brussels-based administrators, feared the demos and despised the idea of government-by-the-people.

Patiently and methodically, they put in place a process of depoliticising decision-making, a process to relentlessly take the demos out of democracy and cloak all policymaking in pseudo-technocratic fatalism. National politicians were rewarded handsomely for their acquiescence to turning the Commission, the Council, the Ecofin, the Eurogroup, and the European Central Bank into politics-free zones. Anyone opposing this process was labelled 'un-European' and treated as a jarring dissonance.

Thus the deceit at the EU's heart was born, yielding an institutional commitment to policies that generate depressing economic data and avoidable hardship. Meanwhile, simple principles that a more confident Europe once understood have now been abandoned:

- Rules should serve Europeans, not the other way around
- Currency should be utilised, not hoarded
- A single market is consistent with democracy only if it features common defences of the weaker Europeans, and of the environment, that are democratically chosen and built
- Democracy cannot be a luxury of creditors, refused to debtors
- Democracy is essential for limiting capitalism's worst, self-destructive drives and opening a window onto new vistas of social harmony and sustainable development

In response to the inevitable failure of Europe's cartelised social economy to rebound from the post-2008 Great Recession, the EU's institutions that caused this failure resorted to escalating authoritarianism. The more they asphyxiate democracy, the less legitimate their political authority, the stronger the forces of economic recession, and the greater their need for authoritarianism. The enemies of democracy gather renewed power while losing legitimacy and confining hope and prosperity to the very few.

This is the unseen process by which Europe's crisis is turning our peoples inwards, against each other, amplifying pre-existing jingoism and xenophobia. The privatisation of anxiety, the fear of the 'other', the nationalisation of ambition, and the rena-tionalisation of policy threaten a toxic disintegration of common interests from which Europe can only suffer. Europe's pitiful reaction to its banking and debt crises, to the refugee crisis, to the need for a coherent foreign, migration, and anti-terrorism policy, are all examples of what happens when solidarity loses its meaning:

- The injury to Europe's integrity caused by the crushing of the Athens Spring, and by the subsequent imposition of an economic 'reform' programme designed to fail

- The customary assumption that, whenever a state budget must be bolstered or a bank bailed out, society's weakest must pay for the sins of the wealthiest rentiers
- The constant drive to commodify labour and drive democracy out of the workplace
- The scandalous 'not in our backyard' attitude of most EU member states to the refugees landing on Europe's shores, illustrating how a broken European governance model yields ethical decline and political paralysis, as well as evidence that xenophobia towards non-Europeans follows the demise of intra-European solidarity
- The comical phrase we end up with when we put together the three words 'European', 'foreign', and 'policy'
- The ease with which European governments decided after the awful Paris attacks that the solution lies in re-erecting borders, when most of the attackers were EU citizens—yet another sign of the moral panic engulfing a European Union unable to unite Europeans to forge common responses to common problems

Our horizon

Realism demands that we work toward reaching milestones within a realistic timeframe. This is why DiEM25 will aim for four breakthroughs at regular intervals in order to bring about a fully democratic, functional Europe by 2025.

Now, today, Europeans are feeling let down by EU institutions everywhere. From Helsinki to Lisbon, from Dublin to Crete, from Leipzig to Aberdeen, Europeans sense that a stark choice is approaching fast. The choice between authentic democracy and insidious disintegration. We must resolve to unite to ensure that Europe makes the obvious choice: authentic democracy.

When asked what we want, and when we want it, we respond:

- Immediately: full transparency in decision-making.

  1. EU Council, Ecofin, FTT, and Eurogroup Meetings to be live-streamed
  2. Minutes of European Central Bank governing council meetings to be published within weeks
  3. All documents pertinent to crucial negotiations (e.g. trade-TTIP, 'bailout' loans, Britain's status) affecting every facet of European citizens' future to be uploaded on the web
  4. A compulsory register for lobbyists that includes their clients' names, their remuneration, and a record of meetings with officials (both elected and unelected)

- First twelve months: address the ongoing economic crisis utilising existing institutions and within existing EU Treaties.

Europe's immediate crisis is unfolding simultaneously in five realms: public debt, banking, inadequate investment, migration, and rising poverty.

All five realms are currently left in the hands of national governments powerless to act upon them. DiEM25 will present detailed policy proposals to Europeanise all five, while limiting Brussels' discretionary powers and returning power to national Parliaments, to regional councils, to city halls, and to communities. The proposed policies will be aimed at redeploying existing institutions (through a creative reinterpretation of existing treaties and charters) in order to stabilise the crises of public debt, banking, inadequate investment, and rising poverty.

- First two years: Constitutional Assembly.

The people of Europe have a right to consider the Union's future and a duty to transform Europe by 2025 into a full-fledged democracy with a sovereign parliament respecting national self-determination and sharing power with national parliaments, regional assemblies, and municipal councils.

To do this, an Assembly of their representatives must be convened. DiEM25 will promote a Constitutional Assembly consisting of representatives elected on transnational tickets. Today, when universities apply to Brussels for research funding, they must form alliances across nations. Similarly, election to the Constitutional Assembly should require tickets featuring candidates from a majority of European countries. The resulting Constitutional Assembly will be empowered to decide on a future democratic constitution that will replace all existing European Treaties within a decade.

- By 2025: enactment of the decisions of the Constitutional Assembly.

Who will bring change? We, the people of Europe, have a duty to regain control over our Europe from unaccountable 'technocrats', complicit politicians, and shadowy institutions. We come from every part of the continent and are united by different cultures, languages, accents, political party affiliations, ideologies, skin colours, gender identities, faiths, and conceptions of the good society. We are forming DiEM25 to move from a Europe of 'We the Governments', and 'We the Technocrats', to a Europe of 'We the people of Europe'.

Our four principles

1. No European people can be free as long as another's democracy is violated
2. No European people can live in dignity as long as another is denied it
3. No European people can hope for prosperity if another is pushed into permanent insolvency and depression

4. No European people can grow without basic goods for its weakest citizens, human development, ecological balance, and a determination to become fossil-fuel free in a world that changes its ways—not the planet's climate

We join in a magnificent tradition of Europeans who have struggled for centuries against the 'wisdom' that democracy is a luxury and that the weak suffer what they must. With our hearts, minds, and wills dedicated to these commitments, and determined to make a difference, we declare that.

Our pledge

We call on our fellow Europeans to join us to create the European movement which we call DiEM25.

To fight together, against a European establishment deeply contemptuous of democracy, to democratise the European Union

To end the reduction of all political relations into relations of power masquerading as merely technical decisions

To subject the EU's bureaucracy to the will of sovereign European peoples

To dismantle the habitual domination of corporate power over the will of citizens

To repoliticise the rules that govern our single market and common currency

We consider the model of national parties which form flimsy alliances at the level of the European Parliament to be obsolete. While the fight for democracy from below (at the local, regional or national levels) is necessary, it is nevertheless insufficient if it is conducted without an internationalist strategy toward a pan-European coalition for democratising Europe. European democrats must come together first, forge a common agenda, and then find ways of connecting it with local communities at the regional and national level.

Our overarching aim to democratise the European Union is intertwined with an ambition to promote self-government (economic, political, and social) at the local, municipal, regional, and national levels, to throw open the corridors of power to the public, to embrace social and civic movements, and to emancipate all levels of government from bureaucratic and corporate power.

We are inspired by a Europe of reason, liberty, tolerance, and imagination made possible by comprehensive transparency, real solidarity, and authentic democracy.

We aspire to:

A Democratic Europe, in which all political authority stems from Europe's sovereign peoples.

A Transparent Europe, where all decision-making takes place under the citizens' scrutiny.

A United Europe, whose citizens have as much in common across nations as within them.

A Realistic Europe, that sets itself the task of radical, yet achievable, democratic reforms.

A Decentralised Europe, that uses central power to maximise democracy in workplaces, towns, cities, regions, and states.

A Pluralist Europe of regions, ethnicities, faiths, nations, languages, and cultures.

An Egalitarian Europe, that celebrates difference and ends discrimination based on gender, skin colour, social class, or sexual orientation.

A Cultured Europe, that harnesses its people's cultural diversity and promotes not only its invaluable heritage but also the work of Europe's dissident artists, musicians, writers, and poets.

A Social Europe, that recognises that liberty necessitates not only freedom from interference but also the basic goods that render one free from need and exploitation.

A Productive Europe, that directs investment into a shared, green prosperity.

A Sustainable Europe, that lives within the planet's means, minimising its environmental impact, and leaving fossil fuel in the earth.

An Ecological Europe, engaged in genuine worldwide green transition.

A Creative Europe, that releases the innovative powers of its citizens' imagination.

A Technological Europe, pushing new technologies in the service of solidarity.

A Historically-minded Europe, that seeks a bright future without hiding from its past.

An Internationalist Europe, that treats non-Europeans equally.

A Peaceful Europe, de-escalating tensions in its East and in the Mediterranean, acting as a bulwark against the sirens of militarism and expansionism.

An Open Europe, that is alive to ideas, people and inspiration from all over the world, recognising fences and borders as signs of weakness spreading insecurity in the name of security.

A Liberated Europe, where privilege, prejudice, deprivation, and the threat of violence wither, allowing Europeans to be born into fewer stereotypical roles, to enjoy equal chances to develop their potential, and to be free to choose more of their partners in life, work, and society.

A Liberated Europe by Raoul Martinez

" We dream of a liberated Europe free from fear and prejudice, where all people enjoy the conditions necessary to live dignified, fulfilled lives; a Europe free from the myths that distort its past, justify its present, or endanger its future; a liberating Europe that works to atone for centuries of colonialism, slavery, and theft by opening its borders and sharing its wealth.

The path from our reality to this dream is obstructed by established systems and influential myths. It is obstructed by capitalism, and its two destructive tendencies: to concentrate wealth and to expand in scale. The first destroys democracy; the second, our natural world. If capitalism overwhelms democracy, that liberated Europe will remain a dream. In its place there will be a Europe of confinement, of fences, borders, and walls that keep at bay those devastated by economic and ecological violence.

Under capitalism, the principle of one-dollar-one-vote determines the future. Those with the greatest wealth have the incentive and means to subvert democracy. Through party funding, lobbying, think tanks, media ownership, and the revolving door that links big business to government, the rich corrupt our electoral systems. Ending their dominion requires a revolution. Where there is no democracy, we must introduce it. Where there is some democracy, we must deepen it. Where the resources and institutions central to modern society have been bought and privatised, we must take them back.

No society will survive if its collective actions are devoid of rationality. A minimum threshold must be met: namely, avoiding conscious self-destruction through ruinous war and environmental degradation. Capitalist civilisation has proved incapable of meeting this basic requirement. Annihilation is highly profitable. Given the depth of the ecological crisis, the challenge for a genuinely democratic Europe is to nurture a culture that can meet this life-sustaining threshold.

A liberated Europe would not only reject capitalism but dispense with the myths that glorify its elites and whitewash its past. Myths of superiority and beneficence conceal the violence that has enabled this continent to seize a disproportionate share of the world's resources and generate a disproportionate share of its waste.

Myths of merit and individualism legitimise inequalities, obscuring the simple fact that the lottery of birth determines who we are, who we hope to be, and the available resources—both material and psychological—that allow us to transition from one to the other.

Generation after generation, we have all been led down well-trodden paths to a familiar destination: a society in which inequalities of power and wealth are reproduced and extended. If the aim of society is to unlock the potential within each of us, we must create new paths to a new world where the resources and rights necessary for individual fulfilment are equitably shared. We must expose the lie that equality of opportunity is compatible with high levels of inequality.

And finally, the myth of separation. Throughout our lives, we all adopt cultural stances that connect us to some but divide us from many. Yet with different influences, any of us could have embraced a group, cause, or belief different from the one we did. Paradoxically, humanity's diversity is a testament to a deeper commonality: we are all products of forces beyond our control, with the potential to be other than who we are. We must remember that our common humanity goes deeper than the identities we inherit—and on that foundation build a stronger continent together. Before we are British, French, German, or Greek, let us be European.

A truly liberated Europe is one in which we unshackle our allegiances from national flags and cultural fictions, and give them instead to universal principles, the natural world, and a shared identity. **99**

A Peaceful Europe by Eyal Weizman

❝ Europe is best seen from its margins. From Roman times until today, whether in the Mediterranean, the eastern Balkans, or Ukraine, the state of the European project is still decided there, for the nature of Europe consists of pacifying its centre and exporting violence to the frontiers.

I offer this observation from a personal perspective, because Israel is one of these eastern frontiers. Though not an official member, it sees itself as part of that culture whose self-imagined function is holding back the orient—maintaining a front beyond which lurks all kinds of danger.

Colonial regimes have always been laboratories in which new technologies of control are conceived and tested for the world—whether to divide and fortify, or to eavesdrop and control. Israel/Palestine is a laboratory of this kind. Not only has Israeli industry generated a huge export market for their spy software and security systems, they have also exported a certain political sensibility from the margin to the centre: an 'everywhere war' against refugees and migrants. When Donald Trump calls for a fortified border with Mexico, he relies on the success of the Israeli border— a 'success' that remains unproven and at enormous cost to Palestinian lives and livelihoods. Hungary and Poland have a close ideological, technological, and economic relationship with Israel. Serbia did the historical job of Europe in Srebrenica. The two states should have been immediately admitted as honorary members.

On the southern edge, the Mediterranean has been transformed into a liquid border for Europe, weaponised to swallow up migrants and asylum seekers from Africa. The same is happening across the Aegean, and in recent years violence has erupted on the eastern frontier with the Ukraine-Russia conflict. The pacification of Europe's centre is a much less challenging task than facing up to the implications of this violence at its edges.

We need to investigate these margins, because the absence of oversight and the destruction of information is a breeding ground to violence. There is no precise record of how many people are trying to cross over to Europe, how many people are drowning in the Mediterranean and along its other liquid frontiers. Instead, there is a perceptual blurring along these edges. Until we begin to see and call to account what we see there, we are not going to be able to speak at all about a peaceful Europe. Peace is not about the relationship between Europe's component state parts, but will be defined at the frontier.

We in Forensic Architecture use various forms of spatial optics, whether cartographic, or based on satellite imagery, or on social media open source investigations, to verify events and capture incidents. These are often used as evidence in legal cases, as well as in citizen tribunals and human rights processes, leading to larger military, parliamentary, and UN inquiries. Each case might start as a technical analysis but is an entry point to reflect on and resist larger phenomena.

We deploy these moments of exposure tactically, because we do not naively believe that it is the law that will save us. We use legal forums in order to connect with certain communities inside and outside Europe. The choice and exposure of specific cases always has to be measured against the longer duration and larger context of these conflicts. We work along the entire trajectory of migration, from the exported misery, climate change, and wars in Syria, Afghanistan, or Mali, to refugees dying trying to make it into Europe, to violence against migrants inside European cities. One of our big cases investigated a series of neo-Nazi murders targeted against migrants in Germany. By selecting cases like these, we can open up the entire web of relations folded within each incident, revealing the broad set of actors that comprise the violence afflicted on migration.

Europe is enacting and integrating various policies intended to increase the precarity of their journey. There is almost an inverse relation between the peaceful image that Europe likes to promote inside its borders—the innovative liberalisation of social relations, the investment in progressive cultural norms, the openness of science—and the violence that it exports to and beyond them. In its colonial imagination, Europe sees itself as a villa in the jungle. But in order to maintain this vision, there is an enormous amount of economic, bureaucratic, and physical violence across the frontiers.

We, privileged citizens of Europe, must be extremely concerned by this destructive firewall burning at its edges as it expands or stems the unwanted incoming flow. It is a firewall felt by anyone who is on the outside looking in. **"**

[*Excerpt of the interview for this volume by Rosemary Bechler, 11 February 2019*]

DIEM VO

We are hearing much
about the vision DIEM has
for the EU. But how is
DIEM planning to include
EUROPEAN
EU / NO-EU countries so we
can achieve a real
paneuropean UNION ?

We Are Hearing Much About the Vision DiEM Has for the EU. But How Is DiEM Planning to Include European/No-EU Countries so We Can Achieve a Real Paneuropean Union?

A Realistic Europe by Katrín Jakobsdóttir

"The current political condition of Europe is marked by cultural anxieties and social insecurities where old truisms and dogmas are being questioned. The party landscape is undergoing fundamental changes, with dominant conservative and social-democratic parties facing a crisis of confidence. In a throwback to an earlier era, anti-democratic right-wing populist parties and authoritarian governments pose major threats to democratic values, human rights, and the rule of law.

Mainstream parties are succumbing to the temptation of either parroting the xenophobic demagogy of the authoritarian right in an attempt to neutralise it, or legitimising it by relying on the support of extremist elements as part of a governing strategy. This regressive trend has not elicited an effective response by the left. But the good news is that many left-wing and green parties are currently undergoing a revival in Europe, and young people are rising up, demanding solutions to climate change.

Thus, while the overall outlook is bleak, we must remember that in such turbulent times, different outcomes are possible. There is no denying that democratic deficits and divisive economic policies have damaged public support for the European project, exemplified by Brexit and the rise of the ultra-nationalist right. It also reflects the lack of institutional reform within the EU, with structures like the European Central Bank having become very powerful whilst remaining outside the purview of democratic accountability. Yet no European future can be built on the reactionary, anti-democratic, and nativist agenda promoted by authoritarian politicians.

In Europe, the left has a tradition of progressive policies, whether in the field of social and welfare policies, the environment, or women's and LGBT rights. Hence, European left-wing and progressive parties need to forge a transnational alliance to promote an ambitious and radical political programme. Within the context of climate change and economic disparities, it should adopt a bold, forward-looking, intersectionalist agenda with emphasis on social justice, gender equality, the green economy and international institutional reforms. Meanwhile, it should also be actively conscious of the historical memory and experience of earlier anti-authoritarian, anti-militarist, and anti-racist struggles.

The European left-wing parties share core values: dignity, peace, universal human rights, and the importance of social protection. They have resisted neoliberal programmes of privatisation and austerity, demanded tighter supervision of cross-border capital movements and the closing of tax havens, and favoured a tax regime designed to reduce the huge disparities of wealth and generate revenue for social infrastructure projects. Many left-wing formations have also been highly critical of military interventions and adventurisms.

While there is no reason to downplay differences on the left, it is our duty in these precarious times to develop a pluralistic alternative which does not shy away from past traditions but is geared toward the present and future. We must initiate radical and democratic political and social changes and create a progressive, transnational venue that will ensure the long-term dominance of the left in European politics. **99**

PART TWO

Democracy

Liberal or 'Illiberal Democracy'? No, Thanks!

Srećko Horvat

A spectre is haunting Europe. The spectre of 'illiberal democracy'.

In 2012, when he was still only two years in office, Viktor Orbán declared the need for a new political system in Europe. "Let us hope that God will help us," he said, "and we will not have to invent a new type of political system instead of democracy that would need to be introduced for the sake of economic survival."[1]

Two years later, in July 2014, the Hungarian leader announced the death of 'liberal democracy' and the arrival of the 'illiberal state', which would abandon fundamental liberal values such as tolerance of minorities or foreigners or freedom of speech.[2] One year later, in May 2015, Orbán went a step further, claiming explicitly that "dictatorial countries are more successful than democratic ones".[3]

The reaction to this in Europe was best embodied at the EU summit that year in Riga, Latvia, where the Head of the European Commission, Jean-Claude Juncker, jokingly greeted Orbán with a "Hello, dictator" and slapped him on the cheek (you can still find the video online).[4] Maybe one day a historian will treat it as unique evidence of the cynicism of European elites.

Although it was already clear back in 2012 when Orbán announced "a new type of political system instead of democracy" that Hungary was openly moving towards some form of dictatorship or what nowadays would be called 'illiberal democracy', the European deep establishment treated this prospect as a joke.

Fast forward to 2018. The European dictatorship is no longer a joke. Rising extremist and right-wing populist movements such as Alternative für Deutschland in Germany or Rassemblement National (formerly Front National) in France are aspiring to grab power in the two most developed and politically important countries of the European Union. In Austria and Italy, parts of governments are already occupied by right-wing and xenophobic forces, while governments in Hungary and Poland are actively transforming their states into 'illiberal democracies'.

The final proof that what is called 'illiberal democracy' is not just something that belongs to the east and south of Europe but to the western 'core-countries' came in

June 2018, when the hardline interior ministers of Austria, Germany, and Italy formed what the Austrian Chancellor Sebastian Kurz poetically called an "Axis of the willing".[5] His choice of words, coincidentally or not, carries much darker historical undertones: a previous 'Axis' between precisely those three countries occupied Europe in the Second World War.

But what is the 'Axis of the willing' without Hungary? Only a month after this official inauguration of the 'Axis', at the end of July, in his annual speech to ethnic Hungarians in Romania, Viktor Orbán announced that the European Parliament elections in May 2019 could bring about a shift toward 'illiberal Christian democracy' in the European Union that would end the era of multiculturalism and immigration.[6]

The question we face today is not so much what the future of Europe will look like. It's more urgent than that. The question is: what if the future is already here? Or to go a necessary step further: what if the 'illiberal' aspect of democracy is not just something characterising those regimes and leaders openly advocating the fight against liberal values, but is becoming a reality of western democracies themselves?

State of emergency

Over the past twenty or so years—more or less since 9/11—the state of emergency has ceased to be an exception. After the Paris terrorist attacks of November 2015, the French government declared a 'state of emergency', which is still in place today. In order to protect against the threat of terrorism, the state imposed unjustified measures restricting freedom of movement and the right to peaceful assembly. According to Amnesty International, between November 2015 and May 2017 the French authorities used emergency powers to issue 155 decrees prohibiting public assemblies, in addition to banning dozens of protests by recourse to ordinary French law. They also imposed 639 measures preventing specific individuals participating in public assemblies. Of these, 574 targeted those protesting against proposed labour law reforms. According to media reports, authorities imposed dozens of similar measures to prevent people from participating in protests after the second round of the presidential elections on 7 May 2017.[7] In other words, peaceful protests are treated as a potential threat such as terrorism, rather than a fundamental right. Similar states of emergency have recently been active in various European countries including Italy, Germany, Spain, Belgium, the United Kingdom, and Turkey. Most recently, at the 2017 G20 Summit in Hamburg, an unprecedented 'state of emergency' was declared, and even the right to protest and show discontent was banned in Hamburg's broad city centre.[8]

All these instances of 'state of emergency' across Europe might seem temporary. However, the sheer volume of European countries declaring them for one reason or another—from fighting terrorism to fighting refugees—indicates otherwise. The situation can rather be described as a 'state of exception' (*Ausnahmezustand*), defined by the legal theorist Carl Schmitt as the right of the sovereign to transcend the rule of law in the name of the public good. In other words, in order to defend the constitution, the constitution can be suspended. In order to protect the people, it is the people's fundamental rights—freedom to assemble, protest, and so on— which are suspended first.

Indeed, the concept of the 'state of exception' is so tightly woven into the history of Germany between the two World Wars that it is impossible to understand Hitler's rise to power without understanding the uses and abuses of Article 48 of the Weimar Constitution.[9] The last years of the Weimar Republic were acted out in a 'state of exception'. As the Italian philosopher Giorgio Agamben points out, Hitler's rise may not have been so straightforward had Germany not been under a regime of presidential dictatorship for nearly three years, and had the parliament been functioning properly.[10] This situation was justified by Schmitt on the grounds that the president acted as the 'guardian of the constitution', but the end of the Weimar Republic in fact clearly demonstrated the opposite: that, in the words of Agamben, a protected democracy is no democracy at all. Instead, the paradigm of constitutional dictatorship functions as "a transitional phase that leads inevitably to the establishment of a totalitarian regime".

In this light, a recent renewal of interest in the years of the Weimar Republic is maybe more than coincidence. Take the success of the popular German TV series *Babylon Berlin*, based on Volker Kutscher's police thriller about the decadence and disintegration of the late Weimar Republic and Germany's slide into Nazism. A direct connection can be made between cocaine dealers, pornographers, nationalists, organised crime, street clashes between the police and the workers so vividly depicted in *Babylon Berlin* with the 'state of exception' and rising Nazism. And if we go back to the future, what if a better parallel to our own times isn't so much the 1930s (now frequently used to warn of the times ahead), but the 1920s and the period of Weimar? What if it is the 'state of exception' deployed during the last years of the Weimar Republic which carries a crucial lesson for our future?

Two sides of the coin

To understand how a democratic order can turn into a 'state of exception', it is not enough to enact the usual verbal gymnastics that portray 'illiberal democracies' as something opposed to the 'open society' which was to be reached after the 'end of history'. We already live after the end of history. When Fareed Zakaria published an essay in *Foreign Affairs* twenty years ago, titled "The Rise of Illiberal Democracy", he proclaimed that western liberal democracy might prove to be not the final destination on the democratic road, but just one of many possible exits.[11]

However, what Zakaria and subsequent liberal critics of 'illiberal democracy' didn't and still don't consider is this question: what if it is just the other side of the same coin? Moreover, what if the choice between 'liberal' and 'illiberal' is fake? What if, instead of being opposites, the two actually reinforce each other?

To put this into the terms of today's political conjuncture: what if the rise of contemporary 'illiberal democracies'—from Orbán to Trump to Salvini to Kurz—is dependent on the inability of the (neo)liberal establishment to handle the 2008 financial crash, just as the failed response of the liberal elites to the financial crash of 1929 helped the 'illiberal' forces of Nazism and Fascism rise to power?

What if, in the same way that the (neo)liberal Hillary Clinton wasn't an answer to the 'illiberal' Donald Trump, the current answer to Europe's crisis of liberal democracy isn't the same old (neo)liberal response currently represented by Emmanuel Macron, who is portrayed by German philosophers such as Habermas and Sloterdijk just as Hegel would describe Napoleon: the 'world-spirit on the horseback of history'?

To understand just how 'illiberal democracy' is inscribed in the very origin of democracy, so that a shift from 'liberal democracy' towards a state of exception or civil war is inherent in the very concept of democracy, we must turn to the ancient Athenian model—not as a blueprint of what democracy should look like, but as the origin of the problem.

Isonomia

In his groundbreaking work, published in English only in 2017 under the title *Isonomia and the Origins of Philosophy*, the Japanese philosopher Kojin Karatani convincingly shows that taking Athenian democracy as a model will never allow us to solve the problems faced by modern democracy. Being the composite of liberalism and democracy, it is not able to resolve its basic contradiction between equality and freedom.[12] If one aims for freedom, inequalities arise; if one aims for equality, freedom is compromised. Liberal democracy cannot transcend this. According to Karatani, instead of idealising Athenian democracy, it is more important to recognise in Athens the prototype of these problems.

While Athenian democracy sought to equalise people via the redistribution of wealth, it was at the same time rooted in the homogeneity of its members. Not only did it exclude heterogeneity, but realised it by relying on both internal exploitation (of slaves and resident foreigners, the *metic*) and external exploitation (the colonisation and subjugation of other *poleis*). In other words, Athenian democracy was already inseparable from the sort of nationalism that resembles Benedict Anderson's famous concept of the modern nation as an 'imagined community'.[13]

Karatani's major contribution, not only to the critique of liberal democracy but to the traditional history of philosophy, is that instead of turning to Athenian democracy, we should return to the Ionian *isonomia* (ἰσονομία: 'equality of political rights', from the Greek *isos*, 'equal', and *nomos*, 'law') and to the philosophy of the pre-Socratic philosophers, who are still dismissed as having only dealt with 'natural philosophy'.

It is assumed that ethical and political questions were not things these philosophers were seriously thinking through and dealing with (a phase that, according to the traditional history of philosophy, only emerged with Socrates). This, to Karatani, is a mistake. Greek political philosophy, and democracy with it, has to be seen as originating from Ionia, and Socrates should be taken off the pedestal. His thought can be better understood as a transition from pre-Socratic to Athenian philosophy, owing many of its ideas and values to Ionian philosophers. Socrates was in fact the "last person to try to reinstitute Ionian thought and politics".[14]

Clans and nomads

But why, according to Karatani, was the political system of Ionia (*isonomia*) a more equal and free system than Athenian democracy? Primarily, the Ionians did not place great importance on their place of origin, which led to a culture free from deep attachment to the traditions of a tribal society that characterised the mainland.

The cities of Ionia were formed by colonists who did not bring the traditions of the clans. Freed from the bonds and restraints of kinship, they restored in the *poleis* of Ionia the nomadic existence that preceded tribal society, which now took the form of foreign trade and manufacturing—itself not simply the exchange of goods, but experiences and cultures in a space best described as Mediterranean. The Greek *polis*, on the other hand, was based on social strata that ascended from the house-hold (*oikos*) to the clan (*genos*) to the brotherhood or kinship (*phratry*) to the tribe (*phylai*).

Athens was no longer a clan society, but the tribal traditions were still alive and well. Even transforming the people into a *demos* didn't prompt the formation of a *polis* based on autonomous social contracts between individuals. Even in the age of Pericles (the zenith of Athens), kinship determined citizenship, and foreigners from the other *poleis* were excluded.

Instead of just belonging to the *polis*, the Ionians considered themselves as belonging to the *cosmopolis*, and it is precisely this kind of political philosophy that can be found in the pre-Socratic Ionian philosophers.

Civil war

In the best manner of historical materialism, Karatani goes to the end. Athenian direct democracy depended on the ruling and plundering of the other *poleis*. It was this imperialistic expansion that set the precondition for Athenian democracy and tied it to the development of the slave system. Meanwhile, deep class conflict drove civil society: namely, the fact that most citizens were poor.

"Democracy in Athens", says Karatani,

> meant the seizure of power by the majority and the redistribution of wealth through taxation of the nobility and the wealthiest members. As one would expect, this was met with resistance by the nobility and the elite. This kind of conflict does not admit

of a solution. This is because it seeks to resolve the problem by redistribution of wealth without addressing the reason for the gaps between rich and poor in civil society and the social conditions which give rise to them. What gives the appearance of solving this internal class antagonism is the imperialistic policies that seek a source of wealth in the exploitation of foreign countries.

This is why democracy at its very origin in Athens was characterised by *stasis* ('civil war'), a growing struggle between the oligarchic and democratic factions which took a particularly virulent form during the Peloponnesian War. In the *History of the Peloponnesian War*, Thucydides describes in detail the experience of *stasis* in the Greek *poleis* (in Athens in 411 BC or Corcyria in 427 BC): fear and confusion, survival struggle and violence, but also distrust and despair, all leading to the dissolution of social solidarity.

In short, the *demos* was inevitably reduced to self-oriented, isolated individuals. What Thucydides describes is known today as 'fake news' ("the ordinary acceptation of words in their relation to things was changed as men thought fit") and 'populism' ("the tie of blood was weaker than the tie of party, because the partisan was more ready to dare without demur; for such associations are not entered into for the public good in conformity with the prescribed laws, but for selfish aggrandisement contrary to the established laws").

The enemy within

Couldn't we use Thucydides' description of *stasis* to understand our current political conjuncture, from 'fake news' to Trumpism? Isn't this Thucydidean *stasis* a defining feature of our own liberal democracies turning into 'illiberal democracies'?

It could be said that even Thucydides himself viewed the Peloponnesian War as a *stasis* between the Greeks: that is, an *internal war*.[15] Why should we not perceive the current proliferation of 'illiberal democracies' around the globe not as an enemy from outside, but an enemy within our very own 'liberal democracy'? Why not consider the current *stasis* as a product of 'liberal democracy' itself?

For the Italian philosopher Giorgio Agamben, *stasis* (civil war) has to be situated in the relationship between the *oikos* (household) and the *polis* (city). It is not simply a relationship between the private and the public. It is more the politicisation of the *oikos* and the 'economising' of the *polis*: the *oikos* is politicised and included in the *polis* through *stasis*. Thus politics, according to Agamben, must be a field of forces whose extremes are the *oikos* and the *polis*. Between them, civil war marks the threshold through which the unpolitical is politicised and the political is 'economised'.

"Athenian democracy is perhaps the place", says Agamben in his exploration of the origins of *stasis*,

> in which this tension found for a moment a precarious equilibrium. In the course of the subsequent political history of the West, the tendency to depoliticise the city by

transforming it into a house or a family, ruled by blood relations or by merely economic operations, will alternate together with other, symmetrically opposed phases in which everything that is unpolitical must be mobilised and politicised. In accordance with the prevailing of one or the other tendency, the function, situation and form of civil war will also change.[16]

It seems like the current rise of 'illiberal democracy' which is transforming the world into a house or family "ruled by blood relations or merely economic operations", is not merely a deviation of 'liberal democracy' but a result of the unresolved contradictions present within democracy itself.

The point of these short prolegomena to the critique of 'illiberal democracy' is the following: If we are not able to confront the fact that modern liberal democracy is based both on internal and external exploitation and exclusion, which in itself is a long-lasting class war ("There is a class warfare," Warren Buffett said, "but it's my class, the rich class, that's making war, and we are winning"), then we will be doomed to live in the world of 'illiberal democracy' which is now rapidly transforming into *stasis* with devastating consequences for the whole of humanity—and the planet.

The only way to come close to true democratic egalitarianism (what the Ionian philosophers called *isonomia*) consists in going beyond the false binary choice between 'liberal' and 'illiberal' democracy.

This is the direction in which DiEM25 is trying to navigate, not only when it comes to the serious philosophical and political debate that has to take place, but also when it comes to the way of organising itself and its different forms of political action.

Notes

1   Népszava et al, "Orbán Considers Alternative to Democracy," *VoxEurop*, 30 July 2012, voxeurop. eu/en/content/news-brief/2437991-Orbán-considers-alternative-democracy.

2   Viktor Orbán, "Full Text of Viktor Orbán's Speech at Băile Tuşnad (Tusnádfürdő) of 26 July 2014", *The Budapest Beacon*, 29 July 2014, https://budapestbeacon.com/full-text-of-viktor-Orbáns-speech-at-baile-tusnad-tusnadfurdo-of-26-july-2014.

3   Christopher Adam, "Viktor Orbán Tells Friends of Hungary That Dictatorial Countries Are More Successful than Democratic Ones," *Hungarian Free Press*, 11 May 2015, hungarianfreepress.com/ 2015/05/11/viktor-Orbán-tells-friends-of-hungary-that-dictatorial-countries-are-more-successful-than-democratic-ones/.

4   " 'The Dictator Is Coming': Juncker Trolls Hungarian PM Orbán," *YouTube*, Russia Today, 22 May 2015, www.youtube.com/watch?v=juFxBhDSK9s.

5   Vassili Golod, "Austria's Kurz Wants 'Axis of Willing' Against Illegal Migration," *Politico*, 13 June 2018, www.politico.eu/article/austrias-sebastian-kurz-wants-axis-of-willing-against-illegal-migration/.

6   Mark Heinrich, ed., "Hungarian PM Sees Shift to Illiberal Christian Democracy in 2019 European Vote," *Reuters*, 28 July 2018, www.reuters.com/article/us-hungary-orban/hungarian-pm-sees-shift-to-illiberal-christian-democracy-in-2019-european-vote-idUSKBN1KI0BK.

7   See "France: Unchecked Clampdown on Protests under Guise of Fighting Terrorism," *Amnesty International*, 31 May 2017, www.amnesty.org/en/latest/news/2017/05/france-unchecked-clamp-down-on-protests-under-guise-of-fighting-terrorism/.

8   Srećko Horvat, "We Came to Hamburg to Protest about G20—and Found a Dystopian Nightmare," *The Guardian*, 6 July 2017, www.theguardian.com/commentisfree/2017/jul/06/hamburg-protest-g20-dystopian-nightmare-security-disunity-politics.

9   The text of Article 48 reads, "If security and public order are seriously disturbed or threatened in the German Reich, the president of the Reich may take the measures necessary to reestablish security and public order, with the help of the armed forces if required. To this end he may wholly or partially suspend the fundamental rights."

10   For this point see: Giorgio Agamben, *State of Exception*, University of Chicago Press Books, 2005.

11   Fareed Zakaria, "The Rise of Illiberal Democracy," *Foreign Affairs*, 1997, www.foreignaffairs.com/articles/1997-11-01/rise-illiberal-democracy.

12   Kojin Karatani, *Isonomia and the Origins of Philosophy* (Durham: Duke University Press, 2017).

13   Benedict Anderson, *Imagined Communities: Reflections on the Origin and Spread of Nationalism* (London: Verso, 2006).

14   Karatani, 134.

15   A thesis put forward by Jonathan J. Price, *Thucydides and Internal War* (Cambridge: Cambridge University Press, 2001).

16   Giorgio Agamben, *Stasis: Civil War as a Political Paradigm* (Stanford: Stanford University Press, 2015), 23.

Europe: For a Transnational Democracy

Sam Hufton

When Europe set about drafting a constitution in the winter of 2002, it did so to great fanfare. The belief that the Old Continent was about to have its own 'Philadelphia Moment' was actively propagated by a political class[1] determined to crown their 50-year-long project to transform Europe with the invocation of that ancient act of political metamorphosis: the constitution.

Yet what actually occurred was one of the greatest acts of theatre in the history of European politics. For what was being drafted at the Laeken Convention was not a constitution in any meaningful sense, but another treaty. Admittedly, one more streamlined and sophisticated than the seventeen treaties and their thirty-six annexed protocols which preceded it, but nonetheless a compromise between Heads of State and Government, negotiated far from their electorates and any democratic institutions designed to set the political agenda and hold presidents and ministers to account.

However, this is not some unfortunate flaw of the European Project. It is the cornerstone on which this complex, obscure entity is built and it is the rot at the heart of the Union that makes its governance opaque and illegitimate. The European peoples' place in this Union has always been on the sidelines: outside the halls of power, below the grand summits. This is the outcome of the choice to build a political system on treaties, and this is why, as Yanis Varoufakis put it, Europe doesn't just have a deficit of democracy: it is a democracy-free zone.

At the end of this spectacle, Europeans were no closer to believing the constitution was real than at its beginning. The French and Dutch electorates rejected it in 2005, and other states planning to ratify it via referenda cancelled them to avoid further embarrassment. The time for make-believe European constitutionalism was over.

Here we look at the causes behind these failures of European politics, failures that leave its public support hollow, provoke deeply authoritarian reflexes, and breed a contempt for democratic politics that feeds the very nationalism this Union was constructed to prevent. The irony is that the people at Laeken had it right; the way to undo all this is to convene a historic Constituent Assembly, and draft a democratic constitution for Europe.

Corporatism and technocracy

According to Europe's constitutional experts John Erik Fossum and Agustín José Menéndez[2], a constitution must perform three roles: it must bring together the rules by which the system runs, make clear the norms and standards by which it operates, and formally present these as the ideas which underpin the system so that they are known. These are necessary components if we are to trust that we are equals in a political community—that we are citizens. Without them, a political system lacks democratic essence.

For a legal order to be democratic, both its constitutional origin and everyday legislation must be democratic. But it is not good enough for citizens simply to be equal under law. They must also be its authors. This is the very idea of a *pouvoir constituant*—the power of the citizens to constitute legitimate political authority. This authority then represents the sovereignty of the citizens, the right to decide on the affairs of the political community, as defined through a constitution. The EU does wield this authority, having the power to make laws which directly apply to its citizens. The treaties gave it this power. The fundamental problem is that this law has no democratic origin: the power of the Union was instead constituted by the nation states. The Union's authority is not democratic.

Does this matter? Couldn't the Union still act as if it had been constituted democratically? An analysis of how it operates reveals that this is no theoretical problem. In practice, the treaties ensure that the Union cannot recognise itself as a *polis*, an area of common interest in the name of which public power is exercised. In fact, the EU categorically rejects the existence of such a polis, and structurally prevents one from forming. What takes its place is a coalition of interests which are assumed as separate: the national interests represented in the Council. Without the recognition of any common interest, all that can emerge from their deliberations is a compromise between isolated demands.

The technocrats of Brussels serve the key purpose of finding the compromises that allow them to present a consensus masquerading as an act in the common interest. It was decided in the 1960s that a consensus was the best way to reach such decisions, rather than the overt victory of some national interests over others. This allowed the EU to create the illusion of common interests.

From this moment onwards, the compromises they reached were immensely significant, as were the interests served by those decisions. The role of the technocrats became crucial in maintaining the appearance of accord. And such an environment, where isolated interests are amalgamated and packaged together as elite compromises, became fertile ground for corporatism.

At the core of corporatism lies the assumption that economic interests are the only basis on which to exercise public power. By finding a compromise between these private interests and incorporating as many as possible, action can be taken in the name of all. It is clear why the technocrats and diplomats in the Union might embrace this: the system began life as a cartel administration, thinking sectorally about managing economic interests. Everyone advocates for themselves and the technocrats must bring peace and order to the resulting free-for-all. The national governments are simply the loudest and most effective lobbyists with the power to decide on the final compromise.

There is the trick of the treaties: national governments remain sovereign, but only exercise power in the black hole at the heart of the Union where there are no political principles, no limits, no common interests. Corporate lobbyists promote fragmented economic interests by influencing national representatives, and are brought to a compromise through technocratic management. Sovereignty is only exercised as the 'Governments-in-Council', as only there can decisions be made on behalf of Europe. In this domain, there are no controls. National governments have full discretion to legislate on whatever they like, far from the prying eyes of their electorates and democratic institutions.

Corporations use this to bypass parliamentary institutions and gain direct access to governments in ways no other sector of the economy can. Corporations have both the wealth and the networking gravitas to access disproportionate representation. Yet this is how technocracy conceives of 'representative government', allowing it to manage economic interests through amalgamating and satisfying them, while relieving it of the responsibility to consider real common interests by engaging with any of the people who rely on their individual voices for representation.

There is no place for democracy here. It is an obstacle to a functional process. Technocracy allows corporate interests to influence policy without finding a mandate for their agendas from the citizens.

This was exactly the premise of Friedrich Hayek's interstate federation. In 1939, he advocated that citizens should be excluded from political decision-making in order to protect corporate interests, forcing them to submit to the homogenising, dehumanising power of the market unbound. Authoritarian laissez-faire: let some be free to do whatever they want to everyone else, and deprive the rest of any power to resist. The global over-class we see today, pursuing its interests without regard for the vast mass of citizens, relies on these mechanisms to do so.

Corporatism takes advantage of the fragmented state of political agency beyond the nation to sideline democratic processes, commandeer national authority, and implement its agendas with the help of technocrats who ensure that it goes enforced.

Economic interests are the only rallying point internationally, which means that the bearers of economic power—corporations—must be allowed to bring this about through a global unification of markets. In this form of globalisation, all sovereignty is lost, since there is no transparency in who takes responsibility for decisions. This dilution of political authority, and the attendant concentration of bureaucratic power, uncouples the authority to decide and the capacity to decide. Democracy is unmade.

As Altiero Spinelli and Ernesto Rossi recognised in the Ventotene Manifesto, corporatism is incompatible with democracy, the essence of which is to recognise our equal agency in a community. Corporatism creates an over-class with full agency. Sovereignty is wielded out of sight so that the question of 'who decides?' becomes irrelevant. The Governments-in-Council is the product of a post-sovereign governance where ministers retain all their power while reducing national democracy to a husk. Around 70 per cent of legislation at the national level is the adoption of EU directives[3], monetary policy is no longer decided separately in the Eurozone, and agreements like the Stability and Growth Pact and Fiscal Compact constrain national room for fiscal manoeuvre. It is no longer the right of citizens to determine who gets to decide, but the prerogative of a distant elite cartel.

In their hubris, the men and few women who crafted the treaties made it easy for the populists who attack the Union today to do so on grounds of distance, opaqueness, and complexity. They did not count on nemesis. In denial of the lessons of Greece, they have failed to take democracy into account. The permissive acceptance of this abuse of power died in the 1990s. The tide of indignation that threatens to replace it might overwhelm everything that has been achieved by the European Project over the past seven decades of peace.

Democracy and the nation

Is this what we want from Europe? To write off any vision of post-national government, and retreat behind the 'Maginot Line' of national sovereignty? It would be a false hope to suggest that there is refuge in the bosom of the nation state, and equally self-defeating to mistake the globalisation underway for the only form in which a post-national politics might emerge.

The years 1914–1945 exemplify what happens if we believe nation states can only relate to each other internationally on the basis that they are isolated and owe no obligations to each other. This rejection of universal humanity and its ideals leads to violence, oppression, and fear, and the destruction of civilisation. This is due to the inherent limitations of the nation state that prevent it from fulfilling universal principles.

Nation states are founded on the idea that a *demos*, the community on which democracy is based, can only emerge if there is a pre-existing *ethnos*. Only that ethnos provides the ability for people to recognise that they have the common interests on which democracy relies. This is why the treaties fail to allow for a common European interest, substituting for it a coalition of individual national ones; because there is no European nation from which a European demos could emerge.

A citizenry empowered to be self-reflective and critical is central to Jürgen Habermas' concept of 'constitutional patriotism'. To be constitutionally patriotic is to be loyal to the ideals articulated in one's constitution. Institutions are established to realise those ideals, hence their actions and our collective memory of their actions must be questioned, so we can judge their success.

The endeavour is ongoing because universal ideals are abstractions. It is an illusion when politicians claim to be in possession of the 'will of the people', like the Jacobins in the 1790s or the Brexiteers after 2016. A common will is like all universal abstractions: we work as if we can reach it. It is never a distinct or fixed reality. It is continuously bringing an image into greater focus, a greater sense of all the different parts, which always provides clarity, even if not *full* clarity.

It is qualitatively different from private interests, because it emerges not from an individual but a social process of realisation. All citizens must always have the equal agency to shape it. We see this unfold in the European Union, which categorically rejects the notion of a truly public European interest and which has descended into a mass of warring national and corporate interests, each trying to constrain and dominate each other through the absolute power of the Council. *Standortkonkurrenz*[4] is the result of national authority being commandeered for the purpose of pursuing corporate interests at the supranational level. Robbed of power, national communities are left to fend for themselves, their citizens losing their ability to participate in politics as the polis disintegrates.

Meanwhile, the nation state rejects diversity in favour of uniformity, creating official national narratives propagated by the state, which naturally exclude critical perspectives. When they arrive, foreigners are assumed incapable of participating. 'National interests' are represented internationally as immutable and devoid of the complexity of reality. National loyalty is still expected as a precondition for belonging. The state traps itself in its own particularity. In such a subservient environment, any constitutional patriotism can decline into civic nationalism, unquestioning subjection to an ossified political system, and deference to an oligarchic ruling class.

What we need is a post-nationalist[5] political community to allow this process to unfold to its full ambition. It cannot rely on the kind of internationalism supported only by an ethno-culturally homogenous democracy. We must reject the idea that life can be integrated within nations but not between them. This is a shallow view of communities, especially democratic ones; a view repudiated by the lived reality of Europe. Yet this is the premise of the international: we can conduct negotiations and establish relations across the border voids, but we cannot cross them. We remain isolated from each other. The only way these communities can interact is in far-off summits where our differences are technocratically managed: nations cannot be socialised together.

But Europe is the home of a 'transgressive civilisation'[6]; where diverse influences, identities, and beliefs, people of multiple communities and loyalties, have long coexisted and confronted each other. Internationalism does not capture this. To prevent it from becoming a nationalist echo chamber, what the Union must facilitate is a transnational politics where the nations themselves open up to each other, cross the chasms between them, and begin this process of critical self-reflection.

This cannot occur through the false unity of nations present in international summits, but through the communities themselves enmeshing with each other. It will not eradicate nations, languages, cultures, and historical memory, but realise their particularity within a whole. This process is embodied in the civic state.

Transnationalism and the civic state

A democratic Europe must draw on a more sophisticated understanding of a political community that can function democratically and peacefully, and it must do so without replicating the mechanisms which create an oligarchic ruling class with the façade of unity and common interest. It must understand that such an interest cannot emerge from a coalition of private interests, but involves everyone as equal agents engaging with each other and realising the mutually reinforcing relationship between the individual and the collective, the particular and the universal.

This civic state relies on an unrealised mode of politics: transnationalism. This maintains that democracy—and other ideals such as justice, liberty, and equality— can only unfold in a meaningful way through the socialisation of nations as a single democratic community. Democracy is not about the 'will of the people' as a sum of individual wills, or the 'general will' as a grand coalition of private wills. When majoritarianism can be used to batter into submission our collectively guaranteed status as equal agents, such a democracy is stillborn.

Democracy is about everyone's will being equally influential on the exercise of public power. This manifests as a community of citizens critically engaging with each other's interests as they relate to their own and their common institutions' ability to carry them out. That process will be conflictual, it will provoke criticism and reflection, and we must all be able to engage in it as equals. Democratic politics can only unfold through this process of peaceful conflict, in which sums of individual wills are required for law and decision-making, but only as part of an ongoing process of realising the common interest. The common interest emerges not through an individual, but a social process of realisation.

The Belfast Agreement of 1998 demonstrates how this can work, having radically transformed the basis of national identity.[7] Those born in Northern Ireland may choose British or Irish citizenship, or both, as they so wish. It is not assigned, not inherited, not monolithic, absolute or immutable. It is not determined elsewhere. It is the product of the individual's interaction with others as they try to realise a common whole. In amending its constitution, the Republic has recreated the Irish nation as something you can join and contribute to.

This is how transnationalism aims to remove the reactionary trappings of the national state-system, creating a new form of state around which can grow the 'new, genuine democracy'.[8] Diversity must be embedded in the community, and they must constitute their sovereignty—the authority to act—together. They then guarantee their agency to determine the aim of the community together, allowing them, through their interaction, to pursue and redefine common endeavours by installing and dismissing governments, passing legislation, and setting the agenda. A shared civic identity will exist alongside various national, regional, and local ones, refining and reinforcing the basis for a common whole.

These are the pillars of the constitution of the civic state. It relies on a post-national, post-ethnic identity based on civic, democratic values and processes, complementing the identities which give us belonging. This provides the basis for peoples to guarantee each other's different languages, cultures, and memories of history; the belief that their differences can be reconciled through a conscious effort to engage in democracy, yielding a dynamic, evolving community.

Transnationalism challenges our opponents on both fronts. It challenges the idea of order through an international concert of nations and a global order of markets. The global overclass created from these interlocking forces must suppress all ideas of a restrained, democratic government serving the public good. We see here why the liberal establishment relies on nationalist populism: to reinforce the idea that only an oligarchic ruling class can force these differences into consensus. The super-rich can then pursue their interests entirely separately from the average citizen. Unrestrained global capitalism emerges from the nexus of technocracy, international diplomacy and corporatism. Here is an alternative which can halt its advance: a transnational constitution to establish a civic state.

Constituent Assembly

The momentum for this can only emerge from the citizens, which is why we must convene the crucible of democratic constitutionalism: the Constituent Assembly. This has been the means by which free peoples have made their voices heard in the exercise of public power for over 200 years, and so we must call for one which will have the full right to draft and propose a democratic settlement for the European Union. This is the epoch-advancing step among peoples who recognise each other as citizens with the ability to find a common will, so that they are not only governed by the law but also the authors of that law. Through discussion, argument, creativity, and the common desire for an accountable, democratic, just, and legitimate government, we will shape the cornerstone of our democracy.

This cornerstone relies on our voices being heard as the constituent power of a political community of common endeavour and commitment to the ideals of civil society. Here we work to a settlement of what this union of nations should be, how we should use it, and what it should be for. There will be no summit, no diplomats or bureaucrats working for hidden agendas, no last-minute fudges, obscure compromises, ignoring of facts, and certainly no exclusion of citizens on the pretence that we don't have the right to decide. We, the disparate and diverse peoples of this turbulent yet mighty continent, claim the right to decide by calling for this Constituent Assembly on a Democratic Constitution for Europe.

Let us spread the call. We must demonstrate to Europe's authorities that our proposal is both viable and of the highest value. We must invite Europe's authorities to recognise the appeal of Europe's peoples to be governed truly democratically and in accordance with the principles of civil government. Where they do not, we must disobey. We must agitate and demand this assembly, and when we have our chance, we must organise it as our predecessors did for their struggles: independently, as citizens.

*   *   *

Democracy is fragile. It relies on a complex set of conditions to work, and these fall apart when the potential for change departs from politics and people feel disconnected from institutions that have ossified and ruling classes who only weigh the interests of the powerful. Continued potential for peaceful change is therefore the principal condition: politics must be a process. That is why politics must be transnational and we propose the civic state to that end.

It is not that Europe is the only place where this can exist, nor is it the only place it should. But Europe is ready now to enter this new epoch. It has been unconsciously engaged in it for centuries, and the culture emerging from it is closest to the kind that transnationalism needs in order to work. Thus, it is our responsibility to draft a constitution on these principles, found a civic state, and demonstrate to the world all that is possible: another kind of politics, another democracy, another Europe—another humanity.

Notes

1 See Joschka Fischer's speech, "From Confederacy to Federation: Thoughts on the Finality of European Integration," Humboldt Universität zu Berlin, 12 May 2000.

2 John Erik Fossum and Agustín José Menéndez outlined the weaknesses of Europe's constitutionalism in *The Constitution's Gift: A Constitutional Theory for a Democratic European Union* (Lanham, MD: Rowman & Littlefield, 2011).

3 Ulrike Guérot, *Warum Europa eine Republik werden muss!: Eine politische Utopie* (Bonn: Dietz-Verlag, 2016).

4 Zygmunt Bauman used this term to describe 'local competition'. When capital is released from its social bonds and obligations, it generates problems globally that are met with impotent local responses, where the only option is to compete with each other to find the least exposed position and weather the storm.

5 Jan-Werner Müller believes that constitutional patriotism is the best route to a post-nationalist identity. More than the post-national, it would be free of all the subservient trappings of nationalism.

6 Bauman wrote that Europe itself has had some of the qualities of the universal, in that is has always been imprecise, undefined, uncertain, and a source of disagreement. Europe resembles an ideal in a way, rather than a fixed reality.

7 Fintan O'Toole gave a series of speeches and discussions in late 2018, in which he talked about the impact of Brexit on Ireland and the peace process in the North. Particularly, the radicalism of the Belfast Agreement which Brexit threatens to unravel. And that radicalism is what the people of Northern Ireland and the Republic agreed to embrace with regards to identity and political community.

8 Words used by Spinelli and Rossi in the Ventotene Manifesto to describe the purpose of the European federation.

Municipalism: Experiments in Autogestion

Bertie Russell

In June 2017, Barcelona en Comú hosted the first international Fearless Cities summit, bringing together more than 700 participants from six continents. This was the first time many of these initiatives had been brought into conversation. With a series of regional Fearless Cities gatherings having occurred throughout 2018 and early 2019 (in Warsaw, New York, Brussels, Valparaiso, and Naples), those four hot days in the classrooms, gardens, and grand halls of the Universitat de Barcelona may become known as the 'coming out party' of a global new municipalist movement.

Each of these initiatives emerged independently, responding to their own particular situation. They did not follow a revolutionary blueprint, nor were they eager to define themselves as liberal, socialist, Marxist, or anarchist. They are 'municipalists', and the ongoing discussions between many of them—not least through the Fearless Cities summits—is leading to a process of collaborative theory-building. From Barcelona en Comú's commitment to carrying out a 'democratic revolution'[1] to Cooperation Jackson's strategy of building 'black self-determination and economic democracy'[2], the municipalist project is unquestionably democratic. Yet when we talk about the struggle of and for democracy, we are not talking about political parties and mayors, even when they are a feature of these movements. So what are we struggling for?

What democracy?

From the election of the neo-fascist Bolsonaro to the right-wing Brexit farce and the racist schemes of Salvini in Italy or Orbán in Hungary, it appears that the failings of democracy have both fuelled and created the space for reactionary, far right and populist forces. When these same forces are driven by a demand to 'take back control', or make promises to "give voice to those populations that are cut down by those who only ever cared about financial outcomes and the multinationals"[3] (neither of which would have sounded out of place in the occupied squares of Syntagma or Plaza del Sol), does it still make sense for progressive movements to talk of democracy? Can we distinguish a democracy of the right from a democracy of the left? And do these terms still make sense when building radically progressive social movements?

It may seem anathema to suggest that building walls[4], closing university departments[5], and letting hundreds of bodies wash up on the beaches of Europe can be equated with democracy. Indeed, it's common to hear people characterise the current western interregnum as a collapse or absence of democracy, or to suggest that the rise of populism poses a challenge to democracy itself.[6] Yet in each case these are democratically elected national governments which, irrespective of the barbarity of their actions or inability to address structural crises, have legitimacy. With the (democratically elected) extreme-centre of neoliberalism having entered a terminal tailspin, various elements of the (democratically elected) extreme-right are vying to take controls.

What all these cases share is an interpretation of democracy fundamentally wedded to the state. We think of the state as a machine—an ever-modifying series of mechanisms, and the associated buildings, weaponry, and technical infrastructure to support it—which is passed from one group to another. Under state democracy (sometimes called liberal or bourgeois democracy), elections determine which group of people should control this machine. They are seen as the least worst way of ascertaining a general will[7] of the people, which is then entrusted to them, but also as a safety valve that guards against excessive misuse of the machine.

This understanding of state democracy is not the preserve of the right. From social democracy through many interpretations of socialism, the democratic question remains who controls the machine, how the population chooses them, and what they do with it. Whilst the electoral process itself may be tweaked (for example, a move to proportional representation) or interstitial 'participatory' processes introduced (such as referenda), the concept of the machine itself as a necessary infrastructure which acts on behalf of society goes unquestioned.

Yet there is another reading of democracy that recognises that "the state, then, is not just an institution. It is a form of social relations, a class practice. More precisely, it is a process which projects certain forms of organisation upon our everyday activity."[8] So what of a democracy that looks for different 'forms of organisation'? When hundreds of thousands of people took to the Spanish squares behind the banner ¡Democracia Real YA! (Real Democracy Now!) or occupied the financial heart of Wall Street chanting "this is what democracy looks like", we know this was not simply a demand for a better government. It was a challenge to state democracy, a restatement of the principle that the *demos* can organise itself, a refusal to wait for the state to deliver its own antithesis, and a belief in the possibility of us beginning to 'freely associate' together *now*.

Municipalism: experiments in autogestion

There are two opposed understandings of 'democracy': one is the idea that we can develop a plurality of approaches to self-governance, and the other is being alienated from governance through the *form* of social relationships we call 'the state'. Writing in 1966, the heterodox theorist Henri Lefebvre referred to the former as 'autogestion', noting that "the state in essence opposes a centralising principle to the decentralising principle of autogestion."[9] As Mark Purcell summarised, the struggle of or for autogestion,

> is a struggle from below by people who have decided to take on the responsibility of governing themselves, who gain confidence through their successes, and who are able to demonstrate, bit by bit, that the state is no longer necessary . . . In autogestion, we do not smash the state and then begin managing our own affairs. Rather we manage our own affairs, we work hard at it, and we get to the point where it is evident that we can truly govern ourselves. Only then does the withering of the state truly kick in. Autogestion thus offers the possibility of a withering from below. It is a clear alternative to a failed model of a vanguard party seizing the state in order to impose conditions that will cause the state to wither away.[10]

Without this interpretation of democracy, it's difficult to register the potency of Debbie Bookchin's assertion, made during the final plenary of the 2017 Fearless Cities summit in Barcelona, that "municipalism is not about implementing progressive policies, but about returning power to ordinary people."[11] The new municipalist movements do want to achieve progressive policies, but that is not what defines them. The remunicipalisation and 'cooperatisation' of essential services to reduce costs and carbon emissions whilst increasing service access and quality is a testament to what can be achieved at the municipal level[12]. Yet these should be seen as positive symptoms of a political project that is not *only* about the policies themselves (which could hypothetically be implemented by a traditional social democratic party), but about the construction of new forms of organisation of our everyday activity.

As Ana Mendez, an activist in Madrid 129 and former cultural policy advisor puts it: municipalism is "not a way to implement the state conception of the world in a smaller scale. It's a way to actually modify this level of the local government into something that is different, that actually operates at a different scale." In other words, many municipalist activists are guided by this principle of autogestion—that we should be able to govern ourselves—and that this means trying to reshape the bundle of social relationships that constitute the alienating state machine in favour of new forms of collective social organisation. As Ana says, "we were sent out like scouts, we were sent like a kind of force into this enemy territory in order to fight, in order to try to change a super complicated machine."

Caren Tepp, a councillor elected as part of Ciudad Futura in the city of Rosario, Argentina, phrases this as a commitment to:

> constructing a different kind of power. Not this power over someone, of oppression, but rather a power of equality, of getting things done, of cooperation, not of competition . . . [but] a new kind of power in society which is precisely in the hands of

ordinary people, but organised ordinary people. Ordinary people that have started down the path of prefiguration. [The aim] is not to take power but to build a new kind of power, from the bottom up, a power to do with others, a power as a creative power and collective capacity to change things.

Whether it's called autogestion, self-determination, or autonomy, it's clear that the radical democratic impulse is to build a new collective social order from within the shell of the old. Yet this commitment to develop the self-organising capacity of society does not mean forsaking working *within* existing state processes (something more akin to 'traditional' anarchist approaches to autonomy). Rather, we can see these movements as functioning transversally, developing strategies for organising in, against, and beyond the state, where the radical democratic impulse is to turn these institutions against themselves through "transforming the institution itself and its mechanisms in order to distribute power". As opposed to the narrow understanding of simply getting elected and passing progressive policies:

> this second kind of municipalism entails . . . giving autonomy to the social movements and opening the institution in order to let them act as a counterbalance. Once you have distributed power you lose the monopoly of the strategy and the agenda, so this second type of municipalism entails losing part of the control of the political process, but enhancing the changing process.[13]

People have committed to these municipalist movements for different reasons, and the tension between these two opposed understandings of democracy continues to play out within the movements themselves. Yet for Giuseppe Micciarelli, a legal scholar and activist with Massa Critica in Naples, the stakes are clear: "We have to imagine how to change institutions, because if we think that we win and we change the world, or our country, or our city, only [by] going to manage it—we fail . . . . You try to change the system, or the system will destroy you." In these terms, it is the permanent commitment to transforming institutions and distributing power outwards, and the constant movement towards 'a withering from below', that defines the municipalist project.

Municipalism beyond the municipality?

If a shared commitment of these initiatives is to enact different forms of organisation, then why not organise at a political level that controls more resources and has greater capacity to produce policy? These movements want to operate in, against, and beyond the state, so why focus on the periphery? If these movements succeed at the municipal level, why not contest power at the national level?

The emergence of a municipalist electoral list for the European Parliament —which promised to pursue a municipalist agenda for a Fearless Europe[14]— suggested that many municipalists are acting strategically and fluidly across political scales. Rather than being caught in a local trap[15] that erroneously considers towns and cities as inherently more democratic or progressive, municipalism is understood as "a means by which to achieve [our] vital goals"[16], finding strategic opportunities in the least city-like places.

Nonetheless, arguments to scale up this municipalist turn are in danger of betraying one of its central characteristics. Municipalism rejects the myth of the state as a machine that can be conquered, and instead sees it as a knot of social relations to be unpicked and differently rewoven. Municipalism did not begin in our towns, villages, and cities because political structures are at their 'strongest' there, or because movements were too weak to claim the centre of the state machine. Municipalism began where people are in their greatest proximity to one another, where there is the greatest opportunity to build new institutional forms grounded in our day-to-day relationships: a "new kind of power in society which is precisely in the hands of ordinary people."

This politics of proximity is not about localism, but about decentralising institutional forms. It is not just about distributing power downwards to cities and towns, but distributing power outwards by developing polycentric systems of ownership and governance. One example of this could be the development of Public-Common Partnerships[17], a diverse institutional form that unpicks the knot of social relations that constitute the state whilst amplifying autogestive tendencies. Such innovative arrangements exemplify what the Mayor of Naples, Luigi de Magistris, refers to as,

> an absolute novelty in the institutional and political panorama: that between civil society, social movements and local institutions there exists a relation under construction, where each has to preserve its autonomy while building new relations and forms of participation . . . and new ways of working together[18].

Rather than a demand for local control or a commitment to progressive policies, the goal of municipalism is to weave a new political geography, a new terrain of distributed power. No longer should we understand democracy as the argument over an expansive fiefdom to be owned and controlled, but as a series of human relationships that need to be collectively co-organised.

Notes

1   "Governing by Obeying: Code of Political Ethics," *Barcelona en Comú*, 2015, https://barcelona-encomu.cat/sites/default/files/pdf/codi-etic-eng.pdf.

2   Kali Akuno, "The Jackson-Kush Plan: The Struggle for Black Self-Determination and Economic Democracy," 2011, *https://static1.squarespace.com/static/59826532e6f2e1038a2870ff/t/5b6655 c86d2a73ce52f8d6ce/1533433296830/Jackson-Kush+Plan.pdf*.

3   Ilaria Polleschi, "Italy's New Political Order: A Green Beard and Mozzarella," *Reuters*, 3 July 2018, https://uk.reuters.com/article/uk-italy-politics-league/italys-new-political-order-a-green-beard-and-mozzarella-idUKKBN1JT1NA.

4   Alan Travis and Heather Stewart, "UK to Pay Extra £44.5m for Calais Security in Anglo-French Deal," *The Guardian*, 18 January 2018, https://www.theguardian.com/politics/2018/jan/18/uk-to-pay-extra-445m-for-calais-security-in-anglo-french-deal.

5   Matthew Day, "Viktor Orbán Moves to Ban Gender Studies Courses at University in 'Dangerous Precedent for Hungary,'" *The Telegraph*, 13 August 2018, https://www.telegraph.co.uk/news/2018 /08/13/viktor-Orbán-moves-ban-gender-studies-courses-university-dangerous/.

6   Yascha Mounk, "How Populist Uprisings Could Bring Down Liberal Democracy," *The Guardian*, 4 March 2018, https://www.theguardian.com/commentisfree/2018/mar/04/shock-system-liberal -democracy-populism.

7   Conceptualised by the French political philosopher Jean-Jacques Rousseau, the 'general will' is considered as one of the foundation stones of Western democratic systems, and was enshrined in the *Declaration of the Rights of Man and Citizen* during the French Revolution.

8   London Edinburgh Weekend Return group, *In and Against the State* (1979), https://libcom.org/ library/against-state-1979.

9   Henri Lefebvre, "Theoretical Problems of *Autogestion*," in *State, Space, World: Selected Essays of Henri Lefebvre*, ed. Neal Brenner and Stuart Elden (Minneapolis: University of Minnesota Press, 2009).

10 Mark Purcell, *The Down-Deep Delight of Democracy* (London: Wiley-Blackwell, 2013), 40-41.

11 "(EN) Public Panel Debate Democracy from the Bottom Up Municipalism and Other Stories," *YouTube*, Barcelona en Comú, 12 July 2017, https://www.youtube.com/watch?v=zohw_IUJUiw.

12 Satoko Kishimoto and Olivier Petitjean, eds., *Reclaiming Public Services: How Cities and Citizens are Turning Back Privatisation* (Amsterdam: Transnational Institute, 2017).

13 Adrià Rodríguez de Alòs-Moner, "Seizing Power Within Global Neoliberalism: Lessons from the Municipal Movement," *Alternative Information & Development Centre*, 13 June 2017, http://aidc. org.za/seizing-power-short-xx-century.

14 Kate Shea Baird, "A Municipalist Agenda for a Fearless Europe," *Kate Shea Baird*, 2 November 2018, https://katesheabaird.wordpress.com/2018/11/02/a-municipalist-agenda-for-a-fearless-europe/.

15 Mark Purcell, "Urban Democracy and the Local Trap," *Urban Studies* 43.11 (2006).

16 Laura Roth and Kate Shea Baird, "Municipalism and the Feminisation of Politics," *ROAR Magazine* 6 (2017), https://roarmag.org/magazine/municipalism-feminization-urban-politics.

17 Keir Milburn and Bertie Russell, "What Can an Institution Do? Towards Public-Common Partnerships and a New Common-Sense," *Renewal* 26.4 (2018), http://www.renewal.org.uk/articles/what-can-an-institution-do.

18 Luigi de Magistris, "Rebel Cities are not Utopia," in *Shifting Baselines of Europe: New Perspectives beyond Neoliberalism and Nationalism*, ed. Daphne Büllesbach, Marta Cillero, and Lukas Stolz (Bielefeld: Transcript Verlag, 2017).

Don't Let Belgrade D(r)own

Marko Anđelić , Aleksandar Mirčov, Vladimir Šestović

In 2014, the Serbian conservative government announced a €3 billion investment from a United Arab Emirates company which was set to transform a large portion of the Serbian capital, Belgrade. An area close to the Sava river and the historic city centre was to become a building ground for luxurious commercial and residential buildings, skyscrapers, and shopping malls. From the start, the Belgrade Waterfront project lacked transparency, excluding the public and experts from the review process. The 'Ne Da(vi)mo Beograd/Don't let Belgrade D(r)own Initiative' formed as a response to the way the government handled the project, with the aim to oppose the construction via institutional means, public debates, and research, leading to media campaigns and acts of civil disobedience.

At first, this project seemed like an extreme case of urban blunder combined with misappropriation of public lands through privatisation. Since the riverbanks were under municipal ownership, the government took control of the lands, aggravating the population. Activists tried to raise their concerns through legal means and at city council discussions, yet the city officials ignored almost all of their amendments and gave the project the green light. Eventually, the government handed over the legal rights of the area to a foreign investor.

Encouraging independent state actors to react

The tipping point came in 2016, when masked thugs mobbed local residents and demolished the houses in the area, all during election night. The act—which remains unsolved by the authorities—was a blatant violation of civil rights and an obstruction of the rule of law, and sparked mass protests across the country. At the height of the protests, 20,000 people took to the streets of Belgrade in the greatest expression of civil disobedience since the fall of Slobodan Milošević in 2000. In addition to regular protests in Belgrade, the Initiative sought legal methods to shut down the project, filing a public complaint to the Public Prosecutor encouraging other state actors (police, judges, courts of justice) to follow the law and investigate the matter.

This incident highlighted the ties between state officials, government-controlled media, the police, and the perpetrators of the demolitions, and the overall decay of Serbian institutions. Even though 'the Savamala case' was not an isolated event, it highlighted the absence of the rule of law instigated by the Serbian Progressive Party. This crime is just one of the many that have occurred since they seized power in 2012, and in all those affairs, citizens, independent media, and NGOs have failed to find clear answers about the perpetrators or any of the investigations. While neighbouring countries entering the EU gradually managed to implement the required democratic checks and balances, Serbia is still facing the crisis of deeply rooted corruption leading to a massive exodus, especially among younger generations.

The Don't Let Belgrade D(r)own Initiative brought together individuals and organisations committed to sustainable city development, improving urban and cultural policies, and the fair use of common resources. However, with the number of cases linked or similar to the Savamala case increasing, the Initiative announced it would run in the next local elections for Belgrade's city assembly. Through urban activism, the Initiative has mobilised citizens around core issues, challenging the neoliberal hegemony expressed through the growing privatisation of public resources.

A citizens' association merging collective aspirations

Eventually, the Initiative launched the drafting of a joint political agenda, taking input from all areas of society. Our common goal was to promote fairness and equality: a city built on solidarity. However, while the Initiative does receive donations, its financial resources can hardly challenge the mass media, and so the organisers decided to spread its message its own way, adopting a yellow duck as the Initiative mascot and transforming an old Renault 4 GTL into the Duckmobile, replete with official social media channels. Instead of paying for billboards, Don't Let Belgrade D(r)own launched its message on wheels. The move sparked the sympathy of locals and soon broke through the ruling party's steely grip on media to raise widespread popular awareness.

In the previous decade, successive governments used political pressure, privatisation, and discreet personal investments to control the Serbian media. Now, beyond a handful of satirical shows, there is a complete lack of content critical of the government, and the public only hears of any opposition through the government's own mouthpieces. Even at emergency press conferences, government representatives only allow 'friendly' media to speak. To tackle this, the Initiative constantly publishes research responding to different aspects of local decisions which fed into the electoral programme. Numerous other protests, debates, and public events were organised alongside the Belgrade Waterfront project, promoted almost exclusively through social media.

In September 2017, the Initiative Facebook page had some 75,000 followers, making it one of the largest political actors in the country. It still regularly disseminates information several times a day, maintaining a constantly open discussion. However, the biggest issue is reaching out to citizens outside the internet. To approach them, the Initiative organised numerous panel discussions and published two editions of its gazette, each in 10,000 copies. Unfortunately, no amount of effort could match the media machinery that the government used not only to defend itself, but to attack the Initiative.

Pressure, smear campaigns, and an answer from the government

Despite being assailed by investigations, fines, and arrests prior to the electoral campaign, the Initiative continued to bring to light the failures of the city's corrupt officials backed by the ruling party. Even though these were only local elections, the government resorted to non-democratic means, openly intimidating opposition candidates. First, they attacked their right to peaceful assembly, taking Initiative activists into custody for organising a protest and using parapolice to follow and wiretap others, including one of the candidates on the ballot. Finally, a government-orchestrated media campaign derided the Initiative as foreign agents funded by philanthropist George Soros: a conspiracy theory popular in various other countries, including Hungary. This combination of elements worsened the situation on the ground, placing activists and members under unrelenting pressure.

Despite all these attacks and smear campaigns, the Initiative did well in the March 2018 elections, winning more than 30,000 votes. Although the elections were described as not transparent and unfair by an independent civil society organisation, the results were endorsed by the electoral committee, leaving the Initiative outside the city council. Nevertheless, these efforts to emerge as a genuine political platform have paved the way for further mobilisations and cemented a foundation of cooperation between different groups of citizens. Starting from late November 2018, protests named '1 Out Of 5 Million' (1 Od 5 Miliona) have brought together hundreds of thousands of citizens.

Changing the way politics is done

The aim of the Initiative is to build a socially and environmentally conscious platform, named 'Citizens' Front', that will allow like-minded organisations across the country to collaborate on local and national issues, such as workers' rights, the protection of natural resources, transparent decision-making, independent media, institutional democracy, and equal rights for all. We strive to bring citizens back into politics by empowering them with resources and tools for critical thinking. We must reaffirm the right of every citizen to claim what they should expect from the State and work collectively to build a sustainable future. The need for a functioning society is strongly felt, and we of the Initiative and the Citizens' Front are out on the streets protesting for it.

While citizens' movements are emerging all across Europe, Don't Let Belgrade D(r)own looks at both domestic and external examples, working towards sharing its experience. To achieve this, the Citizens' Front must act as a citizens' association that changes the way politics is done. Belgrade and Serbia's citizens will reimagine the political arena as a public place, where diverging views can be expressed without fear of censorship or attack. Now is the time to set an example not only for ourselves but for the rest of Europe, and to convert our country into an authentic democracy with functioning institutions and political actors that respond to citizens' needs.

Democracy Has Many Enemies

Brian Eno

Since democracy is based on the idea of utilising the full intelligence of society—not just the intelligence of some rich lads who went to expensive schools—the supporters of inequitable social systems are enemies of democracy. They are limiting the intelligence base of society, just when we need all the brainpower we can get.

Since democracy is based around the idea that people should be able to make informed decisions about their future, the proprietors and producers of biased news are enemies of democracy. They are lying to society, just when we need the best information we can get.

Since democracy is ostensibly the rule of the people by the people—and not just by the wealthy or the powerful people—those who corrupt politics by using their money to swing elections are enemies of democracy. They are crooks, just when we need honesty.

Since democracy is based around the idea that people should share in the costs and benefits of their society, those who don't pay their taxes—the people who take the benefits but not the costs—are enemies of democracy. They are stealing from society, just when we need all the resources we can get.

Democracy has many enemies: those who think their wealth entitles them to a bigger say in how things work; those who assume themselves to be intellectually superior; those who think the law is for 'little people'. They should be identified and shamed, not celebrated. They are selfish freeloaders.

Democracy isn't a complicated utopian idea. It is what naturally happens when people of good will try to reach a decision together. If you are aware of your own limitations, and respect the intelligence of those around you, you will want to solicit their opinion, not out of politeness, but because you want the benefit of their minds.

"Democracy is a political system for people who are not sure that they are right."*

---

* Elmer Eric Schattschneider, *Two Hundred Million Americans in Search of a Government* (1969).

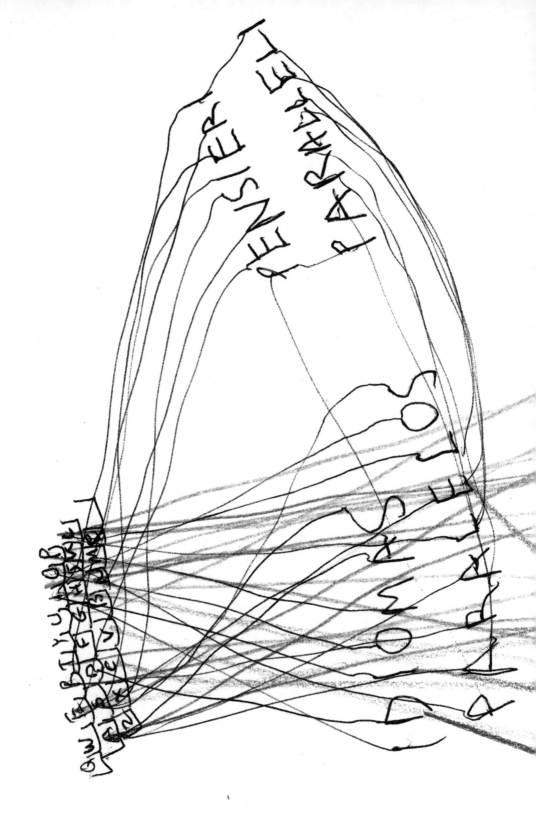

A Decentralised Europe by Gerardo Pisarello

" In 2015, many of us with a background in activism understood that municipalism was the best way to change the way politics is done and achieve concrete improvements in people's lives. And when we were elected, that's what we did. We have shown that it's from cities, from municipalities, that we can build creative, credible alternatives to the politics of austerity and fear, and that with political will we can change priorities, increase investment in our neighbourhoods, fight job insecurity, promote scientific and technological innovation, defend the commons like water and energy, create more breathable, friendly cities, and do so honestly and effectively.

We've also learned that we must defend municipalism from other levels of government. We've fought back against the Montoro Law (restrictions on public sector employment) and called for rent controls in the Spanish Congress. We're insisting on increased investment in education and health in the Catalan Parliament. And, increasingly, we need to be active at a European level to stop the far right, defend basic rights and freedoms, and stand up to global corporations who see our cities only as a business.

To remain on the margins of these battles would be to cede space to those who, if we weren't there, would continue to act against us. That's why Barcelona en Comú has been working with other Cities of Change on a municipalist agenda for all levels of government: from local to national to European. It's a collective project that we believe is innovative and necessary: in the face of narratives of fear and xenophobia, cities have a duty to create alternatives for their citizens. Let's take the experience of the Cities of Change to Europe and, from there, weave networks of solidarity and hope. If we are to have a future, it must be municipalist. "

PART THREE

Transparency

The Greek Files Campaign

Fabio De Masi

In February 2017, Yanis Varoufakis and I sued the European Central Bank.

The aim of the lawsuit was to gain access to a single document with a name befitting the institution: 'Responses to questions concerning the interpretation of Art. 14.4 of the Statue of the ESCB and of the ECB'. This document gives a legal opinion on whether the ECB exceeded its mandate when, in 2015, it cut off Greek banks from the money supply, once the Greek government had decided to hold a referendum on the troika reforms.

This case has great symbolic character, as it questions both the independence of the ECB on political matters of the Eurozone and the accountability of all EU institutions to the peoples of Europe. The ECB is supposed to be a politically independent and purely technical body, ensuring price stability in the Eurozone through a variety of tools. One important tool in the context of the Greek crisis was the Emergency Liquidity Assistance (ELA): it ensures funding to the banks facing liquidity problems. With the European interbank market down in 2015, the Greek banking sector depended heavily upon the ECB for its liquidity provision.

But in its multiple roles as creditor, referee, and lender-of-last-resort, the ECB was faced with a conflict of interest. As part of the troika, it had an interest in the implementation of the conditions tied to the bailout programme to Greece. By cutting the Greek banking sector off the money supply, it solved this conflict in a way that questioned its independence as a central bank. More precisely, the ECB only ensured that the euro would flow into Greece as long as Greece cut wages or pensions. In more technical terms, it only accepted Greek government bonds as eligible collateral if the Greek government implemented the troika reforms that looted the country. As a central bank, it should have ensured the functioning of the Greek banking sector to avoid a liquidity crisis that can quickly turn into a solvency crisis and threaten financial stability. At this point, the ECB overstepped its mandate when it mixed up the tools of its politically independent role as central bank to force Greece to fulfil the conditions of its role as a troika creditor.

The conditionality of the bailout programme by the troika included harsh austerity measures, among them cuts in pensions, tax increases, and fire-sale privatisations. The reforms were based upon neoclassical assumptions and supply-side politics that would ruin the country's economy for many years to come. Pensions were cut by more than 60 per cent, and incomes fell back to their 2003 levels. The unemployment rate skyrocketed and continues to hover at 20 per cent among the general population, and 40 among Greek youth. At the same time, 95 per cent of the credit Greece received for the bailout went to paying back debt to European banks.

These measures were not only highly unpopular with the Greek population, but economically senseless. Austerity reforms—raising taxes, cutting pensions, lowering wages—weaken domestic demand. Any monetary policy measure like lowering interest rates to encourage lending by businesses will be ineffective in a low-demand environment, as there is no incentive to invest. Cheap money will therefore stay in financial markets, with no effect on the real economy. But instead of ensuring the functioning of the Greek economy, the ECB froze its money supply and insisted on these reforms. Clearly, there was awareness of this conflict within the ECB when it requested the legal opinion on the boundaries of its mandate in the case of Greece.

To gain better insight into the negotiations between Greece and the troika, I had applied for an 'internship' at the ECB. They refused my demand, explaining that, as Member of the European Parliament, I would control the ECB and could not be its employee at the same time. They offered me background talks with a member of the ECB executive board instead. There, I learned about the existence of the document. Confident that I could manoeuvre the ECB, I asked for its disclosure. But Mario Draghi refused. Since then, Yanis Varoufakis and I, together with thousands of supporters, have tried to obtain access to the document through several ways without success.

The implication is obvious. If the ECB were convinced of the legality of its decisions in 2015, it would have disclosed the legal opinion right away.

But, ultimately, this case is not just about the ECB's mandate. It is also about the viability of democracy itself—about *which* people and *which* institutions are entitled to interfere in political decisions, processes, and outcomes. The devastation of an austerity policy imposed by the troika gives the Greek population—and all EU citizens—a right to know whether the actions of the ECB were just. Simply put, the ECB became political in Greece. As an unelected institution, it needs to explain its actions instead of hiding inside its black box.

As long as the ECB remains beyond democratic control, any government that refuses to cut wages, trim pensions, or privatise public assets can be cut off from the euro supply. Hence, our quest to open the black box of the ECB is not simply about exposing the financial alchemy of unelected bureaucrats at the ECB tower, but about democracy.

DiEM25 Policy Paper on Transparency

Edited by Rosemary Bechler

It is crucial to put an end to the widespread distrust of the European Union: most Europeans are kept unaware of what is decided in Brussels and Strasbourg on their behalf, often by their own member state politicians. To make informed voting decisions, one must know what one's politicians are up to. Transparency allows the European public to acquire that information and exposes institutions to public scrutiny, leading to more democracy, more access to information, and, ultimately, more justice and more fairness. More transparency also means that citizens make better decisions. They become more involved with the commons and develop a civic conscience which, in turn, leads to higher quality discourse over matters that concern not just a privileged few, but everyone.

DiEM25 proposes a democratic Progressive Agenda for Europe that addresses the systemic challenges the continent is facing. This document is a contribution to that end, with tangible recommendations.

Making European Union institutions fully accountable

One of the basic principles of democratic control is that people have the right to know how and why their elected representatives and public officials make decisions, particularly on issues that affect them. Access to information on the work and the decision-making processes of public bodies is at the heart of accountable governance. The most common arguments against transparency revolve around the need for a 'space to think' or to negotiate freely, potential threats to national security, additional administrative burdens, and, increasingly, business secrets. These concerns are sometimes legitimate but are usually cooked up solely to make decision-makers' lives easier—to the detriment of democratic scrutiny.

The institutions and decision-making bodies we will look at include the European Union Council, the Eurogroup, the European Commission, the European Stability Mechanism (ESM), the European Central Bank, and the troika, as well as member states' administrations as far as they are directly involved in EU decision-making processes.

Even for close observers it is challenging to understand the roles and power distributions *at* and *between* these institutions. Many are enveloped in a cloud of technocratic complexity and secrecy, making it increasingly difficult to keep track of what is happening. Insiders understand the internal communications code of an institution and can fill in the missing contextual knowledge, but outsiders unfamiliar with that code are deliberately kept baffled by what is going on at any given time.

We would like to see the disclosure of all official and informal working groups at the Council, Commission, ECOFIN, Eurojust, Eurogroup, ESM, ECB, troika, and FRONTEX to the general public and the dissemination of their documents—particularly their meeting schedules.

In the case of the European Parliament (the main legislating body with members from all member states) we propose that information such as records of who entered the building and on what business be made public. Name, nationality, and other data are collected at various security checkpoints and are therefore easy to share. Committee and group hearings and expert panels should also be required to fully disclose the identities and affiliations of panellists and external visitors. EU Parliamentary proceedings should also be televised or streamed online.

Party financing is often opaque and secretive and creates plenty of opportunities for private interests to financially influence politics. We propose that all parties running for any kind of office should publish their funding structure online in a standardised, transparent way. Political parties should also clarify where their money comes from and where it goes. Membership fees, party donations, loans: all must be accessible to the public.

The Council of the European Union is the most opaque European institution to external observers—citizens and lobbyists alike. In the interest of furthering transparency, it should consider having Permanent Representatives of Member States in the EU designated by national parliaments. Currently, council representatives are administrative officials from national ministries and diplomats. The parliamentary oversight of their delegations does not follow consistent standards. It often depends on the setup in the national political system. In addition, we should lobby for complete disclosure of all formal and informal working groups at the council using a standardised reporting format, and institutional transparency must become a required task in the job description of the next Council President.

What first must be addressed in the EU Commission is the issue of revolving doors. Heavy sanctions should be imposed on former EU officials with personal links to institutions who could benefit from privileged information. Besides being prevented from participating in meetings with the EU, it should be legislated illegal for former high officials of EU bodies to work for large financial groups or lobbyists within a predefined period—at least five years.

All financial transactions under the European Stability Mechanism (ESM) should be public. At present, banks in need of recapitalisation from the EU's bailout fund can be turned over to the ESM to restructure, recapitalise, and resolve the failing bank, instead of having the national government borrow on the bank's behalf. Decisions under the ESM restrain the options of national democracies.

The European Central Bank (ECB) has an important governing role in the euro currency zone. Decisions of the ECB are sensitive and speculation must be avoided. Yet, more openness is needed if we are to address the democracy deficit. We want to see economists and critics invited to a broad and open scientific dialogue with a view to mainstreaming and debating the weaknesses and shortcomings of the ECB system.

The troika comprises a controversial group of institutions guarding the compliance of national democracies with the budgetary agreements. Their interventions have a considerable impact on the fiscal policy of member states, which is key to national democratic sovereignty. The troika includes both EU and non-EU institutions. In these cases, common practice is to blame the lack of transparency on external players. However, since the European Commission is itself involved, all such obligations and principles of the European Treaties should apply to their work. We expect full transparency, enforced in line with EU best practice under Article 14 TFEU, and the troika should be made accountable to European Parliament members by enabling members of the latter to address written questions to any members of the former.

Implementing transparency

Most institutions, bodies, and agencies are well aware of their transparency obligations. However, since there are no formal rules regarding who to approach, the quality of responses by public officials fluctuates depending on whether one is communicating with transparency specialists. It is essential to raise the awareness of European officers about the rights of citizens and the obligation to work openly.

Public bodies edit their stories for the media, but the public deserves to be governed democratically. Its political bodies are a means to this end. Press coverage of European affairs by independent and pluralistic journalism must be safeguarded to offer the European citizenry a comprehensive picture. Transparency should help technocracies leave their institutional bubble and codes of communications behind them and open their institutions up to diverse views. The very role of media should be to confront institutions with dissenting perspectives.

Meanwhile, online platforms are essential tools. Technological improvements could be as effective as legal improvements. We should seek to expand and harmonise the number of databases open for the public, improve the usability and fitness of online services, and support independent hackathons and open government data initiatives.

Many of the transparency websites are generic in their mission. Displaying parliament questions from Italy is no different from displaying parliament questions at the EU level. Public administrations could promote the reuse of these transparency services on a national and regional level by offering the platforms under an open source licence. This way, the best implemented services would support public administrations in their response to the transparency challenge and raise quality standards. Standards for public sector documents could be mutually exchanged and jointly developed. In much the same way, transparency of information services needs to be further advanced with intelligent proposals to enact the working principle of the European Union to act as openly as possible.

Database schemes in the public sector should be open by default. All software commissioned by EU institutions should be publicly available as open source under the European Union Public License, or a compatible licence, to facilitate reuse and inspection.

EU institutions must open up their data and support the reuse of data using civic tech applications, for instance in the field of budgetary transparency. Data should be made available in open, interoperable, and machine-readable formats.

Digital online services increasingly enable political scrutiny, but proliferating innovation in data provision can be a stumbling block for transparency. As DiEM25 stressed in its first transparency petition, experienced political observers regularly discover common shortcomings with online public information services.

What we need is a systematic review of online services to meet European citizens' needs for technological non-discrimination, platform neutrality, privacy protection, interoperability, and accessibility. New legal requirements for public information services should be based on these principles, together with uniform minimum rules on streaming access to meetings, best practice guidelines, and single points of contact to track issues and publish regular progress reports.

Lobbying unmasked

Democracy is the art of finding a good compromise between conflicting interests. Articulating one's own interest and trying to influence decision-making in one's favour—individually or collectively—is therefore an integral part of the process and not inherently evil. Problems occur when certain interest groups gain privileged access to decision makers and decision-making processes—whether through personal contacts, the resources they can mobilise, or because they can offer favours.

Furthermore, while much political lobbying and campaigning is done in the public sphere, substantial parts remain hidden. Citizens rarely learn how and why these interest groups have influenced laws or administrative decisions.

EU institutions have lobby registers that collect data on who professionally tries to influence European institutions. Lobby registers are being revised to become more useful, and this process is a gradual learning curve with input from civil society. At the same time, we must ensure that no lobby privilege is created, in the sense of not compromising the legitimate rights of concerned citizens and small and medium enterprises to contact their representatives.

The European Union is assisted by external consultants—experts from the member states. Their names are found in the register of expert groups. Many of them also work for other clients and it is important to be able to trace potential conflicts of interests. Expert groups have to comprise a broad variety that reflects the diversity of Europe in terms of diversity criteria, working language, professional qualification, and country of residence. As stated above, in many cases it is not even known that an advisory board exists, and in recent years more and more expert boards have been uncovered.

Lobbying and stakeholder representation on the global level is a grave concern. We have to ensure that acts of bribery of public officials in the global south are not assisted by our tax laws. In the same way, we want to shield our democratic societies against undue intervention in our domestic election and policymaking processes. We have to build safeguards against the meddling of corporations and state actors in the elections or internal affairs of foreign countries.

Secret trade agreements

In recent years, the 'next generation' of trade agreements—TTIP, CETA, and TiSA—have generated plenty of resistance across Europe. Beyond the content of these deals that privilege large multinational corporations over citizens, consumers, and smaller local businesses, the negotiation process has accounted for much of the criticism. Due to maximum secrecy, the general public is not able to discuss these deals, and members of parliaments are not able to exercise their rights to democratic scrutiny, whereas lobbyists are warmly invited to have their say.

When the negotiations end, governments and parliaments are presented with the simple choice of 'take it or leave it'—an open, democratic deliberation about the content is not permitted. No wonder that calls to drop these agreements also include the demand to entirely rethink the way we conclude international trade agreements. This includes not just those that clearly affect European citizens negatively, but also those that the EU—also without public notice—concludes on an unequal footing with developing countries (BITs, FTAs, association agreements).

Secret negotiations should not exist in the first place, and the agreements should be made available to the public. Member states should have free access to everything related to the aforementioned. It is urgent to rethink trade agreement secrecy since it can be dangerous for the EU as well as its citizens. We must rethink the mandate of such far-reaching trade and decide whether it should be made public and if so, how much. We have to determine the kind of access that members of national and regional parliaments and governments and Members of the European Parliament ought to have to ongoing trade deal negotiations. A democratic debate preceding the adoption of such agreements should involve individuals informed in a wide spectrum of relevant fields: professionals, analysts, academics, the non-governmental sector, politicians, etc. All these debates should be public and live-streamed.

Vested interests and whistleblowers

We need to develop tools and ideas to make information on public decision-making and budgets easier to access, process, and analyse; harness people with the knowledge to understand such information; support the work of journalists and researchers who dig up the information on corruption and abuse of power; and protect those who alert the public about corrupt practices. What else do we need to have in place for this to work?

Private companies should be subject to transparency requirements. It should be legally required that private companies reveal information relevant to the public good and human rights. There should be a body/agency/association for transparency protection in the EU which would verify this and constantly work on surveys regarding conformity, environmental impact, etc.

But it isn't just decisions on behalf of the public and their implementation that are being kept from public view. Public money—or money that partly belongs to the public from taxation—is also frequently stashed away, usually through offshore channels. Too often such money becomes a reward for corrupt behaviour. When speaking about transparency in the interest of common good, we also have to address tax evasion, money laundering, and generally all forms of cheating the public interest.

We recommend the creation of a position for a Tax Evasion ombudsman: an annual report to raise awareness about tax evasion tactics, the application of reasonable policies regarding tax shelters and offshore havens, support for investigative journalists, and special funds for data whistleblowers.

Besides the income side of public budgets, there is also a need for more budgetary transparency on the expenditure side, in order for the public to see clearly who the benefactors of public money actually are. This would also enhance its ability to hold accountable those who make decisions on public budgets and to participate in the decision-making about public money in an informed way, so that every European citizen is able to evaluate the priority, weigh the benefits and drawbacks, and the cost of publicly funded projects. A central European Budget transparency web service on which to display the data of public work projects in all relevant programmes would help in this.

Public procurement is the field where the risk of corruption and administrative conflicts of interests is highest. Therefore, transparency needs to be improved. Public money gets spent on external goods and services which are supposed to serve the needs and interests of public authorities, and we could also speak of a public interest. Transparency in tendering needs to be closely matched with budget transparency. We should aim to create a portal for European public procurement grants with end-to-end monitoring and enable opportunities for small businesses to participate in calls and citizens to have a say.

Municipalities and local communities are a good starting point for reform in transparency because best practices in one city could be replicated all over the country. A special focus should be given to the information needs of the users as the main beneficiaries, the citizens in a town. We would like to see appropriate budgetary, research, and scientific resources assigned to Open Transparent City pilot projects, and the development of dedicated open government tools for Open Transparent Cities.

Many facts regarding European governance only became known to the public through leaked documents and administrative whistleblowers, such as the disclosures by Paul van Buitenen from the European Commission of fraudulent practices that led to the demise of the Santer Commission. The current availability of large arbitrary leaks leads to a new culture of openness while at the same time lowering public pressure for legal acts improving lawful transparency and openness. Leaks have shown that more lawful transparency is desirable and benefits the public interest. Lawful access is less harmful to the affected institution because it offers only limited opportunity to use the findings to create major scandals, compared to leaks of classified information under a veil of secrecy.

Transparency will remain an empty right if the knowledge of how to use it in the treaties is not mainstreamed and if citizens remain unaware of their rights and the data available to them.

[*This first green paper on transparency was drafted by André Rebentisch, with comments and feedback from citizens throughout Europe and other parts of the world.*]

The View from Brussels

Olivier Hoedeman

Brussels is the lobbying capital of Europe. Big corporations, industry lobby groups, lobby consultancies, law firms, and corporate-funded think tanks spend hundreds of millions of euros every year ensuring that EU policymaking meets the needs of big business—and it works.[1]

It is estimated that there are over 25,000 lobbyists working in the European Quarter, most in the service of corporations and their lobby groups. Whenever the European Commission proposes a new regulation or the European Parliament votes on a new law, corporate lobbyists are there, outnumbering and outspending public interest groups. On certain issues, the imbalance is staggering. In the lobbying concerning EU financial regulation, the banking sector outspends NGOs, trade unions, and other interest groups by a ratio of thirty to one.[2]

Larger numbers of lobbyists and large lobbying budgets, combined with privileged access to decision-makers, often result in excessive industry influence and the corporate capture of decision-making. One example of such privileged access is when corporate lobbyists dominate membership of the Commission's many advisory groups, or so-called 'expert groups'. This dominance can easily result in biased advice, with very negative impacts on draft EU legislation.

Research by watchdog groups has revealed that 75 per cent of all lobby meetings of Commissioners and high-level Commission officials are with lobbyists representing big business. In such key areas as financial regulation, the internal market, and international trade policy, this figure rises to over 80 per cent. The problem is equally bad for mid-level officials: over 90 per cent of the meetings that officials from the Commission's financial regulation department DG FISMA have with lobbyists are with corporate interests, and only less than 10 per cent with other interests or independent experts.

The revolving door is another important way in which industry gains the upper hand in the battle to influence the political agenda in Brussels. When senior European decision-makers—Commissioners, MEPs, officials—leave office and go straight into lobby jobs, or when lobbyists join the EU institutions, the risk of conflicts of interest and undue influence is great, undermining democratic, public-interest decision-making. And the revolving doors spin fast in Brussels. One-third of Commissioners leaving in 2014 went into industry lobbying jobs. Commission President Barroso's move to Goldman Sachs and Commissioner Neelie Kroes' switch to Uber and Bank of America were among the most controversial revolving door cases. The European Commission's revolving door culture is far from limited to Commissioners: at DG FISMA, four out of five directors who left their post between 2008 and 2017 went on to work for companies they were previously responsible for regulating.

Enabling the privileged access enjoyed by lobbyists is the belief—widespread in Brussels—in marketisation, deregulation, and the idea that what is good for big business is good for society. The irony of such faith in the free market, however, is that it has resulted in the corporate capture of EU institutions.

Lobbying power and the Bolkestein Directive

Many of these problems were clearly present in the decision-making process behind the proposed EU Services Notification Procedure. This directive is a follow-up to the 2006 Services Directive (also known as the Bolkestein Directive), which provoked mass protests in several EU countries due to concerns about its social impact, and was approved only after being scaled down. The proposed directive would radically expand EU Commission powers over national and municipal services regulation and constrain public-interest policymaking in a wide range of sectors, including city planning, affordable housing, water supply, energy supply, waste management, and many others. With the new directive, the Commission would be able to override new laws and regulations developed by national parliaments, regional assemblies, and local governments across Europe—or impose significant delays in order to change proposals. Those authorities will have to submit their regulations to the Commission three months in advance in order to receive prior approval; a far-reaching tightening of existing rules, which only allows the Commission to object after the approval.

The proposed directive is the result of an intimate working relationship between the Commission department responsible for the Notifications Procedure and three major industry lobbying groups, in particular BusinessEurope. Industry has been particularly keen on shaping the proposal, which will give it a backdoor channel to comment on—and lobby against—local legislation before it is enacted. The European Commission has essentially treated big business lobby groups as strategic partners in promoting the directive, including closed-door sessions throughout the negotiations where lobbyists and EU officials met alone. This is in stark contrast to the way the Commission has responded to many of its critics: with deafening silence.

In December 2014, a few months after the Juncker Commission took office, BusinessEurope complained to the Commission that public authorities have 'too much leeway' in implementing the Bolkestein Directive. The 'large area of discretion' creates a 'grey zone', BusinessEurope argues. It is exactly this grey zone that currently allows progressive city governments such as Barcelona and other Fearless Cities to replace failing neoliberal policies with bold municipalist initiatives and thereby achieve speedy tangible social and environmental progress.

The problem is that much of what BusinessEurope considers to be barriers and obstacles are legitimate and much-needed social and environmental policies, democratically decided and introduced to protect the public interest.

As with all EU legislation, a public consultation was held for the Notification Procedure directive in spring 2016. The consultation, however, violated the Commission's own rules as it failed to consult broadly and transparently among stakeholders. Only one trade union and not a single other civil society group participated. Not a single larger city was included, nor any EU-level federations of municipalities. The failure to consult municipalities and critical civil society voices created a bias and led to skewed conclusions.

Such failures have sparked widespread opposition to the directive, ranging from city councillors in cities like Barcelona, Amsterdam, and Napoli to large trade unions from across Europe. A number of governments are having second thoughts about the proposed directive and want to restrict both its scope and the Commission's powers.

For the future of democracy in Europe, one can only hope that the negotiations fail to deliver a deal and that this ill-conceived directive—the result of the European Commission's neoliberal tunnel vision and partnership with big business—is dropped altogether.

Member states are not safe

Examples like the Notification Procedure directive show that EU decision-making is vulnerable to corporate capture. But the problem is not limited to the European Commission, or what is described as 'Brussels'. There is an equally serious risk of EU member-state governments being heavily influenced by corporate lobbying. Very often, capture on the two levels reinforce each other.

A clear example is the Dieselgate emissions cheating scandal, which was exposed in September 2015. The responsible European Commission department (DG GROW), led by then-Commissioner Antonio Tajani, saw it as their mission to advance the interests of the car industry and turned a blind eye to evidence of emissions cheating, evidence which emerged as early as 2010. But this cover-up would have been impossible if it wasn't for powerful member state governments agreeing with this approach.

The most far-reaching degree of car industry capture of decision-making can be found in Germany, where government after government has seen it as its task to promote the interests of the car industry and protect it from unwelcome regulations. Both before and after the Dieselgate scandal broke, the German government did everything it could to delay or water down EU rules and the implementation and enforcement of these rules. Politicians both in Germany and in Brussels still fail to learn the lessons from the Dieselgate scandal and act to protect public policy-making from excessive car industry influence.

Contemporary nationalist rhetoric argues that a strong EU is imposing rules and regulations on nation states—and it often suits member states to play up to this narrative and blame the EU for decisions that are unpopular at home. However, blaming the EU 'apparatus' alone is far too easy. Too often, member state governments, acting individually or collectively, are their own bastion of corporate influence on EU decision-making. The excessive influence of the German car industry on the German government is only one of many examples.[3]

Complex EU decision-making procedures, lack of transparency, the exclusion of citizens in decision-making at the national level on EU matters, and generally weak national parliamentary mechanisms have combined to create a deficit of accountability, which corporate lobbies are happy to exploit. Indeed, many of the ways in which member states feed into EU decision-making are shrouded in secrecy. After some progress has been achieved in (lobby) transparency at the European Commission and Parliament, the Council is now clearly the most secretive of the major EU institutions. In short, the risk of corporate capture of some member states, on some EU dossiers, is very high—and is only getting worse.

What we can do about corporate capture

An essential element in preventing corporate capture of decision-making is the EU-wide mobilisation of citizens against the corporate agenda.

The good news is that this happens increasingly often and on a larger scale than ever before. An example is the 2016–2017 battle over the revision of the European Union's market authorisation for glyphosate, a key ingredient in Monsanto's Round-Up weed killer. In the past, decisions over market authorisation for glyphosate were taken quietly in meetings of little-known EU committees, without any public attention. Not this time. Civil society petitions for phasing out glyphosate due to its negative health and environmental impacts were supported by hundreds of thousands of citizens across Europe. There were demonstrations outside key meetings of the EU officials deciding on the future of glyphosate. And the vibrant public debate and citizens' mobilisations had an impact. After the European Parliament voted in favour of phasing out glyphosate, the Commission and a majority of member state governments decided for a 5-year extension of market approval for glyphosate for agricultural use instead of the original fifteen years. Meanwhile, many EU member states have introduced further restrictions on the use of glyphosate-based products, including a ban on all glyphosate-based herbicides in Belgium.

It's one thing to get one pesticide restricted or banned, but it's another thing to achieve a vast reduction in the overall use of pesticides and other polluting substances. Beyond individual lobbying battles, a deeper change is needed to prevent excessive corporate influence. Until EU decision-makers stop conflating the interests of big corporations with those of the public, profit will come before the environment and public health.

Awareness of the dangers of corporate capture is growing. In the last European Parliament, more than 180 MEPs signed the ALTER-EU 2014 pledge to "stand up for citizens and democracy against the excessive lobbying influence of banks and big business"[4]—a significant number, but still a minority of the 751 MEPs. The European Parliament is itself the target of heavy corporate lobbying pressure and there is no lack of examples of parliamentary voting being influenced by these pressures. But there are also a growing number of MEPs standing firm against industry lobbying. In 2017, MEPs managed to significantly improve the Commission's weak proposal for new EU rules to protect workers from workplace cancer risk, despite heavy lobbying pressure from BusinessEurope and other industry lobbies. And in the first months of 2019, MEPs voted for much stricter CO_2 rules for cars and for major improvements in car safety, repeatedly defeating the car industry and its aggressive lobbying.

If we want policies reflecting the interests of the environment and public health, then the companies most likely to resist them must not be allowed to write them. This applies at all stages of legislation—from ensuring the independence of advisory groups and European agencies like EFSA, to curbing the power of big business players lobbying the European Parliament, and challenging EU member states trying to weaken legislation on behalf of 'their' corporations.

Both the EU institutions and member state governments must adopt rules—and political cultures—which reduce the risk of corporate influence on EU decision-making, including an end to privileged access for corporate lobbies and full lobby transparency. Transparency is a precondition for tackling corporate influence, but not a solution in itself. It's time to go beyond transparency.

We must initiate a broad and ambitious action plan to democratise EU decision-making and reduce the risk of corporate capture.[5] This includes new ways of engaging citizens and those whose voice is less heard. It also includes better equipping the EU institutions to secure independence, reducing the dependency on external—most often corporate—expertise.

Additional measures are needed to protect decision-making from undue corporate influence. This is clearly the case when there is an irreconcilable conflict between an industry's interest and the public interest, and when corporate lobbying has blocked much-needed solutions. The European Commission's health department DG SANTE, for instance, limits the interference of the tobacco industry in public health policymaking (an approach that is unfortunately not followed by the rest of the Commission).

A similar approach is needed for climate policymaking, where fossil fuel industries are using their privileged access to policymakers to ensure ambition remains low, rather than leaving fossil fuels in the ground, where they belong. Both UN climate talks and EU climate policymaking must be protected via conflict-of-interest rules that introduce a firewall between policymakers and climate-polluting lobbyists.

Ultimately, corporate capture is only possible when decision-makers fail to prevent it. Far stronger political will is needed to protect the public interest and prevent corporate capture. Civil society networks such as ALTER-EU and MunicipalizeEurope must team up with other movements like DiEM25, and together they must demand ambitious action to curb corporate influence and rebuild democracy in Europe.

Notes

1   David Lundy, "Lobby Planet: Brussels," Corporate Europe Observatory, 2017, https://corporateeurope.org/lobbyplanet.
2   Rachel Tansey, ed., "Corporate Capture in Europe: When Big Business Dominates Policy-Making and Threatens Our Rights," ALTER-EU, 2018, https://www.alter-eu.org/corporate-capture-in-europe-when-big-business-dominates-policy-making-and-threatens-our-rights-0.
3   Vicky Cann and Belén Balanyá,"Captured States: When EU Governments are a Channel for Corporate Interests," Corporate Europe Observatory, 2019, https://corporateeurope.org/power-lobbies/2019/02/captured-states.
4   Olivier Hoedeman, "ALTER-EU: A Decade of Campaigning for Transparency, Ethics, Accountability and Democracy in Brussels," Corporate Europe Observatory, 2015, https://corporateeurope.org/power-lobbies/2015/09/alter-eu-decade-campaigning-transparency-ethics-accountability-and-democracy.
5   Tansey, op. cit.

Triple Threat to Transparency: a Brexit Story

Adam Ramsay

The main institution which drove Britain out of the EU was the right-wing press. For decades, papers owned by oligarchs like Rupert Murdoch, Richard Desmond, and the Barclay brothers protected politicians that their journalists ought to have been holding to account, shifting the blame for their failures onto a convenient, fictionalised version of the European Union.

Any discussion of propaganda and the European referendum has to start within that context, rooted in a history of lies told not as fake news or Facebook memes, but in so-called respectable national papers, by liars who were not hidden behind anonymous Twitter accounts, but who proudly paraded on the bylines of their articles.

The original Brexit liar was the *Telegraph*'s Brussels correspondent from 1989 to 1994. Already controversial when he was appointed—he'd been sacked by *The Times*—this propagandist for the British establishment used his role to distract people from the struggles of the Tory government of the time by inventing a string of stories about the European Union, creating, as one of his fellow Brussels correspondents would later say, "an entire newspaper genre: the Euromyth, a story that had a tiny element of truth at the outset but which was magnified so far beyond reality that by the time it reached the reader it was false."

Over the next twenty-five years, his genre of Euromyth-making became a central feature of the oligarch-owned press in the UK—from *The Sun* and the *Express* to *The Times* and *The Telegraph*—warping the national understanding of the EU.

Sins of the state

Alongside Euromythology grew another kind of mythology, driven by the shared interests of the tabloids and the state: migrant-bashing. Though the seed had been sown long before 2008, the financial crisis brought with it a desperate need to find someone to blame who didn't have the social power to answer back. And so, in 2010, the newly-elected Conservative government, in concert with the same right-wing press, brought the full weight of the state down onto people of colour and communities of migrants, describing their own policy agenda as having the goal of creating a 'hostile environment' for people who had come from other countries.

The policy had practical and devastating impacts on people living in the UK: black people were rounded up and sent back to the former colonies from which their parents had migrated a generation earlier, in what became known as the Windrush scandal; people whose British partners didn't earn enough were deported; vans were sent around areas with high numbers of migrants and people of colour, telling those without the correct paperwork to "go home or face arrest".

But this brutality had a second purpose: propaganda. It ramped up racism in the country, and then shifted blame for stagnant wages and public service cuts, a decomposing political system and the explosion of the banking system onto people of colour and migrants.

The architect of this hostile environment was the UK Home Secretary. In the manner of an old-school colonialist, she spoke softly but carried a big stick, slamming the power of the British state down like a sledgehammer onto communities of colour. Each thud she delivered added the legitimacy of the state to the idea that migration was responsible for the degeneration of the UK. That was the rhetorical context for Brexit, the environment into which the Leave campaigns stepped. That is a background too often ignored.

The dark money network

The week before the referendum, I stumbled into two Brexit campaigners for Leave carrying placards in Edinburgh. In their smallprint, the placards said that they'd been paid for by the Northern Irish DUP. So why was a Northern Irish party paying for propaganda in Edinburgh?

This question took my colleagues and me down the rabbit hole, which turned out to be a complex warren-system which we explored for two years. Together with journalists at other publications, we've shown how millions of pounds appear to have flowed into the various Leave campaigns from questionable sources. And we've mapped how right-wing think tanks have come in behind a hard Brexit.

We've monitored thousands of pounds worth of Facebook adverts pushing a hard Brexit—paid for by who-knows-whom? Carole Cadwalladr at *The Observer* started from a different angle: looking at online debate, and what is and isn't promoted by web monopolies like Google and Facebook. Together, what we're looking at is the adaptation of elite propaganda to the age of social media and offshore finance.

Of course, legacy media and the state are still at the heart of those propaganda efforts, attempting to shape the agenda and drive politics in their preferred direction. They are determined to ensure that the debate about politics is a debate about which marginalised group is to blame, who's in and who's out, while questions of resource distribution—of housing, wages, and work—are matters for the market and, like the weather, may be cursed, but are not within anyone's control to change.

But alongside these traditional players, we see new agents emerging. At the centre of the warren we've been exploring is a cluster of firms linked to a company called SCL—formerly Strategic Communications Laboratories. You've probably heard of one of its offshoots, Cambridge Analytica, and another company from the same cluster that ran much of the Brexit campaign: AggregateIQ.

To understand these firms, we need to understand that Strategic Communications Laboratories describes itself as a 'security' company, and is essentially the psychological operations wing of our increasingly privatised military. "SCL Group provides data, analytics and strategy to governments and military organisations worldwide", reads the first line of its website. "For over twenty-five years, we have conducted behavioural change programmes in over sixty countries and have been formally recognised for our work in defence and social change." While it's hard to know exactly what contracts they secured, we do know that they've done work in Afghanistan, Kenya, and elsewhere.

Cambridge Analytica (the company which ran Trump's campaign) was a subsidiary of the SCL Group, and the Canadian company AggregateIQ, which received £3.4 million for their work on the Brexit campaign, and has long faced allegations of close connections to the SCL Group. AIQ created Cambridge Analytica's software platform, and the firm was suspended from Facebook in 2018 over concerns about its alleged links with Cambridge Analytica.

This network is therefore best understood as a wing of the increasingly privatised security world, taking lessons from the wars in the Middle East and Global South and applying them to democratic events at home. They shouldn't be seen as having limitless influence, and their own claims about psychometric profiling are based on little evidence. However, they also shouldn't be underplayed. Social media, with its customised messaging, is the communications channel of the era, and it's not surprising that elite networks are using it to shape politics.

Similarly, it shouldn't be surprising that Cambridge Analytica emerged in the UK. Britain, after all, is the world centre for privatised military contractors, with more mercenary firms than any other country. This is a powerful network in the country, holding its own beliefs and interests, and it needs to be analysed and understood as such.

Sitting alongside this network are the people who, in the Brexit campaign, funded them. In a paper for the Transnational Institute (TNI) in early 2019[1], Reijer Hendrikse and Rodrigo Fernandez argued that offshore finance, "together with the wealth of the world's billionaire class effectively constitutes the backbone of global capitalism." And Britain, with its overseas territories and crown dependencies, is a key segment of this backbone, with the British state acting as one of the most important guardians of offshore wealth.

Follow the money which funded much of the controversial online campaigning in the Brexit referendum, as we have, and you find that it soon disappears offshore, into the UK's network of tax havens and secrecy areas. There has been much speculation about whether the money was Russian or American or Saudi or British. But in a sense, this is missing the point. We know the cash came through the loopholes in Britain's broken constitution. We know it came from abroad. That's enough to tell us something important.

If offshore finance is becoming the backbone of the global economy, then we can expect it to continue to find ways to shape politics in its interests. As the elite networks which historically operated through states—like the military and intelligence communities—increasingly shift into private, transnational, and offshore firms, we can expect those networks to act in concert with the new backbone of capital. And as the media is changed radically by the emergence of the internet, we can expect them to use new technology—along with the newspapers they own and governments they can influence—to steer public debate and comprehension.

This is the triple threat we face today: news media, directed by faceless finance, finding common cause with the state, and leaving the task of transparency to a handful of investigative journalists piecing together clues to how the world is changing, and in whose interests.

Notes

1   Reijer Hendrikse and Rodrigo Fernandez, "Offshore Finance: How Capital Rules the World," State of Power 2019, *TNI Longreads*, 2019, http://longreads.tni.org/state-of-power-2019/offshore-finance/.

Next spread: *A Colossal Market Crisis* (left),
The Beginning of a Possibility (right)

A B C D   O P Q R
E F G   S T U
H I J K   V W
L M N   X Y Z

WHY IS THERE
A CORONAVIRUS
CRISIS?
IT'S A COLOSSAL
MARKET FAILURE
' ?

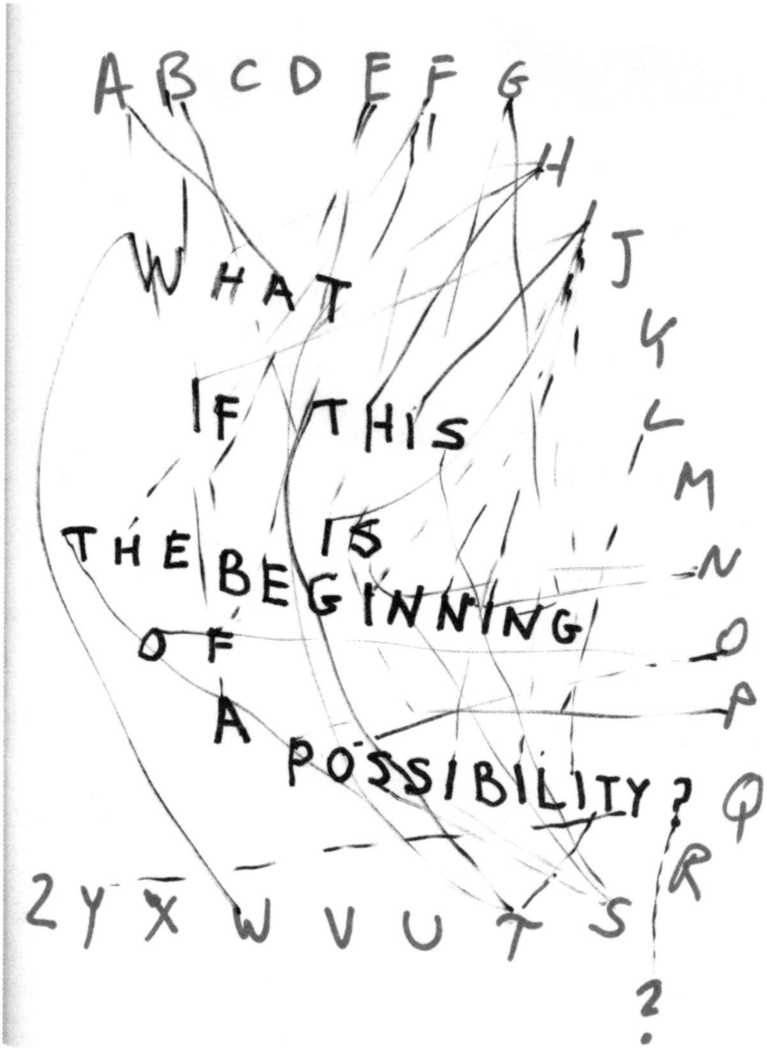

A B C D E F G

H

J

WHAT

K

IF THIS

L

M

IS

N

THE BEGINNING

O

OF

P

A POSSIBILITY? Q

R

Z Y X W V U T S

?

A Productive Europe by James K. Galbraith

❝ The last European Civil War ended seven decades ago. It was followed by thirty years of recovery, balanced growth, and the return of Europe to the position of a great first-tier economy in the world. Much the same happened in the United States for about three decades following the end of our Civil War.

But then, in both cases, came troubles: crises, stagnation, more crises, joblessness, and deflation. On both continents, this was especially true in the south—in the American states of the defeated Confederacy and in the European states of the Mediterranean: Greece, Italy, Spain, Portugal, and parts of France.

Almost seven decades passed before the United States came to grips with the catastrophic consequences of a toxic mixture: poverty and underdevelopment, new technologies producing mass unemployment, financial failure known as the Depression, and ecological mayhem known as the Dust Bowl.

Europe today faces all of these on an even larger scale, with a digital revolution threatening to sweep away jobs and a changing climate promising to dispossess families from their homes.

In these conditions, Europe's first necessity is to admit that ideas, institutions, and policies forged forty years ago in an age of growth and high confidence are unsuitable today. There is no shame in this. When times change, ideas should too. Eternal economic truth is an illusion; it is foolish to believe in it, when the evidence is so clear.

Europe today is weak and divided; the United States is at near-full employment even though the financial crisis originated in the United States. Why is this? It is because the US continues to benefit from continental-scale institutions created in the crises of a century back, the work of our New Deal and Great Society, which Europe has not yet created for itself at the continental scale. Nor can Europe, in its present state, compete with the rise of China, let alone the rapidly-integrating Eurasian landmass, including Russia.

Europeans can see this. Anxious and threatened, they are drawn to retrograde nationalism with authoritarian overtones. But such policies and programmes court disaster. It is easy to see why they are encouraged by nationalists in the United States and Russia, including Donald Trump and Vladimir Putin. Neither wants a strong and independent Europe.

The way forward is to tackle Europe's problems as they are, in the spirit of a European New Deal: a mobilisation of Europe's talents and resources in necessary defiance of the shibboleths and stasis of orthodox economics.

Each of the three major areas must be dealt with.

In Europe's afflicted regions—mostly, but not entirely, in the south—debts must be restructured, written down, and made sustainable, while new investments in infrastructure and human services rebuild the foundations for sustainable economic life. Because of the particular structure of the European Union, each European country must be assured of its own viable future. None should be sacrificed to economic dogmas or to the financial mistakes of recent decades.

Across the entire continent, energy transformation must proceed at a pace forced by pressing necessity. And the inevitable consequences of climate change already underway must be mitigated so far as possible.

In each country, public investments and the Job Guarantee must put an end to unemployment, giving every European who wants a job the right to have one, in his or her own country, at a decent, modest living standard suited to the conditions of the place.

These are the core measures of a European New Deal. Like the American New Deal of 1933–1939, the key is active experimentation, action, dynamism, and the earliest possible showing of results. If something works, pursue it; if it fails, drop it and try something else. But Europe must act; it must spend and invest, get the job done, and persuade Europeans that it can be done. No new taxes should be levied, or heavy burdens imposed on European peoples until they are demonstrably benefiting from a new direction. When they are, people can be persuaded that change is in their interest.

Franklin Roosevelt in 1933 stayed within the United States Constitution, despite many temptations and examples in other countries of political upheaval. In a similar vein, Europe's leadership should act within existing treaties and charters. European voters are rightly sceptical of new constitutional measures—fine! Let those wait until the proof-of-concept has been made.

With brave new action, Europe can break the fatal cycle of austerity and dissolution, restore hope and confidence, and so rebuild an effective and democratic political centre, immune to authoritarians of left and right. It may require—as it did in the United States—a strong new leadership vested with a progressive vision, a bold programme and the courage of its convictions. The American voter made that choice in 1932, and has never regretted it. **99**

PART FOUR

Economy

Why We Need a European New Deal

Edited by David Adler

Europe is caught in a vicious cycle. An insurgent coalition of nationalist forces confronts a political establishment whose failed policies, in a never-ending circle, feed the Nationalist International insurgency. Unless Europe's progressives act now, not only will the European Union dissolve—it will be replaced by something much uglier: the convergence of permanent economic crisis and authoritarian nationalism.

The bitter fruits of austerity

While the origins of Europe's malaise are various, the loss of hope lies at its heart.

Hope evaporated when a majority of Europeans faced the spectre of involuntary underemployment. For at least a decade, millions of Europeans living in affluent countries like Germany have been restricted to the precarious jobs that dominate an increasing segment of the labour market. Meanwhile, those living in Europe's periphery—especially younger people leaving university and older people approaching retirement—are confined to the scrapheap. Thus the young migrate en masse to Europe's core where locals—already in the clutches of discontent—see them, mistakenly, as the root of their problems.

Europe is disintegrating as a result of this perfect storm: involuntary underemployment on the one hand, and involuntary migration on the other.

Involuntary underemployment is the bitter price of austerity. It is the effect of ultra-low investment, of a failure to generate the paid work that Europe needs to meet economic, social, human, and environmental needs, and of the European economic stagnation that concentrates most economic activity in a few regions but drains the rest.

Involuntary economic migration is the bitter harvest of austerity. The vast majority of Greeks, Bulgarians, Spaniards, Romanians, Portuguese, and Poles moving to Britain or Germany do so because they must. With no jobs or prospects at home, with a vast and growing income differential between European countries, what else can they do?

In this fog, a growing number of Europeans need to exert superhuman efforts to provide for themselves and their families. This struggle inevitably breeds political monsters, who are now exploiting the climate of uncertainty to fragment the European continent.

What comes next?

Protectionism is not the solution. Yes, it would have been better if the European Union had sought to develop industries in every country prior to the creation of the Single Market, rather than encouraging mass deindustrialisation in many of them. But those horses have bolted; the industries that died when the borders came down have gone forever. They cannot be recreated by impeding trade now. If we tried to revive them through protectionist policies, the price would be a breakdown of the existing, integrated Europe, with trade wars inflicting vast new losses on our peoples. Anyone promising that the UK, Italy, France, Greece, or Germany would be able to emerge wealthier from this race is peddling false hopes.

Walls and electrified border fences are not the solution. Yes, it would have been better if the European Union had created conditions for Poles, Bulgarians, Romanians, and Greeks not to be forced out of their countries by the lack of employment, housing, and other basic services in their communities. But these migratory waves have happened. And the price of trying to reverse or to stop them will be a boon for racists, religious intolerance, national chauvinism, as well as a vast cultural impoverishment of Europe. The promise that the Nationalist International is making—to restore hope through taller walls—must be resisted fiercely by Europe's progressives.

A 'multi-speed' or 'variable geometry' Europe is shorthand for a defeated Europe

Many EU leaders have been attracted by the idea of a 'multi-speed' or 'variable geometry' Europe. It sounds like a flexible and realistic approach that would allow some member states to integrate further along the lines of common values while others can take a few steps backwards.

However, in substance, this approach reflects a wholesale acquiescence to disintegration. Some member states will use the 'multi-speed' narrative to ditch crucial rights and liberties (e.g. freedom of the press, judicial independence, free movement) while the rest will fail to compensate with greater consolidation (like the Eurozone, the prime candidate for a closer political union). In short, 'multi-speed' and 'variable geometry' are euphemisms for a collapsed and increasingly illegitimate EU.

Should Europe be saved?

Until very recently, proposals to 'save' Europe aroused sceptics who would say, "that's all very well, but can whatever you propose be done?" Indeed, the sceptics ask whether Europe is worth saving at all.

DiEM25 emphatically answers in the affirmative. We have a duty to demonstrate that Europe can and must be saved. The alternative is to impoverish all Europeans—in economic, social, and cultural terms. The world needs a unified Europe committed to authentic democracy, to the peaceful resolution of conflicts, to social protections, to saving the planet, and to the ongoing expansion of human freedoms.

DiEM25's New Deal suggests a blueprint of how Europe can be saved. The New Deal conceives of the necessary investment into people's communities like the Green movement conceives of climate change: a joint responsibility of peoples whose fortunes are intertwined.

Will Europe be saved?

A lost decade has made many Europeans feel that the European Union is beyond the point of no return—that perhaps it is better to let this neoliberal, authoritarian, incompetent, unappetising Europe collapse and then start from scratch, once we have restored democracy in our nation states.

We do not contest the proposition that perhaps Europe is past the point of no return. However, DiEM25 staunchly contests the proposition that we should campaign to dissolve the EU, or that we should let it collapse, to start again from the beginning.

We believe that our struggle to save the EU—by putting forward practical proposals for democratising, civilising, and rationalising it—will prove essential *even* if we fail, because it builds up the transnational network of democrats that will prove invaluable in the event of Europe's disintegration.

By inciting constructive disobedience—leading with moderate policy proposals while disobeying at every level the edicts of the clueless establishment—and getting Europeans from different national and party political backgrounds to struggle side-by-side, we create the Progressive International that can confront both the establishment and its nationalist challengers. This is a movement that could pick up the pieces if Europe collapses.

The narrative of "let this Europe disintegrate so that we can start again once we have recoiled into our nation states" only strengthens the surging nationalists. But DiEM25's call to stick together and reimagine a democratic Europe is their greatest enemy. It is the cement and the glue of the transnational European movement that will oppose barbarism after Europe's collapse.

Stabilisation, recovery, and greater national sovereignty must come first

In response to the crisis, the liberal establishment proposes 'more Europe'—a 'federation-lite' that hands even greater powers to the bureaucrats of Brussels, the Germany Ministry of Finance, the European Central Bank, and the least enlightened parts of the European Commission. Inevitably, under present economic conditions, this federation-lite model would deepen austerity and advance the destruction of Europe.

Federation-lite is not the solution. Had it been established back when the euro was born in 2000, it might have taken the edge off the crisis that followed in 2008. But now it is too little too late. The tiny federal budget that is proposed in exchange for political union will turn Europe into a permanent Austerity Union. Rather than avert the path to dissolution it will speed it up and maximise the human costs.

Today, Europe needs practical steps that can be taken tomorrow morning to end the free fall, stabilise local and national economies, heal the fault lines between surplus and deficit countries, rebalance the Eurozone, and achieve coordination between the Eurozone and other economies falling geographically within greater Europe (e.g. the UK, Switzerland, Serbia, Norway, Turkey, Iceland). These steps need to be taken quickly and therefore within the existing institutional arrangements. Any moves to 'more Europe' now will not only produce a permanent Austerity Union in continental Europe but will also be outpaced by the galloping crisis which will ensure that there will be nothing left to unite or federate.

DiEM25's European New Deal proposes policies within existing institutional arrangements that could bring about this stabilisation. Stabilisation would, in turn, bring greater national sovereignty: once investment flows have been restored, public debt management has been coordinated, the bankers have been restrained, and abject poverty has been addressed at the European level, national governments will suddenly be endowed with more degrees of freedom—proof that the European solution to common problems does not require further loss of sovereignty.

Quite the opposite, actually: Europeanising the solution to issues like investment flows and public debt unsustainability gives greater powers back to national parliaments and regional assemblies. Once this stabilisation is achieved, Europeans must then address the crucial question: How do we envisage Europe in, say, twenty years? Do we want gradually to deconstruct the EU, plan for a smooth, low-cost velvet divorce, and rely more on nation states? Or do we want to build and maintain an open, continental, pan-European democracy in which free men and women can live, work, and prosper together, as they choose?

DiEM25 is committed to the latter. Once Europe is stabilised by means of the modest policies outlined below, a real democracy can be built at a transnational European level. This will naturally require a European democratic constitutional process underpinned by policies for democratising economic life, breaking down the capital-labour division, enshrining shared green prosperity into Europe's institutional make-up, and eradicating all forms of institutionalised discrimination.

DiEM25's European New Deal

DiEM25's European New Deal is an integrated programme for bringing hope back to Europe. It maps out ways by which Europe would:

- Fund its innovators, whose R&D will be the foundation of the green transition to prosperity without growth.
- Back its maintainers: the nurses, carers, teachers, sewer and electricity grid repairers who do the multitude of work needed to maintain communities and existing infrastructure.
- Restore the dream of shared prosperity in an era of automation, exploitation, and inequality.
- Enable democracy at the local, regional, national, and pan-European levels.

To fund the above, DiEM25's European New Deal proposes financial mechanisms that will not only minimise the probability of disintegration but that will also minimise the costs of containing a possible disintegration of the European Union. This is crucial: Unlike those who argue that the current European Union is 'finished' and go on to support a Plan B for its dissolution, DiEM25's European New Deal proposes a Plan A whose implementation will save Europe (by stabilising it), but also deal optimally with the fallout from a collapse of the Eurozone and possibly of the European Union itself.

The New Deal as a prerequisite for a democratic constitution

The people of Europe have a right and a duty to consider the Union's future and to decide between (1) a multilateral cooperation framework and (2) the possibility of transforming Europe into a full-fledged democracy with a sovereign parliament respecting national self-determination and sharing power with national parliaments, regional assemblies, and municipal councils.

However, this debate will never take place as long as Europe is buffeted by economic imbalances and deflationary forces that turn one proud people against another. This is why our European New Deal, and the policies it proposes for bringing about Europe's stabilisation and recovery, can be seen as a first step to, and a prerequisite for, the debate that Europeans must have about Europe's long-term political future.

Once this European New Deal becomes part of our political discourse—giving Europeans a chance to stabilise Europe and stem the centrifugal forces that are tearing it apart—we can move forward with a Constitutional Assembly Process to manage the evolution of Europe into a democratic political entity and the replacement of all existing European Treaties with a democratic European Constitution.

Elements of a European New Deal

James K. Galbraith

DiEM25 was founded in response to a deep crisis within Europe: the failure of the EU leadership to meet the economic, social, environmental, and humanitarian challenges facing Europe, the calamity of Greece and the cock-up of Brexit, and the threat of a Nationalist International leading to a neo-fascist fragmentation of Europe itself.

The movement specifically warns that 'Left Exit', or 'Lexit', is an illusion that will only empower Europe's most regressive and aggressive elements, in the service of oligarchs and outside powers. It therefore proposes a European New Deal, building on existing treaties to develop a strong, independent, peaceful, prosperous, sustainable, and democratic Europe as a community for all Europeans and a distinctive model for the world.

Today, Europe faces a new threat—a threat that is political, economic, and moral. It demands a strong, unified, independent, and democratic response. And it comes not from Russia, which has always posed complicated challenges for Europe, nor from China, but from Europe's historic ally, the United States.

Politically, the Nationalist International is plainly and overtly a project of the American far right. The sympathies of President Trump and the work of Mr. Bannon make this clear. The American nationalist right wants a divided, weak, reactionary Europe and would be happy if the European Union falls apart—as was the case with Yugoslavia and the USSR.

Economically, the present US government is intent on bending Europe to its will. This is obvious with respect to Iran, where a stabilising nuclear pact was scuttled, over ineffective European protests, in the brazen pursuit of 'regime change'. It's obvious with respect to Russia. It's obvious with respect to Trump's trade wars. To this US administration, Europe is a collection of vassal states.

Morally, Europe must find the leadership and the will to establish an independent and progressive path, against the will of the far right now dictating American policy, but in alliance with progressive forces in the United States and, indeed, across the world. Europe must find the leadership and the will to refuse unneeded military spending, to resist dangerous provocations, and to devote itself and its resources to meeting the overwhelming needs for economic stabilisation and conversion to a sustainable green economy—as well as protecting and advancing human rights and social welfare for citizens and immigrants alike.

This paper summarises the key elements of DiEM25's economic policy, the European New Deal—henceforth END. As the name implies, it is a policy with American roots, adapted to European conditions. Like its namesake, it is a comprehensive, transformational policy, composed entirely of practical elements addressed to specific problems. Then in America as now in Europe, a continental society had to confront a crisis of many dimensions: economic, financial, environmental, developmental, and technological. Unemployment, bank failures, the Dust Bowl, the chronic poverty of the Deep South, and the rise of the Machine Age were all elements of that crisis. Each has an equivalent in Europe today. And now, as then, the situation demands a unified, coherent response at a continental level. This is the European New Deal. This is DiEM25's proposal.

The END has three broad operational elements: Green Investment, Basic Goods, and Shared Returns. Integrated into all three is a programme of Guaranteed Jobs. Underpinning all three are three major reforms: Democratic Finance, Fair Taxes, and Fair Trade.

Green investments

Investment is the future. But private investments are not an effective motor for growth and sustainable development in today's Europe—or anywhere in the capitalist world—because the public sector is no longer setting the course or laying the foundations required. The consequence is a natural tendency for industry to concentrate where it is already strong—as in Germany—and for new investments to concentrate on saving labour, thereby worsening unemployment.

To counter this, the END proposes a public investments programme totalling 5 per cent of European GDP each year, aimed at building Green Power, modern post-automotive transportation systems, social housing, enhanced cities, and a restored countryside. The programmes will emphasise the revival of decayed industrial regions—the heartland of the Nationalist International—and especially Europe's south and east. Specific projects will be designed and guided by the European Investment Bank and European Investment Fund, and bond-financed using the European Central Bank's bond-buying powers to assure a stable market. As the Green Transition advances, Europe will build a Green Energy Union, decarbonising with the aid of a carbon tax to be phased in as Europe's exorbitant and regressive VAT rates are phased down.

Basic goods

In line with European values, DiEM25 believes that all Europeans have a right to secure supplies of food, to decent housing, and to education and healthcare. These are the foundations of a civilised life. In today's Europe, they are under attack from unemployment, bankruptcy, foreclosures, pension cuts, and public-sector austerity policies. The END would provide food assistance, foreclosure protection, a right-to-rent for homeowners, social housing, and a common standard of excellence for public schools and universal healthcare. These basic goods must be supported from common resources, to stabilise European families in their home communities, reducing involuntary economic migration. Elements of the manpower required—for instance, in the caring services and in education—can come from the Job Guarantee.

Shared returns

Technology and the resulting monopoly, aided by the power of Big Finance, drives inequality by concentrating returns in new sectors and demolishing the old and obsolete. This is an inevitable process. No society since the Middle Ages has ever stopped it. But the inequalities it generates can be contained. This is the purpose of Shared Returns, the Universal Basic Dividend, and the European Equity Depository. Every European citizen will have an inalienable share, from birth, in the common Depository. Funding of a common dividend will come from a share of initial public offerings (IPOs), a share of central bank profits, a tax on intellectual property (IPRs) and monopoly rents, plus a categorical end to tax havens in Europe, backed by financial sanctions, and an estate-and-gift tax designed to curtail dynastic wealth and to encourage regulated philanthropy on an improved version of the American model. In these ways, DiEM25 proposes to reduce the great oligarchies of Europe gradually, but once and for all. In their stead, DiEM25 envisions a European society of widely-distributed capital wealth—a true commonwealth of Europe.

Jobs guarantee

All Europeans should have the right to a job at a living wage in their community. The cure for joblessness is jobs. People with jobs pay taxes. They do not collect unemployment benefits. Their skills and usefulness increase. And they produce what other people want.

The END proposes that all European countries fund and guarantee jobs for every European in their home country. Such jobs would be created in the public and non-profit sectors, by European states, at the local levels. They would be paid at a common, modest living wage rate at national scale. They would be available on demand for all who want them, in conjunction with city and local councils. The guaranteed jobs proposed could not be used to replace civil service jobs. Nor would they carry tenure. But those in the job guarantee pool would gain incomes, pay taxes, and come off public assistance, saving state funds, while producing goods and services and social investments. As the private economy improves, those in the pool with good work records will be hired away.

Why restrict these jobs to the home country? DiEM25's objective is to stabilise each European country. Clearly, if every European had a guaranteed job in Germany or France at the German and French pay scales, economic migration would increase. European countries should provide jobs for Europeans in their own communities, administered in their own languages, giving a safe and productive employment option to the peoples of all European countries, while preserving the right to migrate and the right to work for any and all who are motivated by opportunity rather than compulsion. So the pay scales should be national, but common to the standards of each country—a modest living wage, better than welfare, but not a substitute for civil service jobs. Europeans will, therefore, take these jobs when they need them, and move on to better jobs when the occasion appears.

Democratic finance

Europe today lives, like most of the world, under an oligarchy not merely of persons but of banks; banks that teeter on the edge of bankruptcy, held up only by their ability to exact bailouts, at public expense. END will end this, just as the New Deal did in the United States for forty years following the Great Crash and the banking crises of the early 1930s. In its place, DiEM25 proposes a stable democratic financial system with the following elements:

- A European Public Depository and Digital Payments Platform. END will terminate the monopoly of private banks over basic banking and payments services, restoring, in modern form, and accessible to all European taxpayers, a safe and secure means of making payments, free of 'bail-in' risk and protected against loss of liquidity should the euro fall apart. The PDDPP would permit cancellation of arrears between the state and private sectors, direct sale of public bonds (effectively CDs) to small investors, and prepayment of taxes at a discount. It would create fiscal space for governments, directly reduce the scale of the private banking sector, and set a standard for efficient and affordable banking services on a purely digital platform.
- A European Bank Regulator with the power to take control of any and all banks operating in Europe that are in danger of collapse or otherwise destabilising the system, to replace the management, to refer fraudulent behaviour for prosecution, and to divide the bank into a good bank and a bad bank, so as to write down unpayable debts, and to manage those concerns in the public interest. The EBR would have full powers to supervise and limit the risks of derivatives transactions and transnational speculations, especially in foreign exchange, and such risky activities as mortgage lending in non-national currencies and other systemically risky practices.
- A European Deposit Insurance Fund, adequate to protect the deposits of most private households and small business transaction accounts, tied to the European Bank Regulator.
- A Bank Restructuring Agency, charged with developing strategies to decentralise, diversify, and bring back public purpose to the private financial sector,

making effective regulation possible. The BRA would also establish appropriate capital requirements, limit the exposure of insured European banks to external risks (such as from subprime mortgages in the US or elsewhere), and end the doom loop of zero-weighted risk capital for the public securities of each nation's government in their own banks.

- To support public debt without the doom loop, END proposes that the Maastricht Compliant Debt (MCD) of each European country be refinanced through the ECB, with servicing handled by the nation state through a super-senior debit account at the ECB. In this way, excessively indebted European countries can work their way back toward financial sustainability over time, without bringing down their own banking systems.

Fair tax

The END proposes a Fair Tax system to underpin the new European economy with the following elements:

- Complete elimination of European tax havens backed by strong sanctions against financial institutions based in tax havens or doing business there. The threat of sanctions alone should be sufficient to bring this anomalous and indefensible feature of European life under control.
- Reduction of VAT rates and introduction of a carbon tax, thereby substituting a necessary step toward climate sanity for a regressive, anti-business, anti-employment tax on which Europe has for too long relied.
- Strong progressive income taxes and equal treatment of income from all sources, including capital gains. These will continue to be administered nationally, but DiEM25 proposes that they be coordinated across all EU member states, to reduce tax arbitrage.
- An effective estate-and-gift tax, aimed at preventing dynastic accumulations and at fostering a culture of intra-vivos transfers to the qualified non-profit sector.
- A financial transactions tax, aimed at curbing speculation, high-speed trading, and other unproductive financial activities.

Fair trade

A Europe that is productive, sustainable, fully employed, and rebuilt needs a trade policy that advances and protects European interests. Chief among these is the pursuit of peace. DiEM25 declares that Europe must not be drawn into provocations, let alone into wars, but must seek stable trading and other relations with all of its partners on the basis of European values and priorities. This means:

- European firms must be protected legally and effectively from coercive measures and sanctions operating against European interest.

- European workers must enjoy reasonable job stability and managed transitions as patterns of industry and technology change.
- Europe must be able to regulate trade so as to maintain environmental, labour and social standards.
- Europe must be prepared to regulate or control capital flows outside and into Europe, reducing the risks of financial contagion and as a lever against aggressive trade policies from outside.
- Europe must have a fair, humane, welcoming immigration policy for refugees and asylum seekers, and an effective development policy to minimise purely economic migration.
- Above all, Europe must not militarise, but use its resources for sustainable development, and rely on diplomacy, mutual benefit and good trading relationships to keep and preserve the peace.

In sum: We propose a practical, coherent, integrated programme to revolutionise and revive the European Project, creating a new and truly democratic Europe with full employment and financial stability, while transforming the physical foundations of European life to support a green and sustainable future. To this end, Europe requires a strong, unified, principled leadership, institutions and policies capable of advancing European ideals and of defending European interests. The European New Deal sets forth the essential elements of that approach.

Postscript on the euro, intra-European trade, and capital flows

The objective of DiEM25 and the European New Deal is to save the European Union through democratic reforms and sensible economic changes. In this context, DiEM25 wishes to clarify its policies with respect to the euro, to the imbalances of intra-European trade and corresponding capital flows, and with respect to capital controls which have been used in Europe (in both Cyprus and Greece, as well as during the crisis in Iceland) in a stopgap manner.

Many of Europe's problems can be traced to the massive trade imbalances within the Eurozone since 2000, with German surpluses matched by deficits elsewhere, and a corresponding pile-up of private and public debts that exploded with the onset of the financial crisis of 2008–2009. In DiEM25's view, Europe cannot be run as a debt collection agency; the imperative policy is to stabilise the indebted regions and return Europe to a commonwealth of common progress.

In this respect, the euro poses a dilemma. It is plainly not sustainable under current policies, as political developments in numerous European countries—most recently Italy—make clear. Moreover, there are parts of Europe that will not join the euro, and other countries that aim to join, but only on an indefinite schedule. And yet, where it exists the euro nevertheless retains strong popular acceptance and support, both among businesses that prefer a stable unit of account, and among households that prefer a stable store of value.

DiEM25's policy is, therefore, designed to work within the existing currency framework and to make it work. Some pressure can be brought to bear on the economic policymakers of the major surplus countries, and some benefit may be achieved by limiting naked capital flows. DiEM25 has technical proposals in these areas. But one has to recognise that surpluses based on industrial excellence are a chronic issue, not easily overcome by macroeconomic measures or even by exchange-rate adjustments, as the experiences of Japan, Korea, and China—as well as Germany—show.

So the right approach is to recycle purchasing power and to regulate credit flows in such a way as to keep the buildup of inter-regional debts under control. DiEM25's fiscal, social, and regulatory proposals aim to achieve this. It is the only alternative to chronic debt-deflation on the one hand, or the break up of the euro into appreciating and depreciating currency blocks, on the other.

Nonetheless, since Europe is already a multi-currency region, and will remain so, DiEM25 keeps an open mind about its long-term monetary future. Monetary systems are a tool, not a totem; contrary to political statements, the euro is not Europe. Contrary to myth, monetary systems tend to change with circumstances; it is not unusual for a new reform to be required every three or four decades. And yet monetary systems are not toys either; people rely on them in the broad expectation that they will continue to exist, and they should continue to exist, until such time as they are definitely broken and must be changed.

DiEM25 believes that the euro is in danger—and it is obvious from the rise of the Nationalist International that this is the case. Yet the euro deserves one last great reform to make it work. This is what the European New Deal intends to achieve, to the extent possible within existing European treaties and charters, including the common central bank and the common currency in the Eurozone.

Taking Back Capital Control

Ann Pettifor

The year 2016 was momentous for Europe. On 23 June, over seventeen million Britons voted to leave the European Union, shaking its foundations. But they were not alone. Across Europe, millions on both the radical left and the radical right backed political parties that actively repudiated an economic system increasingly detached from the regulatory democracy and accountability of Europe's member states. This opposition to the principle of self-regulating markets has manifested in mounting public rejection of Europe's proposed bilateral trade and investment treaties, and of its mainstream, social democratic politicians.

By opposing global trade treaties, citizens were rightly rejecting the utopian delusions of those that George Soros defines as 'market fundamentalists': powerful interests that believe it is possible to construct a global financial and economic system detached from democratic political scrutiny, oversight, and management—a system that vested interests would prefer to be governed only by 'the invisible hand', in which private authority frees up financial capitalists to exploit a public good.

The ecological economist Herman Daly once noted that democratic public policymaking requires boundaries. Policies for taxation, pensions, healthcare, criminal justice, working conditions, environmental protection—all require boundaries. Citizens within the boundaries of democratic states agree to uphold laws, defend institutions, and fund policies made by their elected politicians.

Finance capital, on the other hand, abhors boundaries. The owners of private wealth wish to be internationally mobile; to avoid laws, regulations, taxes, and other restraints. They wish to operate solely according to the 'laws' of the market and its automatic pricing mechanisms.

At the same time, contradicting so-called 'free market theory', many financiers expect to avoid the much-vaunted 'discipline of market forces': the burden of losses imposed when risk-taking goes bad. Unlike everyone active in other sectors of the economy, and because of the systemic importance of the finance sector, bankers and financiers expect protection from such 'laws' of the market and demand to be bailed out by taxpayers and subsidised by governments.

If Europe's economies, finance, trade, employment, and national incomes are to be stabilised and made sustainable, it is vital for Europe's democratic, accountable governments to manage flows of capital, trade, and labour in and out of Europe—and do so in the interests of their citizens. Such a strategy, if it is to succeed, will require not just European, but international cooperation and coordination.

Such is the challenge for DiEM25's European New Deal.

The European New Deal in historic context

Management of the financial system was fundamental to President Roosevelt's New Deal of the 1930s. The New Deal itself was a mix of dozens of programmes and agencies, in sectors as varied as automobile, construction and agriculture, soil and forest conservation, rural electrification, fine arts, literature and history. The aim was to refocus the US economy on domestic activity, and achieve full employment.

Above all, Roosevelt wanted to end the 1929–32 slump; which, for its magnitude, took some time. His administration proposed to create jobs and generate income, including tax revenues. Central to this was public management of both domestic and international financial systems.

Roosevelt's administration enacted many pieces of legislation for stabilising and regulating private banking. However, the most urgent of his government's economic reforms was made on the day after his inauguration. It was to abandon the 'barbarous relic' (the Gold Standard) that was a fetish for all international bankers. As Eric Rauchway explains, Roosevelt "wanted to establish an international system of managed currencies, with an agreement that would allow them to remain stable for long periods, but adjustable in case of need."

Roosevelt's second world-changing decision was to boycott an international conference called by the global banking orthodoxy in 1933, the aim of which had been to maintain the Gold Standard and its associated policies for 'liberal' (self-regulated) finance.

By doing so, Roosevelt began to stop the control by private authority of international cross-border capital flows into the US. In the future, and later during the Bretton Woods era, these flows would be managed by public authority—as democratically mandated. The consequence of these changes to the international financial architecture and system was an unprecedented period of postwar prosperity between 1945 and 1971—known to all economists as 'the golden age'. And its lessons are as relevant today as ever. To build a better Europe, we must reject the doctrine of capital mobility and recover the radical spirit of the New Deal.

Capital mobility in Europe: winners and losers

Finance capital, through re-regulation and de-regulation, has forced the European economy away from the interests of citizens and democratic states, and towards the interests of the wealthy who are active in global, invisible, and unaccountable capital markets.

To transform Europe and restore high levels of good, well-paid employment and wider prosperity, it will be necessary to refocus attention on the health and stability of the Union's domestic economies. Any attempt at such transformation will face fierce resistance by the international financial sector.

To understand this, it is important to grasp the sector's vested interests in capital mobility and the extent to which the world's economic architecture has transformed over the last forty years.

So, who are the winners?

First, the criminal classes. We need to consider the motivations of drug dealers, fraudsters, elephant trophy hunters, tax-dodging individuals and corporations, common thieves and gangsters amongst the biggest winners of financial globalisation. They prefer financial borders without barriers, checks, or customs staff. Capital mobility gives both the criminal class and corrupt corporations a free pass to move illicit gains around the world.

Second, those who borrow cheap and lend dear. For those whose activities in global financial markets are legitimate, the foremost motive is the ability to quickly move capital away from economies that produce low returns and into ones that offer high returns. Provided the speculation works out well, this is a quick and effortless way of making substantial capital gains. In Europe, private financiers based mainly in northern Europe borrow 'cheap' from the European Central Bank and lend dear to southern European countries. They, too, are winners from globalisation.

Third, money lenders. Another motivation is creditors' determination to recoup financial gains from lending in full. So, if a creditor lends dear to Greece or Portugal or Brazil, he considers it vital to be able to collect profits or capital gains from his speculation in that country's credit markets. To maintain the value of such capital gains, investors demand repayment not in a local currency, but in 'hard' currency that upholds the value of the original loan—usually the euro or the US dollar.

This was one motivation behind the establishment of the euro and monetary union. Greece's drachma, the Portuguese escudo, or the Italian lira were not regarded as reliable, hard currencies. By joining the currency union, these countries relinquished their rights to repay debts in their own currency. Instead, they are obliged to repay debts in the currency preferred by their creditors.

As a result of pressures by investors to recoup debts and profits, countries like Greece are obliged to boost exports to other parts of the Union, and earn euros. These are then stocked in the national bank and used in part for the purchase of vital commodities and services. Priority, however, is given first to the repayment of foreign creditors and investors, and then to the financing of profits made in-country by corporations and individual investors and repatriated to the corporation's country of origin or tax haven.

And who are the losers?

First, deflation victims. The second flaw in this global strategy is well known and much commented on by development economists. If, as has been the case, all debtor countries are forced to reorient their economies towards exports, the result is predictable: an over-supply of exports. Excess supply exerts downward pressure on prices (or: deflation). We have seen this not just for the world's major commodity exporters—many of whom were already impoverished—but for the rest of the world now enduring deflationary pressures. From 1980 to 2000, as governments oriented their economies towards exports, world prices for eighteen major export commodities fell by 25 per cent in real terms.

Deflation is particularly threatening to the European economy, where since 2016, despite a massive expansion of ECB-generated liquidity, core inflation has remained stuck at or below one per cent for three years.

Deflation poses threats not just to indebted European governments, but to Europe's indebted consumers and firms as well. As prices fall into negative territory, the relative value of debt and interest rates rises. Just as inflation erodes the value of debt, deflation increases it. The prospect of debt and interest rates rising in value regardless of the actions of borrowers or central bankers—even while prices fall and incomes remain low—is of grave concern to the European Central Bank and the EU Commission. Unfortunately, prominent European politicians have a poor under-standing of deflation and disregard the warnings emanating from global institu-tions like the IMF, the OECD, and the Bank for International Settlements.

This threat comes at a time when central bankers have very few policy tools avail-able for dealing with deflationary shock. Interest rates are remarkably low and cannot theoretically fall below zero. The negative rates now applied in some Eurozone countries imply that banks are charging customers for depositing sums in the bank. The German government is imposing charges on investors for the privi-lege of lending to them. Both developments are bizarre. An expansion of quantita-tive easing is also not sustainable because of this policy's impact on asset price inflation.

It turns out that reorienting the global economy towards exports and the interests of foreign creditors and investors impoverishes countries, worsens global imbal-ances, and raises the spectre of deflation along with its economic, social, and politi-cal instability.

Second group of losers: exporters and importers. There is another problem with the IMF's global economic model: capital mobility interferes with the efficient func-tioning of trade in goods and services. Mobile capital does not just cause trade disruption and periodic crises, it also uses its absolute advantage over trade and labour flows to fatally weaken both.

These flows face geographic barriers. They also face political, regulatory, physical, and, in the case of labour, even emotional and cultural barriers to movement. By contrast, finance faces few real barriers to its ability to cross borders. Finance, there-fore, enjoys an absolute advantage over trade and labour, and its mobility destroys any comparative advantage enjoyed by different trade and labour markets. It is the absolute advantage enjoyed by international capital markets that causes the finance sector to exercise dominance over the open, domestic economies of Europe.

This dominance has persuaded many industrial capitalists that 'if you can't fight them, join them'. The result is that the European economy, like many others, is becoming financialised. In other words, industrial capitalists are finding ways of mimicking the finance sector's ability to make gains or charge rent on effortless activities like international lending and speculation.

Industrial capital is learning to compete with finance capital by accumulating unearned income from 'rent' on pre-existing assets. These include income from property, vehicles, algorithms, databases, brands, works of art, yachts, etc. Why would they not? To earn income, industrial capitalists like Apple, Siemens, Daimler, or Nestlé have to engage with land—in the broadest sense of the word—and labour. By engaging in speculation on the value of pre-existing assets rising or falling, capitalists can bypass both land and labour and make fantastic capital gains.

Europeans without the good fortune to own pre-existing assets cannot profit from unearned rents on these assets. They are obliged to earn income from their labour. As a result (and as many studies, including those from the International Labour Organisation have shown), the decline in labour's share of the economy in many European economies since the 1980s has been marked and exacerbated by the 2007–9 financial crisis.

Finally, democratic institutions. The result of all this is an increasingly unequal and financialised European economy, where domestic and foreign investors get paid, but the interests of domestic economies and their citizens are neglected. This helps explain why the continent suffers high rates of unemployment, falling tax revenues, and budget deficits. It also explains why income inequality, and populist resistance to the economic system, has risen.

The rise in political extremism is ultimately a threat to the democratic (and also financial) institutions—from political parties and press freedom, through to the judiciary and criminal justice system. So, Europe's democracies, too, are losers from financial globalisation.

The five pillars of financial stability

How would financial stability for Europe be achieved? I would argue that there are five pillars to the architecture of the European Union that should be adopted by the Union's public authorities in order to construct a stable and fair financial and economic system.

- Offshore to Onshore

The management of cross-border flows of money ensures democratic governments enjoy 'policy autonomy'. Bringing offshore capital back onshore allows governments to implement policies for national prosperity and full employment. These include policies for stabilising the exchange rate, keeping interest rates low for the sustainability of domestic enterprises, ensuring the taxation of all homegrown profits, and managing inflation.

- Tax Justice

The second pillar is the ability of public authorities to oblige those that use the Union's currency to pay their taxes in euros—fundamental to the central bank's creation of liquidity, and to maintaining the value of the currency. Taxing everyone who is active in and who profits from the monetary system is essential to social and political stability, because of taxation's role in managing wealth and benefits distribution within states, and the Union as a whole.

Capital mobility enables companies like Apple, Amazon, Starbucks, or Uber to avoid taxation by easily moving their profits or capital gains abroad, to tax havens. On the whole, law-abiding, tax-paying citizens do not enjoy this privilege. If tax systems are to be affordable, and if tax justice campaigns are to be effective, capital controls are vital.

- Managing Currency

Without capital control, a currency can be overvalued or undervalued. These distortions of the exchange rate are caused by the speculative activities of those in capital markets, who may sweep their capital into or out of an economy without regard to economic conditions within that economy.

Economists argue that central banks should not enjoy such control over the valuation of the currency, as 'rent-seeking' governments seek only to make financial gains from such management. This overlooks the rent-seeking of the private sector, for whom manipulation of the currency is fundamental to speculative capital gains.

As we witnessed in 2007–9, globalised, self-regulated markets can act as electric currents and transmit crises caused by imbalances in any part of the world to anywhere else. Unbalanced exchange rates—whether overvalued or undervalued—place the greatest strains on the globalised financial system. Managing the exchange rate to properly reflect the health or otherwise of the domestic economy is vital, not just to the prosperity of individual countries, but for the global economy as a whole.

- Managing Investment Booms

The fourth pillar of financial and economic stability is the management by public authorities of price stability, for goods, services, and assets. To manage inflation, central banks, the ECB, and governments must regulate the level of private credit or debt created and issued by bankers, shadow bankers, and creditors of all types. Too much credit chasing too few goods or assets is inflationary. It is especially so if credit is used for speculation on gambling activities as opposed to productive, job-creating, income-generating investment.

So it is also important for authorities to regulate the purpose for which credit/debt is issued. And if debtors are unable to repay the excessive amount of debt issued, the second likely outcome is a rise in defaults and bankruptcies. Both of these outcomes—inflation and defaults—harm financial stability.

Rapid and massive inflows of foreign capital can cause inflation and lead to consumption and investment booms, as Britain and other EU markets have recently experienced. Governments must be able to stabilise inflation, and ensure that consumption and investment levels are sustainable. They cannot do this if capital flows remain offshore, under the management of private authority.

It is also essential for the authorities to manage public debt. However, a rise in public debt is not so much a failure of regulation, as a consequence of rising unemployment caused by private sector weakness or failure and the resulting fall in tax revenues.

A reduction in public debt is therefore achieved by government investment that compensates for the collapse in private investment and spending, until the private sector is once again operating at full employment. Full, well-paid employment can increase tax revenues, cut public debt, and restore government budgets to balance. "Take care of employment," Keynes said, "and the budget will take care of itself."

- Rate of Interest

The fifth pillar of financial stability is the interest rate on all loans across the spectrum of lending: short- and long-term loans; safe and risky loans; and loans in real terms, i.e. allowing for inflation and deflation. If rates on loans exceed the gains likely to be made from the investment of those loans, then defaults will be inevitable. A low interest rate is essential for innovation and risk-taking, and also vital to the sustainability of the ecosystem, as it lowers the extraction rate of earth's scarce assets used to finance the repayment of debts—subject to the laws of mathematics, not thermodynamics.

Moneylending at high rates of interest can help stratify wealth and poverty across Europe. The rich owners of assets effortlessly become richer, and the poor and indebted ever more entrenched in their debt. Rapid outflows of capital make it impossible for central banks to manage interest rates across the spectrum of lending: for short- and long-term loans, safe and risky loans, and in real terms (i.e. adjusted for inflation).

What is to be done?

Governments can make good use of macro-prudential tools to act as forms of capital control. These can strengthen the supervision and regulation of risk-taking behaviour by foreign investors operating within a domestic banking system. They can also discourage investors in the home country from making risky investments abroad, or using borrowed money for speculative purposes.

If we are to restore stability within Europe and defeat the authoritarian ambitions of extreme political forces, restoring policy autonomy to democratic governments by managing capital mobility is essential. Economic forces cannot be untangled from democratic political institutions. Any attempt to do so is utopian, and has triggered the Polanyian countermovements that are leading the people of European countries to seek protection from the predatory behaviour of self-regulating markets. Unless mobile capital is subordinated to democratic interests, such 'protection' will be offered by strong, authoritarian leaders—who will likely reverse the extraordinary progress made across Europe since the Second World War.

There is a great deal at stake. And there is very little time.

Tax Wars or Tax Cooperation?
Europe's Fate Hangs on This Question

John Christensen

Tax policies are largely to blame for the rise of the far right in Europe. The liberal fixation on cutting taxes for wealthy people and corporations did not yield new investment or growth, but exacerbated inequality and accelerated the demise of welfare states. The widespread obsession with tax 'competitiveness' has driven an absurd race-to-the-bottom dynamic which serves no useful purpose other than to transfer wealth to the owners of capital. To make matters worse, EU member states operating as tax havens have engaged in protracted tax wars against other countries, undermining their taxation regimes and supporting criminal tax practices and anti-market tax avoidance. The threat of a post-Brexit British government committed to a deregulated tax haven development strategy, known as 'Singapore-on-the-Thames', can only make matters worse. Radical measures are required to push back against this toxic form of liberal economics.

Europe's 'Hamilton moment'

Europe faces what we might call its 'Hamilton moment', the point in its evolution when it must either commit to enhanced political cooperation, or surrender to the current beggar-my-neighbour trajectory. Choosing the latter will inevitably lead to further erosion of national tax bases, slower growth, deeper inequality, and social division. Facing a similar crisis moment in 1790, US Treasury Secretary Alexander Hamilton recognised the potential harm caused by fiscal competition between states and advocated for deeper union on the grounds that it would, in his words, "contribute in an eminent degree to an orderly, stable and satisfactory arrangement of the (union's) finances."

A festering question

The question of whether the EU should adopt a fiscal union, and what type of union that might be, has festered for decades. The political intractability of a fiscal union has contributed to prolonged fiscal crises facing most member states, and Eurozone members in particular. At the macroeconomic level, the quest for some form of fiscal stabilisation tool within the Eurozone—possibly along the lines of the IMF proposals for a 'rainy day fund'—has been fruitless. On the issue of tackling harmful tax policies, critics correctly accuse the EU of not adequately pushing back against member states operating as tax havens. Despite mounting evidence that the existing rules on taxing transnational companies (TNCs) cannot be made practicable, some member states reject measures designed to tackle tax avoidance by corporate giants (for example, the Digitax proposal), and resist attempts to shift to alternative methods for taxing TNCs, such as unitary taxation (UT). The latter approach discards the current rules based on the OECD's separate entity principle and arm's length method, instead treating a TNC as a single legal entity with profits apportioned to different countries on the basis of real economic substance. This approach has been recognised as the logical way forward as far back as the League of Nations meetings in 1932, although at that time the imperial powers resisted measures that would allow other countries to tax corporate profits.

The requirement that all matters relating to tax policy garner unanimous member-state support has placed the EU at an impasse, threatening the integrity of both the Single Market and the Eurozone. When Commission President Jean-Claude Juncker proposed in January 2019 that the right of a single member state to veto tax policies be replaced by qualified majority voting, the idea was predictably rejected: one senior diplomat said the proposal had "not a hope".

Proponents of a deeper fiscal union argue that combining supranational monetary policies with national fiscal policies is unsustainable, preventing the EU from tackling macroeconomic imbalances while also leaving individual member states vulnerable to the tax haven activities of spoiler states. Without deeper fiscal integration, they argue, the Eurozone will remain vulnerable to asymmetric shocks, and potential efficiency gains from the Single Market will be distorted by tax competition to the benefit of large, rent-seeking TNCs.

Opponents argue that a fiscal union would undermine the ability of governments to react to domestic problems, while also raising concerns around democratic accountability and national 'competitiveness'. The latter aspect is challenged, however, by those who regard the very concept of tax 'competitiveness' as having no meaning in normal economic discourse, recognising an ideology-driven agenda to encourage or force governments into deeper tax cuts and more reliefs, to the benefit of owners of capital. The tax 'competitiveness' agenda, they argue, will inevitably worsen the fiscal crisis while also deepening inequality and harming social cohesion.

Europe's spoiler states damage democracy

Without deeper fiscal cooperation, the EU project is vulnerable to the actions of 'spoiler' states, including member states like Ireland, Luxembourg, the Netherlands, and the United Kingdom, which extract wealth by enabling and encouraging profit shifting and tax evasion while using their political veto power to block attempts at strengthening the framework of international tax rules, regulations, and information sharing processes. Faced with capital mobility and massive lobbying from powerful corporations, political leaders feel incapable of defending domestic tax sovereignty and resisting race-to-the-bottom pressures. In response, they have shifted tax charges away from capital by largely abolishing wealth taxes and lowering corporate income tax (CIT) rates, while at the same time increasing value-added and similar consumption taxes and cutting back heavily on welfare provisions. Inequality has risen dramatically as a result, and social and political cohesion is threatened.

The discontinuance of capital controls since the 1970s, and the removal or reduction of withholding tax provisions, has increased capital mobility and the ease with which profits can be shifted to tax havens. Improvements in communications technology have contributed to this trend. TNCs have adapted their tax strategies to take advantage of this enhanced mobility through sophisticated profit-shifting mechanisms and by exploiting political access to lobby for lower tax rates, tax reliefs, and subsidies. This has called into question the sustainability of operating a Single Market economy in the absence of agreement between member states on how to block 'spoiler' states from using their fiscal sovereignty as a weapon to extract tax revenues from other countries. Examples of such weapons include patent box measures aimed at attracting royalties from intellectual property rights and secret special treatments targeted at corporate treasury operations such as those revealed by the 2011 LuxLeaks scandal.

The EU Code of Conduct Group (CCG), launched by the Council in 1997, made some early progress in addressing egregious abuses, especially those relating to ring-fencing arrangements that provided preferential treatment to subsidiary companies used for booking profits from operating companies located elsewhere. But the CCG did not effectively tackle the issue of secret tax rulings and the widespread use of reliefs to subsidise companies. The 2011 LuxLeaks scandal revealed the inadequacy of relying on non-binding commitments from member states to remove secretive preferential tax regimes. This situation has not been improved by the failure of the Competition Commissioner to investigate the LuxLeaks and develop policies for tackling what are essentially subsidies which contravene rules on illegal state aid.

When it was launched in the 1990s, the CCG was able to make progress across a range of issues because concerns about tax competition had political salience ahead of the imminent accession of several Central and Eastern European countries. This expansion raised concerns about compliance with state aid rules and their application to the existing EU-15 member states. But the early progress of the CCG in tackling issues like ring-fencing was not taken to its logical conclusion, which would have required an accord between all member states to protect national tax regimes from tax wars.

Tax havens v. Westphalian sovereignty

Tackling the threat of tax wars will require resolution of the political tensions that arise when countries insist that principles of Westphalian sovereignty are respected on tax matters, without acknowledging that in the absence of effective international rules and cross-border cooperation to curtail tax evasion and avoidance, free movement of capital erodes domestic tax sovereignty. Mounting concerns about tax avoidance have revealed the tensions between the Westphalian principle of non-intervention in the internal affairs of other states on the one hand, and the harmful 'spillovers' on the other that arise when a tax haven state adopts tax measures or secrecy provisions intended to undermine or nullify the domestic sovereignty of a third-party state.

The EU therefore faces a historic choice between allowing tax wars to erode the CIT, or adopting a common tax base for TNCs and a harmonised minimum rate. If the former route is taken, allowing erosion of the CIT will compromise the viability of the personal income tax, since the majority of wealthy people use offshore companies to protect their wealth and earnings from income, capital gains, and inheritance taxes.

The logical way forward

The long-standing EU project for creating a harmonised base for taxing TNCs, known as the Common Consolidated Corporate Tax Base (CCCTB) is key to protecting domestic tax sovereignty. This project was first considered by the European Parliament in 2005 and subsequently developed by the European Commission in consultation with business representative groups and technical specialists. Following a period of technical scrutiny by the Council of Ministers, in June 2015 the Commission announced an action plan to proceed with the project. The CCCTB, combined with UT, would simplify most of the complexities in the current system and allow for a more rational way for allocating profits to source countries based on the economic substance of where sales take place, where labour is employed, and where capital is invested (rather than registered for tax purposes). The UT approach has been used successfully for decades in the United States and other countries.

The difficulties associated with making UT practicable are relatively minor, especially if the process of adopting this new approach is made gradual with a well sign-posted strategy for transition. Four key components are necessary for a successful shift to UT and to block race-to-the-bottom dynamics:

The first is country-by-country reporting (CBCR) to the tax authorities of each relevant country. This includes consolidated worldwide accounts for the TNC as a single entity, excluding internal transfers, details of all entities forming the group, plus data on the sales, physical assets, and numbers of employees and payroll, as well as actual taxes paid in every country where the TNC has a business presence. CBCR has already been adopted by the European Commission, albeit with a high threshold for the reporting requirement, and after considerable civil pressure.

Second, CBCR provides the necessary information to decide on apportioning profits between the different countries where production or sales take place. Many countries will already have experience of applying so-called 'allocation keys' used to apportion profits under the profit-split method allowed under existing OECD transfer pricing guidelines, and this experience can be combined with further research to identify the most equitable formulae for specific industries.

Third, cooperation on taxing TNCs must also address the deficiencies in conflict resolution between states. Mutual Agreement Procedures (MAP) laid down in existing tax treaties already provide for resolution on disagreements over transfer pricing. However, these are rightly criticised on the grounds that they currently seek to apply rules that patently disfavour some countries, especially developing countries. Their procedures are also shrouded in secrecy, which means rulings involving many hundreds of millions of euros are not published. The OECD BEPS programme includes a provision for compulsory and binding arbitration, which could be built into a European UT policy framework, preferably without the secrecy that surrounds existing MAP processes.

Finally, harmonising the tax base would inhibit countries from offering special tax treatment to attract investment, but by itself would not eliminate tax competition since it would allow states to engage in a race to the bottom on nominal tax rates. This race would probably lead to zero tax rates, effectively abolishing the CIT within the coming two decades. What was previously a relatively slow burn issue grew more urgent after the US Congress adopted Trump's tax reforms in December 2017, increasing the need for the EU to establish a minimum rate to block a race-to-the-bottom sprint.

Countermeasures

EU member states have found their tax sovereignty eroded to the extent that tax havens pose existential threats to democracy. Countermeasures are needed to resist tax havens which use beggar-my-neighbour tactics to undermine the tax and anti-money-laundering regimes of other countries. The EU needs to conduct an expert independent spillover analysis of the external risks that the tax and secrecy regimes of one country might pose for other countries.

In the case of the United Kingdom's 'Singapore-on-the-Thames' proposal, the EC should require spillover analyses of the entire British ecosystem of tax havens and secrecy jurisdictions to identify its weakest points. In the post-Brexit scenario, under no circumstances should London-based banks and other financial services providers have access to the Single Market on the basis of either mutual recognition or equivalence of regulatory standards without the UK government finally delivering on its promises—such as requiring its overseas territories and crown dependencies to make their company ownership registries fully transparent and accessible to public enquiry.

Nothing demonstrates clearer the EU's political failure to address the tax haven problem than the total uselessness of its attempts to create a tax haven blacklist.

Fortunately, help is at hand: the Tax Justice Network publishes two indices, one covering financial secrecy, the second covering corporate tax havens, which identify and rank the main spoiler countries. The EU should take the lead in imposing the strongest countermeasures possible on the principal secrecy jurisdictions and tax havens, *pour encourager les autres.*

Conclusions

The current framework of tax rules did not come about suddenly or by accident. They were developed over the course of decades and shaped by huge lobbying efforts on the part of special interests. Corruption played a part: not just in the form of tax deals done behind veils of offshore secrecy—as LuxLeaks revealed—but through extensive intrusion by major accounting and tax advisory firms into the very heart of policymaking process. Too few politicians understand international tax matters, and far too many political parties are captive to special interests. When it comes to tax policy matters, revolving doors between the private sector and political office spin very fast indeed. Urgent action is required to end the multiple conflicts of interest that have captured tax policymaking.

I am regularly told that the tax justice agenda for pushing back against tax wars is 'federalist' and anti-democratic. This accusation ignores the ways in which, in a world of mobile capital, tax havens and secrecy jurisdictions undermine the ability of democratic governments to shape the tax policies they were elected to deliver. The tax justice route, which rejects tax and regulatory wars in favour of international cooperation, will enhance democracy and national sovereignty on tax matters.

It is said that the history of economic and social justice is written in the tax codes. In the case of the EU, the historic failure to agree to a framework of rules that protect tax sovereignty has harmed social justice and threatens the democratic norms of most member states. How serious has the threat become? Fascists are gaining ground in many countries, and European history demonstrates how fast extreme inequality and political polarisation can kill democracy.

Unless measures are taken to protect domestic tax regimes from tax havens, tax wars, and the overbearing power of TNCs to shape tax policies to their advantage, democracy in Europe may well succumb to extremist politics in less than a decade.

It's Time for Europe to Tackle the Finance Curse

Nicholas Shaxson

If there is anybody who symbolises the incoherence of Europe's centre-left political parties, and of the European project more generally, it is Germany's finance-friendly finance minister Olaf Scholz. For years he has promoted policies favouring large multinational enterprises and banks, sabotaging corporate transparency initiatives,[1] rejecting efforts to tax Google and other digital giants, and undermining efforts for a Financial Transaction Tax.

In September 2018, in an article entitled "Berlin Falls in Love with Big Banks"[2], the *Financial Times* reported that Scholz, who is from the centre-left Social Democratic Party, "has time and again stressed that the German economy needs strong and globally competitive banks to support its export-oriented economy . . . Berlin is warming up to the idea of eventually merging Deutsche and Commerzbank." Scholz, for his part, stated baldly: "We want to be perceived as a country that appreciates when banks create jobs in Germany and bring over capital and know-how." And in February 2019, Scholz and his deputy, the former investment banker Jörg Kukies, were exposed as having been huddled in clandestine meetings in the City of London with grandees from some of the world's biggest investment banks—Goldman Sachs, Bank of America, and several others—to discuss how to encourage the Deutsche Bank/Commerzbank merger, and how to develop Germany's banking sector.[3] "We are very happy to have a lot of international banks acting in Germany," said Scholz, "but also to have a stable banking sector in Germany that is able to go with any company abroad."[4]

The competitiveness agenda

This needs some unpacking, but it boils down to three big and interrelated ideas. First, Germany should boost its financial sector (helped, perhaps, by an exodus of banks and bankers from London after Brexit). Second, Germany should promote a merged 'national banking champion' big enough to go head-to-head with the Americans and the Chinese in global financial markets. Third, that both these things promote something called 'national competitiveness'.

This kind of thinking pervades European policymaking, far beyond Germany. It is all tied together by something I call the Competitiveness Agenda, which has suffused much if not most of European economic policymaking. Now the idea of national (or regional) competitiveness is a tricky area. You can take the word 'competitiveness' and get it to mean whatever you want. You can argue, for instance, that upgrading education, building strong social protections, controlling capital flows across borders, or adopting protectionism are the best ways to achieve 'competitiveness'. You could insist that it must meet the test of productivity, good jobs, and a broad-based rise in living standards, or recommend carefully targeted industrial policies of nurturing domestic economic ecosystems to support sectors where the country might have comparative advantage—the concept pioneered by the eighteenth-century British economist David Ricardo, where countries play to their strengths.

There are strong, respectable arguments along all these lines. The Competitiveness Agenda is a particular, pro-finance and pro-multinational strain of this: the idea that you must always shower tax cuts, lax laws, and financial regulations, weak antitrust enforcement and other goodies on big banks, insurance firms, phone companies, oil producers, shell companies, or oligarchs—or they'll run away with their money to Singapore or Geneva.

This agenda assesses the many trade-offs between the interests of large banks and multinationals, on the one hand, and the interests of Europe's broad populations, on the other—and when there's a clash, comes down hard on the side of the big corporations. This was solidified under the Lisbon Agenda to make Europe "the most competitive and dynamic knowledge-based economy in the world." Although this particular strain of competitiveness isn't official explicit policy in euro-land (things are much more nuanced than that) it has in practice been the guiding approach for much of what happens, helped by heavy lobbying in Brussels and in European capitals. The Commerzbank/Deutsche saga is just the latest episode.

This agenda is often an easy sell to large parts of the public, particularly in heavily financialised countries like Britain, because, well, who would want to oppose something called 'competitiveness'? So it is, as a result, enormously influential. Fortunately, these ideas—that European countries can become more 'competitive' through building 'national champions', or that they can grow faster by attracting more financial activity—rest on an interlocking array of elementary but gigantic intellectual fallacies. This Competitiveness Agenda is an intellectual house of cards, ready to fall. If this becomes widely understood, the door to profound reform can open. But if this agenda continues to rule policymaking, the European Union will collapse under its own contradictions.

From resource curse to finance curse

All the fallacious and bankrupt arguments underlying this Competitiveness Agenda can be understood via a concept I've helped develop, called the Finance Curse.

Back in 1993, just as the European Single Market was being established, I was the *Reuters* and *Financial Times* correspondent living in war-ravaged Angola, whose oil-rich government army was fighting against Jonas Savimbi's bloodthirsty UNITA rebels, who mined diamonds to pay for their war effort. Oil and diamonds made up over 99.5 per cent of Angola's exports back then, yet despite the billions of dollars cascading into national coffers, most Angolans were among Africa's most destitute people. The war was a big reason, but something deeper was going on, too.

Academics at that time were just starting to put together a thesis now known as the Resource Curse, which afflicts mineral-rich countries like Angola. It's a complex phenomenon, but if you understand one thing about the Resource Curse, it's this: it isn't just that corrupt elites steal the mineral wealth, though that certainly happens. It's worse than that. Countries dominated by oversized oil or mineral extraction sectors are often even worse off than they would have been without these resources. The resource-rich countries were likely to suffer lower economic growth, a higher risk of war and conflict, greater despotism and authoritarian rule, steeper inequality, and higher levels of poverty than their resource-poor peers. Some countries, like Norway, have escaped the curse, but back then nobody doubted that Angola was being cursed by its minerals. Too much money, it seems, can make you poorer. That's why this phenomenon is also known as the paradox of poverty from plenty.

In 2007, long after I had left Angola, I had a peculiar conversation with John Christensen, then a former Economic Adviser to the British tax haven of Jersey. He had given up his job and, disgusted by what he had seen, helped set up the Tax Justice Network to campaign against tax havens. As I recounted my experiences in Angola, and of the Resource Curse, he said "but this is Jersey!" Similar things were happening there, on an island dominated not by oil but by finance. In both Angola and Jersey, the best and brightest people were being sucked out of industry, out of agriculture, out of civil society, and out of government, and into the highly-paid sector. This brain drain, and other finance-related things, generated shocking levels of inequality. In both places, foreign dollar earnings cascading in from outside were pushing up local price levels in a 'Dutch Disease', making it hard for other tradable sectors—mostly agriculture in Angola's case, and mostly tourism and agriculture in Jersey's case—to compete with imports. Those sectors withered. Massive volatility—oil boom-and-bust in Angola's case, and the Global Financial Crisis, in Jersey's—threw economic and political policymaking into turmoil.

Vast opportunities for rent-seeking (copious easy oil dollars in Angola, and copious easy foreign fees for handling dirty money attracted by Jersey's secrecy laws) were encouraging people to turn away from genuinely productive and entrepreneurial activities, and towards the lazy, easy pickings from oil or offshore finance. And, of course, the entire political system and policymaking apparatus seemed 'captured' by the dominant sector, so that its interests were prioritised, often at the expense of broader populations.

Christensen and I resolved to call this phenomenon the Finance Curse, and we set about studying, putting out our first joint position paper in May 2013.[5] Just then, as it turned out, academics were putting out the first of a slew of recent papers showing a simple, clear relationship between the level of a country's financial sector development and that country's long-term economic performance.[6] On a graph, that relationship looks like an upside-down 'U' shape. Here's one, from the IMF:

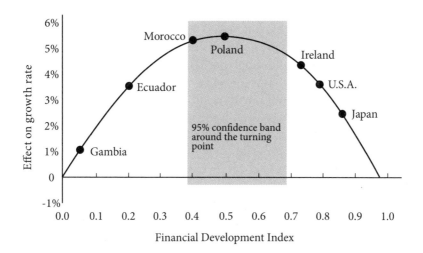

In short, we all need finance—to pay our bills, to provide the ATMs, to channel savings into productive investment, and so on. But this is only true up to an optimal point (the highest point on the graph) after which finance starts to turn nasty, and the finance curse starts to bite. The reasons are many and complex, but the key point is this: if your country is on the wrong side of this graph, then attracting more financial activity to your country is likely to harm economic growth—and cause many other harms. If your financial sector is oversized, then a core and brazen public policy goal should be to *reduce* the size of the financial sector, not increase it.

Here, then, is the first foolishness at the heart of Scholz's message. Germany, like most mature western democracies, lies on the wrong side of these graphs. Attracting more banking business to Germany is likely to deepen the finance curse, reduce economic growth, worsen inequality, deepen corruption and financial crime, and, yes, damage the car industry.

National banking champions and competitiveness

This brings us to that other big source of incoherence and inconsistency in European policymaking I mentioned at the outset: the quest for something called German (or European) 'competitiveness', and the closely related pursuit of competitive 'national champions' in banking and in other areas.

The first fallacy here lies in the idea that whole countries or regions can 'compete' in a way we would recognise. *Companies* compete in markets; *countries* don't. To get a first sense of this, ponder the difference between a failed company, like Enron, and a failed state, like perhaps Syria or Venezuela. They are utterly different beasts.

Tied up with this confusion is a second fallacy, which confuses the fortunes of one sector of an economy—let's call this sector 'big banks and multinationals'—with the fortunes of a whole country. (Economists call this 'the fallacy of composition'.) You can certainly make the big players in this sector more globally competitive by giving them subsidies (corporate tax cuts and tolerance for tax havens, ways to undermine labour unions and otherwise reduce workers' wages, permissions to increase their monopolising market powers, financial deregulation, government contracting favours and subsidies, and so on) but this does not obviously make Germany or Europe more 'competitive'. It merely involves transferring wealth away from German or European taxpayers, workers and consumers, and towards the 'Big banks and multinationals' sector. The corporations win, at the expense of broad populations. This isn't an obvious benefit to 'Europe', or an obvious route to anything you might call 'competitiveness'.

You might still try to argue this, if you could show that getting European populations to hand vast goodies to large banks and multinationals promotes broad-based overall economic growth, which then trickles down. But all the evidence shows that it will do precisely the opposite. That's not just because of the finance curse, but for a host of other reasons: not least because such policies will tend to increase inequality, which not only harms majorities of populations but also is now known to sap long-term growth—something even the International Monetary Fund now admits.[7] And such policies subsidising the rich tend to trigger nasty political shocks, like Brexit.

Inequality and bankruptcy

These are some of the reasons why Scholz's love-in with Big Finance is so dangerous, and so intellectually bankrupt. And this brings us to the more specific nonsense at the heart of his proposal: the quest for greater German competitiveness through building a 'national banking champion' constructed from Deutsche Bank and Commerzbank. In fact, nineteen European countries in December 2018 signed a statement urging a Europe-wide 'national champions' approach,[8] and a weakening of competition rules, in order for Europe to 'maintain its competitiveness'.

So here's the bankruptcy at the heart of this idea. A bigger, merged entity is likely to be a stronger entity, the thinking goes. How will it be stronger? Well, at the expense of others in Europe. For one thing, it will be even more of a too-big-to-fail bank than either of those two banks already is. It will thus have greater ability to take profitable risks at the ultimate expense of German, and European, taxpayers, when the next crisis hits and they face bailouts. (In fact, Germany's Monopolies Commission warned about exactly this kind of thinking in 2004, ahead of the global financial crisis, pointing out that similar policy ideas underpinned and fed the rise of Nazism in the 1930s.)[9]

But there is more. The effect of any merger—often the main idea behind a merger—is to reduce competition in the market and increase monopolistic power. That boosts profits and, again, can make for a stronger combined entity. But that strength is derived from these entities' ability to 'streamline' (or cut) jobs and, more importantly, to use monopolising market power to extract more wealth from consumers, workers, taxpayers, suppliers, and so on.

Once again, the idea is that these behemoths must be allowed to exploit European consumers, workers, taxpayers, and suppliers more effectively, so that they can compete better in global markets. That same transfer from populations to big banks, which is not a net benefit to Europe, does nothing to improve genuine productivity, and is likely to harm overall economic growth in Germany and in Europe.

In fact, we can summarise this 'national champions for competitiveness' strategy in an even shorter, pithier way: the strategy is to increase national 'competitiveness' by reducing competition. If that sounds ridiculous and incoherent, that's because it is.

It's time to pass the baton

None of this is rocket science. It can all be understood through the prism of the finance curse, which goes far beyond the banking and shadow banking sectors, and touches on something that academics call *financialisation*. This is about the conversion of more 'normal' businesses—selling shoes and hotel reservations and film content and widgets, and so on—into financially-engineered vehicles whose core purpose has been narrowed from the task of making profits while serving society, down to a single-minded focus on using special techniques to extract maximum wealth from these activities on behalf of the mostly wealthy owners of these vehicles, many of them foreigners. Those techniques include tax cheating via havens, monopolisation, wage suppression, and the prodigious use of debt to juice up financial returns. That's what we're up against.

In February 2019, Brad DeLong, one of America's best-known economists, accepted the bankruptcy of the conventional wisdom that has ruled western economic policymaking for so long. "We failed to produce enough large-scale obvious policy wins to cement the centre into a durable governing coalition", he said. "And so, the baton rightly passes to our colleagues on our left. We are still here, but it is not our time to lead."

Similarly, it is time for Olaf Scholz and Europe's mainstream governing classes to recognise their failure. Doubling down on the finance-driven Competitiveness Agenda isn't the answer. It's time for European leaders to pass the baton to a new, younger generation.

And to be honest, it's not even necessary to pass the baton to the left. Europe's central economic problem is that markets are *rigged,* in favour of a billionaire class, and in favour of large multinational banks and enterprises. Markets, and political systems, have been corrupted wholesale by tax havens, by monopolies, and by the rise of overweening finance and criminalised offshore finance. People on the left will naturally fight against these things, as they have always done. But there are large numbers of people on the right who hate rigged markets and crime, too. There is a large and powerful coalition for change, right here.

A powerful coalition for change

Here are three big areas of focus, for starters:

First, we must embrace the reduction in size of our financial sector as an explicit policy goal, particularly in places like Britain or Ireland or Luxembourg, where the finance curse is strongest. Obviously, it matters which bits of finance get reduced, and which bits get preserved, but getting political traction for this elementary idea in the broad national self-interest opens up many possibilities for change. Fight the Finance Curse.

Second, we must pay particular attentions to tax havens. Europe hosts some of the world's most important havens—from see-no-evil Luxembourg, to crooked little Jersey, to rapacious corporate tax haven Ireland, to Britain itself. Elsewhere, the United States must be tackled, as must places like Panama and Dubai, two of the muckiest havens on the planet. We must crack down on them hard. John Christensen's article in this book lays out a useful agenda for change.

Third, Europe needs to wake up to the importance of monopolies and corporate power. Right now, there's an amazing, thrilling rise in antimonopoly fervour in the United States, spearheaded from a civil society perspective by groups like the Open Markets Institute, which are energising progressive politicians such as Elizabeth Warren, Bernie Sanders, and Alexandria Ocasio-Cortez. Europe has nothing like this—partly because of a misguided belief that our competition authorities under Margrethe Vestager are solving the problem. They aren't. Those fines against American technology giants are better than nothing, but still pinpricks. Europe isn't tackling its too-big-to-fail banks—it's encouraging them to get bigger.

European competition authorities have done nothing to rein in the appalling litany of monopolising market abuses and tax haven shenanigans at the hands of the Big Four accounting firms.[10] They haven't broken up Facebook, Amazon, or Google—even though they could, and should. They have approved merger after merger after merger. Commerzbank and Deutsche are just the latest in line. Monopolism has pushed Europe towards fascism before, and it could do again. Wake up, European civil society. Get into this fight.

The good news here is that we can use the finance curse to properly and clearly expose the fallacies and misunderstandings that underpin Europe's current economic consensus and change the minds of people of wildly different political persuasions. Once we have done that, we can outflank the right-wing extremists, and reclaim Europe for its people.

Notes

1 Markus Meinzer, "Why is Germany Siding with the Tax Havens Against Corporate Transparency?" *Tax Justice Network*, 13 July 2018, https://www.taxjustice.net/2018/07/13/why-is-germany-siding-with-the-tax-havens-against-corporate-transparency/.

2 Nick Shaxson, "Is Germany's Finance Minister the Puppet of Big Finance?" *Brave New Europe*, 5 September 2018, https://bravenewweurope.com/nick-shaxson-is-germanys-finance-minister-the-puppet-of-big-finance.

3 Stephen Morris, David Crow, and Olaf Storbeck, "Deutsche and Commerzbank: Why Berlin is Backing a Merger," *Financial Times*, 4 March 2019, https://www.ft.com/content/fd55d086-3b52-11e9-b856-5404d3811663.

4 Steven Arons, Birgit Jennen, and Stephanie Flanders, "Germany's Scholz Signals Support for 'National Champion' Banks," *Bloomberg*, 8 February 2019, www.bloomberg.com/news/articles/2019-02-08/germany-seeks-deutsche-bank-merger-plan-by-may-magazine-reports.

5 Nicholas Shaxson and John Christensen, *The Finance Curse*, 2013, *Tax Justice Network*, www.taxjustice.net/cms/upload/pdf/Finance_Curse_Final.pdf.

6 See the selected articles and papers in "The 'Too Much Finance' Literature," *The Finance Curse: How Global Finance is Making Us All Poorer*, October 2018, https://financecurse.net/research/academic-papers-too-much-finance/.

7 See the various papers of the "IMF's Work on Income Equality," *International Monetary Fund*, https://www.imf.org/external/np/fad/inequality/.

8 Jorge Valero, "Nineteen EU Countries Call for New Antitrust Rules to Create 'European Champions,'" *Euractiv*, 19 December 2018, https://www.euractiv.com/section/economy-jobs/news/19-eu-countries-call-for-new-antitrust-rules-to-create-european-champions/.

9 Nick Shaxson, "Is Germany's Finance Minister the Puppet of Big Finance?" *Brave New Europe*, 5 September 2018, https://bravenewweurope.com/nick-shaxson-is-germanys-finance-minister-the-puppet-of-big-finance.

10 Richard Brooks, *Bean Counters: The Triumph of the Accountants and How They Broke Capitalism* (London: Atlantic, 2018).

The Far Right's Gold Fetish

Quinn Slobodian

In September 2019, the German tabloid *BILD* (Europe's bestselling newspaper) ran a headline accusing 'Count Draghila' of "sucking our bank accounts dry." The article ran with a photomontage of European Central Bank head Mario Draghi with triple-bagged eyes and fangs leering over the popped collar of a crushed velvet cloak. The idea was that the negative interests that have been ECB policy since its outgoing head Draghi took over in 2011 had eroded the savings of ordinary Germans—and one man was to blame.

The image and analogy seemed extreme but predictable in Germany's version of the *Daily Mail* or the *New York Post*, designed to shock the pearl-clutching liberals of the 'serious press'. Surprising then to find the image had run before—this time in the sober news monthly *Cicero*, which ran a near-identical image on its cover one year earlier. The idea of the European monetary system as a parasite feeding on a host body of German prosperity was somewhere in the cultural air.

The rise of the far right in Germany—and Europe in general—is usually narrated by way of immigration policy and the handling of millions of asylum seekers to the continent in 2015. Yet the story of money tells an unfairly overlooked tale that runs parallel. One need only recall that the 'alternative' called for by the leading far right party Alternative for Germany (AfD) when it was founded in 2013 was not an alternative to open borders within Europe, or even an alternative to the mainstream parties, but an alternative to the common currency of the Euro.

The AfD are part of the far right that advocates 'hard money', though what this should look like differs. All demand a reversion to the Deutsche Mark, returning control of the currency from the ECB lost in 1999, but one faction goes further by imagining a new Deutsche Mark backed by gold. The latter group, called goldbugs, are long-time denizens of the online fringe, of whom Ron Paul might be the highest-profile member.

Goldbugs see the twentieth century as a period of continual economic and moral decline kicked off by the decision of the leading economic powers to end the gold standard, first during the Great War and second in the 1930s. Although the US re-established its own dollar's peg to gold after the Second World War, this too was ended by President Richard Nixon in the 1970s, leading to a period of so-called floating exchange rates. To goldbugs, the move from gold-backed money to so-called fiat currency paved the way to government profligacy and the purchase of votes through ever-expanding entitlements to marginalised groups that would eventually destroy the world economy.

The AfD's leading goldbug is precious metals blogger, gold consultant, and former Booz Allen Hamilton employee Peter Boehringer, who brought his outsider beliefs to the German Bundestag in 2017, where he has since become chair of the parliament's budget committee. An image posted to Boehringer's blog in 2010 captures his peculiar worldview: it shows Karl Marx's head floating over Frankfurt, the home of the ECB, whose printing presses were the primary weapon of 'monetary socialism'. Fiat money, he wrote, was "in a literal sense the tinder that will set the world on fire."

The gold fetish of the far right does not often appear in the tsunami of takes on the current 'populist wave'. Why? It may be in part because gold does not fit cleanly into the common framework that casts the far right as avatars of a 'closed society' against advocates of an 'open society' defending the centre and the status quo.

Historically, gold has been the symbol of connection, not isolation. The gold standard was the bedrock of the First Age of Globalisation that lasted from the 1870s to the outbreak of the First World War, enabling exchange and contract across continents and oceans. To many classical liberals, it was the metal that bound the world economy together. The mythology of gold is that it is the natural vessel of value arrived at across millennia of trial and error and profiting from an anthropological mystique impossible to replicate.

The far right's fixation on the metal expresses both a desire to ground morality in traditional conceptions of economic value but also a more recent link back to an era before the ECB, the Bank of International Settlements, and the U.S. Fed—a time of finance and commerce unburdened by supranational governance and regulation. It is one of the many ways that the far right's capitalism combines aspects of the open and the closed.

Gold has had a wild ride in the new millennium. Its value more than sextupled from 2000 to a high point in 2011. The biggest factor driving the price up was the Global Financial Crisis of 2007–8 and the associated Eurozone crisis that followed it. German savers, in particular, have fled to gold in droves as a safe haven in times of uncertainty and of zero interest rates. Already in 2008, Germany overtook India, gold's long-standing champion, in private gold sales as nervous savers put their money where they hoped it would be stable.

The far right cannily picked up on the rising price of gold as an index of anti-establishment anxiety. In the United States, Tea Party cheerleaders Glenn Beck and Rush Limbaugh pitched gold on their respective shows, with Beck's favourite company eventually charged with fraud.

For AfD thinkers, gold was more than just a reliable store of value. It was also a filament of cultural and social order. Long-time member of the AfD federal board—and professional opera singer—Dirk Driesang wrote in 2014: "The fatal effects of fundamentally fake money (Falschgeld) on our society and politics, our family and our values, are destructive and undermine the fundamentals of our civilisation as well as our western culture."

To hazard a neologism from the Latin prefix for gold, we could call what some AfD thinkers promote an auripatriotism—a national feeling whose referent is not a territory, ethnos or language but whichever monetary system backs its currency with the precious metal they perceive to be the natural currency of modern humanity. It's a peripatetic patriotism, alighting where it is safe and fleeing when it is in danger.

What world does this auripatriotism envision? Although the AfD rejects the slogan of open borders, they offer, by definition, an ideology of open borders for gold. The nation nests within a golden globe where precious metals flow freely. Far from rejecting globalisation, their vision deepens it, subjecting the actions of the state to the continual audit of asset-holders with the ability to move.

Boehringer made his clearest public mark in the 'bring our gold home' campaign he launched in 2012, demanding the return of German gold reserves held by the Fed in downtown New York. Within months, the Bundesbank relented, announcing its plans to bring back a portion of its overseas holdings. In 2017, the first repatriated gold bars were put on display—and Boehringer promptly denounced them as fakes. Instead of direct democracy, where the mediating institution of the legislature is removed in favour of popular referendum, the gold display was a quixotic bid for 'direct economy', where the citizen-investor receives unmediated encounter with what they (falsely) perceive as the final guarantor of value. Boehringer perfected here a double gesture—at once a middle finger to the monetary masters in Frankfurt and a welcoming spread of the arms to the world market where the value of gold is set.

With monetary policy, as with other matters, we can only understand the far right as a creature of our present moment, not as a throwback to a supposedly autarchic past. The far right is not blind to how the world works. They are turning its weaknesses into their strengths. They see instinctively that money is a matter of trust and that the turn to gold is a sign of diminishing trust in state-managed money. The euro seems distant, the plaything of technocrats—and possible vampires—in the gleaming towers of the ECB.

Remaking Europe means, in part, taking the offensive caricature seriously and rethinking the lines of communication from the managers of Europe's money to its users. A strengthened Europe needs a democratic central bank: Draghila with a human face.

Greek Tragedy in Times of Austerity

Vlassis Missos

Austerity is related to a set of policy initiatives undertaken by governments aimed at reducing public deficits. Other elaborate synonyms of austerity, such as 'fiscal consolidation', 'adjustment', or 'discipline', have also been used by political elites, while highly skilled technocrats have learnt to communicate using an abstract esoteric codified jargon that deviates substantially from common peoples' understanding.

'Rationalisation of public expenditures', for example, refers to cuts, and 'improving one country's competitiveness' stands for devaluation of labour. These ideological fragments of neoliberal policy, found permeating the main policy documents and treatises of the EU (Stability and Growth Pact, Lisbon Treaty, etc.)[1], imply a particularly biased interpretation of the modern state of social affairs.

Since the late 1990s, neoliberal thought has been built upon a growing literature concerning the main postwar causes of the economic crises of advanced capitalist countries, providing a consistent policy framework for their resolution. Blame is mainly placed on 'fiscal profligacy', i.e. governments. High public debt and deficits are considered to be signs of low confidence that will eventually lead to the devaluation of government securities (bonds), upon which all private speculative bubbles have been inflated.

In this context, even though the 2008 crisis was triggered by excessive US Private Sector borrowing, which was further based on a highly leveraged and enormously unregulated financial system, by early 2010 it had been transmitted to the Eurozone as a 'fiscal' problem[2]. Let us examine the impact of austerity policy as it was implemented in Greece.

During the first three months of 2010, Greek government bonds were gradually being devaluated as market rumours spread regarding the anticipated announcement of the official level of its annual deficit. The latter was finally set at 15.1 per cent, initiating a heated internal political debate with reference to the past managerial responsibilities burdening the two major political parties that had governed the country since 1974.

Within a few weeks, the cost of refinancing public debt was hiked, and access of the Greek government to international capital markets was lost. Public debt was at an uncommonly high level of 126.7 per cent and its projected trend path was expected to move upwards. Greece had actually been defaulted, and its public debt was urgently in need of a large, courageous 'haircut'. Instead, the European institutions and the IMF agreed on a more costly option, both in terms of social impact and the loss of GDP.

In May 2010, the Greek government signed its first out of three Economic Adjustment Programmes, committing itself to an excessively demanding set of structural reforms (privatisations of public property and market-oriented social security) along with permanent spending cuts and tax increases, in exchange for a low-interest loan of €110 billion. This huge bailout was condemned to failure, as it was overloading an already over-indebted country with a new long-term debt.

From this perspective, the ultimate purposes of these loans can in no way be attributed to pure sentiments of international solidarity but were rather like a 'rope to hang ourselves'—Varoufakis's words[3]. These amounts were loaded on the shoulders of the Greek people, undermining the economy's future prospects and provoking a rather profound transformation of society that had to be violently adjusted towards a less commodious way of life.

Between 2010 and 2018, Greek governments had borrowed the exorbitant amount of €320 billion, scheduled to be gradually disbursed in a series of tranches as a reward for the progress of the reforms included in the Memorandum. According to the IMF[4], all Greek programmes implemented during this period can be codified along the following lines:

- Measures to improve competitiveness through internal devaluation to boost exports.
- Fiscal adjustment based on expenditure cuts and improvements in tax collection.
- Measures to restore financial sector stability.
- A combination of private and official sector involvement to deliver debt relief, to place debt on a trajectory to reach 120 per cent by 2020.

Until early 2019, apart from fiscal adjustment, all other targets were missed, generating a severe deterioration of the people's general standard of living. During assessment of the first programme, the IMF admitted the following:

There were notable successes . . . Strong fiscal consolidation was achieved and the pension system was put on a viable footing . . . However, there were also notable failures. Market confidence was not restored, the banking system lost 30 per cent of its deposits and the economy encountered a much-deeper-than-expected recession with exceptionally high unemployment. Public debt remained too high and eventually had to be restructured with collateral damage for bank balance sheets . . .

Competitiveness improved somewhat on the back of falling wages, but . . . productivity gains proved elusive.[5]

In sharp contrast to the IMF's projections concerning the trend that the GDP would have followed after the implementation of the programme, the actual GDP in Greece had receded substantially more, losing a total 27 per cent of its value. The figure depicts the immense divergences that occurred between the actual and the projected values, estimated at 2010 and 2014, respectively, by the IMF. As is observable, even after its daring admission that the programme did fail to address the major issues of the Greek crisis, it ploughed on with another misperception, underestimating, once again, the aggression of its neoliberal mandates.

For more than eight years in a row, in a period stamped by political turmoil and social upheaval, GDP was kept shrinking along with increasing and persistent unemployment, poverty, income inequality, and a great mass of low-paid workers. In parallel, the budget balance was shifted from an extremely negative amount into a minor surplus (0.5 per cent), after having fully complied with the rules of fiscal discipline adopted by the EU to lower the level of Social Welfare.

Moreover, and due to the architectural structure of the Eurozone, as long as any government was—and is—unable to depreciate its currency (external devaluation) or to sustain a fiscal deficit to boost internal demand and employment, the burden of adjustment has to be carried exclusively by the labour market (internal devaluation). As a consequence, the unemployment rate was gradually and steadily increasing and in 2016, it was estimated at 23.6 per cent, while more than half of the people unemployed were 'long-term' ones and belonged to the group of over-forty-four years of age. Many of those who were in dire need of keeping their job were forced to share the cost of their social security with their employers or were officially declared self-employed, even though they were working as full-time employees, so that their social security costs were paid out of their wage. Almost half of the job contracts were involuntarily turned into part-time ones and approximately one million people lost their jobs. The minimum wage went down and a great part of the young and educated people began immigrating, in search of a better, and decently paid job abroad, mostly in Germany, France, and the UK.

In the meantime, the Greek debt was never actually reduced. The process of debt restructuring (PSI) that took place within the first trimester of 2012 did not change the amount of the debt; it only significantly extended the maturity period and altered its structure to secure the financial sector from a potential 'credit incident'. As a first step, almost one-third of the gross debt in the form of government bonds was having a 'haircut', causing its holders a real loss of 75 per cent of its value. A few weeks later, however, the Greek government agreed on an additional loan of €130 billion to be disbursed gradually as reforms were progressing, thus annulling the effect of the previous 'haircut'. Concomitantly, the debt-to-GDP ratio moved upwards from 159.6 per cent in 2013 to 178.5 per cent in 2016, signifying that the austerity policy did not aim at dealing with a 'debt crisis' but, instead, its purpose was to secure the interests of the financial sector. According to a special report conducted by the European Court of Auditors concerning the international intervention in the Greek crisis:

> Under the second programme, an amount of 50 billion euros was earmarked for bank recapitalisation and resolution costs via HFSF. An additional buffer of up to 25 billion euros was envisaged for the same purpose under the third programme.

In other words, private banks' losses due to the PSI and austerity policy mixture were indirectly transferred onto the shoulders of the taxpayers, for they became part of the public debt. On the other hand, the respective losses relating to public pension funds and the bondholders who had placed their trust and credit upon the public sector had been left out, indicating this grave financial bias of the implemented programmes.

Most strikingly, even though the value of economic activity (GDP) in Greece had sharply receded, overall public revenues in per capita terms seemed to be remarkably persistent since they were only slightly diminished, by about 2.9 per cent. This was principally the result of an excessively heavy tax system that was imposed not upon the annual income created, but on the stock of private wealth, mostly on residences and land property as well as vehicles and offspring. Each child was considered as adding up to €3,000 on the household's taxed income (imputed income), even though the household's declared income was zero.

As far as the aspect of public expenditures (also in per capita terms) is concerned, they were reduced by 30.8 per cent between 2009 and 2016. Social Welfare was contracted at an extremely low level (for example, public health expenditures were decreased by 45.6 per cent) leaving enough 'market space' for private pension schemes to step in. The quality of public health services in general also deteriorated and the beneficiaries had to contribute financially for their medicines and medical checks. The same also holds for public education, since the teaching staff suffered significant wage losses and many public schools in more remote areas were forced to merge due to excessive costs. In 2016, it was estimated that 71.7 per cent of Greece's population was considered 'poor' according to German income standards.

A lot more remains to be said about this unprecedented episode of political battering. During those tragic years, peoples' living standards in Greece scaled down even further, decelerating the country's speed of 'convergence' with the core European countries, and eventually shifting it towards a path of 'divergence'. Few can deny that the Greek public debt, or deficit, need not have been managed thusly, but few have also argued that the austerity policy implemented in Greece has been focused on the symptoms, rather than the causes, of this crisis. Austerity in Greece was institutionalised and was rooted within the legislation, daily behaviour, customs and hearts of the people who suffered this immense 'doing over' by their international allies. The case of the Greek crisis will always place a stigma upon the history of Europe and will exist to remind us of the false ethics of the developed world's leadership.

Figure: Actual v. IMF-projected GDP in Greece

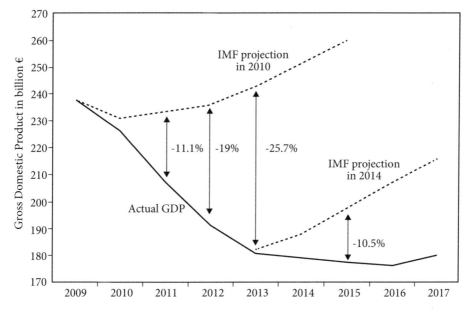

Source: Eurostat, IMF

Table: Data, Greece and Germany (in parentheses), showing the level of economic adjustment between 2009 and 2016. Amounts in € are in current prices and per capita terms.

	2009	2013	2016	% change from 2009 to 2016
Budget balance (as a % of GDP)	-15.1% (-3.2%)	-13.2% (-0.1%)	0.5% (0.9%)	- -
Public Debt (as a % of GDP)	126.7% (72.6%)	159.6% (77.4%)	178.5% (67.9%)	- -
Annual interest payments (per capita, in €)	1,079 (792)	661 (689)	521 (455)	-51.7% (-42.6%)
Trade balance (as a % of GDP)	-9.8% (4.9%)	-2.8% (6.0%)	-0.7% (7.8%)	- -
Total public expenditure (per capita, in €)	11,578 (14,274)	10,228 (15,685)	8,007 (16,876)	-30.8% (18.2%)
Public HEALTH expenditures (per capita, in €)	1,459 (2,134)	846 (2,470)	793 (2,742)	-45.6% (28.5%)

Public EDUCATION expenditures (per capita, in €)	884	752	695	-21.4%
	(1,292)	(1,499)	(1,610)	(24.7%)
Public MILITARY expenditures (per capita, in €)	709	353	344	-51.5%
	(339)	(379)	(397)	16.9%
Total public revenue (per capita, in €)	8,336	8,068	8,093	-2.9%
	(13,303)	(15,636)	(17,225)	(29.5.%)
Unemployment rate	9.6%	27.5%	23.6%	-
	(7.6%)	(5.2%)	(4.1%)	-
Percentage of the population in Greece, living under the 'poverty line' of Germany	35.6%	67.7%	71.7%	-

Source: Eurostat

Notes

1 See Achim Truger, "Austerity in the Euro Area: The Sad State of Economic Policy in Germany and the EU," *IPE Working Papers* 22 (2013).
2 See Mark Pagano, "Understanding the Eurozone Crisis," *VoxEU*, 15 May 2010, https://voxeu.org/article/understanding-eurozone-crisis.
3 Yanis Varoufakis, "Open Letter to a Friend and Colleague," *OpenDemocracy*, 28 June 2012, https://www.opendemocracy.net/en/openeconomy/open-letter-to-good-friend-and-colleague/.
4 International Monetary Fund, *Greece: Request for Extended Arrangement Under the Extended Fund Facility*, IMF Country Report 12.57 (Washington D.C.: 2012).
5 International Monetary Fund, *Greece: Ex Post Evaluation of Exceptional Access under the 2010 Stand-By Arrangement*, IMF Country Report 13.156 (Washington D.C.: 2013).

Shaking off the Burden

By Jerome Roos

For five years, from early 2010 to mid-2015, the eyes of the world were transfixed on a peripheral region of the European continent that normally receives little attention from the international media. As official lenders forced highly unpopular austerity measures, particularly on Greece, where hundreds of thousands of protesters gathered in front of parliament in Athens to stop their ratification, international news agencies beamed the images of violent clashes right across the globe.

A decade on, the world's attention has shifted; fresh crises demand it. The brief infatuation with Syriza as a great challenger to global capitalism has given way. In these new circumstances, one could be forgiven for thinking that Europe's long-forgotten debt crisis is now well and truly behind us: a distant relic of the early 2010s.

If only it were so. Greece's debt may no longer fill the front page of Europe's newspapers, but its burden remains a stubborn reality for millions of Greeks—including those yet to be born. While public debt stood at 110 per cent of GDP on the eve of the crisis in 2008, it grew to 180 one decade later. To repay this mountain of debt, Greece has been forced into a fiscal straitjacket that will see its current and future governments run primary budget surpluses of 3.5 per cent until 2022 and 2.2 per cent until 2060, condemning the Greek people to 40 more years of austerity—an unprecedented feat anywhere in the world.

A slightly less dramatic but generally similar story holds for the other Southern European members of the Eurozone. Spain's public debt-to-GDP ratio stood at a mere 40 per cent in 2008. A decade later, after the bank bailouts and the years of crisis and austerity that followed, it stood at 97, having remained more or less stable since 2014. Italy's public debt also rose from 102 to 132 per cent over the same period, again remaining largely unchanged since 2014. Portugal is the only one of the so-called 'PIGS' countries to have slightly reduced its debt burden in recent years, thanks in large part to the unorthodox refusal of its left-led government to abide by the EU's strict austerity doctrine. But even then, the country's debt-to-GDP ratio has remained well above 100 per cent, up from around 70 at the start of the crisis.

If there is one reason these countries have been able to sustain these enormous debt loads in recent years, it is the unprecedented decision by the European Central

Bank to flood the markets with cheap credit by slashing interest rates and providing an almost limitless outlet for European banks' toxic assets through its quantitative easing (QE) program. The resultant wall of money has driven the yields on many European government bonds into negative territory, enabling these governments to borrow cheaply to refinance their existing obligations. But as soon as the ECB begins to raise interest rates and unwind its QE program, borrowing costs will inevitably rise and the ability of the heavily indebted peripheral countries—especially Italy—to repay their debts may once again be called into question.

Central bank intervention therefore does not resolve the problem; it merely pushes it into the future. If the purpose of international crisis management is not just to stabilise market expectations but also to reduce actual debt burdens to sustainable levels, then the official policy response to the European debt crisis has clearly been a miserable failure. But if the purpose was simply to make private creditors whole by staving off a series of disorderly defaults and, in the Greek case, delaying and diluting an inevitable debt restructuring as much as possible, then the success of the official policy response knows no bounds—for this is precisely what Europe's 'extend and pretend' strategy achieved in practice.

Consider the International Monetary Fund's own evaluation of the original Greek bailout program, which concluded that "in retrospect, the program served as a holding operation" for private creditors—especially French and German banks—to reduce their exposures, "leaving the official sector on the hook." A review by the Fund's Independent Evaluation Office noted that at the outset of the crisis "many commentators considered debt restructuring to be inevitable", but given the strong opposition by the French and German governments this option was not even considered. As a result, the IMF's decision to participate in the EU bailout "allowed many private creditors to escape."

Since the initial round of bailouts, EU leaders have doubled down on this strategy, putting in place a highly disciplinary institutional framework that actively insulates economic policymaking from democratic pressures or alternative economic theories by legally forbidding member states from pursuing expansionary fiscal policies in response to future economic crises. The European Fiscal Compact, signed in March 2012, is a particularly notorious example of this Germanic ordoliberalism in action. It effectively entrenches the prevailing orthodoxy about 'expansionary fiscal contractions' to the level of constitutional law, while outlawing the type of counter-cyclical policies proposed by Keynesian economists.

This is why legal scholars have widely criticised the Fiscal Compact for its interference into the democratic processes of individual member states. Loïc Azoulai, Professor of European Law at Sciences Po Paris, has rightly called the treaty a "legal monster" for its abrogation of national sovereignty in the determination of spending priorities. An editorial in the *European Constitutional Law Review*, the leading journal in the field, similarly declared that it "strikes at the heart of the institutions of parliamentary democracy by dislocating as a matter of constitutional principle the budgetary autonomy of the member states."

It is clear, then, that the problem of Europe's unsustainable debt overhang is closely connected to the question of its fraying democratic institutions. This should not come as a surprise, for debt and democracy have long been tied at the hip. The classical Athenian poet and statesman Solon recognised as much when he repealed the draconian laws of his tyrannical predecessor Draco and decreed the city-state's first democratic constitution in the sixth century BC. Recognizing that there could be no democracy without freedom, and no freedom in the face of slavery, Solon promulgated his famous *seisachtheia*, or 'the shaking off of burdens', which cancelled the debts of the Athenian peasantry, abolished the prevailing practice of debt slavery, and freed those held in bondage by their creditor-landlords.

Today, freedom and democracy are once again under threat—this time from a draconian form of *sovereign* debt bondage, and the morbid political phenomena it has spawned. Over the past decade, the widespread insistence on austerity, privatisation and neoliberal reform has gutted the last remnants of the postwar European welfare state, further hollowed out the continent's weakened democratic institutions, and dramatically widened pre-existing socioeconomic inequalities. The result has been to fan the flames of a burgeoning anti-establishment backlash, giving rise not only to a number of progressive new political forces—from municipalist movements taking root at the local level to the Democracy in Europe Movement organised at the transnational level—but, much more disconcertingly, also to a resurgent nationalist right.

The political tumult currently gripping large parts of the continent, therefore, cannot be seen in isolation from the unresolved debt crisis that preceded and continues to underlie it. Insofar as the wealthy European creditor powers succeeded temporarily in staving off the market turmoil of the first half of the past decade, they have in reality only transformed a *financial* crisis into a *social* and *political* one. As millions of people see their living standards stagnating or falling, and rightly continue to lose faith in the capacity of Europe's democratic institutions to represent their interests and improve their quality of life, a desperate need for an alternative democratic project imposes itself upon radicals and progressives alike.

It is in this context that the lessons of Solon's original democratic experiment regain their world-historical relevance. In this brave new world of rising 'populisms' and negative real interest rates, Europe's unsustainable debt burden may no longer be keeping investors up at night, but the social and political consequences of a decade of dispossession and disempowerment continue to make themselves felt across the continent. It will take nothing less than a modern-day *seisachtheia*— shaking off the burden of oppressive debt loads and bringing an end to the nefarious practice of sovereign debt bondage—to truly set our peoples free and give a new impulse to the historic project of building a unified and democratic Europe.

Shouldn't Europe Deal With Its Colonial Past Before Building a Future Fuelled by Emancipation? Q DiEM Voice Brussels 9 Sept 2017

SHOULDN'T EUROPE DEAL WITH IT'S COLONIAL PAST BEFORE BUILDING A FUTURE FUELLED BY EMANCIPATION?

An Egalitarian Europe by Alice-Mary Higgins

" The European Commission published in 2019 a somewhat ambiguous paper on how the Sustainable Development Goals may or may not influence Europe's post-2020 strategy. The goals resonate partly because, thanks to pressure from countries in the global south, they have equality as their heart and frame. Equality, not just of opportunity but of outcome, must also be recognised as key to Europe's future. This is particularly important as we come out of a period which exacerbated social and economic inequality, both within member states and between them.

There are many intersectional layers to equality. I will focus on gender equality. European institutions have often been instruments of progress on gender. In my own country, Ireland, Europe helped us win maternity leave, end the marriage bar for working women, and decriminalise homosexuality. However, in recent years, some European institutions seemed to slow down or even roll back on gender equality. Progressive Directives stalled, and Europe's Strategy for Equality Between Women and Men was downgraded to a 'strategic document' lacking real power.

Women were also deeply impacted by measures imposed during the years of austerity. They were often hit hardest by cuts in welfare and public services, expected to fill gaps in crumbling social infrastructure and expected to remain throughout at the frontline of new forms of precarious work. In many countries, the recession was exploited by opportunistic employers to erode pay and conditions. Hard won 'flexibility' was twisted into insecure, unpredictable working hours.

Still, despite difficult circumstances and institutional ambivalence, movements for gender equality have been gathering momentum. Women have been making themselves heard. In the arts, sciences, education, sport, and politics, the habits and patterns of oppression are being identified and challenged.

There is a strong demand for equal representation at every decision-making level, including the European Parliament and the Commission. Women are not only seeking seats at the table, they are putting issues and ideas on the agenda. They bring voice and vision and seek both participation and transformation.

Social movements have been strengthened by diverse participation and feminist social and economic analysis. I often refer to the Women Workers Union as the first in Ireland to make paid leave a priority and win two weeks' holiday for all workers. Similarly, women are driving the advocacy for parental leave, predictable working time, and decent childcare. Successful campaigns to introduce gender budgeting at local and national levels have opened up new spaces for debate and accountability in resource allocation that should be reflected in the European Budget.

Deep, often hidden, layers of violence against women are also being peeled back. Fundamental Rights Agency research based on tens of thousands of women across Europe has shown the scale and spread of violence, while the Council of Europe's Istanbul Convention has forced many countries to debate and address these issues.

There has also been further breaking of the silence around bodily autonomy and reproductive rights, including in Ireland where, after decades of campaigning, a Citizens Assembly, a cross-party committee, and a difficult but ultimately compassionate national conversation, access to free, safe, and legal abortion was finally introduced. At the same time, in Spain and Poland, women and men have had to take to the streets to protect the reproductive rights they already hold.

Unfortunately, as old patriarchal powers realise they are losing ground, they sometimes turn to authoritarianism. In a number of European countries, we are seeing a rise in divisive, hostile, deeply regressive parties and governments who use the laws of the state as instruments of inequality and intimidation. As a former member of the European Women's Lobby, I have seen the importance of international solidarity. The nurturing of strong cross-border connections between women's groups and wider civil society has never been more important.

Patriarchy, capitalism, racism, and other historic hierarchies are complex and entwined. So, as activists who meet or work with others who are struggling with different aspects of those embedded systems, it is important to listen to and recognise the many forms inequality and oppression can take.

Feminism, like every movement, is stronger when it reflects the diversity of women's lives. Women may be parenting alone, may be transgender, homeless, immigrant, managing a disability, or from an ethnic minority, and this will shape their experience and analysis.

It is important to welcome that insight and place our stories alongside each other, even when it challenges our own familiar narrative. Thinking in an intersectional way allows us to identify patterns and strengthen the collective work of transformation. It deepens our understanding and our effectiveness. This is true across countries, as well as within them. Intersectional thinking and internationalism are, of course, deeply complementary to each other. Those of us who wish to work together for a better Europe will embrace them both, as we embrace the future. **99**

A Social Europe

by Caroline Lucas

"In 2016, over seventeen million voters delivered a well-deserved blow to the UK's establishment. Many people interpreted the referendum question to mean "Should the country go on being run in the way that it is?" And with a collective howl of rage, they voted "No!" That response was justified then and it's justified now. For a huge number of people, the status quo in the UK is intolerable. The social contract is broken. The political system is rigged. It is right and reasonable to be furious.

The UK, like much of Europe, is divided—between classes, regions (North and South), and within the same region (thriving cities and failing towns). Every single one of our thirty worst 'coldspots' for social mobility voted for Brexit. For many, there was a genuine sense that *any* change would better than the status quo.

People were right to give the ruling class a kicking—but I fear leaving the EU will only make matters worse. Not only because, under every Brexit scenario, there will be less money to spend repairing our torn social fabric, but also because the EU has generally been a force for good, pushing the UK forward on workers' rights, social and environmental protections, and giving us the remarkable gift of free movement. In my view, it's no exaggeration to say that, for all its flaws, it's the greatest international venture for peace, prosperity, and freedom in history.

But in this moment of flux, with the far right on the rise, this progress is at risk. Those of us who believe in building a truly social Europe must urgently learn from the failures of the UK's Remain campaign and be bold in our work towards a society that puts people first.

Instead of making a hopeful case for a fairer country in a more democratic EU, the Remain side in the referendum campaign, Britain Stronger in Europe, pursued Project Fear—warning that leaving would make life worse. What they did not understand was that millions of people felt they had nothing to lose. By obsessing over economics, leading Remainers reduced what should have been a wide-ranging conversation about the UK's place in the world to an argument about the cost of a trolley of shopping.

Meanwhile, Leave campaigners found success in playing on people's sense of powerlessness and fanning the flames of hatred. So it was not just a political failure, but a moral one which saw the Remain campaign avoid talking about migration. By refusing to engage with people's concerns about free movement, and to offer them hope that they too can enjoy its benefits, they allowed the far right to dominate the conversation.

In the end, Remainers lost the most important vote in a generation—putting at risk rights that people had spent decades fighting for. Now, instead of campaigning for something better, we are scrambling to defend principles that once seemed untouchable. But for the sake of communities across Europe who've rightly had enough of the status quo, progressives can't afford to be on the defensive. Those of us who believe in a social Europe must be proud to champion it.

We should admit the fact that the EU is far from perfect, and make the case for bold democratic reform. Simple changes like live-streaming of meetings and publishing trade negotiation documents can make its work more transparent and within reach. And exciting ideas like calling a constitutional assembly could begin a process of democratic renewal that could ultimately dismantle the domination of corporate power. In 2016, people in the UK rightly voted to 'take back control'— and across Europe, people deserve more of a say over decisions that affect them.

We must argue for policies that not only protect people from exploitation, but allow them to live more fulfilling lives. The stark inequalities both within our countries and between them are a grave injustice, and have been exploited by the far right to divide communities. Progressives must call out this hatred, point to the wealthy elite who are truly responsible, and demand positive changes. Working towards an EU-wide living wage, set at appropriate levels according to national circumstances, could help end inequality, deliver decent living standards, and empower workers across the bloc.

Rebalancing our economies in favour of the majority goes hand in hand with protecting and enhancing freedom of movement. Our precious right to live, study, and work across twenty-seven other countries is one of the EU's greatest gifts. But for many people, the opportunities it offers are out of reach. By reversing inequality, we can make that right a reality for everyone.

I believe progressives have the solutions to heal our divided continent—but across the EU, nationalists are gradually gaining ground. If we are to build a fairer, more democratic Europe, we must learn from the UK's mistakes and deliver the hope people need. **99**

PART FIVE

Work

Let There Be Light

Paul Laverty & Ken Loach

I met Dave on 29 July 2017 inside a Tesco's cafeteria in Dunfermline, Scotland, while we were wrestling with a film idea that eventually became *Sorry We Missed You*. Dave drove a white van, and had worked for several courier companies, including Amazon.

Typically, he would get up at 4.45 a.m. He would leave home at 5 a.m. He would get into a holding car park at the giant warehouse, and try to make sure he would be there early enough to get a good position so he wouldn't be crowded out on the first wave of 'loading up' by the other 400 drivers.

In the car park, he was not allowed to mingle with the other drivers. The company said this was for 'safety reasons' but Dave had other ideas: "Best to keep us separate, easier to control us."

Dave would often wait up to two hours before loading his van. Only then would his official working day begin. Each day would be different but sometimes he would deliver over 200 parcels at the busiest times. His record was 218.

The handheld device, HHD, nicknamed 'a gun', was his constant companion. It scanned every parcel, photographed each item if left in a place of safety as instructed by the customer, received calls and messages, and, by GPS, monitored every step Dave took. It bleeped if he was outside his van for more than two minutes. It worked out a route and gave an estimated time of arrival (ETA), and flagged orders that had to be delivered within a window of one hour (known as 'precisors'), sometimes causing havoc, zig-zagging his route to make the deadline. Such were the relentless demands of his HHD, he would often jog to make sure the parcel was scanned and delivered to the client on time.

Dave carried a plastic bottle in his van to piss in. On exceptional occasions, when luck went his way, he could finish his work in the early afternoon, but usually he finished between 7 p.m. and 8 p.m., then drove home for fifty minutes. Dave worked six days a week. He had one day off per week, but many times the day off would change by text at short notice according to the needs of the company. He had no holidays, no sick pay. Dave had a pale grey complexion and sunken eyes.

Algorithm, creativity, imagination, and technology had pushed Dave to the extreme limits of physical and mental endurance. He felt dizzy one day and nearly passed out driving. His body and mind worked to meet the relentless deadline, and he spoke like a man scooped out from the inside. "I feel like a tube of toothpaste." In law, Dave was self-employed, in control, and master of his own business. In reality, he was a man on the brink.

Two days before meeting Dave, there was a fluctuation of share prices in Amazon which meant that its owner, Jeff Bezos, became the richest man in the world, with a fortune of just over $90 billion. But it took the newspapers a few days to catch up. I passed Dave that day's newspaper with the smiling photo of Jeff Bezos. Dave was silent for a long time as he stared at the image and digested the contents.

Bezos named his company 'Amazon' after the river because it began with A, the first letter in the alphabet. How many Daves were there around the world, white vans on roadways like streams, swelling into fulfilment centres and finally profit-thundering at breakneck speed in unimaginable quantities into the wide open arms of Mr. Bezos at the far, far end of the tens of millions of handheld devices?

A year later, Bezos became the first 'centi-billionaire' with a fortune of over $150 billion, putting him ahead of the GDP of some ninety-eight countries. Dave cut a forlorn figure as he left the cafeteria. Two sides of the same coin; unimaginable inequality and systematic exploitation of labour. Perhaps the greatest challenge of our times alongside climate change.

I followed Dave five minutes later down the same road which brought me close to a modest stone house. It was the original home of Andrew Carnegie, who left Dunfermline an impoverished child and went on to make his fortune in the States. It now serves as a museum.

Carnegie sold his Pittsburgh Steel Company in 1901 to JP Morgan for $303,450,000, making him the richest man of his time. He then proceeded to buy a 64-room mansion in New York, and Skibo Castle, part of a 22,000 acre estate in the Scottish Highlands. There was a great deal of information on Carnegie's philanthropic work over the last eighteen years of his life, during which he gave away over 90 per cent of his fortune and built over 3,000 libraries around the world, and, of course, Carnegie Hall in New York.

Unsurprisingly, I don't recall much information on the Homestead Strike in one of his factories in Pennsylvania. This was an infamous bloody confrontation with the Amalgamated Association of Iron and Steelworkers of the United States, (generally seen as a very moderate union at the time) in 1892, lasting over 143 days. Carnegie's partner, Henry Clay Frick, virulently anti-union, led the action while Carnegie was in Scotland. Carnegie always tried to minimise his role in this battle though clearly stating to Frick before leaving that they should not hesitate to close down the factory if the workers didn't agree to their changes. He wrote to Frick, "We all approve of anything you do, not stopping short of approval of a contest. We are with you to the end." Frick hired the infamous Pinkerton National Detective Agency: armed agents, well-known strike breakers to protect scab labour, mostly made up of immigrant workers. In the violence, seven workers were killed—including three Pinkertons—and hundreds were injured. The State sent in paramilitaries. The union was crushed. Profits gushed in as business as usual was restored.

The photos of the factories are stunning and set the imagination flying; the furnaces, molten flames, and great coke ovens. Thousands of men packed in together in one dramatic setting. There were many horrific accidents and explosions. One 'puddler' wrote of his work with a 25-pound spoon stirring the fiery liquid: "I am like some frantic baker in the inferno kneading a batch of iron bread for the devil's breakfast." Les Standiford, from whom I got the above quote, wrote that it was generally accepted that a 40-year-old man in this work was "all worn out".

Carnegie lived until he was eighty-three. As he opened a stunning sandstone library in the United States he addressed those present. "Believe me, fellow work-men, the interests of capital and labour are one."

Bezos doesn't need the Pinkertons. Amazon hires employee relations managers that, according to an advert, "must have at least seven years direct experience in . . . union avoidance work, or labour law with an emphasis on union avoidance." Amazon doesn't need the overseer. It has the algorithm and the handheld device.

We are blind to an army of Daves, hundreds of thousands of white van drivers weaving in among us and knocking politely on our doors. They don't get scalded by liquid steel, but I do wonder how many have crashed after hours of exhaustion. I did hear from a bona fide journalist that an Amazon transport manager had resigned at the number of road accidents, but I was never able to confirm this allegation. I do wonder, however, whether the government will do some rigorous research.

Carnegie would have marvelled at present-day lawyers and publicists, these masters of disguise. Bogus self-employment transfers risk from the company to the worker, hidden behind new words like 'onboarding' instead of hiring, and 'fees' paid instead of a wage. Technology, finance, contract, language—all genuflect before these giant corporations. Public perception is carefully sculpted; the cult of wealth and philanthropy dance as one. Exploitation sold as freedom.

William Blake warned us of 'the mind-forg'd manacles'.

Technology changes, but not the age-old questions.

The central library in Edinburgh was built by Carnegie, too.

Cut into the sandstone above the main door are the words:

LET THERE BE LIGHT

Paul Laverty: Edinburgh, 18/1/19

An afterthought

The degree of exploitation that Paul describes is not an aberration. It is not a mark of capitalism's failure, but of its inexorable development. Harsh competition between giant corporations in a global market forces them to cut labour costs, discipline their workers, and instruct their politicians to fix the rules in their favour.

Blake's 'mind-forg'd manacles' keep us shackled to an idea of a world in which the few have wealth and power and the many suffer the consequences. While the left sings the Internationale, the right promotes a narrow nationalism, while acting on an international scale.

The questions are always the same. How do we fight back? What is our strategic aim? What are our strengths?

Given the increasing dangers of the environment, we do not have the luxury of time. We used to think that if we lose one battle, we might win the next. We know now that the present danger of climate change is urgent. Can it be alleviated without planned economies? The evidence suggests that the answer is 'no'.

The problems we face are not new: poverty, exploitation, alienation, lack of political power, and, to a large extent, absence of political leadership. The answers are written in history, if only we open our eyes to see them. Coexistence with capitalism does not work. Social democracy has failed, and the parties that promoted it have all but disappeared.

Our task has surely to be directed toward organisation in the workplace (or wherever workers find themselves, at home, on the road, or at sea) and in communities, defending what remains of our public services. We need strong unions and principled political parties. Then leadership becomes critical. There must be an understanding of, and commitment to, the independent interests of the working class. That means developing economies based on common ownership and democratic control, with the ability to plan the careful use of the earth's resources.

Easy to write, but a Herculean task.

Answers on a postcard, please.

Ken Loach: London, 25/01/19

DiEM25 Policy Paper on Work

Edited by David Adler

There is a radical promise at the heart of the European project to unite workers across the continent—to abolish, as Article 45 of the Treaty of Rome sets out, "any discrimination based on nationality of workers". The intention of the Treaty's framers was, of course, not to echo the call of the *Communist Manifesto*; they hoped to create a frictionless labour market to the benefit of employers in Europe's core economies. But DiEM25 aims to redeem this radical promise, with a policy vision to build worker power across the continent, and share the gains of the twenty-first-century economy.

A decade ago, a devastating economic crisis unleashed new forces of fragmentation among Europe's workers. In its fallout, both the European establishment and their right-populist challengers sought to pit one group of workers against another. North against South. Germans against Greeks. Even in countries with a shared experience of the crisis, national sentiment tended to win out over transnational solidarity. Old and nasty national caricatures of sloth, greed, and stupidity were trotted out to obscure the shared struggle between workers across Europe. DiEM25 is a movement to bring these workers together—to see their common interests, common experience, and common hopes for Europe's future.

The experience of work is increasingly similar across Europe. At the signing of the Treaty of Rome, economic development was highly variable among today's member states. The differences in their economies were a matter not of degree, but of category. Today, workers across the continent are suffering from a similar crisis of insecurity and wage stagnation, with a young generation of workers facing fewer prospects for social mobility than their parents. Meanwhile, an increasingly transnational oligarchy continues to accumulate wealth. In other words, the economy today is defined by precarity for the many, and prosperity for the few.

This diagnosis is transnational because the European economy is transnational as well. The Single Market provides for the free movement of goods, services, and capital. And corporations take advantage—from engaging in wage arbitrage to pursuing the lowest-tax jurisdiction. If we are to challenge the power of transnational corporations, DiEM25 believes that workers must also organise themselves transnationally.

The implications of doing so are not simply European in scope. By building worker power here in Europe, we can develop a model that can scale around the world. The goal of this policy vision is simple: to democratise the economy. This programme must act at every level, from the mid-size firm to the transnational corporation. Workers should enjoy the fruits of their labour, and workers should have the power to decide where to invest them.

In the process, these reforms aim to create enduring equality between workers across Europe—and around the world. The European project cannot survive if its regional inequalities remain so stark, with some workers earning half as much money or enjoying half as many vacation days as their neighbours. DiEM25 sets out the reforms, policies, and programmes necessary to bring these conditions into greater harmony.

In short, our vision is to flip the status quo on its head: to guarantee prosperity for the many, while democratising the vast resources of the few.

Guaranteeing good jobs

In 2018, many European officials celebrated the return of the unemployment rate to pre-crisis levels. But throughout large swathes of the continent, an unemployment crisis continues to roil—one in six Spaniards are out of work, for example, and one in five Greeks. The crisis is particularly acute among the youth. For workers under twenty-five, the unemployment rate in Spain and Greece rises to 35 and 44 per cent, respectively. The result is that young Europeans are leaving their home countries *en masse* to pursue economic opportunity elsewhere, leaving behind homes, families, and communities.

Such sustained unemployment is merely a natural outcome of the financial crisis ten years ago. It is the product of austerity policies engineered to prevent member states from responding to the employment needs of their citizens. With these constraints, it is little wonder that countries like Greece have never fully recovered.

DiEM25 believes that all Europeans have the right to a job at living wage in their community. That is why we believe in a jobs guarantee to all those who seek employment—calling for all European countries to come to a multilateral agreement to fund and guarantee jobs for every European in their home community.

Our Green Investment Programme is designed to breathe life into this jobs guarantee. By ploughing €500 billion each year into Europe's green transition, DiEM25 believes that we can end the crisis of unemployment, devolving resources to member states and municipal governments to initiate new projects in infrastructure, industry, and agriculture.

But our jobs guarantee also aims to ensure that workers who are currently uncompensated (in areas like social care) receive decent wages. To do that, we propose to provide much greater fiscal space for member states to invest in their workers. Our plan for a digital payment system, set out in the European New Deal, effectively ends the austerity straitjacket that has prevented member states from directly addressing unemployment issues.

DiEM25 puts particular emphasis on youth unemployment. Alongside the jobs guarantee, we propose to strengthen the EU Youth Guarantee. The Youth Guarantee has supported many young people to enter work and acquire skills—but many young people still lack access to opportunities for training or decent work. We would look to enforce higher rates of investment across member states in order to expand access to training and meaningful work; call for greater oversight of Youth Guarantee placement in order to ensure that jobs are not only decent but also offer the opportunity to pursue a professional career; and directly coordinate with youth organisations to help deliver this improved Youth Guarantee, empowering them to launch their own ventures.

Other solutions to the crisis of youth unemployment provide targeted opportunities to students leaving university. We propose the creation of a European apprenticeship contract that will provide greater mobility to young workers to pursue opportunities abroad. The common contract will be valid in all countries in the European Union, allowing young people to do an apprenticeship in any company registered in the EU.

And we are proposing a Europe-wide initiative to train a new generation of teachers. The European Teaching Corps will support university graduates to teach in primary and secondary schools across the EU. The goal is both to provide new opportunities to young people to become teachers and travel the continent, but also to increase the multilingual resources in Europe's primary and secondary education system.

Finally, DiEM25 proposes to insert the mandate for full employment at the very heart of the European Central Bank. That means extending the ECB's mandate beyond price stability toward the maintenance of a low unemployment rate. The Federal Reserve of the United States already operates this 'dual mandate'. It is time for the ECB to join them, and take responsibility for sustained unemployment across the Union.

Protecting worker rights

The ambition of a jobs guarantee is, however, incomplete. We must also ensure that all workers are entitled to decent working conditions.

Europe today suffers from social dumping: employers seeking to profit from low wages and poor protections in different regions of the Single Market, forcing a race to the bottom in working conditions. Such uneven conditions undermine the principle of solidarity, and encourage involuntary migration from peripheral countries to Europe's core, where wages and benefits are far more generous.

We propose a European Workers' Compact to reinforce worker rights across Europe. We recommend the introduction of a new European minimum wage legislation that includes criteria for the convergence of wages across Europe, applying especially to member states where there are no collective agreements, thereby creating a backstop for in-work income to bring it to a living wage. That minimum wage legislation would require full wage transparency in order to ensure equal pay for equal work. And it would call for the harmonisation of social contributions for employees, in order to make social dumping impossible between European countries.

But still, wage growth is not enough—we must build better working conditions for all. DiEM25 proposes the creation of a new EU working standard, with a maximum of thirty-five hours of work per week and a minimum of thirty-five days of vacation leave per year. The compact will also fund a new all-European Work Inspection Agency that will coordinate and monitor member-state institutions to oversee employers' compliance to labour laws and fair treatment of employees.

Such attention must be paid to groups that are most vulnerable to labour market violations. DiEM25 believes that all migrant workers should be entitled to the same rights, benefits, and protections as European citizens. It is not migrants who lower wages, but a system that keeps them illegal, unskilled, and under threat of deportation. The fight against exploitation begins by creating a special body that investigates wages and working conditions in migrant communities.

The same goes for the culture industry, where artists are routinely underpaid and left without legal recourse. We want to see an end to artist exploitation. When artists are preparing works for institutions, they should be hired on the basis of contracts that ensure they are granted social security, leave, and all other workers' rights. Artists cannot work without pay.

Self-employed workers often fall outside regulatory frameworks in similar ways. For many workers, self-employment provides freedom and flexibility. But some companies—in particular, online platforms offering transport and delivery services—circumvent worker protections by substituting employees for contractors.

DiEM25 believes that self-employed workers should have access to the same rights to minimum wages and working conditions as all other workers. We advocate the reform of competition law which limits the potential for self-employed workers to collectively negotiate fees and working conditions. We wish to see the expansion of existing labour regulations, social protections, and employer contributions to include self-employed workers.

Finally, young workers merit special protections. DiEM25 is calling for an end to both unpaid internships and underpaid internships that cut wages under the legislated minimum. Any European labour regulator like our proposed Inspection Agency must reserve special resources to investigate the conditions under which young people are finding increasingly precarious and underpaid work.

Building worker power

Rights and protections for individual workers are fundamental to a fair labour market. But to build a democratic economy—the core aim of DiEM25's vision for labour—we must build the institutions that allow for workers to come together and make their own decisions about the direction of their firms, industries, and economy at large.

DiEM25 is calling for a Transnational Workers Commission that will strengthen collective bargaining across the continent. The Commission will act as a 'union of last resort' for workers that currently lack access to a labour organisation. And the Commission would support the formation of new transnational unions to challenge corporations that rely on precarious labour.

By organising transnationally, we can challenge the power of footloose corporations. Multinationals continue to play off workers of different countries to lower costs. A Transnational Workers Commission can check this race to the bottom.

But DiEM25 also believes in much more local economic democracy, bringing it down to the level of the individual firm. One of the most common myths about contemporary capitalism is that the problems of precarity and inequality are primarily a function of technology—digital platforms that magically funnel profits to shareholders and away from workers. In fact, the real problem is one of ownership. Those who own assets in the contemporary economy are winners, while those who do not own are shut out.

That is why we are proposing a plan to bring firms under partial control of the workers they employ. Our plan would support medium-to-large companies to create Worker Ownership Funds that distribute an annual percentage of their shares to their employees. Such funds will not only provide annual dividends to workers. They will also increase workers' say over company decisions as shareholders. As such, they are an important step toward democratising the European economy.

The creation of new ownership funds must be tied to a broader transformation in corporate governance. Over the last half-century, firms have become captive to the cult of the shareholder. DiEM25 will fight to change the balance of power between workers and management in European firms. We are calling for legislation that strips corporate bonuses and strictly regulates executive pay, bringing it within a multiple of the lowest-paid employee. And we believe that company boards must include directors that are directly elected by the workers themselves, giving greater representation to workers' interests in corporate governance. Representation is, of course, a fundamental component of democracy.

Sharing the gains

One of the primary goals of democratising the European economy is to safeguard against the inequality that has soared over the last three decades. Such inequality can be contained, in part, by bringing firms back under the direction of their workers. But we also need a more proactive strategy for reigning in the runaway levels of inequality that already preside in our economy today—and redirecting those gains to all European citizens.

To do so, DiEM25 is proposing the institution of a Citizen Wealth Fund which is owned collectively by the European public. This portfolio will include assets purchased by central banks, a percentage of capital stock from initial public offerings (IPOs), and revenues from intellectual property rights, among others.

Feeding into this Citizen Wealth Fund would be a pan-European inheritance tax that could directly and efficiently target wealth inequality. We are calling for all member states to come to a multilateral agreement on an elevated inheritance tax. The majority of European billionaires today inherited their wealth from their parents—to arrive at a fairer, more democratic society, we must end this toxic transmission of inequality.

Each year, the Fund would distribute a Universal Citizen Dividend that allows each and every citizen to enjoy the fruits of economic activity. The proposed Dividend is independent of social assistance payments, unemployment insurance, and other welfare programmes.

We believe that the dividend is the first step toward the creation of a universal basic income, which can provide freedom and dignity to all Europeans, regardless of employment status.

The logic of the market—that wage is worth—has penetrated European society. Unemployed people are the objects of scorn, even when they fulfil necessary roles like social care. The 'lazy' worker who does not flog himself toward an 80-hour workweek is often trotted around by the political class as the scapegoat for economic woes.

The goal of the Universal Citizen Dividend is precisely to liberate workers from the ludicrous pressure to ramp up their working hours even as technology enables us to level them down. And even more important, such a dividend ensures that unpaid labour of all kinds—from care to creativity—is both compensated and encouraged as a legitimate livelihood.

Binding workers of the world

For centuries, the wealth enjoyed by European citizens has come at the expense of other regions of the world. As colonialists, Europe extracted wealth, resources, and labour from countries of the world. As corporations, Europe has done little to redress these colonial legacies, instead exploiting the disparities in regional development and riding roughshod over basic worker rights wherever regulators turn a blind eye.

DiEM25 believes that a democratic economy in Europe cannot be built on the backs of workers beyond its borders. Europe must stand for peace and solidarity, and Europe's policies must serve to curb exploitation around the world.

This commitment implies major changes in EU trade agreements. We believe that 'just' trade should be the basis of EU trade policy, not 'free' trade. We will fight to end the system of 'dumping' on developing countries by defending higher standards to protect all workers and fighting to terminate existing agreements that pose a threat to these high standards.

DiEM25 also rejects all mechanisms that create special privileges for multinational corporations against workers rights to fair wages and working conditions. We oppose the Investor State Dispute Settlement (ISDS) and the Investment Court System, which give international investors unfair legal powers to sue local authorities for implementing stricter regulations. We also reject any attempt to create a Multilateral Investment Court. Instead, we will demand full regulatory freedom for environmental and social policies without the threat of international investment litigation.

These multinational corporations must be accountable for their human rights violations. DiEM25 supports the UN's Binding Treaty on Transnational Corporations and Human Rights. We call on the UN to push for an enforceable mechanism that allows all affected people—including workers who have suffered as a result of exploitative and dangerous working conditions—to bring corporations to court.

Conclusion

Democracy, in the vocabulary of the European Union, is a very narrow concept. It refers primarily to a process of political decision-making—the act of placing a vote on a ballot paper, and little else.

DiEM25 is fighting to expand this notion of democracy in Europe deep into the economic sphere. By democracy, we mean ensuring that all workers have access to their fundamental rights to safety and security. By democracy, we mean providing new avenues for workers to make decisions about the direction of their firms. By democracy, we mean ensuring that the gains generated in economic activity are shared by the workers who drive it.

At its core, our vision of democracy entails giving control to the workers of Europe to determine how, where, and when they choose to expend their labour. At one end of the spectrum, this means reclaiming the sphere of work on behalf of the worker: building the power of employees to challenge employers. At the other end, this means reclaiming the spheres of care, leisure, and creativity, as productive, worthwhile, and socially necessary. The universal dividend aims precisely to allow workers to focus less on fighting for wages and more on dedicating themselves to the people, and the projects, they value most. In this sense, ours is a post-capitalist vision, in which the great divide between capital and labour dissolves as the economy becomes more deeply embedded in society and its fruits widely shared between all of its participants.

The ultimate goal of DiEM25's vision for labour is therefore to recover humanity from the wreckage of the capitalist economy. All workers are entitled to a decent job with decent conditions for a decent wage. But they are also entitled to a decent life, and the right to choose what, precisely, that means for them. By setting out this broad vision for policy change in Europe, DiEM25 takes the first step toward this radical notion of self-determination.

Building Shared Prosperity in the Twenty-first Century

Yanis Varoufakis

The idea of an unconditional basic income is gaining steam, with new pockets of support in the radical left, the Green movement, and even the libertarian right. Cheerleaders for such schemes argue that universal basic income would support those who already contribute priceless value to society, mainly women in the caring sector—or, indeed, artists producing great public works for next to no money. The poor would be liberated from vicious welfare-state means testing, and a safety net that can entangle people in permanent poverty would be replaced by a platform on which they could stand before reaching out for something better.

The cause of this new push for unconditional basic income is the rise of machines that, for the first time since the start of industrialisation, threatens to destroy more jobs than technological innovation creates—and to pull the rug out from under the feet of white-collar professionals.

But if the idea of a universal basic income has returned, so has resistance to it. Rightists point to the impossibility of raising enough revenue to fund such schemes without crushing the private sector or seeing drop in labour supply and productivity, as a result of the loss of work incentives. Leftists worry that a universal income would weaken the struggle to improve people's working lives, legitimise the idle rich, erode hard-won collective bargaining rights, undermine the foundation of the welfare state, encourage passive citizenship, and promote consumerism.

The key to moving forward is a fresh perspective on the connection between the source of a universal basic income's funding, the impact of robots, and our understanding of what it means to be free. That implies combining three propositions: one, taxes cannot be a legitimate source of financing such schemes; two, the rise of machines must be embraced; and, three, a universal basic income is liberty's main prerequisite.

Ken makes a decent living operating a large harvester on behalf of farmer Luke. Ken's salary generates income tax and social security payments that help finance government programmes for less fortunate members of his community. Alas, Luke is about to replace Ken with Nexus, a robot that can operate the harvester longer, more safely, in any weather, and without lunch breaks, holidays, or sick pay.

Some commentators believe that, to ease the inequality and offset the social costs implied by automation's displacement effects, either Nexus should pay income tax, or Luke should pay a hefty tax for replacing Ken with a robot. And this 'robot tax' should be used to finance something like a universal basic income.

There are three problems with this approach. For starters, whereas Ken's income would have changed over time had he not been fired, the reference salary cannot change, except arbitrarily and in a manner setting the tax authorities against business. The tax office and Luke would end up clashing over impossible estimates of the extent to which Ken's salary would have risen or fallen had he still been employed.

Second, the advent of robot-operated machines that have never been operated by humans means there will be no prior human income to act as a reference salary for calculating the taxes these robots must pay.

Finally, it is philosophically difficult to justify forcing Luke to pay 'income' tax for Nexus but not for the harvester that Nexus operates. After all, they are both machines, and the harvester has displaced far more human labour than Nexus. The only defensible justification for treating them differently is that Nexus has greater autonomy—and however advanced Nexus might be, it can be thought of as autonomous only if it develops consciousness. Only if Nexus (like the Nexus-6 replicants in the 1982 film *Blade Runner*) achieves that leap will it have earned the 'right' to be thought of as distinct from the harvester he operates. But then humanity will have spawned a new species and a new civil rights movement, which I would gladly join, demanding freedom for Nexus and equal rights with Ken—including a living wage, minimum benefits, and enfranchisement.

Assuming that robots cannot be made to pay income tax without creating new potential for conflict between the tax authorities and business (accompanied by tax arbitrage and corruption), what about taxing Nexus at the point of sale to Luke? That would, of course, be possible: the state would collect a lump-sum tax from Luke the moment he replaces Ken with Nexus.

But a lump-sum tax on robots would merely lead robot producers to bundle artificial intelligence within other machinery. Nexus will increasingly be incorporated within the harvester, making it impossible to tax the robotic element separately from the dumb parts that do the harvesting.

Either the robot sales tax should be dropped or it should be generalised into a capital goods sales tax. But imagine the uproar against a tax on all capital goods. Woe betide those who would diminish domestic productivity and competitiveness!

Ever since the emergence of industrial capitalism, we have been terrible at differentiating between property and capital, and thus between wealth, rent, and profit. This is why a wealth tax is so difficult to design. The conceptual problem of differentiating between Nexus and the harvester it operates would make it impossible to agree on how a robot tax should work.

But why make life under capitalism more complicated than it already is? There is an alternative to a robot tax that is easy to implement and simple to justify: a universal basic dividend, financed from the returns on all capital.

Imagine that a percentage of capital stock (shares) from every initial public offering (IPO) be channeled into a Commons Capital Depository, with the associated dividends funding a Universal Basic Dividend (UBD). Effectively, society becomes a shareholder in every corporation, and the dividends are distributed evenly to all citizens.

To the extent that automation improves productivity and corporate profitability, the whole of society would begin to share the benefits. No new tax, no complications in the tax code, and no effect on the existing funding of the welfare state. As higher profits and their automatic redistribution via the UBD boosted incomes, more funds would become available for the welfare state. Coupled with stronger labour rights and a decent living wage, the ideal of shared prosperity would receive a new lease on life.

If a universal basic income is to be legitimate, it cannot be financed by taxing Jill to pay Jack. That is why it should be funded from returns on capital. A common myth, promoted by the rich, is that wealth is produced individually before it is collectivised by the state through taxation. In fact, wealth was always produced collectively and privatised by the propertied class. Farmland and seeds—premodern forms of capital—were collectively developed through generations of peasant endeavour that landlords appropriated by stealth. Today, every smartphone comprises components developed by some government grant, or through the commons of pooled ideas, for which no dividends have ever been paid to society.

So how should society be compensated? Taxation is the wrong answer. Corporations pay taxes in exchange for services the state provides them, not for capital injections that must yield dividends. There is thus a strong case that the commons have a right to a share of the capital stock and associated dividends, reflecting society's investment in corporations' capital.

The first two industrial revolutions were built on machines produced by great inventors in glorified barns and bought by cunning entrepreneurs who demanded property rights over the income stream 'their' machines generated. Today's technological revolution is marked by the increasing socialisation of the production of capital. A practical response would be to socialise the property rights over the large income streams capital is now generating.

Fear of machines that can liberate us from drudgery is a symptom of a timid and divided society. The Luddites are among the most misunderstood historical actors. Their vandalism of machinery was a protest not against automation, but against social arrangements that deprived them of life prospects in the face of technological innovation. Our societies must embrace the rise of the machines, but ensure that they contribute to shared prosperity by granting every citizen property rights over them, yielding a UBD.

A universal basic dividend allows for new understandings of liberty and equality that bridge hitherto irreconcilable political blocs, while stabilising society and reinvigorating the notion of shared prosperity in the face of otherwise destabilising technological innovation.

Anyone still not reconciled to the idea of 'something for nothing' should ask a few simple questions: Would I not want my children to have a small trust fund that shields them from the fear of destitution and allows them to invest fearlessly in their real talents? Would their peace of mind render them layabouts? If not, what is the moral basis for denying all children the same advantage?

In short, forget about taxing either Nexus or Luke. Instead, place a portion of Luke's equity in the farm in a public trust, which then provides a universal payment to everyone. And while we are at it, let's improve the wages and conditions of every human still in employment, and bring a lasting peace between humans and the artificial intelligence on the horizon.

Digital Socialism

Evgeny Morozov

First, the bad news. When it comes to Big Tech, we have lost the plot. By we, I refer to those of us who, in one way or another, feel a relationship with social democracy or socialism. And by the plot, I don't mean just our understanding of the dynamics of the digital economy and digital capitalism, but also of capitalism as such and the role that social democracy and socialism should be playing in either countering or counterbalancing it.

These days, it is all too easy for social democrats and socialists to get a false sense of priorities, and no more so than when it comes to Big Tech and Silicon Valley. Although it is true that social democrats and socialists have traditionally worried about questions of power, rule of law and legality, these things have never been at the top of the social democratic or socialist agenda. The values that have actually driven the social democratic and socialist project have always been egalitarianism, social justice and, I would argue, institutional innovation.

Institutional innovation is not fully understood even by those inside the social democratic and socialist project. But it was precisely by inventing new institutions and new practices that social democracy managed to achieve so much. They include the welfare state and workers' co-determination, as well as institutions that exist somewhere between capitalism and the public sector.

Take the library system. It's an institution that works on an ethos and rationale different from those of the market. We do not try to encourage competition between fifty different libraries in order to produce the best results. We recognise that libraries are a public good that require an infrastructure and adequate funding. And we use that public good in order to promote a set of values, some of which have to do with solidarity, cooperation and egalitarianism. We assume that our background and our class should not be obstacles to our accessing certain resources.

But many of these interventions, from the welfare state to co-determination to institutions like the library, were not just about promoting egalitarianism and solidarity. They were also about making society function more efficiently and prompted a significant amount of social and economic innovation. The welfare state was created not only in order to level the playing field; its founders also believed that it was the most efficient and effective way to structure relations in society. People with something to contribute could take full advantage of the resources available to them and have their say in how society was governed and shaped.

The long history of social innovations for which the social democratic project was responsible has almost been forgotten. Instead, over the past few decades, social democracy has seen its main task as being to defend whatever is left of those institutions from the neoliberal assault. Necessary though this has been, the result has been to limit the capacity of social democratic and socialist forces to think about technological change and the kinds of institutional innovation necessary in order to place the economic dynamics involved on a path that is not only more egalitarian but also more efficient and productive—just as social democracy has succeeded in doing in the past.

Today, we face multiple constraints on our capacity to engage in the kind of social and institutional innovation that would enable the persistence of social democratic values in society. The conditions for the possibility of the social democratic project are being undermined, if you like. The threats to those conditions have many sources. One is the tempo and structure of global capitalism as such. Ever since the financial crisis, there has been too much idle capital lying around searching for an outlet that can guarantee a return of at least six to seven percent. Much of this capital is held not in rapacious hedge funds, but in funds set up by social democratic governments and organisations. The same capital that is being invested in the likes of Facebook, Google, and Amazon is guaranteeing the pensions of many Europeans. Unless there is a quick fix to the global economy, this is a structural condition that will not go away. For the foreseeable future, many people will not be able to get the money they were expecting to get from anywhere other than technology startups and technology platforms. The reality is that the 200 billion dollars eager to be invested in anything that will guarantee a return are the structural condition that we have to confront.

We can dismiss the idea of a European technology fund as hierarchical or draconian. But if we don't face up to reality, the entire European technology sector, from startups to big companies, risks being overtaken by Chinese capital, Gulf capital, American capital, Japanese capital—you name it. This is something we have been seeing in the last few years.

This is not a plea for economic nationalism. I am not suggesting that we control those industries because they are German industries or French industries. All I'm pointing out is that the prerequisite for a more sophisticated institutional innovation is the ability to shape the path and the direction in which our digital infrastructure develops. At present, that infrastructure, by and large, is in private hands. This applies to data, and it applies to artificial intelligence and to robotics. Without a massive structural intervention of some kind, which we might not like because it smells of corporatism or something else, we will no longer have any control over the situation.

Artificial intelligence beyond digital capitalism

Of course, there are many conditions that make institutional innovation harder, not least the difficulty that European states have in coordinating fiscal and industrial policy. But if nothing is done, there will be no opportunity for more radical structural or social innovation. That would mean that the neoliberal project succeeds in its ultimate goal: to prevent any other forms of non-market coordination from scaling up. You can coordinate as much as you want in your family, in your church, in any other unit of social organisation, in ways that do not rely on markets. But the moment you present a threat to capitalist accumulation, you get taken out of action.

For me, this is what neoliberalism is all about. It's about preventing forms of social coordination based on values that have nothing to do with the market and competition from occupying the kind of spaces that institutions like libraries currently do in society. Imagine the neoliberal alternative to the library, where readers are provided with Kindles from twenty-five different companies and charged for every word, rather than paying a yearly fee and being able to borrow as many books as they want—or paying for that with their taxes. Ultimately, the neoliberal project is about constraining our very diverse repertoires of interventions to just one: competition. How do we solve a problem? We introduce more competition into it.

That's not to say that competition is bad *per se* or should not be part of the solution. But very often it is seen as the default solution. And when it comes to Big Tech, much of the debate we are having right now is deeply grounded in this neoliberal episteme. The problem solvers are either Big Tech or startups. There is little space for imagining alternative configurations of social forces, whether trade unions, worker cooperatives, municipalities or national forces. There is very little effort being put into imagining what kind of legal, political and technological infrastructure would allow us together to create projects equivalent to the welfare state or the many institutions in its proximity. This may seem abstract, but abstraction is precisely what we need in order to take stock of the hegemony of neoliberalism.

I don't think socialism has lost. But I do think neoliberalism has managed to shrink our imaginations and tie our hands. The challenge now is to survey the new digital ecosystem and get a very basic and blurry outline of what a new set of institutions might be. An idea about where we would be collaborating, where we would be producing new sets of knowledge, where we would be deploying a new kind of public good. Not only in order to promote solidarity, justice and egalitarianism, but also to make our society more efficient and effective.

Just think about artificial intelligence. This is a field where ten companies, five of them Chinese and five of them American, are dumping roughly ten to twelve billion dollars per company per year on research. This intensity of economic concentration is indeed problematic. But does it really make sense to switch to a landscape where you have a hundred firms each dumping two billion dollars into AI? The answer is clearly no. Instead, we need to be asking how much of the current spending is completely wasteful. The answer is around ninety per cent.

Artificial intelligence is almost a classical public good, something you need to develop once and then make accessible to others. Not only will this drastically reduce costs, it will also potentially increase quality, because you will be able to take advantage of network effects. Today, you have ten AI companies developing an identical set of skills for algorithms and machine learning. All of them are training their systems to distinguish photos of cats from photos of dogs, photos of traffic lights from photos of cars, photos of men from photos of women, photos of dark-skinned people from photos of light-skinned people. They are all replicating the same set of functions. There is no better argument for the wastefulness of capitalism than the current race for artificial intelligence.

The situation won't get better if you simply increase the number of firms from ten to one hundred. What is needed instead is a centralised approach, where artificial intelligence is conceived as an infrastructure with a political economy behind it. You engage in a well-planned way of funding and developing it, and you find a way to make it accessible to different players in the economy—perhaps on different conditions. Big companies may have to pay a higher fee, smaller companies a lower fee, and NGOs, activists and startups nothing at all. All of that suddenly becomes possible when we manage to take that one big step towards legal, political and financial institutionalisation. This is precisely the kind of institutional innovation that we should associate with the social democratic and socialist project.

Unfortunately, our mental framework is so dominated by the everyday sins of these firms—their tax evasion, their interference in the legislative process, their surveillance of activists and critics—that we have a very hard time thinking at the more abstract level and relating our interventions to the basic goals and functions of social democracy. I have absolutely no doubt that whatever social democratic or socialist project we build on the ruins of Big Tech and Silicon Valley, it will need to resolve one big question. And that will be the ownership and control of the infrastructure that can then be repurposed for different projects.

We have built the welfare state on a very important assumption: that certain services are so important to human wellbeing and society that they must be decommodified. That is why we have decommodified healthcare, education, transport and a few other areas. Unfortunately, capitalism has found a way to penetrate the most intimate domains of our existence. To use an expression often used in German philosophy, 'it has colonised the life world'. I don't think that is an overstatement. There has been a systematic effort to commodify every single part of our everyday life, our every single interaction, whether with like-minded people, or political groups or institutions. A pushback against that is long overdue. These digitally mediated social relations must be decommodified to a point where they can actually build solidaristic, egalitarian relationships and promote those values.

The challenge for social democracy

Whatever project social democracy and socialism morph into, they cannot continue to ignore the crucial importance of reconquering that infrastructure. And yet, given the current composition of the European Commission and the European Parliament, as well as the overall crisis of many social democratic parties, we need to be very sober. The challenge at present is to preserve at least the possibility of reconquering that infrastructure. We have to be completely clear that the social democratic impulse towards institutional and social innovation has today found its outlet in regulatory tinkering. And I think at regulation we do a very good job. The entire European Commission is informed by the idea that we have rules that we have to follow. Every time a politician associated with a social democratic party talks about regulation, we should applaud them. But we should also ask what else they are planning to do, given the immense political-economic and cultural challenge of digitisation. Do they have a particular kind of infrastructure or economic agenda in mind? My feeling is that they don't, partly because they have found solace in the many possibilities that European regulation offers them.

I am not against regulation. But the idea that some kind of technocratic regulatory agenda can get us out of this mess is a myth. What's missing is a much more ambitious political project that can completely redefine what social democracy is in the twenty-first century. This encounter with digital technology provides a life-saving opportunity, because ultimately it allows us to completely reimagine what the social democratic attitude should be beyond merely defending the achievements of the twentieth century.

This agenda does not preclude the possibility of breaking up Big Tech. But breaking up Big Tech to get Small Tech is not the goal. It might be the goal for liberals, but it cannot be the goal of social democrats. That should be something else, something that might also involve—if not require—reducing the power of Google and Facebook. A tactical alliance between socialists and liberals is possible, feasible, and might actually be necessary.

However, if social democrats and socialists enter into such an alliance without fully understanding the political and philosophical dynamics involved, they will be swallowed up. There is no way they will do a better job talking about competition than liberals. If they keep doing it, the question is why social democracy should even exist. You might be able to use it tactically and strategically to advance your own set of agendas and your own set of goals, but then you need to be very clear about what those goals are. Here there is a gaping hole in the agenda of social democratic parties. It's a hole they have maybe three or four years to fill. At most. If it isn't filled, a life-saving opportunity will be missed.

On a practical level, there are two tasks for the next few years. First, we need to specify precisely what the necessary conditions are for this newly constituted social democratic project even to be feasible. That might mean a very different policy on data ownership, it might mean trying to roll out prototypes in cities where a very different digital economy can function based on solidarity and citizen participation. These projects need to adopt a very anti-hierarchical stance and support genuine entrepreneurship. Of course, there are startups and there are startups. Some are predatory by default. But there are also those that pursue a more noble set of goals and do so in a dignified manner.

These need to be tried and be encouraged. Because unless there are real working prototypes for these new digital infrastructures, which deliver the kinds of values that we want at the local scale, we can forget about convincing anyone to try them out nationally or at the European level. For that, we will need funding and we will need politicians who are willing to take risks, in the face of opposition from the real estate industry, in the face of opposition from Uber, Google, Amazon and the rest. Clearly, there will be a lot of opposition. These companies are very powerful, they know what they want and have their project almost completely mapped out on the neoliberal project of preventing any other non-market form of social coordination from actually scaling up.

The second task, in addition to these two or three years of digital but non-neoliberal experimentation, is to embark on an ambitious intellectual journey in which we try to rethink what social democracy in the twenty-first century might mean. None of the social democratic parties in Europe, North America or Latin America have managed to do this well. Instead, they are beset by an ideological and intellectual inertia that stands in the way of inventing the forms of institutional and social association that would allow us to reformulate a vision for social democracy in the twenty-first century.

The neoliberal contradiction

If we manage to achieve some progress on both of these fronts, there is a good chance that social democracy will not just survive, but prosper. Because, despite the fact that everything is going well for the neoliberal project, despite the fact that companies like Uber, Airbnb, Google and the rest are doing so much to entrench this idea of entrepreneurship and competition—despite all that, the costs of continuing with the current system are high. So high, in fact, that neoliberals don't know how to manage them. Markets can no longer solve that problem, if they ever could have. You cannot just create markets for solutions and another set of markets to solve the first markets' problems. You end up with an infinite regression, in which the problems not only remain unsolved, but actually accumulate.

While we should not underestimate the resilience of our adversary, there will be tactical opportunities to move forward. But unless there is a clearly articulated idea about what it is that social democrats and socialists want, we should expect no progress. It is not a confusion about Big Tech that is the cause of our problems. It's a confusion about the role and the meaning and the future of social democracy as such. Our confusion about the tech industry is the consequence, and not the cause, of our problems. If we really want to get a clear head on this, we have to get a clear head on what social democracy means under the conditions of twenty-first-century capitalism.

[*With thanks to Evgeny Morozov and the Friedrich-Ebert-Stiftung for permission to reproduce this text, delivered as a keynote speech at the 2019 Digital Capitalism Congress.*]

The Yellow Vest Revolt

Cole Stangler

This time, they couldn't be ignored. When thousands of workers flocked to traffic circles across France in the fall of 2018, they forced Europe's political establishment to pay attention. And, with great effort and sacrifice, the gilets jaunes won impressive concessions. Not only did the government agree to their original demand, cancelling an unpopular hike in the fuel tax. But in the face of continued protest, President Emmanuel Macron also announced a series of additional measures: the expansion of a subsidy for low-wage workers, the elimination of a tax hike that hit low-income retirees, and the scrapping of taxes on overtime pay.

After years of cynical retreat from the political sphere, the Yellow Vests remind us that power ultimately resides with the people: direct action still gets the goods. But as the climate crisis continues to deepen, they might also be a warning of what's to come, in France and across the European Union. Working people will not bear the burden of the green transition. If Europe's governments fail to recognise this basic fact, the Yellow Vest revolt will be at their doorsteps, too.

**

Outside of major cities, most French people drive cars. It's an activity that consumes a major chunk of their income, more so than that of drivers in the United States, where gross pay is higher and state governments maintain astonishingly low tax rates on gasoline. French people earn a monthly median income of €1,700, according to the state statistical agency. Meanwhile, diesel fuel, which most drivers use, costs more than €1.50 a litre. It grew even more expensive over 2018, with costs spiking by about 25 per cent.

Frustrations with fuel prices began building in the summer of 2018. But they reached a new level in September of that year, when the government announced in January 2019 that it would be hiking taxes at the pump by as much as 25 cents a gallon. By the end of October, a Change.org petition demanding a decrease in fuel prices had garnered 500,000 signatures. After stumbling upon the petition that same month, lorry driver Éric Drouet created on 17 November a vaguely worded Facebook page calling for a "national movement against tax increases".

It was unclear what would happen. Eventually more than 282,000 people responded to Drouet's call—many of them manning traffic blockades in parts of the country that had scarcely ever seen protests, from sparsely populated villages in Brittany to working-class suburbs on the Mediterranean coast. Since then, the number of weekly demonstrators declined. Just 106,000 nationwide turned out for an 'Act Two' on 24 November, and 75,000 for an 'Act Three' the following Saturday. In February 2019, weekly turnout had dropped well below 50,000. By French standards, these figures are modest. When unions turned out at least 160,000 for a 'day of action' to defend the 'French social model' on a weekday in October 2018, both the press and the government hardly blinked.

Nevertheless, the Yellow Vests managed to seize the national spotlight, instilling a sense of fear among the political establishment not seen since the days of Nicolas Sarkozy and the unsuccessful 2010 protests against an increase in the retirement age. This was partly due to the violence, shown to the whole world in circulating images of burning cars in central Paris and anti-government graffiti staining the Arc de Triomphe. Still, an even greater factor was the movement's seemingly spontaneous origin story—a haphazard discussion on social media that took off without the support of political parties or unions. While Marine Le Pen of the far right and Jean-Luc Mélenchon of the left both endorsed the gilets jaunes movement and clearly hoped to capitalise on its success, their respective parties played a minimal role in the planning of the hundreds of nationwide protests.

Further contributing to the cloud of dread that subsumed the Élysée was the fact that the gilets jaunes enjoyed broad public approval—a rarity for any political movement in France. Not a single leading party enjoys close to majority support, and yet even a poll conducted *after* a protest-turned-riot in Paris in December 2018 showed that, while most disagreed with the use of violence, seven in ten responders still backed the gilets jaunes movement as a whole. Support closely tracked class lines. According to a separate study released in November 2018, about four-fifths of working-class respondents—those defined as blue-collar and service-sector workers in France's detailed socio-professional classification system—expressed sympathy or support for the movement. Just 56 percent of managers and white-collar professionals in that poll said they felt the same.

If the movement managed to win such broad support, it is because its demands tapped into a deeper sense of social injustice. While that sentiment is shared nationwide to varying degrees, the protests themselves sprung up largely in rural areas and in what's known as *le périurbain*: the outer bands of suburbs and metropolitan areas. These are parts of the country that often suffer from high joblessness and rely heavily on state investment to keep their communities afloat, from unemployment benefits to the public rail network that connects them to larger cities.

High expectations of the state also come with close scrutiny over its actions. This attitude can be misinterpreted as hostility toward the very idea of public intervention in the economy—and, unsurprisingly, right-wingers from abroad projected their own libertarian fantasies onto the wave of protest. But the fact remains that most gilets jaunes sympathisers in France were never opposed to the state's role in the economy—they simply wanted it to act more fairly. Over the past decade, they've witnessed hospital closures, postal service cuts, and rail reforms laying the groundwork for privatisation and higher ticket prices similar to the United Kingdom. Much like spiraling fuel costs, these are not the sorts of things that keep wealthy people up at night.

Meanwhile, since taking office in June 2017, Emmanuel Macron has mandated further belt-tightening for the working class. In the name of fighting the budget deficit, local governments have seen subsidies for part-time jobs slashed, low-income people have suffered cuts in their housing aid, and retirees have been dealt reductions in their pension checks. The rich receive a very different sort of treatment. Overseeing his very first budget as president, Macron rushed to repeal France's wealth tax, which had applied only to those with over €1.3 million in assets. This is why the notion of *justice fiscale*—'tax justice'—figured so prominently among Yellow Vest sympathisers. Why should ordinary people, they asked, be forced to fork over another couple hundred euros each month while the super-rich are rewarded simply for being super-rich? Likewise, as outlandish as it may sound, many protesters called on the President to resign. Through both his policies that disproportionately benefit the rich and his tendency to ignore his critics, Macron exemplifies the state's abdication of responsibility toward the least well-off.

At the same time, a non-negligible share of the Yellow Vests' appeal flowed precisely from their lack of clear demands. When two movement spokespeople appointed via Facebook met with then environment minister François de Rugy in late November and called on him to scrap the fuel-tax hike, they presented a larger platform of forty-seven demands. Also built through an online poll, it was a document fraught with contradiction. It called on the government to cut payroll taxes for employers but also called for a hike in the minimum wage and more progressive income taxes; it demanded that immigrants better 'integrate' into French society, but also that the government improve its treatment of asylum seekers. Other points of the platform took aim at France's political institutions: abolishing the Senate, which is not directly elected by voters, and authorising national referenda on questions that earn above a certain number of signatures.

**

The dust has since settled on the demonstrations. A hardcore group continues to take to the streets every weekend, but draws a very limited amount of support. Meanwhile, polls show the broad popularity once enjoyed in late 2018 no longer exists. Nevertheless, the questions raised by the gilets jaunes remain as relevant as ever. Whether in France or elsewhere, states shouldn't forget their obligations to the working class, nor should they expect the latter to swallow the costs of the environmental crisis.

The anger of the Yellow Vests stemmed, in large part, from a feeling of abandonment: a sense that most people are being screwed by tax policy and that public services and social programs aren't being adequately funded. To be sure, France has a particularly expansive safety net as well as a rich tradition of popular uprising—factors that help explain why the gilets jaunes began in the land of Robespierre and Jean Moulin rather than elsewhere. But other European leaders are not in the clear. When people have high expectations of what they're owed, they're all the more likely to revolt. This should weigh heavily on governments across the Continent as they gradually chip away at their respective welfare states.

Unfortunately, until deeper changes in Brussels that pave the way for more public spending happen, working-class animus at national governments—and at the European Union—will increase. In the case of the EU, the hostility all too often comes with traces of xenophobia, as people's anger over their declining statuses finds redemption in narratives that pin the blame on foreigners. And it cannot be denied: while they were never close to a majority, there was a non-negligible share of Yellow Vests who found comfort in this sort of discourse, allured by the false promise of 'national sovereignty'. This was best evidenced by the collective freak-out in some corners of the movement that followed the United Nations General Assembly's vote to endorse the Global Compact for Migration. Finalised in December, this non-legally binding pact had literally nothing to do with taxes, the cost of living or the funding of public services in France. But when confidence in government runs low—and an ultra-national institution is watching over to make sure nothing changes too much—conspiracy theories can run amok.

Finally, there is climate policy. While many gilets jaunes didn't explicitly address the environment—to the disappointment of those of a certain political bent—it was implicitly at the heart of the movement. To that end, the images of burning cars on the Champs-Élysées ought to be seared into the brains of everyone involved in the crafting of climate policy over the next decade. Those who seek to address the crisis through taxes that fall disproportionately on ordinary people do so at their own peril. What's likely needed instead is deeper structural change—a program that convinces society, as a whole, to see benefits in the transition away from fossil fuels. At the moment, as governments face severe constraints on public spending, environmental policy can often feel like an annoying collection of rules dictated by bureaucrats who share markedly different interests than the rest of the population.

This doesn't mean that everybody needs to win from the rapid decarbonisation on which the fate of the planet relies. Of course, there will be losers. But instead of low-income commuters on welfare who live hours from the closest major city, perhaps they should be the ones who actually pollute the most: that is to say, oil and gas producers and the super-rich. Likewise, any successful plan to abandon fossil fuels and radically overhaul the economic order will all but require intense coordination on an international level. If it works, it should lay waste to the notion that reinforcing national sovereignty will solve anything.

When the gilets jaunes first erupted onto the streets, they often spoke of the struggles they faced at the end of each month: the bills that piled up, the bank accounts that seemed to drain so quickly and the all-consuming stress that followed suit. And when they joined with climate protesters on more than a handful of occasions, their coordination gave birth to a new slogan: *Fin du mois, fin du monde, même combat.* It's a timely message with the fates of the welfare state and the planet both in doubt: "End of the month, end of the world, same struggle."

A United Europe by Lorenzo Marsili

"You are destined for a great Monday! Pity that Sunday will never end."

" It is this line in Franz Kafka's diaries, penned in one of his regular moments of melancholy, that appears today as the only response that governing elites have offered to those demanding progressive change. The exit from a rigged economy in a rigged democracy, from a scandalous globalisation built upon unspeakable wealth and enduring misery, continues to represent a Monday that will never arrive.

The years since the implosion of the financial system in 2008 have made one thing clear: national democracies are increasingly unable to transform popular requests for change into alternative policies. There are many causes for this, not least the capture of our democratic systems by organised wealth. But dig deeper and the real cause for a politics out of joint can be found in the absence of political rights beyond the narrow confines of the nation. As paradoxical as it may sound, it is precisely the twilight of the nation state that is the source of the great nationalist uprising of our time.

This paradox is something that Hannah Arendt identified in her famous study on the origins of totalitarianism. It is the international decline of the European powers following the destruction of the First World War that summons totalitarianism as the morbid reaction to a loss of control. Like a weakened animal, scared and therefore ready to bite, nationalism is the response of a body that has lost its vigour. If we look into the great global resentment of our time, what we find is impotence. The global crisis of our era sees a complex of economic, ecological, technological, and migratory challenges that no nation is able to control. The result is an extraordinary provincialisation of our political forms with respect to the new planetary powers confronting humanity.

In this situation, the fate of Europe becomes the metaphor of the world of the future. If the most politically and economically integrated continent reverts to a situation of irrelevant nation states pitted against each other, this will be a dramatic preview of the new global disorder to come. If, on the other hand, Europe turns into a giant nation state, with even greater state powers for control within and projection of power abroad, saying 'Europe first' and militarising its borders, then Europe's horizon of politics is simply more of the same but on a larger scale.

If, however, Europe was able to build a real politics beyond borders, if it was able to demonstrate that unity of action across national divisions were possible, this could transform the world. Not simply because a politically united Europe would be large enough to have its voice heard in the international arena. That, in itself, may mean very little, or even be counterproductive. But here is the rub: for Europe to acquire such a voice—for Europe to become a credible political actor—it would need to surpass the inconclusive cacophony of intergovernmental diplomacy and the competition between its states. There is no strong, united Europe without establishing, for the first time in history, a genuinely democratic political space that surpasses the mental and material confines of the nation.

The establishment of a transnational democracy in Europe would undo one of the most powerful mechanisms through which the subservience of politics to the markets operates—the scandalous gap between a globalised economy and a provincialised politics. It would usher in the kind of post-national, democratic debate that the world so desperately needs today. Whether it is artificial intelligence or climate change, migratory or financial flows, a transnational democracy would return control over the great challenges of the future to hundreds of millions of people and their democratic deliberations.

Europe has the opportunity to demonstrate that unity of action across national divisions and jealousies is possible. It would, in this sense, be the most powerful metaphor for a possible, alternative world to come. Given the size and economic significance of the European Union, this would be a move with global implications. It is ours to make. **99**

PART SIX

Environment

The Game-changing Promise of a Green New Deal

Naomi Klein

It was March 2009, and capes were still fluttering in the White House after Barack Obama's historic hope-and-change electoral victory. Todd Stern, the newly appointed chief climate envoy, told a gathering on Capitol Hill that he and his fellow negotiators needed to embrace their inner superheroes, saving the planet from existential danger in the nick of time.

Climate change, he said, called for some of "that old comic book sensibility of uniting in the face of a common danger threatening the earth. Because that's what we have here. It's not a meteor or a space invader, but the damage to our planet, to our community, to our children, and their children will be just as great. There is no time to lose."

Eight months later, at the fateful United Nations climate summit in Copenhagen, Denmark, all pretence to superheroism from the Obama Administration had been unceremoniously abandoned. Stern stalked the hallways of the convention centre like the Grim Reaper, swinging his scythe through every proposal that would have resulted in a transformative agreement. The U.S. insisted on a target that would allow temperatures to rise by two degrees Celsius, despite passionate objections from African and Pacific islander delegates who said the goal amounted to a 'genocide' and would lead millions to die on land or in leaking boats. It shot down all attempts to make the deal legally binding, opting for unenforceable voluntary targets instead (as it would in Paris five years later).

Stern categorically rejected the argument that wealthy developed countries owe compensation to poor ones for knowingly pumping earth-warming carbon into the atmosphere, instead using much-needed funds for climate change protection as a bludgeon to force those countries into line.

As I wrote at the time, the Copenhagen deal—cooked up behind closed doors with the most vulnerable countries locked out—amounted to a "grubby pact between the world's biggest emitters: I'll pretend that you are doing something about climate change if you pretend that I am too. Deal? Deal."

A decade later, global emissions continue to rise alongside average temperatures, with large swathes of the planet wracked by record-breaking storms and scorched by unprecedented fires. The scientists convened in the Intergovernmental Panel on Climate Change have confirmed precisely what African and low-lying island states have long-since warned: that allowing temperatures to rise by two degrees is a death sentence, and that only a 1.5-degree target gives us a fighting chance. Eight Pacific islands have already disappeared beneath the rising seas.

Not only have wealthy countries failed to provide meaningful aid to poorer nations to protect themselves from weather extremes and leapfrog to clean tech, but Europe, Australia, and the United States have all responded to the increase in mass migration—intensified by climate stresses—with brutal force, ranging from Italy's de facto 'let them drown' policy to Trump's war on an unarmed caravan from Central America. Let there be no mistake: this barbarism is how the wealthy world plans to adapt to climate change.

In short, the metaphorical meteor that Stern evoked in 2009 is not just hurtling closer to our fragile planet—it's grazing the burning treetops.

And yet, I feel more optimistic about our chances of averting climate breakdown than I have in years. For the first time, I see a clear and credible political pathway that could get us to safety, a place in which we avoid the worst climate outcomes and forge a new social compact radically more humane than anything on offer.

But as the report's summary states in its first sentence, pulling that off is not possible with singular policies like carbon taxes. We need "rapid, far-reaching and unprecedented changes in all aspects of society." By connecting the dots between energy, transportation, housing, and construction, as well as healthcare, living wages, a jobs guarantee, and the urgent imperative to battle racial and gender injustice, the Green New Deal would be mapping precisely that kind of far-reaching change. This is not a piecemeal approach that trains a water gun on a blazing fire, but a comprehensive and holistic plan to put the fire out.

The ground has been prepared for decades, with models for community-owned and community-controlled renewable energy; with justice-based transitions that ensure no worker is left behind; with a deepening analysis of the intersections between systemic racism, armed conflict, and climate disruption; with improved green tech and breakthroughs in clean public transit; with the thriving fossil fuel divestment movement; with model legislation driven by the climate justice movement that shows how carbon taxes can fight racial and gender exclusion.

What has been missing is only the top-level political power to roll out the best of these models all at once, with the focus and velocity that both science and justice demand. That is the great promise of a comprehensive Green New Deal.

Of course, there is no shortage of pundits ready to dismiss all of this as hopelessly naive and unrealistic, the work of political neophytes who don't understand the art of the possible or the finer points of policy. What those pundits are failing to account for is that, unlike previous attempts to introduce climate legislation, the Green New

Deal has the capacity to mobilise an intersectional mass movement behind it—not despite its sweeping ambition, but because of it.

If you are part of the economy's winning class and funded by even bigger winners, as so many politicians are, then your attempts to craft climate legislation will likely be guided by the idea that change should be as minimal and undisruptive as possible. After all, the status quo is working just fine for you and your donors. Leaders who are rooted in communities that are being egregiously failed by the current system, on the other hand, are liberated to take a very different approach. Their climate policies can embrace deep systemic change—including the need for massive investments in public transit, affordable housing, and healthcare—because that is what their bases need to thrive.

As climate justice organisations have been arguing for years, when the people with the most to gain lead the movement, they fight to win.

Another game-changing aspect of a Green New Deal is that it is modelled after the most famous economic stimulus of all time, making it recession-proof. When the global economy enters another downturn, support for this model of climate action will not plummet as it did for every major green initiative during past recessions. Instead, it will increase, since a large-scale stimulus will become the greatest hope of reviving the economy.

Having a good idea is no guarantee of success. But here's a thought: lawmakers who want it to happen could consider working with civil society to set up some sort of parallel constituent assembly-like body to get the plan drafted anyway. This possibility is simply too important, and time is just too short, to let the usual forces of political inertia shut it down.

As the surprising events of the past months have unfolded, with young activists rewriting the rules of the possible, I have found myself thinking about another moment when young people found their voice in the climate change arena. It was 2011, at the annual United Nations climate summit, this time held in Durban, South Africa. A 21-year-old Canadian college student named Anjali Appadurai was selected to address the gathering on behalf (absurdly) of all the world's young people.

She delivered a stunning and unsparing address that shamed the gathered negotiators for decades of inaction. "You have been negotiating all my life," she said.

> In that time, you've failed to meet pledges, you've missed targets, and you've broken promises . . . The most stark betrayal of your generation's responsibility to ours is that you call this 'ambition'. Where is the courage in these rooms? Now is not the time for incremental action. In the long run, these will be seen as the defining moments of an era in which narrow self-interest prevailed over science, reason, and common compassion.

The most wrenching part of the address is that not a single major government was willing to receive her message; she was shouting into the void.

Years later, when other young people are finding their climate voice and their climate rage, there is finally a handful of political leaders able to receive their message, with an actual plan to turn it into policy. And that might just change everything.

The Scale of the Problem Itself

Bill McKibben

Two particularly baleful trends have begun to dominate life on this planet: the steady destruction of our natural world and the steady rise in inequality.

These are each incredibly dangerous: the climate and environmental crises have us on the brink of a global extinction event on a scale not seen in many millions of years. Inequality is helping destabilise our political life in countries around the globe. These trends are, of course, linked in many ways, not the least of which is the need for effective and immediate government action to help slow the rising temperature of the earth.

This is why DiEM25's proposal for a Green New Deal is such a remarkably important document. It is the first attempt at a political response to climate change that is on the same scale as the problem itself, and it recognises that any response to the climate and sustainability crisis must necessarily also deal with the austerity and economic short-sightedness that currently paralyse our societies.

This is by no means impossible—in fact, compared with trying to ride out the status quo it is easy.

The engineers have done their job, dramatically lowering the cost of power from the wind and sun and opening up the prospect of a workable future. Now citizens must do their jobs with the same prowess. We must set the stage for rolling out those new technologies at a pace that actually catches up with the physics of global warming. And we must use the economic opportunity that rollout represents to reverse the tide of inequality and instead start a trend in the other direction, towards economic justice.

The institutions envisioned in this document will at least get the job started. But one of its crucial postulates is that the response to these crises must be living and dynamic.

I am reminded of the original New Deal, a response to the Depression announced by Franklin D. Roosevelt almost a century ago. Under his leadership, a period of intense experimentation tried one solution after another, discarding those that didn't work and honing those that did. In many cases, these policies deepened social and economic inequalities, between races as between genders. But the original New

Deal enshrined the principles of democracy and justice. We must emulate it—and radically improve on it—in that regard.

Roosevelt famously inaugurated the New Deal by saying "There is nothing to fear but fear itself". We don't have that assurance, sadly. There is a great deal to fear, on a planet whose ice caps are melting, oceans rising, and cities baking. But there is also a good deal to hope for: above all the human solidarity that can rise above the tawdry exploitation of the last few decades and aim instead for a world that can be both cherished and sustained.

The Ten Pillars of the Green New Deal for Europe

We are running out of time. The oceans are heating, the soil is degrading, the ice caps are melting, millions of species are at risk of extinction, and Europe's economy is crumbling under a decade of underinvestment. Across the continent—and the world—people are marching by the millions to demand a just transition.

Following the 'green wave' of the 2019 Parliamentary elections, Europe's leaders were handed a historic opportunity—and a clear electoral mandate—to put forward an ambitious and pragmatic plan to transform Europe in the transition to renewable energy.

With that mandate, the idea of the Green New Deal took hold around Europe. From Spain to Germany, political parties are echoing its promise to deliver a green transition that also addresses social inequalities.

But not every environmental policy counts as a Green New Deal—even if it attempts to steal legitimacy from its name. To qualify, such policies must do more than tax and tinker: They must transform, creating an economy that is more prosperous, more just, and more sustainable than ever before. A Green New Deal must live up to these ten basic pillars—or it is not a Green New Deal.

Ten Pillars
1. Meeting the Scale of the Challenge

The science is clear: We must limit the global temperature rise to 1.5 degrees and reverse the collapse of our natural systems, or risk it all.

A Green New Deal for Europe must meet the scale of this challenge, investing at least five per cent of Europe's GDP each year in the transition to renewable energy, the reversal of biodiversity loss and other environmental breakdown, and the shared prosperity of all European residents.

It must build an economy that enables Europe to flourish while respecting planetary boundaries, restoring natural habitats, clean air and soil health around our continent.

Responding to the Great Depression in 1933, Franklin D. Roosevelt recognised the need to go beyond small-scale reforms to initiate a radical transformation of the American economic system.

A Green New Deal for Europe must bring this ambition across the Atlantic and into the twenty-first century. It calls not only for a reduction in carbon emissions. It demands a wholesale transformation of our systems of production, consumption, and social relations—rewiring our systems of material production for reproduction: recycling, reuse, repair and care.

Nothing short of this ambition can call itself a Green New Deal.

2. Pressing Idle Resources into Public Service

The Green New Deal calls on public institutions to drive the economic and social transformation away from a fossil fuel society.

Like the US one century ago, Europe remains caught in an extended period of economic instability. Even in its most prosperous economies, precarity has risen while households struggle to find a productive place to invest their savings.

The Green New Deal provides the answer.

Like the original New Deal, its proceeds from the Keynesian premise that a fiscal stimulus can guide economic recovery.

In Europe, the proposal calls on the European Investment Bank to provide this stimulus by issuing green investment bonds that can deliver a return to Europe's ailing savers.

In other words, the Green New Deal must press Europe's idle resources into public service—without placing the burden of the transition on the shoulders of everyday Europeans.

3. Empowering Citizens and Their Communities

Europe's green transition will not be top-down. It must empower citizens and their communities to make the decisions that shape their future.

The Green New Deal is infused with democracy. It provides clear mechanisms for citizen assemblies and local governments to make meaningful decisions about the development of their communities, municipalities, and regions.

And it must ensure that, wherever possible, Europe's new energy systems are publicly owned and democratically controlled.

Like Roosevelt's Works Progress Agency, a Green New Deal for Europe must create a new public body that puts citizens in the driver's seat of Europe's green transition.

In particular, frontline communities most affected by the climate crisis must have adequate resources to redress the degradation of their living conditions.

The democratic principle of the Green New Deal also applies in the workplace. The jobs created by green investment must protect worker rights and build greater control over the firms so workers share in the value they create.

4. Guaranteeing Decent Jobs

Europe today is mired in a mix of unemployment and underemployment. Precarious jobs are on the rise, and millions of people have been forced to leave their communities in search of jobs that will support their basic needs.

The Green New Deal must invest in communities across Europe to ensure that green investment will create high-quality, skilled and stable jobs that enable all citizens to support their families, leaving no community behind.

More than that, it must ensure a just transition for all workers in high carbon industries—promising secure employment, well-paid training opportunities and homes for all who need them.

And the Green New Deal must finally recognise the role of care in our economy, ensuring not only that housework, childcare and care for the elderly are recognised and rewarded, but also that activities which contribute to the regeneration of our natural systems play a central role in our economy.

5. Raising the Standard of Living

The Green New Deal must go well beyond a job guarantee. It must raise the standard of living across our continent in numerous ways, from investments in health and education to investments in arts and culture.

By reclaiming unused homes for public use, the Green New Deal will address the crisis of housing insecurity that has left so many people homeless or at risk of eviction.

By rewiring Europe's energy grids, retrofitting homes with good insulation, and providing clean, public transportation for all, the Green New Deal will reduce the cost of living for all households.

By reversing biodiversity loss and eliminating pollution, the Green New Deal will allow all communities to enjoy clean air, fresh water, and local nature reserves.

And by investing in a more sustainable economy, the Green New Deal will reduce the number of hours we work each week and provide more space for community engagement.

In other words, a Green New Deal for Europe will create public prosperity in place of private wealth, substituting consumption for what really matters for Europe's communities.

And, in the process, it will help build resilience for communities at the frontlines of the climate and ecological crises.

6. Entrenching Equality

The Green New Deal must combat financialisation and entrench equality at the heart of Europe.

Social and economic inequality remains far too high—both within countries and between them. Over the last four decades, wealth inequality has dramatically increased within European countries: the top one per cent captured as much economic growth as the bottom fifty per cent.

Between countries, too, the standard of living remains extremely uneven, with significant variations in income, unemployment rates and pollution. Meanwhile, our societies remain stratified by race, sexuality, gender, age, and ability, creating durable barriers to social justice and collective wellbeing.

The Green New Deal attacks the forces of inequality and builds a new society of solidarity.

Just like Roosevelt's New Deal, the programme will overhaul the financial system. Rather than privatising the gains from the green transition—as the Juncker Plan of 2015 has done—the Green New Deal must ensure that public investments build public wealth.

But unlike the original New Deal, the programme will target social barriers, eradicate discrimination against minorities, and ensure that the ecological transition is inclusive to all.

7. Investing in the Future

The Green New Deal is more than an environmental adjustment programme. It is an investment in the future of our societies, and an opportunity to reimagine it.

Decarbonising our economies means developing new tools and rediscovering old sources of knowledge: from new modes of public transport and more efficient battery storage, to agricultural practices that revitalise our soil and forestry that replenishes our forests.

That is why the Green New Deal for Europe must include a research and development initiative that can bring together the scientific, indigenous and technology communities to develop exciting new solutions to climate and environmental breakdown.

The greatest advancements in technology have happened through public research and funding—from the internet to touch screens, jet engines to rockets, GPS to search engine algorithms. But the way our economy is structured means that while the state invests in research and carries all the risk, the private sector reaps all the rewards—and pays almost no taxes on its profits.

The Green New Deal must ensure that society benefits directly from the investments that it makes in new tools, using the proceeds to invest in further innovation and deliver on the promise of greater social liberation from the working week.

8. Ending the Dogma of Endless Growth

The obsession with economic growth, as measured by Gross Domestic Product (GDP), is not only a primary driver of the climate and environmental crises, encouraging countries to pursue reckless economic policies while ignoring their environmental and social costs. It is also a misguided measure of our collective wellbeing.

The Green New Deal must move beyond the dogma of endless GDP growth and adopt more holistic measures of human progress. Equality, environment, happiness and health: there are scores of indicators that we can and should incorporate into our assessment of Europe's progress.

The Green New Deal must focus Europe's institutions on stimulating areas of social, moral and educational improvement, while designing an economy that privileges social reproduction over material production.

Not only does this take pressure off our living planet, it also makes it possible to accomplish the rapid energy transition we need.

9. Supporting Environmental Justice Around the World

The environmental crisis is global in scope, and the Green New Deal must be, too.

Europe has a historic responsibility to lead this global effort. For over two centuries, European countries have encouraged aggressive pollution and resource extraction that have directly harmed other countries around the world.

The Green New Deal for Europe must redress this colonial legacy.

It must redistribute resources to rehabilitate overexploited regions, protect against rising sea levels, and guarantee a decent standard of living to all climate refugees. And it must ensure that Europe's green transition does not simply export pollution elsewhere in the world, or rely on the continued extraction of resources from the Global South. The supply chain for Europe's energy transition must be committed to principles of social and environmental justice.

Even as we pride ourselves on delivering aid to the Global South, European corporations extract much more in interest payments, resource theft, and wage arbitrage. To support a global green transition, the Green New Deal must put an end to these exploitative economic practices and, at last, respect the rights of communities everywhere—paving the way for environmental justice around the world.

10. Committing to Environmental Action Today

Even if every country in the world fulfilled its commitment to the 2016 Paris Agreement, we would be on course for 3 °C of warming in this century and untold suffering as a result.

But no country has even come close to honouring its promises. This is what we have after nearly thirty years of global negotiations under the United Nations Framework Convention on Climate Change.

But the Green New Deal is not a framework, a treaty, or an agreement. It's not a soft political commitment for change. It's not a piece of paper signed by participating states. It's not a multilateral meeting or the photo opportunity that always follows.

The Green New Deal must graduate us from negotiations to action—putting forward a set of specific, credible measures targeted at every area of society. It is a package of measures that rapidly transitions us to a sustainable economy, pushes our democracies to new frontiers, creates shared prosperity, and builds a fairer world beyond our borders.

Nothing less will do.

Decarbonisation without Democracy

David Adler and Pawel Wargan

Following a decade of severe crisis and stagnation, the European Union prepared to embark on an ambitious reform programme to "rediscover [its] unity and inner strength". Such is the promise made by European Commission President Ursula von der Leyen in the political guidelines for her five-year mandate, entitled A Union That Strives for More.

Von der Leyen's vision statement contains key pledges to address the sources of discontent rising across the continent. "I want Europe to strive for more in nurturing, protecting, and strengthening our democracy", von der Leyen sets out, calling for a Conference on the Future of Europe that promises citizens a chance to "have their say" in the direction of the EU's democratic reform. "I want Europe to strive for more by being the first climate-neutral continent", von der Leyen writes, pledging to deliver a European Green Deal and a "just transition for all" away from fossil fuels.

Within this new framework, the question of democracy and the challenge of a changing climate—of the Conference and the Green Deal, respectively—are set apart as entirely distinct. To be sure, the Commission has promised a 'European Climate Pact', which proposes to convene "local communities, civil society, industry and schools [to] commit to a set of pledges to bring about a change in behaviour". But the Commission's plan for the Green Deal makes no reference to democracy; indeed, the word does not appear anywhere in its twenty-four-page communication. On the contrary, the Green Deal is set to deepen the European Union's democratic deficit, even as it drives the decarbonisation of its economy.

Over the past two decades, a growing literature has examined the relationship between democracy and climate action. Several studies have documented a link between democratic institutions and efforts to mitigate environmental breakdown, suggesting that, even in these troubled times, democracies remain the best political systems to address humanity's most pressing challenge. The fact that the European Commission has pledged a Green Deal in the wake of a 'green wave'—in which Europe's green parties rode the 'Greta effect' to a strong showing in the 2019 European Parliament elections—is strong evidence of this democratic response mechanism.

But the causal arrow does not necessarily run in reverse. Climate action can either enhance democracy or constrain it; drive participation or restrict it; socialise ownership or consolidate it; expand the spaces of common ownership or enclose them. In the Green Deal, the EU is pioneering a model of what we call *decarbonisation without democracy,* in which the green transition may even enflame Europe's massive imbalance of power and wealth—and paving the way for a denialist backlash in the process.

Green Dealing in Brussels

'Decarbonisation without democracy' refers both to the process of designing the Green Deal and its product. The policy—its core features and the directions for their implementation—was cooked up by the European Commission, the executive body of unelected officials at the helm of the European Union. Defenders of the EU's institutional design will point to European Parliament's leverage over the Commission above them; the Parliament has the power to adopt, reject, and amend key parts of the legislation.

But the origins of the Green Deal in the backrooms of Brussels—rooms that are out of sight and out of reach of Europe's citizens, rooms where even the Commission admits that oil and gas lobbyists exert exceptional influence by spending millions of euros on lobbying efforts each year—indicate that the EU does not view the Green Deal as a collective project or a driver of political transformation, but as a technocratic intervention to excise carbon from the European economy.

In other words, the Green Deal has been designed from *within* the European Union's democratic deficit. Public participation has been restricted to 'consultations' with little bearing on the design of the overall legislation. Compare this with Franklin D. Roosevelt's New Deal, from which the current EU legislation steals so much of its legitimacy. That New Deal introduced new institutions like the Tennessee Valley Authority (TVA), aimed at facilitating "the active daily participation of the people themselves." The ambition of the Green Deal, by contrast, is to demobilise them—to put an end to all the marching, to get the children back in school and the rebels off the streets.

The structure of the Green Deal—and in particular, the Sustainable European Investment Plan, which is supposed to power the green transition—reflects this democratic deficit. Its stated aim is to 'mobilise' €1 trillion over the next ten years toward strategic investments to shift Europe's economy away from fossil fuels. By 'mobilisation', however, the EU means that it will use public money to guarantee private investments, 'de-risking' them in an effort to seduce capital to participate in the decarbonisation process. In other words, the Green Deal is a privatisation scheme: it seeks to enclose the opportunities afforded by the green transition—to rebuild Europe's infrastructure, to create new sources of renewable energy, to develop technologies that can drive decarbonisation—in service of private capital accumulation, rather than exploiting them to expand public ownership and democratic control.

Here again, the EU's plan appears as an affront to the original New Deal, framed as it was against the "concentration of private power". And it appears equally at odds with the proposals for a Green New Deal that take direct inspiration from Roosevelt's agenda. If the legislation introduced by Alexandria Ocasio-Cortez consistently emphasises the rights of the 'public' against the profit motive of the private sector—in the workplace as in housing markets and hospitals—the Green Deal is silent on such questions of distribution, ownership, and social protections.

Indeed, the silences of the Green Deal reveal far more than they obscure. While pledging to deliver "deeply transformative policies", the Green Deal is largely silent on the question of austerity and the Stability and Growth Pact that enforces it, strangling investment across the bloc and constraining member-states' ability to invest in infrastructure, social services, and employment. EU leaders have long sought to distract the public from the architecture of austerity: they proclaim the end of the crisis and insist on the health of the Union. But the numbers tell a different story: even before the Coronavirus laid waste again to the European economy, youth unemployment remained stuck at a staggering 33 per cent in Greece, 32 per cent in Spain, and 27 per cent in Italy. The mind boggles in considering the depth and duration of economic stagnation in these Eurozone countries. Italy's economic output has not risen in over two decades; living standards for millions of Italians, meanwhile, have declined. 'Transformation' in Europe's Southern member states is not a slogan; it is an emergency.

Decarbonisation Against Democracy?

The quiet affirmation of austerity in the Green Deal is perhaps the clearest evidence of its disconnect with democracy. Most obvious is the formal dimension of this disconnect: the Stability and Growth Pact directly limits the expression of popular sovereignty by dictating the terms of member-states' social policies. The European Commission suggests that "evaluations are underway" to revise the guidelines for what's called 'State aid'—Commission-speak for government support—in order to facilitate a rapid transition to climate neutrality. But even here, the goal is to ensure a "level-playing field in the internal market", not to make room for citizens to address the social crisis in which they are drowning. In other words, it is the market itself—not the workers who create it, toil in it, benefit from it, or get screwed by it—that is served by the Green Deal.

Here, we see the deeper sense in which the Green Deal embodies 'decarbonisation without democracy'—its silence on the social dimension. Roughly 140 million people in the EU are currently at risk of poverty; according to the Commission's own estimates, one in three people inside the EU cannot "cope with unexpected financial expenses". These statistics are inseparable from the green transition, both in terms of energy production—50 million people in the EU cannot afford to heat their homes—as well as in terms of economic justice. Heed the call of the gilets jaunes: communities already shut out from economic opportunity cannot be expected to shoulder the burden of climate mitigation.

The Green Deal comes with a Just Transition Mechanism, by which the EU will invest €7.5 billion over seven years to ensure that it leaves "no one behind". Behind what? We do not know. The money—a paltry sum compared to the trillions of euros with which the EU bailed out its French and German banks—is intended for "regions and sectors that are most affected by the transition", coal-dependent, mining-heavy places that might buck at the prospect of climate neutrality. But as economist Daniela Gabor recently noted, the money is unlikely to trickle down to the workers themselves; "clever local elites", instead, are likely to funnel transition money to their businesses. The burning question is not who will get left behind in Europe's green economy, but who won't.

Such criticisms do not imply that the EU will be necessarily unsuccessful in its attempt to reach climate neutrality by 2050. For our part, we think there is no chance: the size of the investment—by the most generous estimate, €1 trillion over the next ten years—is wildly insufficient to strip all that carbon from the European economy, even by the Commission's own estimates. And that's assuming everything goes to plan. But the Green Deal may at least succeed in cutting large amounts of greenhouse emissions.

On 4 March, the EU unveiled its draft climate law, which will allow it to set binding short-term targets—with or without the support of its member-state governments. The legislative design of the climate law, however, tells it all: the leaders of the EU simply cannot imagine a bargain that would both drive rapid decarbonisation and engender deep democratic support from across the bloc. Instead, they view the concentration of power in the EU's unelected executive as the only route to successful decarbonisation. Member states may argue that this is not 'decarbonisation without democracy', but rather decarbonisation *against* democracy. And they may, in fact, be right.

The danger of the Green Deal, then, is not only that it lacks the speed, size, and ambition to deliver on its promises. By remaining silent on the social dimension of the green transition, the EU may create the conditions for a backlash from denialist forces across the continent—from the Lega to the AfD—who can present the Green Deal as the perfect illustration of a trade-off between democracy and decarbonisation. The movement of the gilets jaunes has made its position quite clear: no climate justice, no peace. The EU ignores this lesson at its own peril.

Greta and the Green Deal

None of these deficiencies has prevented the leaders of the European Union from presenting their Green Deal as an expression of the youth-led climate movement. In

2019 alone, the EU has welcomed Greta Thunberg not once, not twice, but three times to address—and dress down—an audience of public servants. "Only one year ago, no one would have imagined that millions would take to the streets for climate," President von der Leyen said in her speech to Parliament in December 2019. "Our European Green Deal is for them."

The goal here is to co-opt the energy of the movement while stripping it of its substance. For 'decarbonisation without democracy' to work, the EU must be able to convince its citizens that it has everything under control—and that climate strikes are no longer necessary. It is no coincidence that the Commission's proposal employs the same vocabulary as the activists themselves, from the 'just transition' (albeit one that has little to do with climate justice) to the 'green deal' (albeit one with little to do with the New Deal). The rhetorical sleight has paid off. Behold the headlines: *Vox, Mother Jones, Forbes, The Hill,* and *World Economic Forum*—all of them amazed that the EU has 'its own Green New Deal'.

Fortunately, climate activists in Europe are not so easily fooled. Addressing the European Parliament in March, Greta Thunberg herself condemned the Green Deal as 'surrender' to environmental breakdown. "Such a law sends a strong signal that real sufficient action is taking place when in fact it is not. The hard truth is that neither the awareness nor politics needed are in sight", Thunberg said. But the blame lies partly with the movement itself. Repeating the scientific facts—as Thunberg is wont to do—might expand awareness of the crisis at hand, but it does little to shape our political response. Much of this activism is phrased in purely negative terms. Fridays for Future, for example, describes itself as a movement to "protest against the lack of action on the climate crisis". Rarely posed is the question of *what kind* of action it demands, and more importantly, *for whom.* If climate mitigation is 'beyond politics', as Extinction Rebellion insists, who can blame the European Commission for carving democracy out of its path to decarbonisation?

To confront the Green Deal—and to reclaim the green transition as a democratic project—we need a much bolder strategy than plain 'resistance'. Rather, we need to advance a positive project of our own, organising communities to envision their own 'just transition', mobilising them behind that shared vision, and ripping open channels of democratic accountability that the Commission would rather sew shut. In a word, we need a Green New Deal for Europe, not a European 'Green Deal'.

Organised assemblies are indispensable to this strategy. Across Europe's climate movement, the demand for sovereign assemblies of citizens has become a key rallying cry—and for good reason: they are powerful pedagogical tools, they help build consensus, and they ensure durable public support for the decisions they make. In particular, climate assemblies promise to generate a set of concrete and legitimate demands for the movement at large, shifting away from the *reactive* mode of activism that paved the way to the Green Deal toward a *programmatic* mode that can counter it. By training organisers, and sharing know-how, best practices and strategies, climate activists can entrench this approach as a new *modus operandi* of the broader climate movement.

But assemblies alone cannot fill Europe's democratic deficit—not least because, without a change to the EU treaty system, they carry no legal authority. Absent treaty change, a European climate assembly is little more than an informal gathering; politicians can heed its demands or bury them, while stealing legitimacy from their mere existence. More fundamentally, a lack of legal mandate would deprive these parallel assemblies of their ability to engage a broad and representative demographic. Workers, the disabled, parents, the poor: so many people may struggle to participate for lack of time, resources, or ability. Self-organised assemblies therefore run the risk of excluding the voices of the marginalised—the very people whose needs must be at the forefront of a just transition. A truly emancipatory response to the climate and environmental crises is not the product of participatory democracy; it is a necessary precondition.

The missing piece in Europe's climate movement, then, is *politics*. The shift toward a programmatic mode of activism is not only about developing policy proposals; it is also about developing a political strategy to implement them. This process does not begin in Brussels, but in the communities themselves. In 2019, the municipality of Barcelona announced a climate emergency and a robust policy response that married climate and environmental concerns with questions of social justice. Our campaign is now working with representatives from Barcelona en Comú to advocate a Green New Deal for Barcelona, to which similar municipal movements could connect in a Green Solidarity Network. Such a project would not only reclaim the banner of green politics from the Commission; the existence of an actual Green New Deal in Europe would also expose its rhetorical co-optation of the just transition.

The strands of local climate politics, however, must then scale up to the European level. We cannot simply cede the Green Deal to the lobbyists; the politics must enter those backrooms in Brussels. But it will not do so by knocking on the door or marching in the streets outside. On the contrary, a *politicised* climate movement must target the strategic roadblocks to a just transition. One such roadblock is the so-called 'black zero'—EU member-states' obsession with a balanced government budget with no new borrowing. If the movement did not merely call for climate 'action', but a break with the economic orthodoxy constraining it, they could unlock significantly more money for the just transition. That could disarm opposition from Polish miners, the French gilets jaunes and other groups rightfully suspicious of the climate agenda today, and open the door to a wholesale transformation of Europe's financing architecture, creating the fiscal space for EU countries to mount their own responses to the social and ecological crises.

A politicised climate movement can make a similar strategic intervention in partnership with labour. Using productivity gains to reduce the working week rather than to make more useless stuff would have obvious environmental benefits;

by reducing material and infrastructure use throughout, it would relieve pressures on natural systems and reduce aggregate energy demand, significantly cutting per capita emissions. Here again, a strategic partnership between climate activists and communities across Europe that have not seen living standards rise in a generation would shift the politics of the Green Deal away from market reification and toward public service: decarbonisation with democracy.

Fork in the Road

We seem to return—over and over and over again—to the fork in Rosa Luxemburg's road: socialism this way, barbarism that. "The capitalist social system has run its course; its dissolution is now only a question of time", wrote Karl Kautsky (from whom Luxemburg would later borrow the phrase) in 1909. "The substitution of a new social order for the existing one is no longer simply desirable; it has become inevitable."

Alas, a century later, the climate crisis is bringing us to that same fork. An existential threat looms on the near horizon: we either mobilise collectively to stop it—putting an end to fossil fuel production and the profit motive that keeps us addicted—or we make way for the violence, dispossession, and death that two degrees of global heating will deliver. "Our choices," write Thea Riofrancos, Robert Shaw, and Will Speck, "are eco-socialism or barbarism." In the parlance of the climate movement, the alternative is either system change or climate change.

Yet the EU Green Deal suggests that it might be just as possible to forestall Luxemburg's dilemma. As we have learned—over and over and over again— capital is creative. If some will cast its demise as 'inevitable', given the unsustainability of its current configuration, its managers nonetheless find increasingly clever ways to avoid it. There can be no doubt that Europe's political-economic system is driving unprecedented environmental destruction. But the Green Deal forces us to consider: will our rulers be able to avert climate change while staving off systemic change?

Decarbonisation will reshape the economy in so many fundamental ways— disposing of old industries, making way for new ones, and producing a slew of knock-on effects that are impossible to predict. But it is foolish to assume that these rapid changes will also reshape the distribution of winners and losers, of opportunities, of voice or power. Like industrial revolutions past, it may well consolidate that power for a few, while putting millions of people out of jobs made redundant, and condemning millions more to suffer the consequences of ecological destruction at the margins of society.

For a new system to emerge—for us to walk down the road toward eco-socialism—we need to move beyond an obsession with climate targets and degrees Celsius to develop a real climate politics, one that grapples with the green transition as a field of conflict in which capital holds a strong upper hand, backed up by powerful institutions like the EU. Once we understand the green transition in this way, democracy can return as the guiding principle of the climate movement: only an organised mobilisation of working communities can secure their gains from the green transition, and only their active participation can ensure it stays that way.

One thing is clear: there is nothing neutral about climate neutrality. Decarbonisation is what we make with it.

Different Voices: Building the Environmental Pillar for DiEM25

Ksenia Gerasimova

Freud described two contradictory instincts of human nature: love and destruction, or *Eros* and *Thanatos*.[1] The love instinct, Eros, relates to unity and the desire to do good; the destruction or death instinct, Thanatos, represents egocentric moves to satisfy individual needs and desires over collective needs. Ecology is good terrain on which to explore how both instincts work. On the one hand, people care for and appreciate nature; on the other, human development driven by unchecked greed and the desire to endlessly expand presents a real threat to nature's finite resources.

Caught in the push and pull between these two instincts, humanity ends up suppressing both, and the price is neurosis. This fuels a profound desire for liberty, potential revolt, and creates a struggle between individual desires and the needs of a group. Ecology demonstrates how ego-instincts, often in sadistic form, come into confrontation with object-instincts, and lead us to a dangerous brink which puts at risk the survival not only of our own species, but the whole ecosystem.

It seems then that the world, and specifically Europe, is facing a crisis resultant of losing control over these egocentric instincts. In one of his earlier interviews[2], Yanis Varoufakis pointed out the need to respond to the 'idiotic handling' of Europe's disarray. He identified an opponent whose attitude can potentially lead to destruction in many forms, including the ecological death of the planet:

> We are faced with determined, well-organised adversaries who do not put the good of humanity first. Who want only one thing: business as usual and a world that allows them to make endless amounts of money using the rest of humanity as a tool for doing so. They are not persuaded by rational argument. They are not sensitive to ethical example. They loathe democracy. They know they can intimidate a large majority of humanity. But in their arrogance, like a stupid virus, their business as usual is destroying the organism they depend on.

So, this is why DiEM25 has been created—"to pay any price, bear any burden, oppose any enemy of humanity's hopes".

Who are we?

I joined DiEM25 after discussing the 2016 Greek referendum aftermath and the resulting new ideas for European political development with Italian friends. One of my group, Berardo Carboni, is an envoy and initiator of DiEM25. This is what he says:

> It is fundamental to change the nodal point of society from an eco-nomic prospective to an eco-logic one—not just because the environmental situation is one where if we don't change capitalist's extractive ways earth will become a place where future generations will have difficulties surviving; but, more so, because even in the present, if we don't switch perspective from property and competition to relations between people and nature, we will keep increasing injustice and inequality to a point where they become unsustainable.[3]

Environmental issues figure prominently in most debates about Europe's future development, and many Europeans have keenly participated in developing environmental projects. Perhaps, then, a multi-stakeholder approach would be helpful, in which we would ask members of the movement about environmental issues in their lives and put together a policy agenda proposal. It is completely possible for any member of the movement to participate in shaping this agenda. In the document "Building DiEM25's Progressive Agenda for Europe—Major Principles", this is how concrete policy proposals come about:

- DiEM25 members and the Expert Committee receive questions for discussion;
- DiEM25 members and the Expert Committee draft proposals;
- All proposals are integrated into a first Green Paper;
- DiEM25 members give comments, which are integrated into a second Green Paper;
- DiEM25 members give amendments at an Assembly;
- All proposals are integrated into a third Green Paper;
- DiEM25 members vote, and if approved, a White Paper is born.

Ecological transition

In the Spring of 2018, our group was approved to contribute to the DiEM25 Ecological Transition policy pillar, and coordinate the development of its White Paper. We reached out to them and received their valuable input on drafting the questionnaire. Finally, it was published online for all members. They were called upon to contribute their own experiences and ideas towards a green transition in Europe.

Brando Wild, one of the leaders of the Ecological Transition spontaneous collective, gives his account of his involvement and experiences with DiEM25 work on ecological transition:

The vast majority of DiEM25 members I encountered can agree that the need for an ecological transition is vital for our European and global future. We therefore set up an Ecological Transition in winter December 2017, where we started discussing the topic at our own pace, as the Pillar had yet to be officially worked on by DiEM25 as a whole. We shared ideas with various members and tried within our local groups to ignite some interest in the topic.

However, even for a progressive movement like DiEM25, it was quite a struggle to put ecological transition at the centre of a policy agenda. The topic, which seems more complex and detailed than a New Deal, for example, was formalised only in the summer of 2018 which led to frustration among members of our DSC, with some eventually leaving the movement altogether. The rush to produce a policy proposal in only a few months led to a far less inclusive process (for members) than was initially expected.

We must learn from our experience, and we should allocate more time to creating policy proposals in the future, largely by creating a better basis for inclusion of our members in the process, as this is one of the aspects that makes DiEM25 different. All in all, the experience was positive. I have met some great people from across Europe with whom I have shared opinions and views and look forward to the future of the movement! I do believe our success depends on our ability to be self-critical and strive to improve our internal democracy and processes: we are getting better, but we are not yet perfect.[4]

After a delayed start, responses from the members were processed and became a draft proposal for the Green Paper on Europe's green transition. The chaos of the movement is that there are many like-minded people with great expertise and useful experiences, and they disagree even among each other. Some were very outspoken opponents of nuclear energy, while others were urging leniency. There is no quick fix that will bring them all to one common denominator, but it is an essential part of democracy to try.

In December 2018, Pawel, an artist and policy adviser based in London, reached out to DiEM25, hoping to become involved in policy design for DiEM25, particularly on environmental policy. He kindly helped to progress the second draft of the paper, illustrating that engagement in policymaking in the movement is open for all, both new and long-standing members.

He had been inspired by DiEM25's belief in the possibility of democratising Europe and sensed that the prevailing neoliberal ideology allowed for political decision-making to end up exclusively in the hands of powerful financial interests and technocratic leaders. He believes that this has undermined democracy in Europe.

Context, complexity, and change

Amir Sharif, Associate Dean and Professor of Circular Economy at Bradford University, has offered his input towards the development of green policy in Europe, by outlining what are for him the major policy challenges:

With policy, and policymaking, the main challenge is one of context, complexity and change. Firstly, in terms of context, the range of potential contextual applications and approaches for green policy/sustainability is, on the one hand, immense and, on the other, narrowly-focused and dependent upon the lens and perspective used.

For those who are involved directly in the field, the scope and context encompass everything, yet for policymakers (in the broad sense), there are innumerable policies, conditions, and contents to be considered. Where is the green policy in this mix?

All is not lost, however, since the increasing popularity of green and sustainability issues (including that of the circular economy of course) means that stakeholders across the European policymaking context are all aware of the need for *answers* (i.e. responses, rather than solutions). The inhibiting elements of policy stagnation and driving factors of active momentum in the field are surprisingly, and refreshingly, clear and visible.

Secondly, in terms of complexity, the challenge is not necessarily related to the solutions proposed themselves, but dependent on the way the question is posed: What does green policy mean? What particular (real) outcomes are being sought? What interests need to be safeguarded? What inter-relationships are inherent in the discussion? Where is the funding going to come from? Complexity, as we know, can be inherent, implicit, interconnected, self-organising, emergent and, above all, hybrid.

Green policies, by their very nature, are simultaneously cross-cutting meta-memes that are, and can be, placed in a variety of contexts and arguments. Complexity is thus assured and the use, relevance, and purpose of developing the appropriate policy for 'greening', for sustainable and circular 'whole earth' approaches is embedded in its very nature.

Thirdly, and finally, change is a real obstacle itself. Policymakers are all too aware that whilst regulation, directives, and initiatives from within, across and throughout nation states can be mandated or supported, active participation from citizen demographic groups still requires effort in terms of changing behaviours.

Thankfully, recent popularisation of the excesses of industrialised and emerging economies in creating waste that harms the natural environment (witness plastics waste) is starting to turn the tide towards a better appreciation of the consequences of action (and apathy).

But regional and hemispheric change requires a more concerted effort from nation states—a challenge to which all policy is formed from sovereign interests, whether political, financial, social, technological, legal, or environmental.

We asked him if the Circular Economy economic model might be one right answer.

The Circular Economy clearly has its roots in the past. The notion of reducing waste, consumption, living within means, balancing man-made and natural assets and general stewardship of what Boulding, Lovelock, and others call 'starship Earth' is nothing entirely new. From roots in and across ideologies as varied as industrial ecology, biomimicry, the performance economy, schools of transitions, natural capitalism, complexity, and systems-thinking, to name a few, circularity as an encompassing concept of optimisation, innovation, reuse, regeneration, recycling, looping, cascading, and value extraction has never been more potent or appealing.

And yet, even with this degree of growth of circular economy, the concept has yet to make it into the true mainstream. The challenge remaining for those involved in the field is in translating the aforementioned deep concepts into realisable and visible tools, techniques and, ultimately, benefits. It still feels far too conceptual for most companies and individuals—although that is now changing, since the emphasis and experience of companies, decision-makers and policymakers continues to grow.

Combine this with other recent business and societal shifts in technology, such as artificial intelligence, big data, analytics, social media, influencer marketing, the growth and expansion of north/south and east/west geopolitical threats, risks, and opportunities, and the circular economy seems to be at the cusp and at a crossroads of a very important shift in our relationship with our immediate anthropocentric context. If we can just distil and explain the fundamental link between our quest for consumption, resource dependency, and the ultimate depletion of our natural asset bank, then indeed the circular economy model can become the actual economic model.

Until then, as is the case for green policy as a whole, existing economic models will have to be shifted to include a different range of interests and motives—which requires a paradigm shift as epic as the invention of the lightbulb. And just as enlightening . . .[5]

Sofica Morariu, in her nineties, is an educator and farmer with a lifelong practice of sustainable agriculture in Romania. She does not use the internet, but knows about DiEM25. She has been cultivating land and teaching others to care about their families and the land they live on. For her, "agriculture is a means to enhance people's *living*, not just *survival*—and horticulture is a source of nutrition and contributes to people's health, and as a result a healthy person thinks better and can discover new things, both in agriculture and all of life's domains." Following her parents' view, she promotes support to small-scale subsistence farming for both economic reasons ("it gives money") and cultural reasons ("it helps maintain traditions").

To her family's astonishment, Sofica is very knowledgeable on climate change both from reading about it and from witnessing the changes firsthand:

This year [2018] affected agricultural production. There was too much change, it was quick: too hot, then it rained—again, too much—resulting in flooding, etc. It was really more than usual. And after you work hard and use good quality seeds, you want to see your crops reward you. But this year it was not a good harvest.

She warns that the fertile land of Romania will be lost in twenty years or less. She has developed her own set of recommendations to prevent such loss, inspired partly from the policies of socialist Romania: "to build an automated water system that irrigates fields in a sustainable manner and uses the water which nature generously supplies; to reconsider house and agricultural planning, lest people lost their houses and crops; to build canals, promote both traditional knowledge and appreciation for local agriculture, and support science to improve local seeds; and more."[6]

Another contribution came from Mayra Crean, a DiEM25 UK active member with a diploma in dental hygiene and therapy, who is currently completing a Master's degree in public health from the London School of Hygiene and Tropical Medicine. Mayra suggested a new subtopic for the green paper subtheme: Environment, Housing, and Health. Her suggestion incorporates an outstanding case study of a DiEM25 member who suffered from a dangerous allergy condition resulting from heavy mould in London housing. This is part of her input:

> Housing is important for health in many ways: it results in psycho-social wellbeing, a crucial feeling of safety and security, personal hygiene, preparation and storage of food, it's an environment suitable for comfort and relaxation, private and social relationships—the list goes on. At the same time, it can be the source of a wide range of hazards (physical, chemical, biological) and threaten both human flourishing and that of nature.
>
> It is the built environment where most people spend most of their time. A significant development in recent years has been the development of the UK Housing Health and Safety Rating System (HHSRS) which provides a health-based assessment of housing-related hazards. The wider local environment around the home is also important in terms of fear of crime, the accessibility of services, and the opportunity to be physically active. In an unstable economic and political situation (such as Brexit) the affordability of housing and the potential for individuals to lose their home is high.
>
> The list of hazards includes lack of heat, excessive heat, falls and general accidents, dampness and mould, carbon monoxide, radon, internal and external air pollution.
>
> Future policies will need to address the above issues. At DiEM25 we are looking to create a grassroots movement which ensures that building standards in the UK are improved because current standards meet neither the needs of people, nor the rapid changes in global environment.[7]

A happening process

It is interesting to see this dynamic process of policymaking in DiEM25 taking shape. In the 1970s, while many authors sympathised with the Malthusian thesis of catastrophism, they argued that it was an authoritarian system, not democracy, that would provide the necessary control over unsustainable human activities.[8] The Green Democracy concept emerged as a reaction to such conclusions, and offered a more optimistic approach to achieving two difficult targets: both respecting nature and, at the same time, applying democratic principles of responsibility, grassroots democracy, social justice, and non-violence.

Modern debates on green democracy have moved into looking at empirical case studies about how to achieve this in practice. If such projects are found to be successful, then there need be no conflict between democracy and environmental sustainability, and together we can tame the destructive instincts of consumerism.

Notes

1   Sigmund Freud, *Civilization and Its Discontents* (London: Penguin, 2004).
2   Yanis Varoufakis, "It is Time for Europe's Humanists to Reclaim Europe," *DiEM25*, 10 September 2016, https://diem25.org/yanis-varoufakis-it-is-time-for-europes-humanists-to-reclaim-europe/.
3   As relayed by Berardo Carboni in a personal telephone interview on 18 February 2019.
4   Brando Wild in a written contribution on 19 February 2019.
5   Amir Sharif in a written contribution on 18 February 2019.
6   Sofica Morariu, personal interview, Adjud, Romania: 27 August 2018.
7   Mayra Crean in a written contribution on 28 February 2019.
8   See R.L. Heilbroner *An Inquiry into the Human Prospect*. (New York: Norton, 1974), and W. Ophuls *Ecology and the Politics of Scarcity* (San Francisco: W.H. Freeman Press, 1977).

A Lesson from Denmark:
How on Earth Do We Save the Earth?

Rasmus Nordqvist

When facing the climate crisis or the biodiversity crisis, when confronted by the discomforting science and the distressing facts that define those crises, and when realising the enormity of the task ahead of us if we were properly to address them, many sink into despair and apathy. "It can't be done." "We don't have enough time." "How on earth do we save the earth?"

Indeed, the crisis of the natural systems that sustain not only humanity but all living organisms does present us with a monumental challenge. To be precise, the challenge of a lifetime, the challenge of our generation. From the perspective of Denmark, the good news is that, increasingly, climate is the new and chief battle line of politics.

In Denmark, public demand for climate action is on the rise, new actors are publicly adopting a stance, and citizens are mobilised to express their demands for *real* climate action. However, when considering politics at this time, the gap between the need to act and the willingness to act is still much too wide.

In the face of the scientific facts, it seems as if the fundamental pact between the people and their elected representatives has been broken. The political elite has until now failed to take responsibility. In this sense, climate politics is at its core a question of how seriously we take our democracy.

The question then is: how can we as people and as political actors reinstall this pact, reconnect the political head to the body, and finally act on the undeniable reality of climate change? Perhaps we should look into the experience of the Scandinavian welfare system and the struggle it took to get there. This can inspire us to step up and act in time. We've done it before; we can do it again.

To begin with, what many of us tend to forget, or maybe not even realise, is that, throughout history, humans have managed to get out of the thick alive many times over. Faced with adversity, we are known to have risen to the occasion and beat the odds. We have united under a common cause and have overcome challenges that seemed too big. We have proven over and over again that not only is it possible change a dysfunctional system, but it is entirely within our reach to create a better future for all—assuming we put our minds to it.

We did it in the 1980s, when the world reacted promptly to the facts of science and the grave threats we faced and united to save the ozone layer by signing the Montréal Protocol and phasing out a number of ozone-depleting substances.

If we act *now* we can overcome the climate crisis. We can build cars that run on electricity and expand our networks of public transportation; we can phase out coal, oil, and gas, and we can harvest the renewable energy of the wind, the sun, and the waves in our oceans. We can build smarter buildings, reuse waste, and create circular economy solutions. We can eat differently, test and develop new kinds of low-carbon meat, find new ways to produce the essentials that keep us alive. The Chinese say, "When the winds of change blow, some build walls, others build windmills." I would like us to build windmills—lots of them.

This climate crisis is not just an enormous challenge in itself, it is also a welcome opportunity to fix the very same system that created the crisis. A long-awaited path to lead us back to our core values, our lost sense of connectedness and humanity that has been sacrificed on the altar of trash capitalism and endless consumerism. In other words, we are not only trying to avoid the coming heatwaves, the scorching wildfires, the flooding of our cities, or the host of other natural disasters that threaten our set ways of lives; we are given an opportunity to challenge austerity, and address fundamental flaws of the neoliberal system that fetishises economic growth. It is a chance to acknowledge that we have long been enslaved by the economy rather than using it to achieve greater things—and do something about it.

I am certain that the crises we are confronting offer us an opportunity not only to alter the system, but a great reason, if there ever was one, to reboot our collective mind frame, to enter a whole new paradigm in which we redefine prosperity as something that is no longer focused solely on financial gain and materialistic acquirements.

We must challenge the idea that human wellbeing—satisfaction, even—should be measured by income or fortune. And we must come to the realisation that the most important things in life are not things at all. What about all the other riches that cater to our human needs? Time for living, for being with loved ones, something as simple as clean air, soil, and water, or the beauty of an abundant wildlife and a rich natural world?

What about creativity, art, curiosity, and lifelong education? What about volunteer work and philanthropy? What about community, cross-generational interaction, democratic involvement, and solidarity? A good life is hardly possible in the absence of a community, and what is community if not a wholehearted commitment to the wellbeing of others?

There is a great need for a shift of focus. If we go through life fixated on ourselves and our possessions, we end up leading impoverished lives, deprived of true meaning and purpose. We end up being slaves. Time is scarce but all the ingredients are right in front of us.

Lessons from Denmark

If history has taught us anything, it is that we can only face these daunting challenges if we act together, united.

That, at least, is the lesson we taught ourselves in our continent's north. In Denmark, in Scandinavia, we built the welfare state as our shared response to industrialisation and the rise of capitalism and the systemic challenges it created. Workers organised in unions. Farmers united in co-ops and shared both investments and profits. We made education free and mandatory for all, adults educated themselves—and each other—in the folk high schools that offered non-formal education. We even paid the youth to educate themselves. Health insurance has been free for all, too. And as we invested heavily in humans and in equality and opportunities, furthered our rights and secured better lives for most, if not all. The welfare state laid a new foundation for a progressive and genuinely democratic pact between citizens and the political class.

Later, we deployed these lessons when Denmark was developing into a global frontrunner in the green transition, and by doing so demonstrated that rapid and ambitious climate action wasn't incompatible with a welfare state. On the contrary: it is a precondition for its flourishing. By supporting research, investing in entrepreneurs, creating public demand, and even by creating the world's first ministry of environment, we became a world leader in a community-led, bottom-up green transition.

Thousands and thousands of citizens have united to invest in windmill farms around the country. For example, one windmill farm just outside Copenhagen harbour is the result of investments made by more than 8,500 people, and is believed to be the biggest windmill co-op in the world. Communities, whole islands indeed, united and set and met ambitious targets of independence from fossil fuels and inspired the rest of the country and the world, too, with new renewable energy solutions. Others bought farmland and turned it into more climate-friendly forests. Now, more than half of our electricity comes from renewable sources and green energy solutions is one of our biggest exports—in turn financing much of the welfare state.

As promising as Denmark's green transition has been, it's also painfully clear that we still have a long way to go. Our per capita emissions remain among the highest in the world. The same goes for our ecological footprint. Not only is a majority in the Danish parliament approving billions in subsidies to continued oil and gas extraction in the North Sea, but there is an unfortunate consensus to open up more licensing rounds for continued exploration. We have also seen catastrophic rises in the prices of electrical cars, which means that Denmark is in no way a leader in this field—rather the opposite. We have seen our current government cancelling one climate goal after another, and we have seen measures being passed that make pollution cheaper for big businesses and heavy emitters.

Thus, learning from the Danish/Scandinavian welfare state—a range of overlapping conditions and actions coming into play—would benefit real climate progress.

The effort and ability to capitalise on the growing pressure from organised forces from below, the making of new, unseen even, political alliances, a progressive network of businesses speaking up, the active use of democratic, legitimate actions such as strikes and civil disobedience, organisation at the workplace, the school, and public institutions—all together can create a mounting feeling among those in power, that the future is not theirs unless they show willingness to share their power and to act.

This might sound banal, but considering the need for a thorough overhaul of the organisation of our society and economy, we need to activate all the forces of society to put things in motion.

The public mobilisation we see in the streets of Denmark and all over Europe are the seeds that will set this movement in motion and capitalise on it politically. So, what can we, as political actors, do to help restore the pact between citizens and the political elite?

Restoring the pact: the Green New Deal and Alternativet

From my viewpoint, European Spring is the most prominent example of a serious attempt to restore the pact and join forces with a substantial political programme (including a Green New Deal) and with progressive policy targets based on an ambitious, solidary financial plan. From a national perspective, efforts have been focused on combining the features of a green, progressive movement with a party branch in parliament named Alternativet (The Alternative).

We were elected to parliament with the main task of addressing the climate crisis and the crisis of our democracy head on. We have since focused on transferring the philosophy behind the welfare state to broadly coordinated efforts that face the challenges of climate change. We are using a bottom-up approach with a crowd-sourced political programme and other novel ways of involving citizens in political processes.

Now this struggle needs to be taken to the European institutions so that together we can transform European politics and not only focus on national politics. In many ways, it's already happening. We are seeing efforts to democratise. Efforts to share influence and power. Efforts to tackle the climate crisis more directly. All I know is this: change can happen fast. Old systems, old habits, and old ways of life are on their way out.

Soon there will be no turning back. Just like when we built the welfare state from the ground up, just like when we set out on a path towards 100 per cent green transition, powered by renewable energy, and the will and the strength of communities—in much the same way, after decades of failed politics, Europe is getting ready to fight back.

If we succeed in making a green deal, we can restore the pact between citizens and the political elite for the sake of our climate and of our democracy. Only by uniting around shared efforts and common goals can we meet the challenges of a lifetime and create a better future for all.

A Sustainable Europe by Jeffrey D. Sachs

66 Winston Churchill once supposedly said, "You can always count on the Americans to do the right thing after they have tried everything else." Yet, maybe that witticism applies more aptly to Europe. After trying everything else—centuries of wars, empires, insurrections, revolutions, and civil strife—Europe finally tried a democratic union based on the principles of human rights and a mixed economy. In our Age of Sustainable Development, Europe's democracy and unity are more important than ever: sustainable development cannot succeed on the basis of right-wing nationalism. Indeed, very little can.

The world has entered the age of sustainable development, marked by the seventeen Sustainable Development Goals and the Paris Climate Agreement, not out of some burst of wisdom, but out of a last desperate gasp. For all of the libertarians who fantasise that the world is better than ever, the truth is that humanity is on the verge of destroying the ecosystems that keep us alive and the social fabric that holds our societies together. Yet, for all of the nationalists who would pull us apart, the solutions to the environmental and social threats are unity and directed investments of knowledge and capital, not division and, even less, social conflict.

Global capitalism is producing a riot of environmental catastrophes—global warming, species extinction, chemical pollution, water scarcity—and rising income and wealth inequality far faster than our political systems can adjust. The likes of Donald Trump, and his mirror images in Orbán, Salvini, and Le Pen are both symptoms of and cause for further disarray. They are symptoms because they epitomise the ignorance and ranting that blames our problems on the weak and poor rather than on our own excesses. They are causes because their policies and distractions take us exactly in the wrong direction to solutions.

The facts are plain. Europe is in the best position in the world to achieve sustainable development—if it chooses the right political course. Europe is rich, at least on average; technologically sophisticated; at peace; and blessed with institutions of social democracy (pensions, family support, universal health coverage, free higher education, and the like). These are a powerful basis for moving forward.

Yet the status quo will not suffice. Europe needs to increase its public and private investments in renewable energy, green buildings, electric vehicles, zero-emission industry, and sustainable agriculture. It needs to strengthen, not dismantle, its social protections. It needs to raise taxes on the rich, break monopolies, and end the stranglehold by corrupt banks and insidious tax havens.

Europe needs to promote innovation, not just in a few high-tech centres in Northern Europe, but throughout the entire European Union. Fortunately, Europe has the world's longest-lasting university network at the service of society. And Europe needs to establish its own security and foreign policy institutions so that it is not utterly beholden to the tottering US empire, but is instead the author of its own international relations with China, Russia, India, Latin America, and Africa.

Sustainable development requires solutions at the scale of the European Union, indeed of the whole world, not at the scale of local regions or individual nations. How will Europe decarbonise its energy system? By bringing Greek, Italian, Spanish, and, indeed, Moroccan solar energy to Germany and Scandinavia through long-distance high-voltage transmission. How will Europe convert to electric vehicles? Not through each country guessing when the transition from the internal combustion engine will occur, but through a concerted Union-wide strategy that makes Europe the world's first-mover in twenty-first century advanced technologies. How will Europe remain competitive with China and the US in the new information technologies? By ensuring that the EU takes the lead in e-governance, 5G, smart grids, and other sustainable technologies within reach.

How should Europe respond to the rise of China and Chinese initiatives such as Belt and Road? By being a unified and confident global leader that announces that Europe will join China, Japan, Korea, and India in a massive expansion of infrastructure across Eurasia—the home of nearly 70 per cent of humanity.

In short, Europe is facing existential choices. Will Europe stay democratic and united, or dissolve once again into fractious, petty, and, ultimately, dangerous national divisions? Will Europe choose sustainable development—the path to social inclusion and environmental sustainability—or continue the inertia of dirty air, degraded water, and disastrous climate change? DiEM25 is about a strong Europe, a sustainable Europe, a just Europe, and a united Europe. There is no other viable course. On the contrary, Europe's unity and leadership in sustainable development will not only ensure peace and prosperity within Europe, but will inspire the world to follow Europe's lead. **,,**

The European Far Right's Environmental Turn

Kate Aronoff

The Berlin-based youth wing of the far-right Alternative for Germany (AfD) is furious. In the lead-up to the May 2019 European elections, a race where climate change was many voters' top concern, the leadership of Germany's upstart party had doubled down on climate denial. The party grew modestly, garnering 10.8 per cent of the vote, but fared poorly compared to the Green Party's surge to second place there with over 20 per cent. In an open letter to party leadership, Young Alternative Berlin chair David Eckert urged higher ups to "refrain from the difficult to understand statement that mankind does not influence the climate", warning that the party risks losing touch with younger voters, and that climate issues move "more people than we thought".

They're right to worry. Three big stories have topped headlines about the 2019 European elections: that of a fortified but not altogether triumphant far right, an eroding center, and a 'green wave' that saw the European Greens claim a little over 9 per cent of MEP seats overall. These are currently countervailing forces. Parties aside, the Europeans concerned about the climate crisis tend to be progressives that don't peddle in reactionary nationalism. That may not, as young AfD members hope, be the case forever.

In many parts of the world, the main litmus test for gauging where a politician stands on climate change has been a deceptively simple and entirely apolitical question: "Do you believe in climate change or not?" Considering the scope and scale of the changes needed, it's a dangerously low bar. The picture abroad—where climate denial is relatively rare—is more complicated. With few exceptions, outright climate deniers of Donald Trump's ilk don't have much power outside the United States. The UK has harboured plenty of climate deniers in and outside of government, but even Tory governments have paid at least lip service to curbing emissions, as has most all of Europe's badly bruised center-right.

Until now, far-right parties in Europe have tended to question climate science as just another example of cosmopolitan groupthink, if they mentioned it at all. But some have begun to embrace the fact that climate is on European voters' minds. France's National Rally (RN)—recently rebranded under the leadership of Marine

Le Pen—unveiled a climate change policy platform in advance of the European election. "Borders are the environment's greatest ally," twenty-three-year-old RN spokesperson Jordan Bardella told a right-wing paper in April. "[I]t is through them that we will save the planet." Le Pen herself has argued that concern for the climate is inherently nationalist. Those who are nomadic, she said, "do not care about the environment; they have no homeland".

Among Le Pen's brain trust is essayist Hervé Juvin, who has contended that "the main threat we face now comes from the collapse of our environment", urging that it must become a central focus of European politics. Juvin's analysis has an anti-neoliberal spin. During a wide-ranging speech in Moldova in 2016, he name-checked Hungarian economist Karl Polanyi—a mainstay of social democratic thought—and noted the end of both the market society and "the liberal systems as we knew them", decrying greed and globalisation. Like Le Pen, he called for a nationalistic localism and a return of the commons for "the people of European Nations", whom he calls the "indigenous people, on our land, in our countries, with our traditions, our faith, our common goods we fought for so many times, and we are still able to fight for"—everyone else be damned.

Juvin has called for the creation of an Alliance for Life to "unite European Nations for survival", to assert that "Europe is the land of Europeans" and, among other things, pursue "no-tariff trade" only with countries that have committed to reaching net-zero emissions. It's not hard to see why Le Pen and Juvin get along. The RN and its predecessor, the Front National, have long advocated a strong welfare state—so long as it's defined strictly along nationalist and often openly ethno-nationalist boundaries.

This exclusionary logic has also infected some center-left parties. In Denmark, climate change is at the top of voters' minds, just above another top issue: immigration. Denmark's Social Democrats—running against the country's far-right People's Party in upcoming national elections—adopted a kind of green-tinged xenophobia, promising a 'sustainable future' alongside harsher immigration restrictions. Charismatic forty-one-year-old party leader Mette Frederiksen embraced legislation hardening rules around the official 'ghettos' housing predominantly Muslim migrants, including harsher sentencing for crimes committed within them. She has linked her stance on immigration to climate change: "Denmark and the world are facing a genuinely difficult situation. A new situation. Record numbers of refugees are on the move", she wrote. "Climate change will force more people to relocate. And add to that the fact that the population of Africa is expected to double by about 2050".

The left is talking about climate change too, and in thankfully less craven terms than the Danish Social Democrats. The continent's other socialist and social democratic parties are now greener than they've ever been. Labour in the UK and Spain's ruling Socialist Workers Party (PSOE) have each embraced versions of the Green New Deal, a framework also pushed in the European elections by Democracy in Europe Movement 2025 (DiEM25). In Spain the center-left moved left, and found success in recent national and European elections by melding a broad progressive vision that plans for decarbonisation. France's various left parties offered strong climate plans, but those efforts mostly failed to win over voters, who seem to have voted Green if it was climate concerns that brought them to the polls. If it's not gone entirely, the old productivist left—pushing for carbon-guzzling industrial expansion—has certainly lost some of its charm.

It's fortunate that young people in the places where the Greens have soared—the UK, Germany, and France—aren't generally a reactionary bunch. But support for far-right parties has risen among millennials and Gen Z-ers in countries where they've made an effort to reach younger generations. Austria's far-right Freedom Party is the most popular choice among voters under thirty. Le Pen made gains among millennials, and support among young voters for the similarly xenophobic League party in Italy has more than tripled since 2013. Several of those parties will send millennials to serve in the European Parliament, and young leaders like Jordan Bardella and Belgium's thirty-three-year-old Tom Van Grieken are injecting fresh blood into a resurgent hard right that's so far been mostly ambivalent about the climate. As climate change emerges as a priority issue across the continent, more parties could follow the lead of the RN and offer their own vision for how to deal with the climate threat. In Germany, Berlin's young AfD suggested the national outfit back a one-child policy in developing countries to "counter one of the greatest climate problems, overpopulation".

What the 2019 elections meant for the annals of the mostly symbolic European Parliament is less important than what they mean for future national elections, particularly on the heels of overwhelming right-wing victories in India and Australia, where parties ran largely on their duelling climate politics. Requiring stringent regulations and considerable state investment, it's hard to square any earnest plan for decarbonisation with dogmatic neoliberal nostrums around small government and the all-knowing planning prowess of the market's invisible hand. Many right-wing populists aren't strict neoliberals, though. They in some cases embrace robust social safety nets and protectionist trade policies, promising to defend welfare states for white Europeans against marauding outsiders. It's not that Europe's far-right parties have robust or remotely adequate plans for reaching net-zero emissions along the timeline science is demanding. But those who have considered the climate crisis do at least have a programme to offer: protection from the ravages of climate breakdown for white Europeans. The racist right traffics in fear—and rising temperatures offer plenty to be afraid of.

As climate impacts continue to ramp up, there's no reason to believe an international focus on it will automatically lend itself either to progressive or even democratic politics. In addition to those young people drifting right, weak showings for the left across Europe should cast some doubt on the idea that the next generation are fledgling, inevitable leftists. The Greens have for now capitalised on climate worries—and the momentum built in massive protests like Fridays for Future and Extinction Rebellion—though they've traditionally found their base among eco-conscious middle-class voters and been quieter on more traditional economic issues (they are sometimes derided as neoliberals with wind farms by some on the left for their role in governing coalitions). A Green vote is a vote for climate action, and a vote against the right, but those votes could travel elsewhere if that doesn't materialise.

That ecologically-minded parties have apparently muted the far right's surge is cause for hope, but the fact that the far right maintains healthy representation threatens to cement them as a settled feature of Europe's political landscape. However much they embrace climate rhetoric, no country run by the far right is going to decarbonise as fast as the moment demands, if at all—and may well sabotage the kind of cooperation needed to take on the problem at scale. What's just as troubling is that the roughly one degree Celsius of warming we're already on track to experience could play out in a world in which they carry influence, either directly or indirectly, as nervous centrists adopt xenophobic, exclusionary policies to avoid losing electoral ground.

The horror of climate change isn't in the intrinsic violence of hurricanes or heat waves, but in the ways societies choose to deal with and prepare for them. Calls for a Green New Deal promise not just to bring down emissions as quickly as possible, but to rewrite the social contract that will govern how we respond to climate change. Will we ensure those displaced by rising seas enjoy a dignified quality of life, or turn them away at our borders? Will we enforce cruelly rigid definitions of who belongs and who doesn't as climate change prompts what will likely be the largest mass migration in human history, or build a society strong enough to welcome newcomers with open arms and generous public services?

The climate crisis is the foundation on which the politics of the twenty-first century will be built. Claiming to believe in the science behind it doesn't carry any more rhetorical weight than claiming, proudly and defiantly, to believe in gravity. The xenophobic right is beginning to catch on to what an opportunity this crisis represents for them, and the potent political capital of promising to prevent the end of the world.

ABCDEFGHIJKLMNOPQRSTUVWXYZ

THERE IS

A MOMENT

A SYMBOLIC

BREAK

I DON'T THINK
THIS CRISIS IS GOING
TO END CAPITALISM
UNLESS WE DO
SOMETHING
ABOUT IT

An Ecological Europe by Tim Jackson

“ The title of a paper published some years ago now by one of my closest colleagues was "Rainforests Are a Long Way From Here". The paper reported on a study which explored the environmental concerns of disadvantaged people. The title was a direct quote from one of the respondents in the study. It struck a chord with me at the time, and it has remained with me all these years because it was such a powerful metaphor for the distance between the ecological challenges faced by the world—climate change, deforestation, the loss of biodiversity—and the concerns that shape the everyday lives of the poorest in society.

That message is as resonant today as it ever was. Rainforests are a long way from here. They're a long way from the neglected English communities who voted to leave the EU. A long way from the *gilet jaunes* protesting stealth taxation on the streets of France. A long way from the refugees arriving in their thousands along the southern and eastern borders of Europe. A long way from the lives of those who have taken them in. Talk to us about the limits of a finite planet, by all means. But our everyday reality right here and now is something vastly different. The streets are shabby, the shops are closing, the healthcare system is failing, and the environment is a wasteland frequented by the homeless and the dispossessed.

It's impossible to talk about a green transition without acknowledging these uncomfortable truths. A green transition must be a *just* transition. A just transition can only start from where people are. It must speak to the poorest in society, those least responsible for ecological destruction and most deserving of change. It must promise them something better. It must offer a life worth living. We'll make no progress against climate change without confronting the deep injustice still perpetuated by a hyper-financialised, neoliberal consumerism that has haunted the European project and undermined its sense of value.

But this is also where the promise lies. The challenge of averting climate catastrophe is a formidable one. Weaning the European economy from its addiction to fossil fuels in the space of a generation is far from trivial. Building the architecture and the infrastructure for a new, renewable, regenerative economy means transforming the role of financial markets. It means claiming back the very meaning of the word 'investment' from the grip of casino capitalism. Investment is not a bet laid down for the benefit of the few against the lives of the many and in defiance of the health of the planet. Investment is our commitment to the future. It is our pledge to support our children and their children. Investment is our commitment to renew and to regenerate society.

Fighting climate change, rebuilding financial stability, and confronting inequality all go hand in hand. Courageous policy and relentless innovation are essential. But the dividends will be substantial: better jobs, stronger communities, safer schools, healthier lives; the potential to repair our broken vision of the good life and to rebuild the values that once connected us to each other and to the planet.

Rainforests are a long way from here. Behind the disillusion lies a sense of longing, a fear of loss, a desire for reconnection. This longing is most clearly expressed in Europe today by a younger generation. It finds its most eloquent expression in the schoolchildren striking for climate action. It is echoed by the civil disobedience of Extinction Rebellion and the Occupy movement. But it is remembered, too, by those whose courage forged the vision from which Europe itself was born. It resides in all of us. It is the common foundation from which we can build a genuine and lasting prosperity.

For, at the end of the day, prosperity goes beyond material pleasures. It transcends material concerns. It resides in the quality of our lives and in the health and happiness of our families. It is present in the strength of our relationships and our trust in the community. It is evidenced by our satisfaction at work and our sense of shared meaning and purpose. It hangs on our potential to participate fully in the life of society.

Prosperity consists in our ability to flourish as human beings—within the ecological limits of a finite planet. The challenge for our society is to create the conditions under which this is possible. It is the most urgent task of our times. 99

Previous spread: *There Is a Moment* (left), *Unless We Do Something* (right)
Next spread: *Ας Αρχίζουμε Εκεί Που Μόλις Τέλειωσε* (left) & *"The Left Should Be About Minimizing Harm to Very Vulnerable People"* Yanis Varoufakis, 2018 (right)

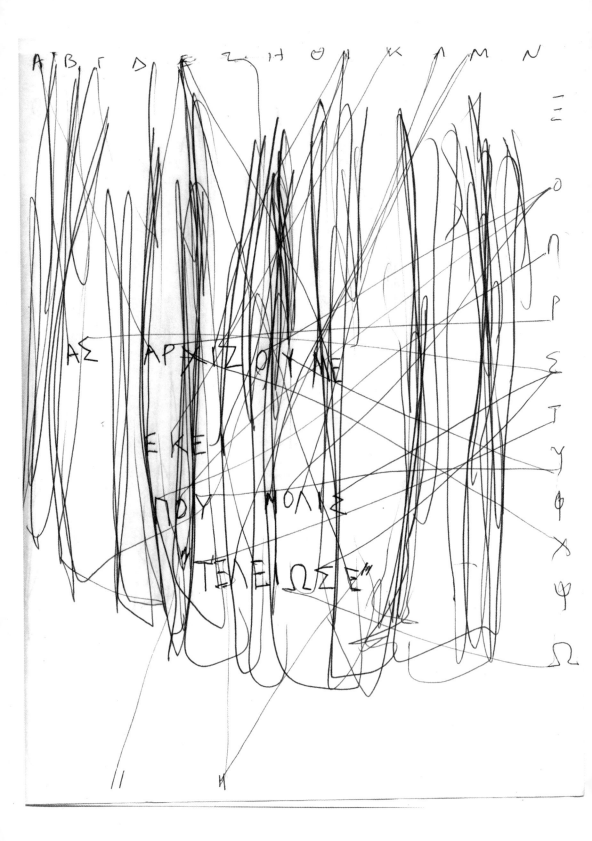

ΑΒΓΔΕΖΗΘΙΚΛΜΝ

Ξ
Ο
Π
Ρ
Σ
Τ
Υ
Φ
Χ
Ψ
Ω

ΑΣ ΑΡΧΙΖΟΥΛΕ

ΕΚΕΙ

ΠΟΥ ΜΟΛΙΣ

ΤΕΛΕΙΩΣΕ

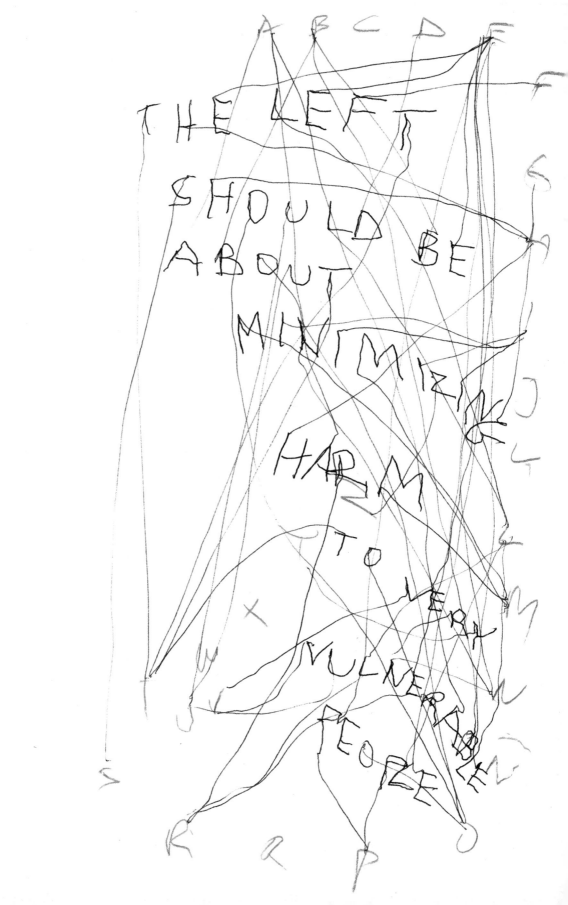

THE LEFT
SHOULD BE
ABOUT
MINIMIZING
HARM
TO VERY
VULNERABLE
PEOPLE

PART SEVEN

Refugees and Migration

Beyond the Familiar: A Third Emergent Migrant Subject

Saskia Sassen

There is a history in the making that has generated a new type of migrant subject, one not recognised in law. She is neither the typical immigrant in search of a better life for herself and family, nor is she a refugee escaping war and persecution. She is forced out of her land or town by new types of 'development' that get registered as a positive under current measures of economic development, such as GDP per capita growth.

These are modes of economic growth that destroy livelihoods, land, and water bodies: developing a mine, a plantation, a new luxury housing enclave; all of these, and more, get reported as 'growth'. Thus, the fact that these are often forced migrations, engendered by massive displacements, is rendered invisible by that other 'fact'—that we still measure any type of growth in terms of GDP per capita, without factoring in the resulting damage.

GDP per capita growth may have functioned reasonably well when there was a sense of endless bounty in nature—no matter the self-deception involved. But today it is clearly a highly problematic measure insofar as new types of economic growth in play have escalated our capacity to destroy vast stretches of land and water bodies.

Here I examine to what extent and in what ways these types of events fail to capture the conditions that result in migrations and are rarely mentioned in immigration research. The dominant *image* is still that of the migrant in search of a better life. But the dominant fact is increasingly the migrant expelled from her land by 'development'. She is caught in a trap that renders that condition of being expelled from land or home invisible.

One prominent factor has been the mix of disastrous development programmes that the IMF and the World Bank implemented in the 1980s and 1990s. Regardless of their good intentions, these programmes helped destroy many an emergent Global South economy. Several of the emigration regions I focus on in this text make this destructive inheritance visible. And yet, law and the rules by which the game is played do not account for the fact that the reported growth was the very cause of destruction.

What we need to do is unambiguously demonstrate that 'development projects' can be extremely destructive for small landholders and modest working- and middle-class enterprises, with emigration one of the very few options left to them.

Most of the poor in the world do not migrate

A fact that is often overlooked when analysing migration is that poverty is not a sufficient factor. If it were, there would be two billion migrants across the world. But the estimated number is at the very most 300 million. And even if the numbers of recognised 'refugees' have grown over the last decade, they are still lower than those of 'migrants'. Both of these designations fail to capture what is happening.

The numbers are relatively small given the escalating expulsion of people from their land and the proliferation of conflicts. Furthermore, most refugees do want to return to their lands and homes. So, both a large share of immigrants and most refugees are not necessarily driven by some abstract desire to leave home, but rather by extreme conditions that push them out. Finally, and too often overlooked by the Global North, is the reality that most migrants and refugees are from the Global South.

In the case of migrants, this suggests that there is a larger context within which migration flows occur; it is not simply an obsession with getting into a safe western country. What interests me is the larger context that remains largely under-analysed, partly because it is far more complicated than simply reporting on the numbers of bodies arriving at a shore. Additionally, our deeply rooted presumptions about the rest of the world make us automatically classify any non-western place as inherently dangerous and undesirable. And, yet, this is contested by the undeniable fact that the vast majority of the poor, and those of lower and middle classes, do not actually ever leave their place of birth. They stay in their rural or urban areas.

Another interesting and little-known fact is that key international development policies promoted by western governments have wound up pushing people out of their lands.[1] Among the major international development organisations shaping these policies are the IMF and the World Bank, organisations not necessarily focused on migration. European and US economic interests have also played a pivotal role in shaping these policies.[2]

These corporate actors should be seen as active generators of migrations and refugee flows—something rarely said or recognised in the debate about immigration in the Global North. It explains how a rapidly growing share of the less developed areas of the world ended up with destroyed habitats because of massive developments like mines, plantations, and water grabs on behalf of big corporations. Directly, and indirectly via their business interests, rich western states—and now also China—have been major players in the destruction of habitats far away from their own lands.[3]

I have long argued that we need to investigate the full cycle of events that explain some of these migrations.[4] As I have written elsewhere, many migration streams actually originate in Global North boardrooms when decisions are made to set up mines, plantations, and building projects in the Global South. And finally, the wars we have launched or supported in the Global South have also been key factors producing new migrant and refugee flows.

Why only a fraction of the poor in the world migrates

New migrations have long been of interest to me because they help us understand why a given flow starts.[5] They tell us something about the larger contexts that generate such flows. The migrant becomes an indicator that there are changes in the area where s/he comes from. This contrasts with a later stage in a flow when it becomes chain migration, which is much easier to explain than how and why a new flow emerges. Once chain migration sets in, it is typically the family that authorises one or another member to migrate for the good of the household. Chain migration has been the dominant mode in the west since the 1950s, as many of those migrations were by then in the second or third generation.

It is these routine migrations that have received most of the attention from immigration experts in the West. Far more difficult is to understand why a migration begins, since the vast majority of people across the world, including the poor, do not migrate.

A concern here is with rather distinct conditions that have led to significant migrations. The larger migrations coming out of Africa into Europe are a good and somewhat familiar example. The case of Africa makes visible the many ways in which western governments—especially from Europe and the United States—laid the ground for pushing local peoples into migration streams mostly for bare survival. The aim of investors and governments was to 'develop' Africa. The result was mostly an enabling of large foreign corporations to extract natural wealth and an enabling of the making of African elites—rather than genuine economic development.

My argument is that these negative outcomes lie at the origins of many African migration streams into Europe.

Migration as expulsion

The massive acquisitions of land by major corporations and governments for their own interests (from mining to growing crops) have contributed to the expulsion and destruction of small-holder agriculture, often enabled by well-intentioned but ill-conceived World Bank and IMF policies. Under these conditions, emigration is often a basic survival move rather than an aspiration to a better life.

But alongside these well-established migrations, we see novel flows that have emerged recently in Central America, Africa, and Asia. These are flows of desperate people. Among the better known cases are the new migration of unaccompanied minors from Central America—specifically, Honduras, Salvador, and Guatemala, all countries marked by extreme violence in rural and urban areas. The other is the expulsion of Rohingya from Myanmar—specifically, the recent expulsion of over 700,000 women, men, and children over three months in late 2017; this amounts to a whole new phase in their long-time persecution as Muslims in a majority Buddhist country.

Each of these types of flows points to a larger context marked mostly by extreme conditions. Factoring in how those conditions came about allows us to see at least some of the larger dynamics generating migration as an option for a better life or for bare survival. Each of these three very different flows emerges from situations larger than the internal decisions of households and larger than the ups and downs of national or local economies. The extreme and sharply delineated conditions from which they arise operate at diverse levels—ranging from individual needs to macro-level dynamics. And they do so with variable degrees of visibility.

Violence is one key vector explaining these migrations. But it is not the only one.

I add a second key vector, one insufficiently recognised: the fact that well over thirty years of international 'development' policies have left much land dead due to mining, land grabs, plantation agriculture, and more.[6] The most extreme case is Africa. The result was and continues to be the expulsion of whole communities from their rural habitats.

Insufficiently noted, and critical for my analysis, is the fact that much of this expulsion of rural people from their habitats gets registered as GDP per capita growth: they are replaced by large-scale modern agriculture and mining. Beyond the expulsion of millions of small holders, the types of large-scale modern 'developments' that replace them—mostly mining and plantations—exhaust the land and poison water bodies. Small holders know how to keep the land alive, but their production is rarely considered in measures of GDP per capita growth. Pushed out of their land across several decades, moving to the slums of large cities is increasingly the last option for the expelled. And, for those who could afford it, leaving their country for Europe and North America, the common destinations.

A massive loss of habitat

This multi-decade history of destructions of rural economies and expulsions dressed in the clothing of 'modernisation and development' has reached extreme levels today: vast stretches of land and water bodies are now dead due to mining, plantations, and water extraction by the likes of Nestlé. At least some of today's localised wars and conflicts in Africa, Latin America, and Asia arise out of such destruction and loss of habitat, with climate change further reducing livable land.

A mix of conditions—wars, dead land, and expulsions of smallholders from their modest economies in the name of 'development'—has produced a vast loss of life options for a growing number of people in more and more parts of the world. This, then, is not the migrant in search of a better life who hopes to send money to the family left behind. This is people in search of bare life.

Important to my analysis is the lack of recognition in law of this third kind of migrant, one evicted from her land to make room for a mine or a plantation. This migrant fits neither of the two established subjects in law: the refugee and the immigrant. She is a third subject invisible to the eye of the law because she is a refugee of what is registered as positive: certain modes of 'economic development'. Nor is there law that recognises the fact that much 'economic development' and wealth are based on land grabs from rural smallholders, destruction of land and water bodies by mining and plantations, and more. Migrants who lose their land or have their water supplies poisoned by nearby mines *are* refugees of such modes of economic development. There should be law that recognises them as such. But, for now, the basic interpretation is that those development modes are good for a country.

In brief, what I seek to make visible are the social and economic conditions that render this third subject invisible to existing law. And my hope is that there are legal scholars who might be interested in making this migrant subject visible in law: not simply as a persona, but as an outcome of development modes we—still—register as positive, no matter what they do to people, to land and water, and to the survival of the biosphere.

One question this generates is whether we can develop legal instruments that recognise this asymmetry between what (a) gets measured as a positive and thereby gains standing in the law and in governmental preferences, and (b) the invisible negatives it also generates, notably accelerated destruction of land and water, as well as failure to recognise the long-standing rights of smallholders to their land.

When 'development' only works for the few . . . and destroys the habitats of millions

Many of today's negative features in Global South countries (e.g. the sharp growth of poverty and the massive expulsions of smallholders from their land) originated partly in the development strategies launched by major international institutions and global firms in the 1980s and the 1990s. Mining and plantation agriculture are among the notable examples of a mode of development that is basically extractive, and leaves behind dead land and poisoned water. Further, by insisting on opening up these countries to imports, much of the international system has wound up enabling large multinational consumer enterprises to enter markets where once local producers and shops were key building blocks of local economies.

The outcome has been a significant destruction of local enterprises and local manufacturing. Opening up these fragile economies to global firms ready to supply all needs gradually reduced them to consumption economies. The extractive sector, mostly under the control of foreign firms, has grown in importance and has become an enabler, not of countrywide development but of the emergence of rich local elites.

A major factor in the late 1970s and early 1980s, rarely mentioned nowadays, was the push by the so-called 'transnational banks' to sell debt to less developed countries[7]. Two clarifications are necessary here. One is that the rise of OPEC (Oil Producing Export Countries) in the 1970s brought with it a vast concentration of money in the oil-producing countries. Instead of 'storing' this money in their countries, the major Arab oil producers decided to work with western banks to 'grow' that money.

That was a time when the many diverse financial instruments available today to multiply the value of cash did not yet exist. Selling debt for an interest rate was the way to gain a quick profit. African governments, especially, were pressured or persuaded to buy such loans—which meant taking on debt. And eventually many, if not most, of these governments wound up paying a very high price for those seemingly cheap loans: local government elites got rich but the economic development of these countries ceased being of interest to their governments and elites.[8]

For much of the 1980s and onwards, indebted poor countries were asked to pay a share of their export earnings toward debt service. This share stood at about 20 per cent, which is far higher than that asked in other cases of country indebtedness. For instance, in 1953, the Allies cancelled 80 per cent of Germany's war debt and insisted on only 3 to 5 per cent of export earnings for debt service. And they asked only 8 per cent from Central European countries in the 1990s when these exited the communist sphere. But the debt service burdens on today's poor countries have wound up being extreme.

It does suggest that the aim regarding Germany and, later, Central Europe, was reincorporation into the capitalist world economy of the time.

In contrast, the aim vis-à-vis the Global South countries in the 1980s and 1990s was more akin to a disciplining of, and extracting from, those countries, rather than enabling their development. One key example was the forced acceptance of loans and restructuring programmes from the international system. Such measures enabled large extractive firms (e.g. mining and plantations) and consumer multinationals to enter these economies on very profitable terms. After twenty years of this regime, the evidence showed little, if any, contribution to the basic components for healthy development. The discipline of debt service payments was given strong priority, while neglect or indifference ruled over basic infrastructure, hospitals, schools, and other people-oriented development goals.

In conclusion

The primacy of this extractive logic became a mechanism for systemic transformation that went well beyond debt service payment. It included the devastation of large sectors of traditional economies, small-scale manufacturing, the destruction of a good part of the national bourgeoisie and petty bourgeoisie, the sharp impoverishment of the population, and, in many cases, the impoverishment and thereby corruptibility of the state even as quite a few individuals in the government and private sector accumulated wealth.

By the early noughts, the rapid growth in the debt of mostly poor countries led global regulatory institutions to implement the so-called 'structural adjustment' programmes. Key to this project were, and are, the International Monetary Fund (IMF) and the World Bank, and, eventually, the World Trade Organisation.

*   *   *

These have shaped the evolution of much of the Global South over the past several decades. Debt servicing was the instrument for this disciplining: it weakened the governments of those countries by forcing them to use growing shares of national revenue for interest payments on their debts rather than for economic development.[83] Further, it made them susceptible to signing unfavourable deals with global firms in extractive industries rather than furthering mass manufacturing and local commerce by national firms.

These arrangements did little to promote the development of manufacturing and commerce, two sectors that could have generated a modest, but effective, middle class. A major outcome has been emigration—not as a result of the search for a better life, but fuelled by the expulsion of people from their land by 'development'.

Notes

1   See also for some of the early pioneering work, notably Andre Gunder Frank, *Sociology of Development and Underdevelopment of Sociology* (Stockholm: Zenit, 1969); Anibal Quijano, "Coloniality of Power, Eurocentrism, and Latin America," *Nepantla: Views from South* 1.3 (2000): 533-580; William I. Robinson, *Global Capitalism and the Crisis of Humanity* (New York: Cambridge University Press, 2014).

2   I have written about this in *Expulsions: Complexity and Brutality in the Global Economy* (Cambridge, MA: Harvard University Press/Belknap, 2014) and "A Massive Loss of Habitat: New Drivers for Migration," *Sociology of Development* 2.2 (2016): 204-233.

3   I develop these issues in great detail elsewhere. See Sassen, "Interactions of the Technical and the Social: Digital Formations of the Powerful and the Powerless," *Information, Communication & Society* (London: Routledge, 2012); 2014, Ibid.; 2016.

4   Saskia Sassen, *The Mobility of Labour and Capital. A Study in International Investment and Labour Flow* (Cambridge: Cambridge University Press, 1988).

5   My work on migration has long focused on that larger context within which a new flow takes off. A key proposition in my work on the subject is that migrations happen *inside* systems, but these systems are not countries: they are the larger operational space within which the powerful countries of an epoch pursue their aims. Examples are the British Empire, the Pax Americana, and such. Today we have multiple specialised systems in play: e.g., high finance has constructed systems that connect the major financial centres across the world in very specific ways, including infrastructures and helpful laws.

6   I develop this at great length in Sassen, 2016, op. cit., and in Sassen, *A Third Emergent Migrant Subject Unrecognised in Law: Refugees from Development*, The T.M.C. Asser Lecture in Palais de la Paix, The Hague, 2018.

7   See Sassen, 1988, op. cit.

8   For a full analysis of how this extraordinarily destructive modus operandi came about, see Sassen 1988, Ibid.; see also Sassen 2016, op. cit.

DiEM25 Policy Paper on Refugees and Migration

Edited by David Adler

DiEM25 is an internationalist movement that stems from democratic and humanist traditions. These values guide our approach to the issue of forced migration and shape our policies to address it.

As a Union, we have committed ourselves to the Universal Declaration of Human Rights, as well as to the EU Charter of Fundamental Rights, and the Geneva Convention. Respecting these international commitments, DiEM25 stands for (1) hosting refugees and migrants, (2) guaranteeing them equal rights, (3) playing an active role in fighting causes of flight, and (4) supporting other countries and communities who host migrants.

We acknowledge both our current and historical roles in contributing to flows of forced migration, through:

- Our colonial history, which to this day has dire ramifications on the developing world;
- Ongoing postcolonial exploitation of resources that leaves many communities impoverished;
- Unfair trade relations imposed by the EU and its member states, hindering development and destroying local markets;
- Supporting dictators that served western interests, while pushing aside democratic aspirations of many populations around the world;
- Ongoing manufacturing and export of weapons which are persistently used in armed conflicts and war;
- The role and responsibility of the member states of the European Union in creating climate change and environmental disasters which are hitting poorer countries harder across the globe.

The consequences of these actions are finally knocking at our door, and we intend to take full responsibility. Justice, not charity, is our guiding principle.

As such, any EU policy should overcome the distinction between economic migrant and refugee. This fake distinction leads to discriminatory policies that deprive many of agency, condemning them to underemployment and exploitation. The economic factor—i.e. conditions in which people are no longer able to provide for themselves and their families—is often the one that leaves families with no choice but to migrate. It is also a form of forced migration.

Intensifying armed conflicts in the Middle East, human rights violations, environmental disasters, and bleak economic prospects in various regions of Africa and Asia will continue to drive refugee and migration patterns for years to come. Meanwhile, Europe is in denial. The people leaving behind poverty, famine, and war to arrive in Europe—one part of the planet mostly spared these high levels of violence—are met with barbed wire, soldiers, cold seas, and a political establishment hopelessly unwilling to untangle its cynical processes.

The term 'refugee crisis' therefore proposes a false narrative. Our current European crisis is defined by unemployment, under-investment, and cuts to social services for all—not the arrival of newcomers to our continent. Therefore, we intend to fight the narrative of scapegoatism, which blames newcomers for our self-made problems, and say no to the poisonous politics of fear.

But our policy framework also extends beyond the European Union—to support the rights, needs, and everyday realities of other host countries. While shedding our legal and moral duties to house many of the newcomers, we placed them in regions with unstable political and economic circumstances. This includes regions in the periphery of Europe that have suffered cruelly under austerity measures, and to a greater extent in communities affected by the EU's implementation of 'hotspot systems'.

Within a more progressive policy framework, host communities would not have to suffer greater economic strain as a result of migration flows. On the contrary, they should be supported against all forms of economic strain.

Therefore, a migration policy framework is incomplete unless it includes policy proposals to induce positive change in the socioeconomic realities of people worldwide. Local economic development is essential to DiEM25's approach, and fundamental to overcoming destructive competition between different groups of people.

This not only applies to competition between newcomers and residents, but also between people from different member states. In migration, as in so many other areas, the EU will democratise, or it will disintegrate.

Towards a policy of coexistence

Our outline argument addresses short-term and long-term policies in order (1) to bring an end to the humanitarian crisis on European soil, (2) to stop the dying at sea, and (3) to address the social, economic, and political developments of a demographically changing society.

Complex migratory fluxes require a migration policy that goes well beyond static regulatory policy. A modern immigration policy that can keep pace with the dynamics of migration and integration must be transparent, adaptive, and interconnected with other policy areas. Under the section of long-term strategies, we outline policies to address root causes of migration, from trade deals to climate change, to the Common Agricultural Policy of the European Union.

Short-term measures

Measures could be taken tomorrow in order to improve the situation of forced migrants on the ground and to mitigate the ongoing humanitarian crisis. We simply urge the European Union and its member states to implement and comply with the existing treaties and humanitarian policies already in place. This would already have a tremendous effect on the ongoing situation. It would save lives tomorrow.

In detail, complying with existing law and obligations means:

1. Respecting the internationally protected fundamental right of non-refoulement by member states of the EU, as well as countries in partnership or collaboration with the Union (e.g. in the case of Libya). Non-refoulement is a fundamental principle of international law that forbids a country receiving asylum seekers from returning them to a country in which they would probably be in danger of persecution based on race, religion, nationality, membership of a particular social group or political opinion.

2. Recognising the inadmissibility of asylum applications based on the concept of a 'safe third country' or 'first country of asylum'. These cannot be imposed, as this means the de facto end of the right to asylum in the EU.

3. Immediately implementing legal and safe passage. Every person forcefully migrating should be able to access safe and legal routes to reach protection, but millions of people fleeing conflict are today trapped in harm's way with no safe escape. Children are stuffed in suffocating lorries, families climb into sinking boats, desperate adults try to scale barbed wire fences. All in pursuit of something to which they already have a legal right, whether it is to reach family members or to be resettled away from conflict.

Every person forced into migrating has the right to access safe and legal routes to a place where they can lead a dignified life, and the European Union and its member states have the obligation to fully comply with the European Convention on Human Rights, the Geneva Convention, and Article 18 of the European Charter of Fundamental Rights.

We, therefore, propose the implementation of these elements:

- Establishing free and legal paths for migration

Implementation of EU-visas and EU-asylum for forced migrants issued in their countries of transit.

- Launching a European Search and Rescue Operation to replace Frontex

Frontex, rather than being cancelled, should be renamed and redefined, and the manpower and resources of the agency used for the launch of a European Search and Rescue Operation in the Mediterranean, which should exceed the capacity of Italy's Mare Nostrum Operation and ensure the full responsibility of state actors dedicated to fulfilling their mandate and saving lives at sea. NGOs have been trying to fill the gap in SAR missions for years and face harsh criminalisation of and constraints on their life-saving missions.

Only through the commitment of the EU to saving lives at sea as a top priority can the current situation be coordinated in a humanitarian spirit and meet its obligations under maritime law. Any military or coastguard intervention in the Mediterranean aimed at targeting the boats of smugglers shipping migrants has to be stopped, as the best fight against smugglers is the opening up of safe passages. The example of the Greek-Turkish border shows that the increased border surveillance supported by Frontex has only led migrants to take more dangerous routes.

- Stopping the externalisation of EU borders and migration controls

The externalisation of migration controls includes extraterritorial state actions to prevent migrants from entering legal jurisdictions or the territories of destination countries by making them legally inadmissible. These can include direct interdiction and preventive policies as well as more indirect actions, such as the provision of support for, or assistance to, security or migration management practices in and by third countries.

Over time, the phenomenon has expanded to regularly include the systematic enlistment of third countries in preventing migrants, including asylum seekers, from entering destination states. States enlisted in the prevention of onward movement of forced migrants are either encouraged to prevent them from entering their own territories or encouraged to apprehend and return them (e.g. EU-Turkey Deal, EU-Sudan Agreement, EU-Libya Cooperation).

We, therefore, call for the immediate suspension of any externalisation of EU borders and migration controls, reject the Global Approach to Migration and Mobility (GAMM), and call on the EU to fully comply with its own responsibility for people asking for protection on European territory, by developing a sustainable long-term strategy based on human rights in consultation with civil society and experts.

- Stopping the criminalisation of humanitarian aid

Fishermen and firefighters, for example, who rescue forced migrants should be rewarded instead of being punished. Ships from private search and rescue NGOs, such as the *Iuventa*, should be released immediately to ensure more life-saving boats along the route.

- Enforcing family reunification

States have an obligation to protect the family under international and European law. On the basis of non-discrimination, holders of subsidiary protection (unrecognised refugees) must have access to the same rights as recognised refugees. To fully respect the right to family reunification, states should apply a broader definition of family members to include non-nuclear families.

Another major obstacle is the significant amount of documentation member states can require of those submitting an application. States must consider the special status of beneficiaries of international protection and the difficulties they have faced in reaching safety. UNHCR could play a role in organising the necessary documentation.

- Allowing for resettlement of asylum seekers across the EU

The decision of a starting point for each newcomer needs to factor in both the preferences of the newcomers as well as the capacities of host communities and the opportunities they offer. Regard for the preferences of asylum seekers based on family ties, extended community links, language and cultural ties, past studies or professional experience on one hand need to be harmonised with the practical requirements of the local context.

European countries shall facilitate mutual recognition of positive asylum decisions and the swift transfer of protection statuses within the EU. This would not only facilitate the relocation and resettlement procedures but also contribute to the non-discriminatory application of the principle of freedom of movement, so that asylum seekers can settle where they have better integration prospects, such as family members, language, etc.

- Improving reception facilities

The current situation tries to make reception facilities more flexible by lowering standards across the Union. Instead of streamlining European reception facilities down to the lowest common denominator, new legislation must introduce minimum standards of quality to be implemented directly across all member states.

The large-scale creation of housing for all people with limited resources is the only answer to the social housing needs of host communities and forced migrants alike, if we want to foster contact and prevent divisions.

Detention centres must be closed down. We need equal and full access of forced migrants to mental and physical healthcare not connected to the administrative burden.

- Implementing fast and fair asylum proceedings

The legal safeguards of asylum seekers must be respected. The bureaucratic separation of asylum claims and asylum applications has to be abolished.

Increased funding for national child protection systems and building mechanisms to protect the rights of children and unaccompanied minors across borders is urgent to ensure that children have access to guardians, education, and family reunification.

Gender-sensitive reform of EU asylum procedures includes introducing gender reasons for political asylum and refugee status and introducing gender-specific training for staff.

Gender-segregated sleeping and sanitation facilities must be established as common standard in the EU. Female interviewers, translators, and interpreters should be provided for all women seeking protection in Europe, as well as trauma counselling for persons who have experienced gender-based violence; childcare during screening and asylum interviews; legal assistance for women on their right to lodge an asylum claim, independently of their spouse, and to have a legal status independent to that of their spouse.

Forced migrants should have access to legal support from the day they enter the EU. They should have access to language courses from the beginning without any distinction between forced migrants with 'good' or 'bad' prospects of remaining, as well as access to education and vocational training and recognition of foreign degrees and vocational diplomas.

- Providing access and right to work

Recognising the principle of unrestricted access to work must be followed by a range of other measures: speeding up the process of recognition of foreign degrees and vocational diplomas, offering professional trainings, language courses that are tailored for labour market integration, strengthening intercultural competencies of the labour agencies staff as well as the employees in companies, dismantling the legal and administrative obstacles for getting work permissions for asylum seekers.

Economic growth cannot be fostered by subordinating migrant work within national economies. All migrant workers must be entitled to the same rights, benefits, and protection as domestic workers. It is not migrants who are dumping wages, but a system that keeps them as illegal, unskilled, and in constant threat of deportation. Increasing public investments to include asylum seekers in the system of minimum wages should be promoted on the EU level and on the level of member states as well.

There should be no exceptions to minimum wages. But at the same time we have to take into account that there is a necessity of some type of bridging mechanism for forced migrants entering the labour market. The positive integrative effects of work are beyond doubt. On the one hand we have to enable short-term apprenticeships and internships and, on the other, we need regulations that prevent the exploitation of that bridging mechanism for getting around the minimum wage and recruiting cheap labour forces.

- Strengthening the capacities of local authorities

Migration funds should be accessible to local authorities directly—not only to national governments. Cities and NGOs should be able to make a pledge to take over responsibility for forced migrants from governments. The involvement and support of local authorities and communities should include the creation of incentives for these communities to apply for receiving forced migrants, thereby creating a positive cycle for resettlement.

- Strengthening the local economic development of host communities

The EU's migration failures are compounded by its economic policy. As a consequence, host communities in the peripheries, austerity regions, hotspots, and poorer communities in surplus regions are being negatively affected by migration flows. These communities are reacting by moving politically to the right, with some tilting towards xenophobia.

A migration policy framework must consider the rights and needs of host communities just as much as those of the migrants. No successful inclusion or integration process is possible otherwise. Integration is a two-sided process.

While a reasonable relocation and resettlement policy will certainly mitigate the pressure on host communities, a migration policy framework is not complete unless it is integrated in a holistic policy framework. The economic reform envisaged in DiEM25's New Deal and green transition is fundamental to the economic development of host communities.

- Endorsing participation

An ongoing and inclusive participatory process is essential to create the necessary measures to achieve all the goals we set in our policy framework. This includes all stakeholders: host communities, local authorities, civil society organisations, and migrants themselves. These are the real experts on the ground who understand the needs, the challenges in their localities, and are best in place to create and implement solutions.

For democracy to be put into practice, an institutional infrastructure has to be in place and clear communication channels between the different stakeholders must exist. Local authorities that are operationally and financially strengthened must be able to implement changes in direct consultation with all other stakeholders.

DiEM25 proposes the implementation of institutional changes that facilitate the practice of direct democracy at the local level and empowers stakeholders as political players.

- Supporting the social solidarity grassroots economy

Especially in communities which host forced migrants, what we call the 'social solidarity grassroots economy' needs to be supported with funding, facilitation, and full-time, qualified support and coordination—in short, financially, institutionally, and operationally.

European civil society and citizens have been inspirational in their reaction to migration flows in terms of offering support on numerous levels to the newcomers.

Such local and decentralised actions, both by locals and the newcomers themselves, are key to the inclusion process. This includes all sorts of social enterprises (such as social cooperatives, associations, NGOs, clubs, etc.), as well as informal voluntary initiatives. The relation between this sector of the economy and the public sector should be one of mutual support and cooperation.

Long-term measures

Speaking of long-term demands doesn't mean we don't have to deal with them right away. Rather, these are topics that will take some time because they involve other institutions, regulations, and policy areas, as well as deeper structural change. We must, therefore, begin to tackle them now, precisely because it will take some time to resolve them.

• Repeal the failed Dublin system

We need a system based on justice in Europe, one that condemns neither a country nor the migrants living in it on the basis of their geographical location within the Union. The current Dublin system prevents the development of any such system.

• Abolish the hotspot system

The implementation of different generations of Dublin systems made it necessary to establish a so-called 'hotspot' system to cope with the influx of people, especially on the islands of Greece and Italy.

As clearly shown by the initial assessments of this hotspot system, its implementation is not in line with EU asylum law and legal standards. Moreover, fundamental rights of forced migrants are not respected. Many newly arrived migrants have been trapped in prolonged detention without access to asylum, have not received the right information, or have been swiftly returned as a result of the hotspots approach.

The hotspots have certainly not helped relieve the pressure from Italy and Greece, as was their stated objective: instead, they have led to an increase in the number of asylum applicants waiting in Italy and Greece, consolidating the challenges and shortcomings already inherent in the Dublin system. Moreover, as it was the responsibility of the member states to implement and run the hotspots, pressure on the member states led directly to the implementation of the EU-Turkey deal and the recent cooperation with the LCG.

• Consider people migrating to the EU as citizens

Forced migrants should be guaranteed civil, social, and political rights, irrespective of their reason for migration, their country of origin, and their socioeconomic status. This includes the provision of democratic rights for everyone based on residence, not on citizenship.

Transparency in Budget and Funds related to migration and refugee policy is crucial. If states receive money, it should be obligatory to check if actions are in line with the EU Charter of Fundamental Rights.

The same is true of the UN International Convention on the Protection of the Rights of all Migrant Workers and Members of their Families (ICMW). Driven by their political interests, none of the EU member states has adopted the Convention, because its ratification would oblige countries to provide the same rights to all migrants regardless of their status. DiEM25 recognises the importance of taking the vulnerability of migrant workers into account and seeking cooperation between the member states and the Union to facilitate the adoption of the Convention.

Tackling the underlying sources of migration

Forced migration stems from many overlapping factors, which culminate in war and conflict, poverty, and famine. Scarcity and conflict will only be made worse by ongoing climate change. As a principle, such global challenges should be resolved in the most inclusive manner possible through the use of multilateral diplomacy.

To meet the systemic causes of flight and forced migration we propose:

- Non-interventionist politics

Stop European participation in wars and military conflict: DiEM25 calls on all European governments to end their direct and indirect involvement in wars and military conflicts. Instead, non-violent conflict resolution between communities needs to be promoted and actively supported by the EU. Efforts must be redoubled to democratise and revive international forums such as the United Nations to bring warring parties together to resolve conflicts non-violently.

- EU-wide curb on weapon exports

Regulation of the arms trade must be strictly in accordance with EU laws that state there cannot be any exports of arms to countries that violate human rights or are engaged in conflict. Weapons exports need to be supervised centrally within the EU and involve all subsidiaries of European corporations based outside EU territory.

- Sustainable policies against global climate change

Since climate change increasingly will be a main cause for forced migration, we need to link this aspect of our migration policy closely to DiEM25's Green Transition policy. In principle, those historically and currently responsible for CO_2 emissions need to be held accountable to fund climate mitigation and adaptation.

- Stopping the exploitation of mineral resources

Corporations based in the EU can no longer externalise the costs of environmental degradation to host communities, but must compensate local communities instead. Furthermore, the use of large-scale agriculture and the advance of deforestation must be re-evaluated in the light of the 2030 Sustainable Development Agenda and the Paris Agreement on climate change.

- International development

The lack of economic development is another root cause of forced migration and needs to be addressed in the reform of economic relations at state and corporate level.

Recognising that there is a net drain of resources from so-called 'developing' countries towards so-called 'developed' countries, DiEM25 proposes to work in cooperation with receiving countries, ensuring that those countries are able to develop economically. Concretely, this entails the renegotiation of bilateral trade agreements and support and cooperation with regards to country-by-country reporting, the closing of tax havens, and cessation of opaque financial flows. This would ensure that profits are taxed where they are made.

European nations should create a substantial international development fund, with a clear emphasis that such development aid is decoupled from any conditionality based on migration control indicators.

The EU should make efforts to enable transnational institutions like the International Court of Justice to hold transnational corporations accountable for their actions. The EU must support initiatives such as UN negotiations on a binding treaty on transnational companies and other corporate actors with respect to human rights.

- International trade and bilateral and multilateral trade agreements

In the years since in the context of the Doha Development Round, so-called 'developing' countries have been completely sidelined by the global powers.

In Africa, in negotiations with the EU, countries have been forced to eliminate tariffs on up to 90 per cent of their trade because no clear rules exist to protect them. At the same time, they kept their side of the bargain and enforced the protection of intellectual property rights, effectively restricting their access to affordable medicine, such as HIV treatment.

True and lasting solutions to global economic problems can only come when the model of global competition between countries becomes one of genuine cooperation.

DiEM25 is calling for a trade system which understands trade as a means to achieving broader social, environmental, and development goals. Multilateral trade negotiations need fundamental reform, to be based on fair negotiations, not power play, so that developing countries have an equal place at the table.

The disastrous impacts of liberalisation on the global financial and food systems are clear to see. Yet, supporters of the so-called 'free trade system' continue to push for deep and fast liberalisation across bilateral and multilateral trade agreements and praise the current trading system as the answer to problems as wide-ranging as human rights abuses, climate change, and food security.

Free trade agreements and development aid programmes run by the EU and its member states should be replaced by fair trade agreements: Europe should renegotiate those agreements for mutual benefit.

- Revision of the Common Agricultural Policy of the EU

We must also look at the policies within Europe that harm countries beyond its borders. DiEM25 is calling to revise the policy of exporting subsidised agricultural products from the EU to African and Asian countries, which destroy the livelihoods of small-scale farmers worldwide.

We should also find ways to differentiate between pure speculation with food and real, sustainable investment in the cultivation, processing, and distribution of food, checking the influence of financial investors on price developments in commodities. The absolute number of futures contracts available for speculation, for example, must be limited, which means that effective limits on positions for trading with commodity futures must be defined and imposed.

- European citizenship

We demand European citizenship for every forced migrant who comes to the EU and wishes to stay. DiEM25's vision is a transnational Europe, and the possibility for migrants to acquire European citizenship should be a step towards this direction.

- Education

It is the duty of general education to create a broad awareness of the European history of colonialism up to the present day. Education policies and the media should not promote the trope of EU society as white, Christian, homogeneous, and static, but give space to historically grounded accounts of it. For example, compulsory school curricula should give appropriate space to the importance that non-Christian cultures have had on the cultural, economic, and political development of Europe.

- Changing the public discourse on migration

The movement of people is an integral part of human history and needs to be seen as a chance for thinking beyond limited, homogenous national frameworks and identity politics, which spread the fear of foreigners and strangers.

We insist on an end to narratives that victimise forced migrants by representing them as passive victims in need of charity, or as criminals who are also stealing our jobs. Instead, forced migrants should be seen as political agents putting into question the injustices and dysfunctionality of the global geopolitical order. Like noxious distinctions between the deserving and undeserving poor, differentiation between 'deserving' and 'undeserving' migrants needs to be rejected, as well as the discourse that differentiates between the citizens, migrants, and refugees.

These divisions legitimise selectiveness in granting the right to protection and asylum and enable the continuation of a narrative in which freedom of movement is seen as a privilege of a small well-off minority, rather than a right and a possibility available to every person regardless of their national background and their social status.

Elimination of the xenophobic, racist, and Eurocentric narrative of 'us' v. 'them' needs to be pursued on a level of public, as well as political, discourse. Getting closer to the vision of one world and free movement for all requires the rejection of the 'clash of cultures' narrative, and the valuing of difference and diversity, underpinned by cultural and religious dialogue.

We have a vision: a world without borders

DiEM25 believes in the dismantling of all barriers—in Europe and around the world—that prevent the movement of people. At the same time, we will fight for policies that allow people to remain safely and prosperously in their place of origin, or wherever they may choose to settle.

No one chooses where and into which circumstances they are born, and no one should be held responsible for their position in this birth lottery. We believe in the fundamental right to decide where to go, and when.

All human beings are born free and equal in dignity and rights. DiEM25 believes it is our duty to respect them.

[*This first green paper on refugees and migration was drafted by Jakob Mohr, Marie Naass, and Sebastian Eis, with comments and feedback from citizens throughout Europe and other parts of the world.*]

Hope Is Out There: Let Them In

Jakob Mohr

The rise of the right has little to do with immigrants: it's the EU's own crisis. Entire parties have been built on the fear that waves of immigrants would sweep away civilisation. But the reason why such fearmongering translates into electoral success all over Europe has less to do with the arrival of refugees and more with the power-lessness we Europeans feel to address the social, economic, and political crises shaping our lives.

Once we endorse this analysis, it becomes clear that the antidote to the right is not to give in to their xenophobic demand to restrict migration, but to propose a radical reform of the EU's architecture and the regime of austerity that drives poverty and insecurity among Europe's working families.

But we must also know how to argue our case without fuelling the populist narrative of naive, do-gooder leftists: to find constructive ways to build popular support for more open borders. Public mobilisations against racism in cities like Barcelona, Berlin, or Milan show real potential for grassroots-led change, but we need a concrete plan for the day after the demonstration.

Seebrücke

Seebrücke, a movement born in Germany, shows us one way forward. This movement developed in response to repression against the NGOs active in sea rescue. When, in 2017, the ships of SeaWatch, Doctors without Borders, and SOS Mediterranée were seized and ship crews incarcerated, a demonstration in Berlin swelled from 200 people to 10,000-strong. They marched together for the creation of safe harbours for all those rescued at sea, while initiating decentralised actions all over Germany. They continue to do so today under the name Seebrücke.

One key element of Seebrücke's success is that participants carry life vests and other orange articles as their symbol, but no further emblems of existing parties or organisations. When you support Seebrücke, you leave your flag at home, your party credentials, your membership badge, or whatever allegiance, and you stand for what humanity demands from our continent and from each of us.

Since Seebrücke's initiation, local groups—no longer differentiated by dogmatic differences or electoral affiliations—have been able to act effectively at the municipal level. The common objective is to pressure city halls into declaring their cities and towns as 'safe harbours', meaning that they will welcome those rescued in the Mediterranean. Until now, they have managed to win statements of support from thirty-five cities and are spreading the movement across the continent.

The idea of uniting for a common goal—without the need for egos and the spotlight—resounds strongly with what DiEM25 has set out to do. Acting on the local level to create *rebel cities* is DiEM25's strategy of constructive disobedience put into practice. It is through these acts of rebellion that we can, as citizens, demand Europe's democratic transformation—and inspire millions of other Europeans to do the same.

Welcoming Europe

Another sign for hope is the European Citizens' Initiative (ECI) known as "We are a Welcoming Europe", a collection of over 170 civil society organisations articulating the demand for more humane migration policy. While the ECI itself failed to reach the required million signatures, we can learn a great deal from their mobilisation efforts.

In the alliance for the ECI, groups working in the field of migration came from different backgrounds to formulate common demands for our continent—an achievement in the fragmented field of migration. This unifying effect was one of the first successes of the campaign that demanded the strengthening of humanitarian corridors for refugees, the abolition of laws "punish[ing] volunteers and civil society organisations for offering humanitarian help or shelter for refugees", and protection for the victims of abuse and exploitation.

The campaign also shifted the organisations' attention to the citizens at the European level: advocacy groups traditionally focused towards EU institutions or national governments went from direct contact with lawmakers to convincing European citizens to support a petition with key demands. Other groups representing refugees in the local setting broadened their field of vision to act together with similar groups across Europe. And a third group of organisations concerned with migration politics on a national level also had reason to look at the European level.

Despite only collecting 120,000 signatures, the ECI did influence the European Commission to investigate the criminalisation of those involved in sea rescue and solidarity with refugees, who are currently prosecuted across Europe under the Facilitation of Illegal Immigration Directive (2002/90/EC). While there is a clause stating that member states can choose not to prosecute when help was given for humanitarian reasons, there are no guidelines when to do so and proceedings are at member states' discretion. The reopening of the discussion on the 'Facilitation Guideline' is meanwhile a sign of hope for the ship crews and others suffering repression from right-wing governments that seek to criminalise them.

The European Parliament also reacted. They are providing more funds for communities supporting the sponsorship of humanitarian visas, and they have asked the European Commission to table legislation for humanitarian visas that can be requested in EU member states and embassies across the globe. Even if the hope of getting such a law through the European Council is slight—any law must be agreed unanimously, and the council features prominent xenophobes like Viktor Orbán, Sebastian Kurz, and Matteo Salvini—the campaign's clear and widespread influence justifies the attempt.

In this sense, the organisers and participants of the Welcoming Europe alliance are drawing positive conclusions: they have vowed to work together to coordinate actions to improve the situation for forced migrants in each of the EU member states and across the globe. Their attention to citizens as the main agents of change when confronted with political stagnation at the top resonates with DiEM25's approach.

Seeds awaiting a European Spring

For DiEM25, the best way of supporting Seebrücke or the Welcoming Europe alliance is to use our networks across Europe and beyond to help spread the message and unify the call for a European response to save migrants dying at sea and protect them from abuse and exploitation around the world.

As a young European movement, our members have been active in the jungle of Calais, at the border crossing of Ventimiglia, in Barcelona and Madrid, in the hotspots of Lesbos, and the streets of Budapest and elsewhere.

It is here where we unite with so many more to struggle for local improvements. The call of our movement is, like the campaign for a Welcoming Europe, to spread these interconnections and out of all the local struggles build a sum that is greater than its parts.

Combining the local with the European level, the potential for a network of disobedient cities becomes particularly vibrant: cities that take actions, often against the laws of their own nations, and exchange support and best practice in managing the costs of moving against the political current. These rebel cities show that a different politics is possible, and they build visible pressure to change policies and spur the European Union into action.

While DiEM25 aims to empower newcomers and improve their living conditions, we remain conscious that such action alone will not ease global migratory pressure and tackle forced migration. Nonetheless, it is our duty to take action in our home environment and, in doing so, to overcome the sense of powerlessness and desperation that predominate when we are confronted with such overwhelming challenges.

It is from the experience of collective mobilisation that we can draw strength to take the next step. And it is by connecting our local struggles and fusing them into pan-European action that we can present a credible, constructive, and realistic solution. In the process, the seeds of Seebrücke and Welcoming Europe can blossom into a European Spring.

Global Compact: Europe's Migration Tourniquet Comes Full Circle

Preethi Nallu

The Rescue

June 2014, *San Giorgio*, Central Mediterranean

"My baby!" A woman being led up from a dinghy screamed, catching her breath as if she were swallowing water, her agony an unsettling contrast to the rest of the group filing out of the vessel with remarkable composure. They were shell-shocked.

Throwing quizzical glances at each other, the coastguard staff tried to find a lone child in the boat. We were aboard the Italian military ship *San Giorgio*, witnessing a rescue at sea, part of Mare Nostrum, the largest ever Search and Rescue (SAR) operation in the European Union.

The rest of the mother's words poured out in Arabic. "It is no more", she tried to explain in vain.

"We will find it. Where was it last?" The marine looked around haplessly for the only translator on board, his English layered with an Italian inflection.

"Here", the woman said, holding on to her swollen belly that was still in a state of shock over the sudden emptying of its womb. She had given birth to a stillborn amid seventy other people in a dinghy—without a moment of dignified privacy to mourn.

We were skirting Libyan territory. Malta was visible as a blob. Over those summer and autumn months, the largest recorded number of asylum seekers would arrive to Italy by sea: around 170,000. The fleet would be tested to its full capacity.

Few things can make one feel more disingenuous than trying to console a mother stricken over the loss of her child. "At least you survived. It will be okay. Please be patient." Platitudes for an inconsolable parent.

Over the next hours, the transfer of the human crush of 1,171 men, women, and children from the seas into the basement of the ship followed a rhythmic sequence: a few minutes of silence as the boats entered, followed by frantic cries, and then a quick calm as they queued up to be registered.

Syria, Afghanistan, Eritrea, Pakistan, Bangladesh, Gambia, Somalia, Nigeria, Mali, Benin, Ghana, Senegal, Guinea Bissau, Ivory Coast, Morocco, Tunis, Sudan—the list was exhaustive. They had been rescued from ten separate boats, all unseaworthy.

"I don't think I have come across people from the Central African Republic and Kashmir in the same group before", the marine jotting down the names and nationalities remarked. He would continue the process, without a break, for the next twelve hours.

Conflict, threats against individual safety, political and religious persecution, general lack of protection, destitution, economic servitude, false promises of work by criminal gangs—myriad motivations prompted their journeys.

After the 'most vulnerable' were registered, the male refugees (a clear majority of this group) were then allowed to disembark, faces lined with fatigue and many with the awkward stubble of adolescent years. The men travelling without families would be the last to get asylum, or any help from humanitarian organisations, but be the first labelled a threat to European security.

In the following years, over the course of reporting on the Mediterranean crossings and beyond, I have watched European governments distort the most natural and age-old phenomenon—migration—into an anomaly. A regressive narrative of the 'encroaching migrants' has coloured the discourse in Europe. Generations of Europeans with migrant backgrounds and newer migrants making their homes on the continent feel tested, while those who came through irregular means are warehoused, their futures held hostage for years on end. All negative experiences related to these communities are amplified by anti-migration politicians and media and seized as exemplary.

A majority of legal migrants in most EU countries have proven year after year to be model citizens yielding tangible returns to the host economies. Refugees, when resettled and given the means to recover, have started contributing in kind. Yet, the evidence is sidelined. European politics have been taken over by a blanket anti-migration rhetoric that deliberately misrepresents both migrants and refugees, portraying the former as job-stealers, and the latter as an unalleviated economic burden.

The following timeline of accounts from my migration coverage since that rescue episode, when the first major Mediterranean crossings surfaced in the media, is an attempt to trace the flashpoints of the *migration tourniquet* that Europe has employed to stymie these human flows. This tourniquet, formed by border closures and deterrence policies, is now unravelling.

A day and a half after that rescue in the summer of 2014, the ship docked at the harbour of Taranto in southern Italy, where everyone disembarked and were put on buses transporting them to reception centres that served as resting stops. Freshened up, they moved on—upwards to Milan—and from there to European countries in the north and the west. Very few would remain in Italy, most of them African nationals who lacked the resources to move on, or felt that they might not be 'favoured' elsewhere. Over 80 per cent of those arriving in Italy in 2014 qualified for asylum, according to the UN.

Most arrivals were not stamped by the Italian authorities, so that they could evade deportation back to Italy under the Dublin Agreement. This was Italy's middle finger to its northern neighbours in Europe for not helping it cope with the increasing numbers of arrivals. The neighbours would respond by closing their borders and, later, with the EU-Turkey deal.

While Italy's Mare Nostrum raised the ire of anti-immigration parties across the continent, Greece silently acquiesced with EU policies, privileging border protection over safe passage.

Greece as the new epicentre

"Before August 2013, we had arrested 6,000 people here. After erecting the fence, by next January it fell to forty-five", explained the chief of border patrol. His statistics were meant to prove the effectiveness of the 12-kilometer-long fence.

Fast-forward to autumn 2015, the Greece-Turkey border at the Evros Crossing: When I visited them in autumn 2014, the border police at Evros had their reasons to be proud. They had successfully thwarted 'illegal crossings' at that infamous border between Greece and Turkey, a decade-long access point for migration. But what my patrolman conveniently failed to mention was that the fortification that would expand in the coming period induced a palpable collateral surge. During the same period, the number of arrivals by sea increased by a startling 450 per cent.

In the absence of options by land, individuals and families started taking to the turbulent waves of the Aegean Sea. Although in much smaller numbers, this continues to the time of writing. Malek and his family were a case in point. From a Yezidi minority community in the Kurdish part of Syria, Malek fled with his wife and three children, travelling from Damascus to Istanbul with the aim of eventually reaching Greece.

Their options oscillated between being sent back to a refugee camp in Turkey or embarking on the dubious journey. As with most who pay large amounts—often their life savings—they were completely trapped at the mercy of the smuggler. So Malek decided to get on the boat with his family. As he recounted the journey in vivid detail, his eyes lowered with shame over the hysteria to which he had 'subjected' them. "I did not realise that I was taking them from one death to another. I could have been responsible for killing the very loved ones who are closest to me."

That Greek authorities push back migrants was no secret. Speaking with asylum seekers in Athens quickly revealed that it was common practice and one that was increasing with the continuing arrivals. But pushbacks, especially at sea, are difficult to corroborate, given that the obligations of individual states are limited to their waters and that the boundaries are difficult to ascertain. Such gross violations at sea continue to this day but without as much scrutiny as in 'pre-crisis' years.

Despite the official policy of not turning back anyone in distress at sea or those who have entered Greek territory, Malek claimed the Greek coastguard repeatedly pushed them back to the Turkish coast, sometimes coming menacingly close to the dinghy. Next time, the family tried by land and failed again. After six attempts and relentless persistence, they finally entered Greece by sea. Like Malek's family, refugees trying to reach Europe find that the more they try, the harder it becomes to stop trying.

The alarming state of detention centres and prolonged waiting periods for asylum seekers in Greece revealed a deliberate policy of dissuading 'irregular migrants' from coming. This continued until the holding centres could no longer cope with the pace of arrivals.

Stories similar to Malek's proliferated over the next season.

Italy halted Mare Nostrum by 2015, while Libya suspended visas to Syrians. The transit country's terrain became increasingly inhospitable, as the country mired in conflict faced its own displacement crisis. Meanwhile, the Syrian conflict also escalated and more refugees fled, desperate to find new routes to Europe.

By the end of 2015, one million migrants and refugees, a majority Syrians, followed by Afghans, entered Europe—collectively billed as the European Migration Crisis. Over 850,000 of them entered Greece by sea. Those arriving on the Greek islands were barely processed before they were allowed to board the ferries to Athens. Most travelled towards Austria, Germany, France, and Scandinavian countries in hopes of better treatment. In reaction, Germany temporarily suspended the Dublin Agreement, opening its doors for asylum. Over 890,000 asylum seekers entered the country in 2015 alone. A majority of other EU countries responded with alarm, shuttering their borders.

One in, one out: the zero-sum game of the EU-Turkey deal

In the following months, EU leaders would serenade Turkey, luring the government with renewed talks of membership and generous financial support for taking in more refugees. Under the EU-Turkey deal, Europe would return all those arriving in Greece from Turkey after 20 March 2016, and relocate one Syrian refugee directly from Turkey for every Syrian sent back. In turn, Turkey would patrol its borders around the clock to prevent irregular arrivals reaching Greece.

Those who arrived after this agreement came into effect, and others who could not leave Greece because of the closed border with Macedonia, became indefinitely stranded.

Fast-forward to summer 2016, Lesbos island, Greece: "The children are trapped under the boat!" The faint cries for help that Ramy Qudmany heard, as he started to swim towards the Greek shore, echo in his ears from time to time.

The 23-year-old from Syria arrived in Lesbos after the EU-Turkey deal came into effect. The fishing trawler that he shared with a dozen others succumbed in the turbulent 6-kilometer stretch between Lesbos and Turkey. When the boat overturned, some of the passengers were trapped underneath, including a little girl, also from Syria. He dived in and managed to bring her to the surface. As he towed them to safety, he realised he was holding a lifeless body. Still, he held onto her. The child is buried in one of the cemeteries created for people who died at sea.

Qudmany and a few others were rescued by a Greek boat that was scouring the coast, looking for distress calls. He then proceeded to one of the reception centres. Despite being in need of legitimate asylum, not to mention psycho-social support for his accumulated trauma—losing family members to conflict, fleeing home, and surviving the deaths at sea—he was now stuck in a reception centre with little visibility over his asylum case. Last time I checked on him in 2017, the computer science graduate was still in Lesbos, which has become a repository for refugees.

Such repositories are expanding in European cities—from Paris to Athens, with squats and tented communities resembling informal refugee settlements. Much of this is the outcome of political inertia from European leaders who had promised to tackle the 'crisis', following the EU-Turkey deal. As member states repeatedly fail to find common ground in distributing the 'burden' of taking in refugees, EASO—the *Common* European Asylum System—has become somewhat of a misnomer.

The deal did indeed reduce migration flows over 2017 and 2018. But, very few asylum seekers have been sent back to Turkey from Europe. They remain in limbo. Similarly, very few Syrian refugees have been relocated to European countries, so far. The 'one in, one out' part of the agreement has failed and the deal itself will collapse as soon as Turkish conditions change, prompting the entry of many of the more than 2.5 million refugees that are in Turkey.

Throughout 2016, as arrivals from Turkey trickled in, yet another negative side effect emerged. Families and individuals started to take to the Balkan route that promptly gained notoriety for the inhumane tactics of its border police and the cunning of its human traffickers.

The treacherous Balkan route

"I am waiting to play the game, to cross this last border to Europe", 11-year-old Abuzar told me. He appeared resolute, despite being on his own. The 'game' is a codeword that smugglers and refugees use when referring to clandestine border crossings between the Balkan countries.

Fast-forward to winter 2017, Belgrade Train Station, Serbia: I found Abuzar among 1,500 men and boys that were biding time behind Belgrade's main railway station while waiting to reach northern Europe. Many had rerouted since the closure of Greece's borders with Macedonia and Turkey. As commuters entered and exited the station, asylum seekers wrapped in layers of blankets walked in and out of adjacent warehouses which had once stored farming tools and animals, now derelict and without heat or insulation.

Over those frigid winter days, Belgrade, which experienced its share of strife during the 1990s Balkan conflicts, appeared a perfect case study of social dissociation—a condition where people can ignore perturbing sights, even when they occur in front of their eyes. Despite sleeping rough and wandering the streets, children like Abuzar were hidden in plain sight to the locals passing through.

The boys in the warehouses could have sought shelter at the local reception centres, but most were determined to reach countries like France and Sweden. Abuzar believed that the Serbian centres would eventually turn into closed detention and that he would be deported to Bulgaria, where the border police had already beaten him up and robbed him of everything, including his only change of warm clothes.

The ripple effect of border closures meant that these refugees, mostly from Afghanistan, were being 'ping-ponged' between different Balkan states, and unwittingly ended up in Serbia, a non-EU country.

Having hiked all the way from his home in Baghlan province, Afghanistan, and through Baluchistan, Iran, Turkey, Bulgaria, and Serbia—Abuzar was determined to press on. He had come too far to turn back. His family had forked out their life savings in hope that he would bring this back in kind.

"Once I cross this last border, I will reach Europe and then be able to bring my family", he told me. The boy bore the weight of being the oldest son in his family on his shoulders as he made his decisions. The next day, he crossed the border to Croatia and disappeared. He remains missing.

In 2016, about 100,000 other children were reported missing in the Balkans. The same year, the highest number of children died in Afghanistan, compared to the previous decade's annual death tolls.

Reclassified as a 'country at conflict' by NATO and its allies, Afghanistan is one of the longest displacement crises in the world and a major source of asylum seekers in Europe. The Afghan conflict is far from over. In fact, it has taken a more tumultuous turn, with increasingly complex bombings and suicide attacks in urban centres forcing civilians to flee.

The source of the wound: Afghanistan

"You cannot possibly help every child in that crowd. I have seen the number of working children in this city mushroom over the years as the war continued and institutions collapsed", the Afghan social worker explained, ushering me into the backseat of a taxi.

Remaining gentle with the children as she shooed away their prying hands, a silent consternation lined her face. Dozens of young hands and faces were thrust against all four windows of our vehicle, pleading for 'spare change'.

Fast-forward to autumn 2017, Kabul, Afghanistan: very few acts induce as much self-loathing as walking away from desperate children. I had been visiting Kabul's sprawling neighbourhoods and it was in the market of an impoverished suburb that despair, masked as panic, got the better of me. Surrounded by the group of boys and girls that had gathered like a maelstrom within the blink of an eye, the bazaar was imploding with abject poverty, government neglect, and malaise. These disparate neighbourhoods surrounding the centre of Kabul were saturated with people that had been repeatedly displaced.

Amid the unceasing hostilities in Afghanistan, the growing demographic classified as Internally Displaced Persons (IDPs) is the most vulnerable, but also the least protected by the humanitarian community and the Afghan government.

A pragmatic and humane European migration policy would address the social, economic, and political realities inside countries like Afghanistan and understand the root causes of displacement, to prevent the cycle from repeating. Instead, the European approach continues to be one of constricting the source of the wound by tightening the tourniquet—i.e. more border closures, less resettlement, and, in some cases, even returns.

Those prematurely returned, particularly in Afghanistan's case, end up in IDP settlements inside the country, suffering yet another round of displacement. Faced with more dismal conditions than before, many get back onto the migration trail to Europe. In newer conflicts like Syria, some refugees are returning 'spontaneously'—in other words, without any UN assistance—from neighbouring countries. A vast majority do not want to go back, and when they do, it is simply because the push away from the host countries, due to prolonged limbo, lack of livelihood, and insufficient education, is stronger than the pull towards their homes.

A growing threat of internal displacement

"This medication is supposed to reduce my anxiety, this one is for the headaches I get when stressed, and these are for my children as they have persistent colds because of the dampness in the camps", Mahmoud said, listing the medicine he was purchasing as he prepared to move back to his hometown in Syria.

Fast-forward to June 2018, Masnaa border crossing (with Syria), Lebanon: the 26-year-old has suffered constant nightmares and was diagnosed with severe trauma due to losing his father. After five years in Lebanon and no semblance of stability, he returned to Syria last June with his wife and two children.

As he coddled his newborn (not registered in Syria or Lebanon, therefore stateless), he paced back and forth, anxiously. It was a sultry summer morning and beads of sweat lined his face as he awaited the vehicle that would transport him and his family across the border to Syria. A handful of other families sat by the road, some stacking their belongings into large trucks and others with scant essentials packed into plastic bags. After several years of being away, Mahmoud's return home felt unceremonious.

He had been forced to choose between the lesser of the two evils—a dismal existence in Lebanon as a stranger, or return to a familiar home, but with several uncertainties. Eight years into the Syrian conflict, "I would rather die in dignity at home than suffer this slow death in Lebanon"—has become a slogan among the displaced. UN agencies were estimating that 250,000 refugees may return to Syria in 2019, while about 6.2 million were already displaced within its borders.

The EU has been evading the Syrian returns issue, instead calling for 'political solutions' to end the conflict. Speaking about returns, reintegration, and reconstruction in such abstract terms is a mere political charade and downright obscene when millions are still awaiting basic services. In parallel, wealthy countries like Denmark are unilaterally deciding to send back Syrian refugees this year, prodding other anti-migrant governments to follow suit. Meanwhile, a vast majority of those who have entered Europe in the past years remain suspended in purgatory, yet invisible to the 'citizens'. Latest EU statements are far removed from stagnant realities, and doused in cognitive dissonance.

Is the European migration crisis over?

Over recent months, the EU Commission launched an audacious public relations campaign declaring "Europe's migration crisis is over".

Fast-forward to early 2019, the European Parliament, Brussels: countries on the other side of the Mediterranean, especially neighbours to Syria who are hosting millions of refugees, often ridicule the European use of the term 'crisis'.

So, what constitutes a crisis? The capacity of the hosts to respond, or their willingness to do so? Or is it the failure of foreign interventions in countries at conflict and 'liberalisation' policies in recovering economies and the dearth of legal migration channels which, together, prompted these human flows in the first place?

For every asylum application that was accepted in the EU in 2019, two were rejected—a pace that ought to enthuse Italian and Danish governments. But despite years of reduced refugee arrivals to the EU and only a fraction of the promised refugees resettled, the rallying cries for stopping the 'influxes' continue unabated. Anti-migration rhetoric has become the lowest common denominator for right wing populist politics in many of the twenty-eight member states.

To transform shortsighted prevention tactics into long-term protection of those in need what is needed is a crisis of conscience among the governments that have evaded their individual responsibilities, followed by collective introspection as a united Europe. The real power to change this status quo and to open humanitarian corridors is ultimately vested in the political will of individual European countries and their citizens. If the EU still holds meaning as the gatekeeper of Europe's liberal order, it must lead by reforming its own migration and asylum policies before mandating member countries.

Awakening from these years of slumber will require concerted, conscientious efforts to move the asylum seekers through the supposedly functioning EASO system. Their futures can no longer be suspended in stasis. We are already inexcusably late.

There have been some suggestions in the right direction among European policy circles, for instance, 'controlled centres' that would determine the asylum eligibility of applicants. But European leaders are at loggerheads over the premise and it is unclear whether these centres will allow freedom of movement, or constitute a new form of detention.

On the international front, European governments have committed to support the recovery of refugees in neighbouring countries. While supporting and stabilising the sources of the outflows is key, the funding has often only led to temporary respite, but little in the way of long-term recovery. This is largely because refugee camps and settlements, whether in the Bekaa or the outskirts of Athens, have become indefinite holding cells. As a result, more and more refugees avoid camps and centres. Instead, they seek smugglers to move forward, or return to their unstable communities. If these places actually aided them in their transition, irregular migration would subside.

The more Europe lags in taking concrete steps, the more they embolden global smuggling rings that have proliferated over the changing seasons of migration. From local middlemen who manipulate impressionable people into making arduous migration choices, to the lower echelons of border patrol that turn a blind eye to crossing migrants in lieu of bribes, to the highest levels of government authorities that rely on these security forces—the rings are intertwined and embedded in the migration landscape. And the former flashpoints are re-emerging.

The tide turns back to the central Mediterranean

Retracing Europe's migration tourniquet, we find ourselves back in the central Mediterranean, where the Strait of Gibraltar experienced a tenfold increase in arrivals in 2018, becoming the latest flashpoint.

Fast-forward to 2019, Strait of Gibraltar, Spain: with border management as its *raison d'être*, Operation Sophia that currently patrols the waters between Libya and Italy makes Mare Nostrum appear legendary. Militarising the Mediterranean has clearly failed to dismantle smuggling networks.

While the mission rescued 50,000 people last year, outsourcing border patrol by supposedly training the Libyan coastguard and navy dominates its mandate. Awaiting a renewed mission, EU officials admitted that dismantling the smuggling networks while working with Libyan naval authorities is an unlikely brief, as the country's various public outfits are intertwined with the smugglers. In some cases, those rescued by Sophia described their smugglers as men in official Libyan uniforms.

While the arrival numbers are manageable at the time of writing, a change in political realities in the Maghreb could unleash a new tide. If the ongoing protests in Algeria were to escalate, several armed groups might fill the political vacuum in the Mediterranean country which neighbours Libya and the Sahel, both riddled with internal strife. The ensuing conflict and displacement would unleash a new wave of migration towards southern Europe. The migration tourniquet is coming full circle. The start and end points are becoming one.

On 29 March 2019, EU member states collectively decided that Operation Sophia would be extended for another 6 months, but without a maritime presence. In other words, search and rescue missions to save those in distress at sea will halt.

We, Refugees

Lyndsey Stonebridge

What kind of people can watch a boatload of people drown in the Mediterranean with pleasure? George Orwell had an answer to that question back in 1948. At the beginning of *Nineteen Eighty-Four*, Winston Smith records his last trip to the movies in his diary—"a ship of refugees being bombed somewhere in the Mediterranean. Audience much amused . . ." Orwell thought that people amused by dead refugees were totalitarian subjects, gorged on nationalism, inhuman. Not like us, then. Not us in Europe, with its much-treasured democratic institutions and human rights. Not us in the United States that once mistook Orwell's anti-totalitarianism for its own. Not us in Australia, with our sharp memories of penal colonies and death by water.

Everyone remembers the rats in *Nineteen Eighty-Four*, but until recently few have had cause to recall the sinking ship. Only the thugs of social and mainstream media promote violence towards refugees and migrants, but elsewhere the assumption that refugees are a 'humanitarian problem' to be dealt with by the securely 'citizened' has settled, largely unchallenged, into public discourse.

Other people are 'our' crises, goes the moral grammar of current political debates about migrants and refugees. If this is a pretty pathetic ethical response to human misery, it is also a cover-up for what is really at stake when people cross the borders not just of nations, but of wealth and privilege.

Undoing meaning

What we are talking about when we talk of refugee or migrant crises is, in reality, a global crisis of moral and political citizenship which can no longer disguise or contain the inequalities of our world. "Emigration", wrote John Berger, "does not only involve leaving behind, crossing water, living amongst strangers, but, also, undoing the very meaning of the world." The world is undone not just for the person who moves, but for everyone.

We've been here before. In fact, we've been undoing the meanings of world citizenship pretty consistently since at least the middle of the last century. "Everywhere, the word 'exile', which once had an undertone of almost sacred awe, now provokes the idea of something simultaneously suspicious and unfortunate", wrote the political philosopher Hannah Arendt, then a refugee herself, in June 1944.

Exiles stopped being awesome once people started identifying themselves, and their core sense of being, with the nation. Placeless people came at best to be pitied and at worst feared and reviled because they reminded the citizens of nation states just how precarious these identities in fact were. This situation became murderous in the 1930s and 1940s when ethno-nationalism overtook the legal functions of European states which then, casually, brutally, 'de-citizened' millions. Colonialism had already established mass population movements as a means of economic and political control. Now, Arendt wrote, casual racist dehumanisation and the habits of treating people as human cargo 'boomeranged' back to the West.

It was at this moment, she also thought, that human rights were exposed for the frail fiction they'd always been for much of the world. The natural rights of men and citizens had been declared in Europe and the US in the eighteenth century. But the placeless people of the twentieth century had a new message: once you were stripped of political citizenship, once you were 'merely human', you had no rights at all. Refugees were not calling for human rights after the war, Arendt pointed out. What they wanted was a community to be at home in again, somewhere to be a citizen, somewhere they could share in making meaning, not simply be pitied. "The passport", wrote Bertolt Brecht "is the most noble part of the human being."

Cleft stick

The big new international human rights regimes that came after the war tried to fix this. In 1948, the Universal Declaration of Human Rights gave everyone the right to nationality and to 'seek and enjoy' asylum. The 1951 Convention on Refugees followed. These were good and largely well-intentioned innovations which have helped push back some of the worst abuses, and kept the idea of asylum alive as a concept.

But as the current pullbacks of refugees and migrants to Libya in the Mediterranean show, for every human rights lawyer putting international law to work, there's a small army of bureaucrats and politicians making sure that whilst European countries can still be seen to talk the talk when it comes to human rights, it's still refugees who get to walk the walk.

From the start, UN declarations and conventions were caught in a cleft stick. The self-determination of nation states was assumed, not unreasonably, to be the best protection for human rights. The problem was what happened when those states went—or were forced—to the bad. Refugee rights were supposed to scoop up those then left to the capricious hospitality of other nations. But, in reality, those safety nets were sewn together with cultural memes of European victims escaping fascism and communist persecution; non-Europeans were, and still are, assumed to be the passive victims of war, state formation and failure, and revolution—objects of humanitarian pity, not subjects of international human rights. By the 1950s, a pattern had been set. Haphazard humanitarianism caught up in political power-plays is largely what is left of human rights for millions of refugees today.

Global exploitation

Another refugee writer who was sceptical about human rights in the 1940s was the philosopher and mystic Simone Weil, who died in exile in the UK in 1943. Weil didn't think human rights would put an end to human suffering because they were too tethered to the history of nationalism, colonialism, and capitalist expansionism out of which they were born. Rights were simply another trade, this time in human virtue. The new human rights might have brushed off some of their earlier sovereign grandeur, but they fatally missed the true source of the misery of modern placeless-ness. "We must put an end to the terrible uprootedness which European colonial models always produce even under their least cruel methods", she wrote in her last book, *The Need for Roots*.

If Simone Weil is a thinker for our time, it is because she understood that refugees and migrants were not a random 'humanitarian problem', but the victims of—and the vanguard against—the global exploitation of millions.

Deciding how to share

When Winston Smith wrote about the drowning and dying refugees in his diary in *Nineteen Eighty-Four*, it did something to him. He began to discover something like his humanity. He began to resist. Orwell didn't simply mean us to understand that if you don't want to be a totalitarian or a fascist you need to be responsive to other people's suffering. Like Arendt and Weil, he understood that human vulnerability was a thing we share and that politics was how we decide how to share it. It is a mistake to confuse our capacity for humanitarian pity with the harder work of being with other people in the world. Different kinds of solidarity are called for, now, seventy years later, more than ever.

Anyone can become a refugee. It just takes a push across a border, or a creation of a new one across what was once your home. It just takes someone more powerful than you to want something that you have—your land, your water—or even something that you do not want, a new industry, regime, or country. "What is a border? . . . My whole life has been impacted by this concept of the border", Behrouz Boochani has written from his prison in Manus Island.

Boochani's suffering is his own, but the concept of the border impacts the lives of us all. If those lucky enough to be citizens want to stop more people drowning or living out their lives in squalid camps, they need to recognise, and confront, the causes of everybody's exile from a common world.

The Temptation of Left Nationalism

By David Adler

In May 2016, at a *Die Linke* party conference in Magdeburg, *Torte für Menschenfeinde* (Pies for Misanthropes) struck again. Sneaking up the side of the conference hall, a member of the anti-fascist organisation threw a piece of cake at Sahra Wagenknecht, a prominent *Die Linke* member in the Bundestag. It was a direct hit: Wagenknecht's face was covered in chocolate frosting, a streak of whipped cream extending from ear to ear.

Torte für Menschenfeinde targeted Wagenknecht for her stance against an open border policy for Germany. In 2015, she challenged Chancellor Angela Merkel's decision to receive over one million refugees, arguing that Germany should cap refugee entry and deport those who abuse German 'hospitality'. The cake attack isolated Wagenknecht in her party, which had otherwise pledged support for Merkel's policy.

But within two years, Sahra Wagenknecht's views on migration had gone mainstream—in Germany, as across Europe. In September 2018, Wagenknecht launched *Aufstehen* (Get Up), a political movement that combined left-wing economic policy with exclusionary social protections. The movement garnered 170,000 members before year's end.

"I am tired of surrendering the streets to the Pegida and the Alternative for Germany", Wagenknecht said at the launch. Onstage, she was joined by allies in Germany's Green Party and the Social Democratic Party. "As many followers of the political left as possible should join," several Social Democratic politicians wrote in a joint statement.

In launching *Aufstehen,* Wagenknecht joined a new vanguard of left politics in Europe. In France, Jean-Luc Mélenchon leads *La France Insoumise*, a left movement that has been highly critical of mass migration. "I've never been in favour of freedom of arrival", Mélenchon has said, claiming that migrants "steal the bread" of French workers.

Meanwhile, the UK Labour Party has expressed deep scepticism about open borders, both under the leadership of Jeremy Corbyn and after. "We are not wedded to freedom of movement for EU citizens as a point of principle," Corbyn said, committing his party to "reasonable management" based on "our economic needs".

The rise of these left nationalist leaders marks a momentous turn against free movement in Europe, where it has long been taken for granted as a basic right of citizenship. Forget the *Communist Manifesto*'s refrain that "the working men have no country": the left nationalists take a radically different view. Free movement is, to quote Wagenknecht, "the opposite of what is left-wing": it encourages exploitation, erodes community, and denies popular sovereignty. To advocate open borders is to oppose the interests of the working class.

In other words, these movements are not only challenging migration policy in Europe. In the process, they are redefining the boundaries of left politics—in a dangerous, and inopportune, direction.

Over the next few decades, global migration is set to accelerate: by 2100, one million migrants will be applying to enter the European Union each year. Right-wing populists have already begun their assault on migrants, from Matteo Salvini's call for "mass cleansing" to Viktor Orbán call to send recent arrivals "back to Africa".

As left nationalist movements charge ahead in the polls, many have been left wondering who will challenge their pessimistic view of migration and fight for the right to free movement.

* * *

In April 1870, from his house on Haverstock Hill, Karl Marx wrote a letter to two German migrants in New York City, imploring them to "pay particular attention" to what he called 'the Irish question'. "I have come to the conclusion that the decisive blow against the ruling classes", Marx wrote, "cannot be delivered in England but *only in Ireland*."

Ireland played a decisive role because of its mass emigration—the Mexico of its time. "Ireland constantly sends her own surplus to the English labour market, and thus forces down wages and lowers the material and moral position of the English working class" Marx wrote. "It is the secret by which the capitalist class maintains its power."

In the century and a half since, Marx's letter has become a key reference point for the left critique of free movement. The passage is cited as evidence of a fundamental tension between the traditional goals of the left—equality, solidarity, working class power—and a policy of open borders.

But critics of free movement neglect to mention Marx's conclusions. "Given this state of affairs," Marx wrote, "if the working class wishes to continue its struggle with some chance of success, the national organisations must become international."

In other words, Marx's analysis of mass migration did not lead him to advocate harder borders. It made him support international mobilisation to protect worker rights in a world of free movement.

After all, Marx was a triple émigré himself: he fled Prussia to Paris, faced exile from Paris to Brussels, and—following brief incarceration by the Belgian authorities—found his way to London. He was hardly a model immigrant: poor, sick, and a notorious procrastinator, Marx was much more of a scrounger than a striver, leeching off the largesse of Friedrich Engels.

Following Marx, then, the concept of internationalism came to be associated with support for free movement on both ethical and strategic grounds. Ethically, open borders gave equal opportunity to workers of all nationalities. But more importantly, the movement of people across borders created new opportunities for a coordinated challenge to capitalism. Internationalists like Marx supported free movement in the same way they supported free trade: it hastened the pace of history; it heightened contradictions.

"There can be no doubt that dire poverty alone compels people to abandon their native land, and that the capitalists exploit the immigrant workers in the most shameless manner", wrote Vladimir Lenin in 1913. "But only reactionaries can shut their eyes to the *progressive* significance of this modern migration of nations … Capitalism is drawing the masses of the working people of the *whole* world … breaking down national barriers and prejudices, uniting workers from all countries."

By the time of Lenin's letter, of course, Europe's Great Powers had been whipped up into a frenzy of nationalist violence. In the First World War, the British soldiers sang *Rule, Brittania!*, the Germans sang *Deutschlandlied,* and they all marched to their deaths. Even the Social Democratic Party of Germany—key players in the Second International—voted in favour of the war. Citing the need for national self-defence, large swathes of the European left abandoned the cause of open borders.

But by the end of the next World War—which left another 60 million dead and 15 more displaced—support for free movement had moved from the left margins and into the heart of the post-war political establishment. When the United Nations convened in Paris to draft its Declaration of Human Rights in November 1948, the Committee considered mobility a matter of 'vital importance'. "Freedom of movement was the sacred right of every human being" the committee reported. "The world belonged to all mankind."

The architects of the European Union took forward this view of free movement as fundamental to the project of European integration. In the 1957 Treaty of Rome, which laid the foundations for a union in Europe, diplomats and ministers included the 'freedom of movement of labor' as one of the four freedoms that would govern the European Economic Community, alongside that of goods, services, and capital. This decision aimed to encourage Europe's reconstruction by enabling workers to move where they were needed most.

Over the next three decades, this fourth freedom shifted from a provisional economic measure to a right of European citizenship. The 1985 Schengen Agreement eliminated internal borders and the customs checks that went along with them; the 1992 Maastricht Treaty established a European Union citizenship, which guaranteed free movement on the basis of personhood, not participation in the labour force.

The ambition was "to turn the whole of Europe into one space," as François Mitterand announced in a Bastille Day address in 1990. "Now the barriers and the walls have collapsed. The storm is not over…but we are getting there."

* * *

The transformation of free movement from a radical demand to a pillar of EU governance was critical to the emergence of left nationalism in Europe. Since the Maastricht Treaty—signed and celebrated by socialists like Mitterrand—the hope for the European Single Market as a force of social cohesion has largely failed.

Today, the European Union looks less like a worker's utopia and more like a neoliberal fortress: demanding, enforcing, and policing a free market order. Banks, corporations, and investors may be free to move their capital across the continent, but national governments are not free to implement the policies that address their local needs.

The new left vanguard formed around the view that, as Jean-Luc Mélenchon once said, the European Union is a "totalitarian project".

In short, the terms of radicalism have changed. A century ago, left movements advocated international integration as the answer to "bourgeois chauvinism under the guise of patriotism", as Lenin put it. Today, they advocate national devolution as the answer to footloose globalised capital.

Both aim to challenge capitalism and advocate for a fairer redistribution of resources. The latter, though, views international institutions as instruments of capitalism, rather than worker power. Their goal is to take back control from those institutions.

For many critics, then, the right to free movement is a mere a casualty of a radical break with the European Union. The priority is first and foremost to build a socialist economy, which they claim is impossible within the constraints of the Single Market. Migrants are collateral damage.

But most left nationalists in Europe view the demise of free movement as an end in itself. These critiques can be broadly divided into three types: economic, cultural, and political. All of them claim to justify the introduction of new border controls, but none stands up to scrutiny.

The most prominent of these critiques, building from Marx's 1870 letter, rejects free movement on the basis of worker exploitation. "The state has a duty to protect men and women from foreign workers who take their jobs away for lower pay," said Oskar Lafontaine, co-founder of *Aufstehen*, in 2005.

The problem is that there is very little evidence to support the claim that foreign workers depress wages and discourage employment of native workers. In 2014, the OECD concluded that migration in Europe has positive effects on productivity—and that migrants contribute more in taxes than they take in benefits.

It is true that any impact is concentrated among low-skill, low-education workers—the most vulnerable in the labour market. But it is entirely unclear why the solution would be to restrict migration, rather than enforcing higher labour standards for all.

Indeed, the real threat to labor standards is not free movement, but its restriction. Hard borders only serve to create an underclass of 'unauthorised' migrants that are far more vulnerable to exploitation than those protected by European law.

The cultural critique is similarly suspect. Some left-wing commentators argue against free movement on the basis that it undermines national culture. In the process, mass migration threatens to incite even stronger xenophobia.

But there is very little empirical basis for these claims, either. In case after case—from the Brexit vote to Germany's general election last year—it is areas with the *fewest* migrants that express the strongest cultural grievances. Restricting migration in order to appease their nostalgia would therefore be futile at best, and counterproductive at worst. Research suggests that contact between different communities is actually a route to more solidarity, not less. In other words, if the goal is to reduce xenophobia, borders are not the solution; interaction is.

The political critique strikes at the core of the left nationalist position. Nation-states require sovereignty: the ability to make decisions according to the democratic will of their voters. Many left nationalists therefore promise to accommodate asylum-seekers fleeing humanitarian crisis, but reserve the right to regulate the inflow of economic migrants in order to serve the needs of their national labour market.

But it is here that left nationalists sound most like the neoliberals they claim to loathe. In making this case for state sovereignty, they make migrants sound like nothing more than lumps of labour.

In truth, the distinction between asylum-seekers and 'economic migrants' is false, and flagrantly so. Every day, scores of young men arrive to Greece and Italy after long and harrowing journeys from their home countries. But the EU only grants asylum to those it deems sufficiently desperate; 'economic' migrants, often fleeing violence and persecution in countries in sub-Saharan Africa and the Middle East, are turned away.

There are certainly reasons to criticise the institution of EU free movement. For one, it is only a partial freedom, restricted by class, ethnicity, and geography. For another, it is an extremely exclusive one, leaving thousands of migrants to perish on the Mediterranean each year.

But it is dangerously foolish to believe that we can destroy EU free movement in order to build something better in its place.

The challenge, instead, is to realise the promise of free movement to bind us together as humans, and to build—as Marx hoped of his friends in New York City—a "coalition of German workers and Irish workers . . . English and American workers" who can fight together for a better world.

* * *

Left nationalists often describe the policy of free movement as naïve. "All successes in restraining and regulating capitalism have been achieved within individual states," Sahra Wagenknecht has said, "and states have borders".

But the evidence suggests that hard borders threaten international solidarity, not strengthen it; fortify inequality, not decrease it; and inflame xenophobia, not reduce it. Europe's new left nationalists may not grasp the likely results of their attempts to curtail free movement: scores of deaths on the sea, an explosion of slums at the borderlands, the continued economic exploitation of desperate migrants, and an increasingly militarised system of passport apartheid.

In the short-term, migration controls might win some votes and throw some sand into the gears of international capitalism. But over the long-term, such controls may well become their own root causes of conflict, persecution, and inequality.

For now, it is DiEM25 and its friends—not Europe's political parties—who are shouting loudest in support of open borders. "Let them in!" we demand. *Cosa Nostra, Cosa Vostra.*

The pie-throwers, for their part, have called for a *Tortaler Krieg*—total cake warfare—until their leaders heed their call. "No activist wants to throw a pie at a politician", they profess. "But a cream pie is a last resort…The pie throw is the last measure at the border of humanity."

Great Migration and the Future of Europe

Franco Berardi

A dark age of misery and violence appears inevitable if a new actor does not emerge to confront the two actors who have overtaken the political scene—neoliberal globalism and xenophobic nationalism.

The populist menace?

I dislike the expression 'populism' because it confounds two very different attitudes. 'Populist' is the name for those who refuse the austerity measures and reclaim a redistribution of wealth, but the same term is also used to define those who reject migrants and promote a politics of aggression. In other words, the word 'populist' suggests a spurious association between anti-capitalism and nationalism.

I also question the use of the word 'racism' for the contemporary fear of migration. The old racism was an expression of the emergence of the young white population urging on colonial expansion, while contemporary xenophobia is the sign of resentment of senescent people who fear the invasion of young males from the territories impoverished by past and present colonialism. The futurist euphoria of fascism has been replaced by a widespread depression at 'no future'—what was once a punk provocation turned into common sense.

The social background

The dramatic rise of the nationalist right in the European continent dates back to the summer of 2015. A deep change in the perception of the Union in the mind of European citizens occurred, and disaffection spread across a wide spectrum of public opinion.

The social violence that the European authorities exerted against Greek society caused a sudden reversal in the popular perception of Europe. Once a promise of prosperity and solidarity, the Union became a menace, a looming danger of impoverishment and moral aggression.

This reversal in the general mood paved the way for the rise of the nationalist right. Unable to defend their salaries, their jobs, and, ultimately, their dignity—conscious of the impotence of democracy in the face of financial aggression—many Europeans have abandoned their liberal-democratic inclination and are leaning towards nationalism in a sway of revenge against democracy's delusion.

This is the background of the sudden rise in hatred and cynicism that is jeopardising the future of the Union, dissolving solidarity, and turning the border of the continent into a war zone.

An underwater graveyard

"Build the wall" is the catchphrase of racist resentment in the United States of Trump, but Europeans do not need a wall: the Mediterranean Sea is a wall of water that in the last years has exacted a frightening toll. The official figures speak of 16,000 persons drowned, but we know that these figures underestimate the real extent of this mass slaughter. We will never know how many people have really drowned in the sea, how many are dying in the desert, how many have been tortured, enslaved, and killed in the concentration camps of Libya. Their destiny is a consequence of past colonialism and present rejection.

Rejection has been the core of European policy: the morally repugnant criminalisation of those organisations whose mission to rescue people is just the last stroke in a long-lasting attempt to dissuade and intimidate people fleeing wars that Europeans have fuelled and the misery that the European's colonialism has sown.

Meanwhile, climate change is shrinking the planet, pushing people to move by the millions. This is the effect of the capitalist devastation of the environment, of the hyper-consumerism of a Western population incapable of facing its historical responsibility.

The colonial roots of migration

Beware: it would be intellectually dishonest to dismiss Europeans' anxiety as machinations of right-wing politicians. We should not belittle the magnitude and the destabilising effects of the great migration looming at the horizon of our time.

When a boat filled with African migrants was rejected by the nationalist government and obliged to float for weeks amid cold sea waves, I took part in demonstrations chanting "Let them disembark", to save lives endangered by the cynical attitude of Matteo Salvini (but also of Emmanuel Macron). "It is just forty-nine people", we said to persuade the government to lift the closure of Italian havens. "Five hundred million Europeans should not be afraid of a few dozen women and children."

I said these words, joining my voice to the voice of anti-racist friends, but I was conscious that these words are not true. They are not forty-nine people. They are millions. And the fear of a migrant invasion, though instrumentally emphasised and exaggerated by the right-wing media, is not illusory, groundless fake news. We must face the dimensions of the historical challenge, while never renouncing humanitarian solidarity.

Last call for Europe

We are not dealing with a temporary emergency. The great migration has begun, prompted by past and present colonial exploitation.

The exploited populations that once upon a time were culturally and technically marginalised now have access to the world mediascape and to the international system of transportation. This paves the way to a migration that cannot be stopped, and that demands a global redistribution of wealth.

This is the crucial point. Thirty years of neoliberal privatisation and financial predation have pushed the world to the brink of a catastrophic collapse, of which the extermination of migrants is only one facet. The only way to escape the endless global civil war is an egalitarian distribution of wealth, and the reduction of work-time around the world.

This agenda is clearly at odds with the current mind frame, so we should expect an apocalyptic precipitation in the coming years.

A Pluralist Europe by Elif Shafak

"I come from a country once regarded as "the sick man of Europe". Turkey was, and some would passionately argue still very much is, Europe's historical, cultural, and political Other.

Born in France, raised in Turkey, but also partly in Spain, Germany, Jordan, and the US, and now based in the UK, always somewhere in between, always a commuter, at different stages of my life I felt compelled to think about this phrase. Why was my motherland, my *mother*'s land, deemed to be 'sick'? And why a 'man'? And how come they said we were 'of Europe' when they also said we surely weren't and never could be?

Putting these questions to myself, I already felt like an outsider in my own homeland. I was on the fringes of the culture, holding on tight to the edge. And Turkey was on the fringes of Europe. So I concluded that my place should be somewhere along the periphery of the periphery. Naturally, I was interested in boundaries. Who drew them? Where exactly did Europe begin, and where did it end?

It is a question that matters greatly to us novelists. Who tells the story? Who claims to have the right to write history, their own version of it? Whose stories are being erased, forgotten, silenced?

Today, no doubt, Turkey is in the grip of authoritarianism. The slide backwards has been at first gradual, and then bewilderingly fast and relentless. Academics, writers, journalists, intellectuals, human rights activists, and cartoonists have been arrested on the most ridiculous charges. Without the rule of law, or separation of powers, or free and diverse media left, and with a civil society that has been massively crushed or intimidated, Turkey's AKP government has become the world's leading jailer of journalists, surpassing Russia's and China's dark records in this field.

What is happening in Turkey holds important lessons for progressives everywhere. It shows us that history does not necessarily go forward, that tomorrow won't necessarily be more advanced than yesterday. It also demonstrates that there is a crucial difference between 'democracy' and 'majoritarianism'.

For a democracy to exist and survive, the ballot box alone is not enough. Democracies that solely rely on the ballot box are bound to crumble. In addition to fair and free elections, a country must enjoy rule of law, separation of powers, diverse media, independent academe, women's rights, and minority rights. Turkey's trajectory shows us that democracy is far more fragile than generally assumed—it is a delicate ecosystem of checks and balances. In the hands of populists and nationalists, that ecosystem is shattered.

The purity of Europe is a myth—and a dangerous one. Europe always was a mixture of ethnicities, cultures, dialects, traditions, and belongings. The charm and internal strength of Europe as a continent was never its homogeneity, but its ability to offer a set of shared egalitarian values and democratic rights to people of different backgrounds. Europe's stories were always plural and pluralistic, and these stories were told and written by locals and exiles alike. James Joyce in Trieste, Seferis in London, Samuel Beckett in Paris.

Instead, we are now being told that we must each go back to our tribes. There is a systematic erosion of complexity, multiplicity, and nuance underway. We are being promised that we will be safer if we are surrounded by sameness. And that is a shameless lie. Populists claim to represent 'the people' but they only divide and, contrary to what they say, have no problem with elitism so long as they are the elite.

Europe is haunted by a toxic nostalgia. Narratives about 'a golden past' that never really was are circulating in Austria, Croatia, Hungary, Poland. Countries that were once empires are even more susceptible to the toxicity of post-colonial nostalgia. The past is being rewritten, reconstructed through the filter of nationalism and tribalism, and memories that do not fit into the ascendant narrative are being quietly erased.

As I am writing this piece, breaking news confirms that right-wing populists have won the elections in Utrecht. Their first official statement has been: "We are standing in the rubble of what was once the most beautiful civilisation in the world." This alarming victory has emerged in the aftermath of a terrorist attack by a Turkish-born man. A vicious circle spins in front of our eyes. Hatred breeds terrorism, terrorism breeds fear, fear breeds populism, populism breeds divisions, and divisions breed further extremism . . .

We must break this vicious circle. And for that to happen, each and every one of us, and each in our own way, needs to become engaged in today's political discourse and civic space. We cannot afford to be silent.

As one era comes to an end and a new one begins, the impetus for social change and a better, fairer future must originate from the civil societies. We must all become active citizens, activists for core democratic principles. This requires us to move beyond echo chambers and 'safe spaces', into new conversations, new narratives. One thing is clear: faith is way too important to leave to the religious. Patriotism, way too important to leave to the nationalists. The digital world is too important to leave to profit-oriented tech monopolies. And politics too important to leave to career politicians. **,,**

PART EIGHT

Technology

Democratising Technology and Innovation

Renata Avila

DiEM25 believes that Europe can become a beacon of hope if it unites political, social, and technological progress. If it fosters a new enlightenment and puts the flourishing of all human beings in the centre of technological change, it could generate a transformative force with global reach.

The technology we have today in Europe and across the world mirrors, sometimes even amplifies, the deficiencies of our democracy and the fragility of a sovereignty that places markets and big businesses before the interest of citizens. Such deficiencies include poor resilience, depending on companies and services developed elsewhere, often with European funding, via expertise and research that the tech giants privatise. Europe is becoming increasingly dependent on a system, insecure by design and non-private by default, that is merging at an accelerated pace with its military apparatus, led by a government which no longer espouses democratic values. It is a volatile, unreliable ally.

Technology, ultimately, is politics. Thanks to Edward Snowden's revelations, Europe received a wake-up call: it was when journalists unveiled the massive surveillance of European citizens by US corporations and the government, and the existence of data collection centres in main European cities, and the criminal hack that targeted Belgacom, Belgium's largest telecommunications provider.

Further evidence published by WikiLeaks in its under-reported Vault 7 publication revealed not just passive spying but systematic hacking that had left key infrastructures exposed. This was a challenge to values, to ideas, and to principles of fairness, and it demanded not only a change in regulation but an accelerated process to lead the world towards an entirely different approach, one that addresses and thwarts surveillance capitalism not just by dismantling Big Tech monopolies but by promoting, designing, and funding a wholly different code of practice. While a General Data Protection Regulation was approved, it was like giving aspirin to a cancer patient. The practices, incentives, and funding are ever more aggressively following an extractive, rights-eroding logic.

The technology sector in Europe today is exploitative and focused exclusively on maximising profit. It is obsolescence, rather than sustainability, that determines services and products. It is privatised, but taking full advantage of public funding—and barely paying any taxes. It is also concentrated in the hands of few, whereas the wealth it generates is at the expense of its users. Further innovation, repair, even audit, is locked in and opaque. The digital infrastructure Europe relies on is built around a surveillance and control centre. Security, especially the security of the citizens, comes second. Its funding favours those who subscribe to the values it represents, and criminalises a culture of sharing. It is a model that is rapidly becoming a threat to European independence and to democracy itself. The virtual platforms where political parties do their campaigning is just one example of abuse that can turn entire nations prey to the companies who control the data. If you can predict the behaviour of a collective, you might be tempted to manipulate it.

The alarm for Europe has been sounding loudly for more than half a decade. As the two leading digital empires, USA and China, enter a merciless trade war to capture the 'next billion' market (meaning, to unlock the data potential of those still disconnected), and to be the first to train their AI system that surveys all thoughts and actions of every human on earth, Europe lags behind.

Yet it still embraces this extractive model. The European strategy has been to erect regulation walls that will protect its citizens, while at the same time trying to emulate the tech empires. Limiting itself and its allies with ancillary copyright regulation, slow, complex, and outdated antitrust processes, and impractical data protection, Europe is no longer leading in any single area of digital transformation, locking itself up with rules which belong to a different century and respond to a different logic.

Building a progressive agenda for Europe and the world

DiEM25 wants to reverse this course and challenge the world by putting Europe again in a forefront position: designing the institutions of the future for a prosperous, inclusive, and sustainable tech future for everyone, one that preserves rights and is focused on citizens' needs. The policy paper in this section of the book was the product of a collaborative process that took more than two years, with the active participation of the DiEM25 membership and the leadership of Joren De Wachter, Kate McCurdy, Christoph Schneider, and David Schwertgen—with comments and feedback from citizens all over Europe and other parts of the world.

DiEM25's blueprint challenges three enclosures we are facing today: the first enclosure is the ownership and control of data, followed by the precarity of informal workers and, finally, the protections of intellectual property rights, including, but not limited to, copyright.

It puts forth an ambitious plan to achieve technological sovereignty. This means the right and ability of citizens and democratic institutions to make self-determined choices regarding technologies and their innovation. The paper proposes two focal points for achieving this. The first is to create a Digital Commonwealth for the twenty-first century, which will not only give back the control of data to citizens, but will enable society to take advantage, in democratic terms, of the potential of data to help people prosper and thrive. The second is free knowledge and the democratisation of innovation, including a comprehensive reform of both intellectual property rights and education curricula, where the role of the economy and the future of digital business models all play their part.

Principles, rights, and governance of the technological future

We are proposing a digital future with democratic participation *by design*. We start with the claim that no political movement can succeed without a strategy on how to deal with the changes that digitisation and technological innovation have wrought on state, society, and labour alike.

The departing point proposed by DiEM25 covers rapid regulatory actions to be taken in the next few years. For Europe to reposition itself as a technological leader, it has to take strong measures against the platform monopolies that dominate the market today and elevate as a priority alternative economic models, such as platform cooperatives. This can be explored as part of a new foreign policy, trade policy, and municipal policy, that promotes Europe and its products as ones with fundamental rights baked into their design and deployment. Europe needs to turn what its competitors perceive as a disadvantage—regulation, safeguards and higher privacy standards—into its central strength and competitive advantage. And this can be exported as a viable alternative which is also complementary of and enforcing our proposals on financial and environmental reform.

The Achilles heel of the tech giants is its disregard for human dignity, which translates into weak privacy and data protection, poor security, and the entire opaque design of its automated decision processes. First steps should include having an active role in approving the best ePrivacy Regulation in the EU; a push to enforce platform interoperability and to expedite stronger antitrust processes; and a transformation of intellectual property rights. This must be done at a local level, relying on the network of rebel cities, and then at a transnational level by leveraging the power of data unions and the European Digital Commons.

Going deeper into the strategies to preserve human dignity and freedom in the digital age, the paper explores new rights that preserve and promote human dignity: the right to encryption, the right to computation (defined as the right of unconditional and unlimited access to public computing resources and infrastructure), the right to an algorithmic opt-out, etc. New rights declared in the proposed paper would then be followed by the creation of institutions that could enforce them.

But, crucially, DiEM25 is looking to inspire a shift in principles. The principles are simple, and close to people's daily interaction with technology. Beginning by considering technology a positive force that serves humanity, and insisting that every technological development is the result of (political) choices; rejecting the idea of technocracy and embracing sustainable practices such as the right to repair hardware instead of rendering them obsolete; and finally introducing Open

Standards, which refers to technical standards becoming documented so that inter-operability is ensured and nothing is subject to IP monopolies.

Let's look at two specific examples:

One, reversing the extractive data model that tech giants impose today by collec-tivising data producers through the creation, and legal recognition, of data unions (representative organisations of data producers on digital platforms who are granted powers to structurally redress the balance between a monopoly platform and its data producers in different ways—negotiate, for example, terms and conditions, or take collective legal action on behalf of data producers, etc.).

Two, extending antitrust measures: platform monopolies should be required to pay for the setting up and running of data unions without having a say in them, while the latter would enjoy the right to be involved in negotiating major changes in the running of the platform. This is necessary to counterbalance the power of the owners of the platform with the interests of its users and data producers.

These policies show a commitment towards institutions that demand a participa-tory governance of technology. European citizens must be given an opportunity, not only to understand how technology works, but also to participate in ways that shape it for the common good.

Sustainable innovation, distributable benefits of technology: How DiEM25 plans to fund the proposed changes

Is this viable? Can we shift away from the Silicon Valley-type model without harming the economy? Who is going to pay for all the costs of implementing this Tech Policy at a pan-European level? One of the weakest areas most urgent to tackle is the public funding dedicated to innovation and, more importantly, how that innovation con-tributes directly to society instead of subsidising corporations, Big Tech included.

The EU's research and innovation funding suffers from a major deficit. It is premised on a 'high-tech for growth' mentality, directly dancing to the tune of big industry. This must change. The EU's funding needs to be opened up to purposes which serve the social good. Innovation that is funded by public money should remain accessible to all and under the most permissive licence systems.

In practical terms, we propose the following principles and practical steps:

DiEM25 is proposing a comprehensive strategy of sustainable public funding, investments in knowledge commons benefiting public solutions. The starting point is taxing the tech giants immediately, regulating against their tax evasion strategies ,and making it more difficult for them to hide their wealth and assets in tax havens. The second move is a significantly higher investment in technology and innovation, matching or even surpassing the investment of USA and China. No alternative model will be able to prosper without a heavy investment from the European Union.

The allocation of funding should follow both the rights and the principles described above. This system should furthermore obey democratic principles, maximising the inclusion and participation of citizens, so that they have a say in how we all want to shape our technological future, democratising its benefits and investments, as well as its innovations. It is proposed that one part should be allocated through a participatory budget system, not only designing technology but funding the projects that people think reflect the values of the society towards which they aspire. As the policy paper states:

> Technological messianism is not the right approach. Technology is a tool that can help to solve technical problems. But it is humans who must direct how technology is used, and its purpose must be to solve human problems and the problems of all lifeforms that humans are responsible for. Justice, equality, fairness, or the lack thereof, will not be solved by technology alone. Without human and moral guidance technology has as much opportunity to make problems worse rather than better. Already, we see how prejudice and bias can be strengthened through technology, making technology part of the problem, rather than the solution. In the end, technology is and remains a tool. And we must choose how to use it. DiEM25 believes that technology must be used as a tool to address problems of human society, and firmly rejects technological messianism.

Decisions about technology should not be irreversibly delegated to technocrats, corporations, and tech monopolies, assisted or not by their lobbyists in Brussels. The radical proposal by DiEM25 puts a stop to tech solutionism, but also to tech pessimism, depositing the future in the hands of European citizens, citizens who would be equipped with the tools to decide the technological future they want.

Europe should aspire to democratise technologies and innovation, and put citizens before companies, sustainability before narrow profit, and responsibility before technological feasibility. The alternative is to become overwhelmed by the undemocratic technologies and society models of, among others, Silicon Valley and China. We are running out of time.

DiEM25 Policy Paper on Technological Sovereignty

Edited by Rosemary Bechler

Technology is essential. Our civilisation heavily depends on technology. Technology provides us with the possibility to feed more than 7.5 billion people, to prevent or cure sickness, to multiply social and cultural interaction and creation, to care for those in need, to learn and teach more, to provide safety and security and to improve the quality of life and increase happiness in many ways for all. But it is only that: a possibility. Not a certainty, and, today, often not a reality.

For democracy to be possible, technology must be democratised

DiEM25 is the one political movement that wants to create, shape and drive political debate and democratic process around technology, based on the concept of Technological Sovereignty. Technological Sovereignty in our definition means the right and capacity of citizens and democratic institutions to make self-determined choices on technologies and innovation. Why? Because technology affects us all, and all of us, not just a powerful few, must have a voice in its development. For DiEM25, it is clear that without the introduction of technological sovereignty through the democratisation of technology, democracy itself is no longer possible.

The examples are manifold. We see monopolistic digital platform providers with tremendous powers to shape what we see, whom we hear from or how we think, without any democratic accountability for that power. We become subject to automated decision-making, wrongly labeled 'artificial intelligence', functioning as a black box without any transparency or accountability.

But there's more. We see how the costs of technology's development and its usage are socialised, but the benefits are privatised to a very small group. We see how decisions on technological development are made by powerful, unaccountable private actors, and kept away from transparent and public debate. Research and innovation must be beneficial for society and the prosperity of mankind. We must fight the absurd notion that the purpose of innovation is to make rich investors richer still.

We believe that startups and entrepreneurial process should not solely depend on venture capital and other financialisation schemes. The purpose of innovation is not only the aggregation of capital. To approach long-term solutions, we'll need sustainable public funding and the democratic inclusion of citizens. And we are told that we can change everything at any time, as long as we play by the rules of the status quo and come up with the next 'disruptive' innovation by ourselves. But these rules do not allow us to put common goals first—and they exclude democratic participation by design.

DiEM25 has a different vision. We know innovation can be beneficial to all. We want to end the practice of socialising the costs and privatising the profits from technological change. Instead, we want to foster innovations for the common good. We want to see an inclusive innovation ecosystem where all stakeholders, such as users, employees, citizens, and authorities are equally important. An inclusive system where women and other historically marginalised communities are empowered to participate actively in shaping our common technological future. A system in which society as a whole benefits from the liberated energy of socially responsible and democratically accountable entrepreneurs who are no longer shackled by the financialisation of their efforts. We believe in a positive and strong partnership of the public and private sector in creating and sharing knowledge, creativity, research, development, and innovation, to the benefit of the whole of society. And we also see the vast opportunities of commons and cooperative approaches that can be fostered with new technologies.

We are convinced that technological sovereignty through democratisation of technology is an absolute necessity for real equality in the technological era. We believe that Europe can become a beacon of hope if it unites political, social and technological progress—if it fosters a new enlightenment and puts the flourishing of all human beings in the centre of technological change. This could have transformative impact on a global scale.

The relationship between people and technology

Today people are increasingly defined as users or consumers of technology—sometimes even as the product itself—rather than citizens. Remember, when the service is free, you're not the user, you're the product. But, as users, consumers or products, people are not empowered. They are not citizens who have a voice on how technology is shaped, who pays for it, and who benefits from it. They don't get the real benefits of the knowledge, research and development funded by their tax money. They are effectively powerless against the monopolies of the platform giants.

DiEM25 wants technology to reflect the values and diversity of the society to which we aspire. Our different genders, ethnicities, capabilities, values and—most importantly—our dreams, shall be supported by technology. Technology has to be set up in such a way that it liberates and empowers each of us to fulfil our vast potential, both as individual citizens and as contributors to the collective good. And it must support the ecological and democratic transformations necessary for our society's future.

That is only possible if we, as sovereign citizens, reclaim the ability to make self-determined choices, argue for different values and change the social and economic processes and powers that shape technologies. We can and shall develop technological citizenship in the twenty-first century, based on principles such as the commons, the capacity of self-organisation, and the development of counter-power held by citizens and democratic institutions. Technology has become a central form of power in society. This power must ultimately belong to the sovereign citizens of a technologised society.

Technology in DiEM25's Progressive Agenda for Europe

DiEM25 believes that, in a technologised world, Europe must occupy an important place of humane and responsible technological progress in cooperation, not competition, with others. Europe must use its assets, such as its strong research and innovation landscape, its public traditions, the knowledge of its citizens and NGOs, its humanistic culture, its diversity and its inventive capabilities. Europe must democratise technologies and innovation, put citizens before companies, sustainability before narrow profit and responsibility before technological feasibility. The alternative is to become overwhelmed by the undemocratic technological and social models we see in Silicon Valley and China. These models favour the few and exploit the many and the living world. They benefit huge corporations who exploit publicly funded technologies, which they aim to optimise, with global reach, for their private profit. In these models, the values of a powerful minority shape the technological futures for the vast majority. They are models with contempt for democracy.

DiEM25's Progressive Agenda for Europe demands a break with this model, and lays claim to technological sovereignty. Our European Green New Deal demands green innovation and a common share in the benefits of technological progress. Our European constitutional process will create a new digital public sphere. Transparent government requires transparent technologies. A dignified future for labour demands responsible technologies and a collective share in the benefits of automation. An ecological transition has to stop and prevent harmful technologies and foster sustainable alternatives. Culture shall be freely accessible, while cultural creation should be respected and rewarded. An open society that welcomes refugees and migrants needs to welcome technologies that can take part in human development. A feminist society committed to equality calls for technical solutions by, and for, people of all genders and sexualities. Our vision of Technological Sovereignty demands that all of these perspectives shape innovation for the common good.

Last but not least, there is also a strong strategic case for Technological Sovereignty. No political movement will succeed without a strategy on how to deal with the changes that digitalisation and technological innovation have brought upon state, society and labour. In this paper DiEM25 presents ideas and strategies to democratise technology.

More and more, all that we do—our activities online, offline, at home, at work, with friends, with families, with strangers—and all that we are—our physical, psychological, and social identities—is captured in digital form, only to resurface in aggregate as the data driving mass social transformation and unprecedented accumulations of value. Though we all contribute to this process and feel its effects, the decision-making power is retained by a handful of powerful actors, notably platform monopolies.

Democratising Platform Monopolies

Our access to knowledge is growing, it is easier to communicate and connect with others, and novel creative spaces have opened up. The digital economy has created many new products and services and strengthened connections across the world. However, this transformation has also yielded ambivalent and negative effects. The communication revolution has brought us overwhelming complexity, the spread of misinformation and collective nervousness. The digital economy is automating jobs and consolidating monopolistic structures.

Many of these negative aspects, however, do not follow from the properties of digital technologies as such, but rather from the ways in which they are used and governed, i.e. the societal structures and contexts of these technologies. The current state of capitalism has led to surveillance and platform monopolies forming technological empires with illegitimate power over the lives of billions of people. The market dominance of a handful of platform businesses relies on two core principles— the network effect and the lock-in effect.

The network effect is quite simple: the more people use a certain platform, the more valuable it becomes for everyone. The lock-in effect is also well known to people using, for example, social network platforms: the more you integrate the service in your daily life, the more dependent you become on the service. Extraction of big data from the growing user base is key to this huge market dominance. Every person who uses digital services is creating a valuable economic and social resource in the form of personal data.

The underlying economic structures, worldviews and cultures—which have gone global—take their users' attention as the product to be sold to the highest bidders. The data that is extracted and privatised is used to constantly manipulate individual and collective behaviour. These systems sell our freedom to destroy it. In a standard Silicon Valley sales pitch, people are not citizens with rights, virtue and dignity, but consumers to be manipulated by marketing, and data points to be tracked and sold as commodities.

Vast digital infrastructures and datasets have been built and privatised in the hands of a tiny and largely unaccountable economic elite. These very datasets are then used to shape and train automated systems that are being offered back to us 'as-a-service'. Work formerly executed by both experts and low-skilled workers is now done by users, who create valuable data that is constantly fed back into the system. Workers are not compensated for the data which they generate on the job, and in so doing, train their own robotic replacements.

How can we constrain their power?

The basic step to tackle the dominance of platform monopolists is to regulate the use of personal data, strengthening user rights and empowering Data Protection

Authorities to enforce these rights. The General Data Purpose Regulation (GDPR) and the upcoming ePrivacy Regulation are steps into the right direction but certainly not enough.

The ePrivacy Regulation is supposed to protect confidentiality of communications and personal data (such as location data, browsing data, device usage patterns, mobile app use, search queries, etc.) in the electronic communication sector by complementing matters covered in a general way by the General Data Protection Regulation (GDPR). The ePrivacy Regulation is meant to be the main framework to protect online communication. We must ensure that in the final version privacy, data protection, and other fundamental rights are fully respected.

To re-open the monopolised social network ecosystem for competition we demand to legally enforce cross-platform interoperability for communication across different platforms. Telecommunication providers are forced to open their network to smaller players and to interoperate—this is how we can call each other across different providers. There is no reason why social networks should not be subject to the same policy.

Mandatory cross-platform interoperability could be achieved by, e.g., standard basic services with end-to-end encryption to which different services could attach, supporting data portability. In practice, this would mean that you could communicate with people on different platforms without having an account for these platforms or handing them your personal data.

Social media should be seen and regulated as a public utility. This includes substantial public funding for the development of open and decentralised alternatives.

To enable fair competition in the realm of Platform Capitalism and the Digital Single Market we need stronger EU Competition Laws. Regulative bodies like anti-trust divisions and cartel authorities shall ask for strong data protection compliance upon corporate mergers. In addition, regulators require additional criteria to evaluate abuses of market power. An effective valuation of market power has to keep the whole economic ecosystem in check. Key regulative measures of these agencies will include splitting up platform monopolies and other businesses that have become too large; sharing (anonymised) datasets of big players with public entities or NGOs—to create a public/municipal data commons; overseeing businesses and corporations; and collecting fines.

To further limit the negative impact of platform monopolies and automatisation it is necessary to close the tax gap. We have to fight the tax evasion of platform companies and create a digital tax on the collection/processing and sale of personal data.

A key characteristic of platform monopolies is the structural power imbalance between the platform and those who produce the data harvested by the platform, be they users or workers. (To clearly illustrate the imbalance we will refer to platform users as 'data producers' in this paragraph.) This imbalance is very clearly illustrated in the bargaining power of data producers in respect of the terms and conditions: there is no such bargaining power. A data producer must simply accept, or be banned from a platform that may be essential for certain aspects of their lives (in which such platforms resemble public utilities); a platform worker must simply accept having their data collected, or risk losing, at worst, the income they need to survive.

The proposed solution is the collectivisation of data producers through the creation and legal recognition of Data Unions: representative organisations of data producers on digital platforms, who will be granted power for activities such as negotiation of terms and conditions, collective legal action on behalf of data producers, and other measures of structural redress.

In an extension of anti-trust measures, platform monopolies will be required to contribute funding for the organisation of Data Unions, although any attempt to use funding to exert influence must be strictly curtailed. Data Unions retain the right to be involved in negotiating major changes in the running of the platform. This is necessary to counterbalance the power of the owners of the platform with the interests of its users and data producers.

Towards a Digital Commonwealth: on data collection, algorithms and AI, or "Automated Decision-Making"

The problem is not limited to the platform monopolists, but also applies to the state and other actors who collect and use data. This includes all aspects of algorithmic automated decision-making (often mislabelled 'Artificial Intelligence'). In order to be clear, this paper uses the term 'Automated Decision Making' (ADM) instead of 'Artificial Intelligence' (AI), because the use of this concept helps much better to set out the issue clearly: how are those automated decisions made? And who decides how they are made? We see today how the expansion of information technology has not been accompanied by expanded democratic control, resulting in a massive concentration of power and surveillance capabilities in a few hands, and little accountability or oversight by the public.

Artificial intelligence is, today, often neither artificial—its 'magic' veneer obscures the all-too-human labour and decisions that shape its development—nor intelligent, as it reflects a blinkered set of powerful interests over all others. Instead of opening our eyes to new possibilities of a free and equal society, ADM is used to consolidate existing hierarchies and explore new mechanisms of control.

Need for a new paradigm

It is time for a new paradigm of the digital economy. A paradigm through which we establish new forms of ownership and governance of data and digital technologies, guided by democratic principles. A paradigm that unleashes the power of data and digital technologies for the common good and that helps to usher in an innovative, democratic, socially just and ecological transformation of our societies and economies. Moving towards such a digital commonwealth in which we will collectively benefit from the digital transformation will help us create a mixed and democratic economy. It will help us gain more democratic rights and to become free and sovereign in our technological choices, as individuals and societies.

For DiEM25, citizens in a digital commonwealth know, and can exercise, their clearly defined rights as data subjects; democratically govern the use of data, setting its scope for private purposes, and harnessing its power for the public good; have recourse to institutional means of enforcing their rights, such as independent, public data audits; and can democratically counter imbalances in economic power through alternative business models such as platform cooperatives.

Democratising structures of economic ownership can counter the consolidation of power of today's platform monopolies. Platform cooperatives are models of economic exchange which are owned and governed by workers, users and other stakeholders, and often have social and ethical objectives. The EU should support such economic approaches.

The value of data relies on aggregation: data becomes more valuable when collected and shared. As a private commodity, data can be used in unaccountable ways, potentially facilitating manipulation, surveillance, and control; however, as a common good, data can contribute much to cooperative and collective purposes.

Data Commons are a way to aggregate data in a safe, anonymised, transparent and democratically controlled way. Data Commons may incorporate a combination of personal data, city open data, public research data and private data. Decommodified data could unlock the power of data-driven technological innovation in the service of common goals and ends—under the direction of public interests rather than private profit. The main challenge for Data Commons is to create a legal and economic framework in which people want to share their data—and its potential economic value—in a controlled way for the common good. This needs to be backed up by technological solutions that enable the enforcement of rules for data sharing and prevent the misuse of data.

The long-term vision here is the concept of shared personal data with strong democratic governance as a common resource for innovation. Users would host their private data in Personal Data Storage—a secure location of their choice—and have full control on how to share data and interact with online services. Personal Data Storage may be—for instance—a decentralised, anonymous and encrypted peer-to-peer network that takes user data and splits it up into encrypted chunks, which get processed by hundreds of other computers across the network. The crucial aim here is that no raw data is revealed to third parties.

Besides democratic governance, such a European Data Commons needs to ensure democratic ownership of data which is collectively produced. Third parties wishing to use the data would be subject to licensing requirements, taking into account factors such as company size, intended purpose of data processing, and mechanisms to ensure accountability. The income of the Data Commons would flow into the fund for a universal basic dividend, proposed in DiEM25's Green New Deal for Europe. Citizens, research institutions, public institutions, small companies and non-profit organisations could all use the Data Commons as their free, common resource.

Introducing Digital Rights

We demand that a new framework for digital citizens' rights be recognised, enforced, and democratically governed by the inhabitants of Europe:

- **Right to encryption**: All citizens have the right that their digital information and communications be conveyed to the intended targets using strong encryption, to prevent interference or eavesdropping from governments or other third parties.
- **Right to computation**: All citizens have the right of unconditional and unlimited access to public computing resources and infrastructure.

With regard to the use of algorithms in everyday life, we demand that the following rights be recognised:

- **Right to an algorithmic opt-out**: An 'algorithmic opt-out' rule shall be established: for any algorithmic service, a user can choose to receive an outcome with a 'default' profile (i.e. with the user's personal/demographic attributes removed from calculation).
- **Right of interaction**: Citizens have the right to know when they are or aren't interacting with an algorithm.
- **Right of equal treatment**: Citizens have the right to be free from algorithmic discrimination. If algorithmic services provide outputs of consistently lower value or quality to or about users coming from historically marginalised backgrounds, this constitutes discrimination. Users should be able to compare outputs based on different demographic profiles (e.g. "would this search result be the same if I were to change the gender or age the algorithm has inferred for me?").
- **Public audits**: the EU shall develop an independent public institution to conduct algorithmic audits in a transparent manner, with resources allocated proportional to estimated scope of a) affected citizens and b) potential harms.

Free knowledge for democratic innovation—the role of intellectual property and education

Innovation depends on high quality public life and public services. Creative societies and economies need the infrastructure to support them: well-functioning education and research systems, guaranteed protection of rights, and various other forms of state support such as targeted monetary subsidies. Knowledge has always been a product of human collaboration. Our vision of technological change must reflect these needs, and contribute to public life and the common good in turn.

Transforming Intellectual Property (IP)

Intellectual Property (IP) is a system of government-created and -enforced exclusive rights (legally created monopolies) on certain aspects of creativity and innovation. They include, to name a few, patents, copyright, trademarks, trade secrets, database rights and other similar rights.

There are two standard justifications for IP: recognition and reward. The reward justification argues that IP protects the creator or innovator, by providing them a monopoly that is limited in time and scope, so they can benefit from the ability to recover their investment. After a time, the monopoly lapses, and the invention or creation becomes part of the public domain—the classical freedom of enterprise, where everything that is not forbidden is allowed, regains its normal place in the market. The recognition justification consists of the argument that IP recognises creators and inventors, and their contribution to society.

There are a number of problems with IP today. First, there is the continued expansion of the monopoly rights. Copyrights, originally eighteen years long, now last at least until seventy years after the death of the last contributing author (and for Disney a bit longer). Patents used to be for narrow, technical applications ('downstream' aspects of technology), but now apply ever more to 'upstream' aspects of technology: methods (i.e. ideas), protocols, discoveries (e.g. in the field of biology), software and many other aspects that used to be non-patentable. In addition, the standards for 'novelty' are sometimes laughable. To give a classic example, in Australia, after a patent law reform, someone managed to obtain a patent on the novel invention of the 'wheel'. Furthermore, new IP rights are invented on a continuous basis—examples include database rights, trade secrets, performers rights and the new secondary copyright for publishers in the draft Copyright Directive. The public domain is under continuous attack from privateers.

Second, the link between the creator/innovator and the IP right is no longer functional. The full transferability of IP rights has the practical effect of allowing monopoly rights to cumulate where they produce the least benefit: with marketers and distributors. The actual creators/innovators typically get little to no benefit from or recognition for their contributions.

The consequences are seriously problematic. For example, while public money provides for most Research and Development (R&D) in developing new drugs, we see that the R&D budget of large pharmaceutical companies is a fraction of their marketing budgets, and most of their R&D budget is spent on researching 'me-too' patents: patents on slightly different versions of drugs that already exist, in order to artificially extend their monopoly position artificially (and charge higher prices). It is a classical example of socialising the cost and risk of developing new drugs, while privatising the benefits. The same is true for other innovations and research at universities and other research centres funded with public money. Far too often, the results of such publicly funded research are privatised, often in opaque and non-transparent ways, through the creation and transfer of IP rights to privately held spin-offs.

Third, IP rights have a number of negative effects on the economy and society. The rent they extract generates huge transfers of money to a limited number of corporate monopoly holders and their shareholders. This leads to a very regressive income distribution and drives economic inequality, as people who work pay rent to those who hold government-created monopolies on the proceeds of that work. In addition, in many countries IP monopolies enjoy tax exemptions or preferential treatment. This allows large multinationals to shift their profits and benefit from tax forum shopping, driving further inequality as these revenues are hoarded rather than taxed and redistributed for the public good.

IP rights, today, seem to slow down innovation significantly. Through IP claims, large established businesses use ever-growing monopoly rights to block access to their market to newcomers or competitors. Initiatives like the draft Copyright Directive allow copyright to be used as a way to censor content, further reducing the freedom of communication that the Internet originally promised. In the discussion on the draft EU Copyright Directive, the monopoly holders of content (the entertainment industry) are fighting with the monopoly holders of the tech industry. But who defends the interests of consumers, citizens and creative people?

Fair IP rights

Reversing the tax treatment of IP is the easiest immediate step to take. This means that any preferential tax treatment of royalties or other income (rent) deriving from IP, such as lower tax rates or higher exemptions on such income, must immediately be withdrawn. They should be replaced by the opposite: income from IP (rent) must be taxed preferably at higher rates, and more progressively, than income from selling actual goods or services.

In addition, the draft EU Copyright Directive must be fundamentally reviewed, in order to obtain much more balanced rights of users, re-users, creators and innovators. A European 'fair use' concept must be created, with broad applications, and based on the fundamental principle of freedom of speech. Introduce a general principle of IP release: any IP belonging to a legal entity which either goes bankrupt, is liquidated or otherwise ceases to function, must be released into the public domain. Equally, any IP ceases to be valid on the death of the inventor/creator.

With immediate effect, public authorities must switch, where possible, to using free and open source software. Any patent on software functionality may only be awarded subject to full disclosure of all source code related thereto. Public funding of free and open source software platforms or core technologies should be envisaged.

Mid- and long-term measures around Intellectual Property are all based on the same principles: the cycle of 'socialising costs and privatising benefits' that currently exists must be broken; the privatisation of benefits through the state-enforced monopolies of Intellectual Property rights must be reduced in terms of scope and duration; innovation that is funded by public money should remain accessible to all, by default under the most permissive licence systems.

In practice, we propose the following principles and practical steps:

Any technical development, including software code, that is funded by public money should be made available under licences equivalent to Free and Open

Software licences. (Note: DiEM25 does not have any a priori preference for any category or set of licences. We are aware that there is a whole ecosystem of software and creative commons licences, and, depending on context and the area, the choice of the appropriate licence will have to be made. We do not believe in a 'one size fits all' approach in this context.)

This has several benefits: it provides for independence from non-EU based suppliers, it increases the security and stability of the software and it breaks the de facto monopoly of many technical platform providers. While exceptions can be possible under strict circumstances, any such exceptions must be accompanied by a practical mechanism to ensure returns to the public from the proceeds of any monopoly granted. For example, the EU might require that any spin-off created to monetise the result of publicly funded research has to grant, on incorporation, twenty per cent of its shares as non-voting shares to the authorities that funded the research.

In addition, DiEM25 wants to put barriers around the public domain and prevent the enclosure of the commons of knowledge, by establishing certain areas of knowledge outside the reach of IP rights. This will include a ban on the concept of IP rights on anything invented or created by machines, and the introduction of a principle that any information 'found in nature' will be and remain at all times in the public domain. Biological information carriers such as DNA or RNA must be classified as Open Content languages, and not subject to any IP right.

DiEM25 will introduce a fundamental Right to Repair: the buyer of a product or service has the right to repair any aspect thereof (or have it repaired for them) and IP rights cannot be used as a means to block such Right to Repair. The Right to Repair includes the right to alter the technical standard in which something is made or captured. This means that if you buy something in one technical standard, you have the automatic right to convert it into another technical standard.

DiEM25 will introduce the principle of Open Standards. Technical standards must be documented so that interoperability is ensured, and they may not be subject to IP monopolies.

Planned obsolescence is the practice of designing and selling products with an artificially limited useful life. They are programmed to break down much earlier, and repair is made expensive, so consumers need to replace them. This leads to a substantial amount of waste. In line with our ecological goals we want products that are durable, repairable and/or upgradable.

DiEM25 wants to alter the approach to copyright fundamentally. This includes the harmonisation of exceptions to copyright, by introducing a fair use concept with broad application, based on freedom of speech.

In addition, DiEM25 proposes a fundamental reform to the Berne Convention on Literary and Artistic Works of 1886, by updating it and making it suitable for the digital age. This includes measures such as making copyright subject to registration, and payment of a fee that increases with time, forcing collecting authorities to provide full transparency on the rights they claim to represent, the costs they charge, and how much they pay to the right holders, and reversing the burden of proof in copyright: unless something can be shown to be clearly under copyright, it must be in the public domain.

DiEM25 wants to open a debate on the patent system: should it be abolished, or should it be reformed so that it can fulfil its original ambition of rewarding inventors and sharing their knowledge and innovations throughout society? In any case, it should become much easier and cheaper to disable a patent when it does not cover something that is actually novel.

DiEM25 wants to limit the enforcement of IP rights so that it benefits the actual inventor/creator, not their assignees/licencees when they do not contribute economic value. This will increase the inventor/creator's recognition, and ensure that they actually benefit from the IP monopoly that government creates for them.

Finally, DiEM25 wants to abolish any tax incentives to create, transfer or collect IP rights, and create a special tax on the rental income of existing IP rights as contributory funding for the Universal Basic Dividend as proposed in the European New Deal.

Education and technology

Knowledge is power. If we want to democratise technology, and start the debate around how society determines which technologies are developed, which are supported, how they are regulated and whether some should be banned, we need to ensure that informed debate is a priori possible.

Leaving everything to the experts is not a solution. Their expertise always comes imbued with opinions and values, containing an implicit view of society and how it should function—in other words, with a political view. Even if they deny it (especially if they deny it), the political views of technical experts should be viewed with normal democratic scepticism.

Decisions are never without value. But in order to be able to judge the values that are applied in decisions on technology, it is often necessary to understand, at least to a certain extent, the technology concerned.

Education plays a key role in democratic debate. Education, not just of the young, but the elderly as well, who are sometimes lost amidst the new technologies emerging around them. And of the civil servants, who must frame and administer the political discussions around technology. How a problem is presented within a certain bureaucratic system is often key to the solutions that are deemed 'possible'.

Also, we know there are serious issues of gender equality and representation in science and technology, and in the many government, quasi-government and private bodies that take key decisions in this area. So the key issue is: how do we, as a society, promote and ensure the knowledge necessary for a proper democratic debate around technology?

Introduce a general principle of transparency: any EU regulatory process (legislative, administrative or otherwise) that relates to how technology affects society should be fully transparent, not only in relation to the content of what is decided, but also with respect to the process (e.g. meetings with lobbyists, etc.).

Education systems and curricula should be updated to ensure an education in technology matters. This means not only teaching the basic principles underpinning technology as such (a minimum requirement of STEM for every student), but also explaining the relationship between technology and society, e.g. by pointing out alternative systems such as the commons and other economic models of technological development and management.

It is clear, in this respect, that our education systems should reflect, and educate, much more regarding the interaction of technology and society, and the concept of Technological Sovereignty. Approaches such as MOOCs (Massive Open Online Courses) can play a crucial role in this respect, providing a publicly available repository of knowledge and understanding.

Education via the internet revives a classical social topos: educating and empowering people. Today, courses by the best experts and most renowned teachers are accessible to many people across the globe. While this is a fantastic development, the accelerating technological change requires a more systematic approach to allow lifelong learning, e.g. via extended sabbaticals and learning credits. Rather than burdening individuals with the obligation to use their own time and resources in learning and gaining new technical skills, public and private support is needed to ensure flexible education can truly serve everyone. Access to lifelong learning is a right. Not a duty.

The principles of open standards and the Right to Repair lead us to a possible 'right to understand'. The EU should investigate a potential requirement for owners of technology to provide sufficient information to the public such that the general principles of how their technology works can be understood by people with sufficient training in the relevant area.

Of course, there would be justified concerns around safety and security, but, as we know from the real life experience of open source software, it is typically proprietary (and secret) technology that presents the highest risks to security, with increased vulnerability to hacking and potential abuse of flaws.

Technology for everyone

Public authorities should ensure that the debate on technology's development and regulation is conducted, not in backrooms full of industry lobbyists, but with participation of all stakeholders. Initiatives for technology assessment and public participation in science and technology need to be strengthened and in some cases made mandatory.

In addition, other stakeholders (e.g. consumers, workers, the public at large, public authorities) should have observation functions or guaranteed representation in the decision-making bodies (boards of management) of companies that make technological decisions with a significant impact on society—similar to how, under certain conditions, governments are entitled to appoint observers to the boards of financial institutions.

There is a growing sphere of organisations that foster public and open uses of technology. Europe has hundreds of maker spaces, FabLabs, museums and educational institutions that experiment with technology and knowledge oriented towards commons and society. New ways to support such projects should be found.

Democratising innovation and the economy

Every technological development is the result of choices. Choices made by governments, researchers, investors, consumers, manufacturers, distributors, users and many others. No technology is God-given or given by the 'invisible hand of the market', and no technology is neutral: it is always value-laden. The way we fund, adopt, use and regulate technology, or not, reflects society's choice of its values and priorities. However, decisions in research and innovation currently reflect the worldviews and interests of technocratic researchers, policymakers and above all venture capitalists that want to take research 'to the market', i.e. want to maximise their profits.

To every technological option there are always alternatives—including non-technological forms of change and problem solving. We must establish the necessary democratic instruments and institutions capable of addressing the complexities of inclusive twenty-first-century technologies. How do we define the problems that technologies should solve? How do we govern the risks and ambivalences of technologies? How do we make sure that their benefits are shared amongst the many?

An agenda to democratise technologies must address the fundamental structures that shape and govern technologies. To democratise Europe we need to also transform the societal, political and economic systems that innovate, shape, regulate and make use of technologies. How can these become more democratic and inclusive? How can we democratise the innovation processes that shape decisions about our future?

DiEM25's European Green New Deal proposes a Green-Investment-driven Recovery and a new agency for managing and funding Europe's Green Transition and Green Energy Union. These measures make use of the risk-taking, mission-oriented funding powers of public institutions and put idle financial wealth to socially useful purpose by boosting a transition into a greener economy that works for the many.

The European Union is already a major funder and decision-making body shaping the research that affects our lives. In the ongoing program Horizon 2020, the EU aims to spend €80 billion to fund research and innovation in the years 2014 to 2020. The following programme Horizon Europe entails €100 billion for research and innovation funding in the years 2021 to 2027.

While the programmes are proposed by the European Commission and debated in the European Council and the European Parliament, the individual funding decisions are taken in a technocratic manner by Brussels bureaucrats, lobbyists and scientific experts. It gets even worse when we consider venture capitalists, whose deep influence on the startups and entrepreneurs pursuing creative new technologies pushes investment based on the short-termist and narrow pursuit of maximum profit.

We need to build alternative and democratic forms of funding research and innovation, so that the technologies of the future will be democratically determined right from the start. We have to put citizens in charge of the decisions that shape technology: research and innovation need to become accountable to citizens and their needs and expectations. This explicitly includes decision-making by separate executive bodies as long as they are transparent, accountable and elected democratically.

The EU's research and innovation funding has a major deficit: it is premised on a 'high-tech for growth' strategy, directly playing the tune of big industry and a 'technology first, society second' symphony. This needs to change. The EU's funding needs to be opened up to purposes which serve the social good. We need to fund social and cultural innovation in concert with technological innovation. Different forms of creativity and transformation need to be combined to move into a brighter future, and funding should be distributed among a broader group of recipients. EU funding for research and innovation must be more easily attainable for civil society organisations, non-profit technology projects, cooperatives and others with a clear mission of green and social change. We need to fund purpose before profit from public money. There must furthermore be democratic oversight of the funding process. The EU should hold stakeholder assemblies for each funding instrument, involving citizens, researchers, NGOs and others in assessing impact.

Furthermore, the returns on research and innovation funding should recognise and support the public life and public institutions on which they depend, e.g. universities, and the collaboration and collective creativity that made them possible. Today if a product is innovated with EU funding, the profits of its marketisation are completely privatised. We propose that a dedicated percentage of returns from these publicly supported products contribute to the fund for the Universal Basic Dividend as set out in DiEM25's European New Deal. This gives society a fair return on its public investment in technological development.

We propose a digital platform for participatory budgeting on a transnational level. This platform will be a twenty-first-century institution that democratises the funding of research and innovation within the EU, giving citizens and civil society a stronger say.

Democratise funding: citizen crowdfunding

The platform needs to contain a crowdfunding system that allows European citizens to allocate public money, e.g. from the EU's Horizon Europe, through their decisions on the platform. The projects apply with their proposals and a sum of money that would allow them to start the work. As in crowdfunding, if enough citizens allocate public money to a proposed project, it is successful and gets money from the fund. A significant proportion of public funds for research and innovation needs to be put into this platform to give citizens a voice.

Innovation starts with problems that should be solved. Who defines the problems is a major issue in every innovation journey. In a democratic society, citizens should define the problems that innovations should help to solve. Therefore, the platform should also enable citizens to identify problems to be addressed through research and innovation. Problems would be freely submitted, then democratically ranked on the platform. Researchers and innovators can then apply with proposals targeting specific problems. In this way, purposes for innovation can be democratically defined by citizens rather than steered by unaccountable private interests.

To democratise research and innovation we also need to find ways to democratise the economy and to foster more decentralised economic arrangements, collective decision-making and structures for shared responsibilities. In short, we need to democratise economic decision-making and ownership of technology and organisations. DiEM25's labour pillar addresses the need for worker participation in companies.

Digital technologies are already being used to coordinate and to govern economic processes. This hints at a big opportunity to shape economic systems in the twenty-first century. We need to democratise these technological capabilities, and shift their application from the accumulation of profit to a radically different challenge: to shape economies that foster social justice and help to keep our production and consumption within planetary boundaries. Technologies such as the Internet of Things, robotics and machine learning offer vast potential to transform how we coordinate our lives and activities. It is imperative that this revolution in coordination is democratic at its heart.

If not, technological authoritarianism will further emerge. We must envision how ideas for real progress, such as that of an 'economy for the common good', can be implemented and democratically governed in such systems. Concretely this boils down to questions such as: whose values and interests will programme automated traffic systems, smart grids for sharing energy or automated agricultural technologies, and who will benefit from these technological powers? The capacity of these technologies is too vast to remain in private hands. It must belong to citizens.

[*The volunteers of the coordination team who structured the discussion, gathered feedback, and synthesised different inputs to create* Technological Sovereignty: Democratising Technology and Innovation, DiEM25 Green Paper No. 3, 2019, *are Joren De Wachter, Kate McCurdy, Christoph Schneider and David Schwertgen. The point person in the DiEM25 Coordinating Collective is Renata Avila. This version was edited by Rosemary Bechler.*]

For a Political Praxis of Algorithmic Sovereignty

Denis Jaromil Roio

We live in a world where more decisions are taken by algorithms than by humans. Even those still without access or those who refuse to use computers are affected. As a result, people have no idea how algorithms govern their lives; they just know they do. The space where rules are made is technological, no longer political. Algorithms can be negotiated only by specialists, then imposed top-down or introduced just by clicking on the agreement. This leads to situations where mere 'users' have no power over the rules that regulate them, but also no insight into the rules themselves, since they are hidden behind trade secrets.

Algorithms have an enormous power over users: they can inflict injustice, induce affective and psychological breakdowns, and exploit labour.

Three main types of failures have occurred so far:

- False positives
- Human psychosis
- Alienated labour

Let's look closer at these three failure scenarios, then point to solutions that are being adopted by policymakers and activists when discussing the topic of this article: that is, the governance of an algorithm by its own participants (no more 'users'!)—for which we have proposed the term 'algorithmic sovereignty'.

False positives

An algorithm can be thought about thus: it processes large amounts of data according to its directives, then marks some samples as positive matches. This happens when an article in our social media newsfeed is marked as 'relevant' for us. A false positive is an error that occurs when the algorithm marks something or someone who was not really supposed to be marked, leading to the dissatisfaction of a reader in the case of 'relevant articles' or the inappropriate treatment of a person in the case of risk assessment.

It is reasonable to consider the living world as an infinite source of unknowns: nothing is absolutely secure, there is no perfect system. The possibility of error is always there, only various degrees of accuracy may statistically lead to fewer errors. Additionally, in the real world when a subject is a false positive, then the error affects the entire subject, not just a statistical fraction of it. So, if we have a one-in-a-million probability to kill someone by mistake, when that occurs we still have killed someone innocent.

In the case of facial recognition programmes, the tragic story of Jean Charles de Menezes is exactly this: shot at Stockwell tube station in London on 22 July 2005 by unknown specialist firearms officers, he was a false positive. What is disturbing in this episode is not just that an innocent has been killed as a result of being confused with a terrorist by the growing apparatus of surveillance cameras, but how law enforcement officials made use of his image post-mortem on mainstream media to justify their error.

Shortly afterwards, in 2008, the Security Service of Great Britain (MI5) decided to mine all information about public transportation. All private data about each person travelling in England has since been, and continues to be, made available for computational analysis conducted by law enforcement agencies in order to search for hints and match patterns regarding terrorist activities. Many other countries followed suit, bypassing legal obstacles and constitutional laws. In the Netherlands, the 'sleepwet' campaign managed to gather enough signatures to mount and win a referendum against that practice. Nevertheless, the government ignored it and went ahead to implement this data mining.

While this may seem just a quantitative change in terms of information processed, it is important to understand why this is a deeply political, *qualitative* shift in the way algorithms are applied in law enforcement. From the necessity of a legal mandate issued by a judge to obtain private data about a specific subject, we have now moved to a situation where hidden algorithms process all data obtainable about any subject to assess risks and deviance patterns.

In mathematics the errors grow exponentially when we increase the number of dimensions. The standard mean error formula resumes this concept:

$$SE_x = \frac{s}{\sqrt{n}}$$

While contemporary security research concentrates on automatic pattern recognition in human behaviour, soon enough mass analysis will be exercised on the totality of data available and at unprecedented depths in the human brain. Yet algorithmic models fail to incorporate the risks of systemic failure: they can barely contemplate the ethical costs of killing an innocent. To keep campaigning for individual privacy is rather pointless at this point: what is really at stake is how our societies are governed, how we rate people's behaviour, individuate deviance, and how we act upon it.

Human psychosis

What we observe today in contexts where algorithms are deployed is a condition of subjugation. The living participants in these systems do not even access knowledge of the algorithms governing their own spaces.

The logic of algorithms is often invisible; only their results are manifest. The cognitive advantage or knowledge capital they offer is up for sale to advertisers. Cases such as that of Cambridge Analytica have uncovered highly questionable practices of political manipulation exercised in this way, through a hidden organising process to which the user is unwittingly exposed.

This condition has now extended beyond search engines: for an individual participant, hidden algorithms govern the rating of their visibility online, of success in dating someone, of the possibility of getting a loan, and, soon, will establish just-in-time prices for everything being bought, matched to a subject's desires and needs.

The resulting psychosis can lead to tragedy such as the one on 3 April 2018, when Nasim Aghdam, a content creator who operated a number of channels covering art, music, and veganism entered the YouTube headquarters in San Bruno, California, and opened fire on a number of YouTube employees, severely wounding three, before turning the gun on herself. Her claim was that changes in YouTube's rating algorithms were hindering her visibility and unjustly removing her from her audience.

Psychopathology emerges in the breakdown of the barriers between lives lived excessively on screen and the external, sensory, and emotional world. This is a dimension where injustice, prevarication, and conflict as seen on a screen can be projected directly into real life—with dramatic consequences. Psychopathology stems from a negative, irrational, poorly-tuned response to the affective environment; and affect is directly linked by algorithms to the social and cultural expectation of participation in mediated environments, where the logics of appreciation, remuneration, and punishment are hidden.

Alienated labour

Going beyond the affective dimension, it is the activity of human labour that nurtures algorithms, while being less and less labelled as labour. Human activity online is often alienated in the domain of games or social interaction, and, at the same time, exploited for its value on numerous markets.

So-called 'platform work' basically consists of online platforms using hidden algorithms to match the supply of and demand for paid labour. For the workers exploited by crowdsourcing platforms, there is no possibility to negotiate their own ratings, or to understand and influence the algorithms that validate the work being done.

If we can consider the labour conditions of 'platform workers' as analogous to what Italian Autonomous movements have called 'precarious workers', it may be possible to nurture the trade-union consciousness of large and growing multitudes of workers. But even if it seems easier today to organise and communicate with a large amount of people, it is still difficult to devise platforms that can facilitate the necessary independence, integrity, and confidentiality for such communications.

The journey is still too long. But rather than regress into a primitive rejection of algorithms, let's try to envision a positive horizon where the humanisation of digital labour occurs, encouraging cooperation, co-ownership, and the democratic governance of algorithms.

Going beyond the empire of algorithmic profit

Following the dotcom boom era and the vertiginous rise of capital in financial markets, human dynamics (including the application of laws, affective space and labour conditions) are increasingly abstracted from the algorithm governing them. Through the decades, this has created huge asymmetries between the agency of humans and that of the empire built by profits from algorithms.

Global corporations are ruling the world at unthinkable speeds and with seemingly infinite resources, for which (algorithmic) clouds are an apt metaphor: omnipresent and intangible, they seem to connect the sky to the ground by carrying the water needed by the living world. And they offer it at a price that is not measured in money, but in souls. Following this metaphor, let's not forget that water is a common good. It should be fair access to match offer with demand in the digital economy.

Historically, public institutions are an important bastion of rationality that transcend the mere logic of profit and stand for peace and prosperity of a particular society and of the living world as a whole. As in similar struggles for food sovereignty, trade unions, and workers' associations, social institutions have the important role of stewards of the commons. Let's now imagine a new mission for them: to empower participants to know the rules of algorithmic systems, to facilitate democratic participation also through algorithms, to be able to appeal algorithmic decisions, and to grant human intervention on life-critical decisions.

Going in this direction, a bright example for Europe is the institutional work achieved in the heart of the fearless city of Barcelona by its CTO Francesca Bria during the mandate of mayor Ada Colau, calling for a new form of municipal rationality that takes technological sovereignty fully into account.

This narrative is echoing through the world's biggest municipal administrations as we speak: a stance against the colonisation of dense settlements by complex technical systems that are far beyond the reach and political control of citizens. The "Manifesto in Favour of Technological Sovereignty and Digital Rights for Cities"[1] is now considered a standard set of guidelines for ethics in governance by many cities of the world.

Finally, being a software developer myself, I'd like to call to action fellow programmers out there: We need to write code that is understandable by other humans, as well as animals, plants, and all the living world we inoculate with our sensors and manipulate through automatism. Good code is not what is skillfully crafted or what is most efficient, but what can be read by others, studied, changed, and adapted. Let's adopt intuitive namespaces or simple metaphors that can be easily matched with reality; let's make sure that what we write is close to what we mean. Common understanding of algorithms is vital, because their governance must be an inter-disciplinary exercise and cannot be left in the hands of a technical elite.

It is also important to rethink the meaning of 'innovation' in light of its side effects on legacy systems that are already well understood by a larger portion of participants. Innovation often introduces complexity and technical debts that are not only economic but political, since they affect the safety of systems, their ease of maintenance and accessibility to communities.

When compelled to innovate, let us ask everyone the question: Does anyone really need to substitute what is already in use with something else? Before chang-ing an algorithm, shall we ask first: How did it work so far? And if it worked well, why? Using what languages? What sort of people operated it? What ethos did they cultivate? Legacy systems often stratify an enormous quantity of knowledge built through the years by many people. As such, they may seem chaotic at first sight, because they aren't the result of top-down planning. But they can still be simple to navigate. Algorithms can embed ethical choices made through decades and chang-ing them may falsely assume that many important governance choices are simply obsolete. If maintaining an old algorithm comes at a high cost in human labour, then so be it: what we cannot really afford is to lose control of what governs our societies.

Notes

1 Currently hosted by Barcelona Municipality at https://www.barcelona.cat/digitalstandards/manifesto/0.2/.

The Right to the (Digital) City

Francesca Bria

The structural shift to the digital economy and the fourth industrial revolution should trigger deep thinking. Artificial intelligence, massive computation, robotisation, and automation are quickly transforming our industry and society, with digital platforms capturing key markets such as healthcare, education, transport, and housing. This rise of digital capitalism brings many challenges: from questioning monopoly power to the need for a new tax for digital platforms, from trade regulations to automation-caused unemployment, raising various questions around civil liberties and fundamental rights.

Large tech firms have a combined market value of $4 trillion, and have offshored around $1 trillion in the last decade, while they are issuing debt on the US public market at a very low interest rate and using it for shares buybacks so that they can pay high dividends to their shareholders. This means that 80 per cent of corporate wealth belongs to just 10 per cent of firms, leading to an increase in corporate profit and wealth inequality. Furthermore, the public sector is increasingly dependent on the tech industry.

Repoliticising the question of technology

Still, we rarely ask where this power and dependence comes from. Why is the immense value that such a digital revolution represents accruing exclusively to technology firms—and not to ordinary citizens or public institutions? And what can we do to return some of that value back to citizens, while empowering them to use technology to participate in politics—a process from which they justly feel excluded—as well as to offer better and more affordable public services?

It is obvious that we need to repoliticise the question of technology and have this discussion in terms of redistribution of assets and power, and the management of future welfare services and critical infrastructures.

Given the gloomy state of politics on both sides of the Atlantic, this might seem impossible. And yet, there's one bright spot on the horizon: cities. They can't, of course, solve all our digital problems—many of them need urgent attention at the national and global level—but cities can become laboratories for democracy and sustainability. They can run smart, data-intensive, algorithmic public transportation, housing, health, and education—all based on a logic of solidarity, social cooperation, and collective rights.

Cities can deliver on the promise to take back the city for the people, and this also means democratising the ownership of and access to digital technologies. As I argue in the booklet written with Evgeny Morozov, *Rethinking the Smart City*, cities can initiate a radical democratic process that puts people's digital sovereignty first.

Reclaiming technological sovereignty

When we talk about urban technology and data, we are dealing with a meta-utility composed of those very sensors and algorithms which power the rest of the city. As cities lose control over said meta-utility, they find it increasingly difficult to push for non-neoliberal models in supposedly non-technological domains such as energy or healthcare. One useful concept for cities seeking to preserve a degree of autonomy in this digital world is that of technological sovereignty: an idea which denotes citizens' capacity to participate in how the technological infrastructure around them operates and what ends it serves.

The notion of sovereignty—whether of finances or energy—permeates the activities of many urban social movements, including those transitioning into leadership positions in their respective cities. Concepts like energy sovereignty may be easily grasped and capable of mobilising large sections of the population, but what does energy sovereignty mean once we transition onto the smart grid, and firms like Google offer to cut our energy bills by one third if only we surrender our energy data? Does the struggle for energy sovereignty mean anything if it is not intricately tied to the struggle for technological sovereignty? Probably not.

A fight for digital sovereignty should be coupled with a coherent and ambitious political and economic agenda capable of reversing the damage inflicted by the neoliberal turn in both urban and national policy. Well-targeted, pragmatic interventions can have a big impact. Insofar as signing smart city contracts requires purchasing software licences, every effort should be made to demand free software and open-source alternatives—a measure which many cities would be well-advised to codify into law. Barcelona is a pioneer on this front, having defined a Digital City Strategy, with a manifesto for technological sovereignty pledging to drop Microsoft products from its system, and investing over 80 per cent of its IT new development budget in free software and open-source services, while also introducing data sovereignty clauses in public procurement contracts and defining ethical digital standards that need to be followed by public officials in the digitalisation process.

The right to enjoy rights

The right to the city might need reformulation as the right to enjoy rights altogether, as the alternative means risking that digital giants will continue redefining every right. What, for example, does a right to the city mean in a city operated by technology companies and governed by private law, with citizens and social communities unable to freely and unconditionally access key resources like data, connectivity, and computing power, which could allow them to pursue self-management?

And to what extent would losing control over the information-powered meta-utility undercut successful remunicipalisation campaigns, whether to reclaim energy, transport, or water infrastructure, allowing the utilities in question to transition to their own 'smart' consumption model with a new set of private intermediaries?

Ultimately, brave cities that want to deploy key resources and digital infrastructures under a different legal and economic model—which produces outcomes benefiting local residents and local industry—must show that the economic models proposed by the likes of Uber, Google, and Airbnb do not deliver the promised results. At least, not without causing considerable damage to the cities, from the rise of the speculative economy and gentrification to the precarity of labour in the gig economy and the blockage of social innovation by those without access to data. Many of these alternative experiments to achieve digital sovereign cities must happen working jointly with other like-minded cities and with stronger synergies at national, continental, and global levels, as demonstrated by promising projects such as the Cities Alliance for Digital Rights initiated by Barcelona, New York, and Amsterdam.

A new deal on data: city data commons

Changing the data ownership regime may be an affordable option, if only because it would not require massive financial commitment, and because it represents an agenda with intuitive popular appeal: cities and citizens, not companies, ought to own the data produced in cities and should be able to use said data to improve public services and put their policies into action.

In the fourth industrial revolution, data and artificial intelligence (AI) are essential digital infrastructures that are critical for political and economic activity. Data has become the most valuable commodity in the world. It is the raw material of the digital economy, and it fuels AI. Companies in every industry are counting on artificial intelligence to drive growth over the years to come. Data cannot be controlled by a handful of tech giants. Business models that exploit personal data to pay for critical infrastructures are broken. We need to democratise data ownership and artificial intelligence, and move from data extractivism to data commons.

Taking a firm stance on data ownership may accomplish several goals at once. Firstly, it would make the rampant real estate speculation facilitated by the likes of Airbnb much more difficult: cities and ordinary citizens would be able to check whether the claims frequently made by Airbnb in its defence—that it primarily benefits ordinary users—are empirically verifiable. Secondly, placing cities in charge of their own data would remove one of the main bargaining chips firms like Uber now have when negotiating with regulators. In Boston, for example, Uber offered the authorities access to traffic data, expecting in return lighter regulation. Thirdly, it seems highly unlikely that cities could stimulate growth of an alternative digital economy with robust local and decentralised alternatives to Uber and Airbnb without a robust alternative data regime. Without the troves of data available to these giants, these smaller contenders may prove unable to compete.

The immense economic value that such data represents should be returned back to citizens. By helping citizens regain control of their data we can generate public value rather than private profits. To take one of the most ambitious examples, Barcelona is betting on a new approach to data called 'city data commons'. This involves striking a New Social Pact on Data to make the most out of data, while guaranteeing data sovereignty and privacy. Data is a key city infrastructure, and can be used to reach better, faster, and more democratic decisions, incubate innovation, improve public services, and empower the citizens.

DECODE

Barcelona is experimenting with socialising data in order to promote new cooperative platforms and democratise innovation. This is the objective of DECODE, a project Barcelona leads with thirteen partner organisations from across Europe, including cities like Amsterdam. The DECODE project develops decentralised technologies (such as blockchain and attribute-based cryptography) to give people better control of their data, in part by laying down rules on who can access it, for what purposes, and on which terms.

By helping citizens regain control of their data, we aspire to generate public value, rather than private profit. Our goal is to create data commons from data produced by people, sensors, and devices. A data commons is a shared resource that enables citizens to contribute, access, and use the data (e.g. about air quality, mobility, health) as a common good, without intellectual property rights restrictions.

Barcelona envisions data as public infrastructure alongside roads, electricity, water, and clean air. It is a meta-utility that will enable us to build future smart public services in transportation, healthcare, education. However, we are not building a new panopticon. Citizens will set the anonymity level, so that they can't be identified without explicit consent. And they will keep control over data once they share it for the common good. This common data infrastructure will remain open to local companies, co-ops, and social organisations that can build data-driven services and create long-term public value.

Involving citizens in Amsterdam and Barcelona, DECODE addresses real-world problems. For example, it's integrated with the participation platform 'decidim. barcelona', already used by thousands of citizens to shape the city's policy agenda, with over 70 per cent of the government actions proposed directly by citizens. Rather than using the personal information of voters (furnished by the likes of Cambridge Analytica) for manipulation, data-intensive platforms are used to boost participation and make politicians more accountable.

Data commons can also help cities develop alternatives to predatory on-demand platforms like Uber and Airbnb. Introducing fair regulation and algorithmic transparency to tame the on-demand economy, as many cities are currently doing, is necessary but insufficient. Barcelona has launched a variety of initiatives to empower sharing economy alternatives such as platform cooperatives and experiments with next-generation collective platforms that work for the public interest.

A people-centric, rights-based framework for digital Europe

We can start from cities to challenge the current narrative dominated by Silicon Valley's leaky surveillance capitalism and dystopian models, such as China's social credit system. A New Deal on Data, built around a rights-based, people-centric framework, which does not exploit personal data to pay for critical infrastructure, is long overdue.

Europe just passed new data protection rules based on worthy principles such as *privacy by design* and *data portability* and *the right to be forgotten*. Coupled with new regulatory instruments in the areas of taxation, antitrust, and digital trade, such bold interventions can create alternatives where citizens have greater power over their data and the future built with it. As we ask how we could create a financial sector that serves the real economy, we should be asking how could we create a digital sector that serves the people? We need a New Social Pact for digital society that will make the most of new technologies, access to data, and artificial intelligence, while guaranteeing citizens' fundamental rights, workers rights, environmental standards, and gender equality.

This new social pact will require rethinking the economic model for digital society, making sure that it can create public value and it is not confined only to private profits, reconquering critical digital infrastructures—long surrendered to the likes of Facebook, Alphabet, and Microsoft—and protecting citizens' digital sovereignty.

This is a matter of democracy, and cities like Barcelona can show the way and open a path for a network of digital sovereign cities reclaiming democratic governance of twenty-first-century infrastructures, including data sovereignty and ethical AI for citizens.

Alternative forms of public and common ownership for platforms and infrastructures, as heralded by the wave of remunicipalisation rolling across Europe in energy, water, and waste management, will help create a more democratic economy, transcending the logic of short-termism and rent extraction. Rather than trying to stop innovation, we should think about how to harness this technology-driven transformation to improve our society and welfare for the collective benefit. In this way, we will shape a digital future for the many, not the few.

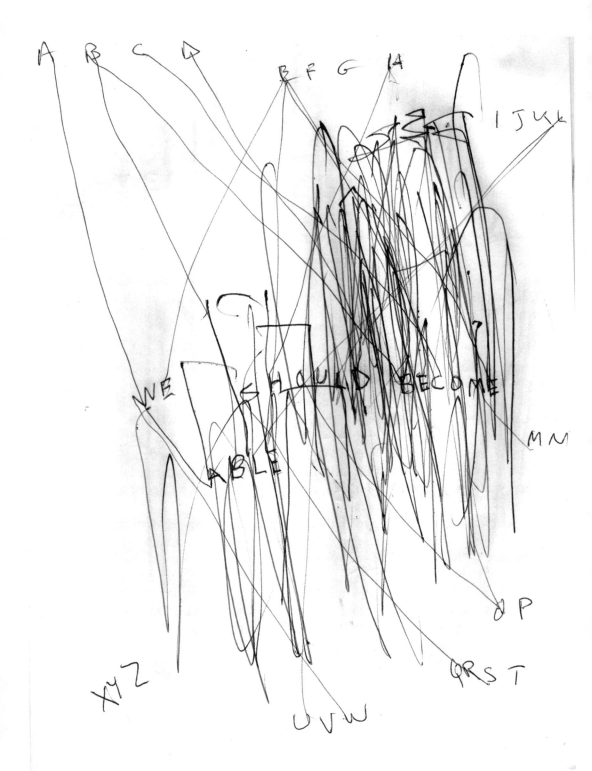

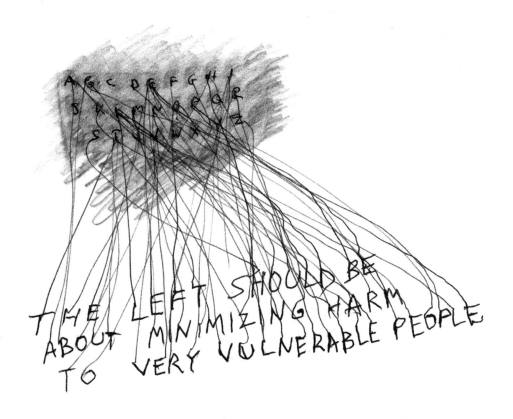

We Should Become Able (left)
*"Left Should Be About Minimizing Harm to Very Vulnerable People"
Yanis Varoufakis, 2018* (right)

A Technological Europe by Shoshana Zuboff

66 Surveillance capitalism is a human creation. It lives in history, not in techno-logical inevitability. Surveillance capitalism was invented around 2001 as the solution to financial emergency in the teeth of the dotcom bust, when a fledgling company faced the loss of investor confidence. Operationally this meant that Google would repurpose its growing cache of behavioural data, now put to work as a behavioural data surplus, and develop methods to aggressively seek new sources of this surplus.

The company developed new methods that could uncover data that users inten-tionally opted to keep private, as well as infer extensive personal information that users did not or would not provide. And this surplus would then be analysed for hidden meanings that could predict click-through behaviour. The surplus data became the basis for new predictions markets called 'targeted advertising'.

Here was the origin of surveillance capitalism in an unprecedented and lucrative brew: behavioural surplus, data science, material infrastructure, computational power, algorithmic systems, and automated platforms. As click-through rates skyrocketed, advertising became hugely important. Eventually, it became the cornerstone of a new kind of commerce that depended upon online surveillance at scale.

Surveillance capitalism quickly became the default model for capital accumula-tion in Silicon Valley, embraced by nearly every startup and app. By now, it has spread across a wide range of products, services, and economic sectors, including insurance, retail, healthcare, finance, entertainment, education, transportation, and more, birthing whole new ecosystems of suppliers, producers, customers, market makers, and market players. Nearly every product or service that begins with the word 'smart' or 'personalised', every internet-enabled device, every 'digital assistant', is simply a supply-chain interface for the unobstructed flow of behavioural data on its way to predicting our futures in a surveillance economy.

Surveillance capitalists were the first movers in this new world. They declared their right to know, to decide who knows, and to decide who decides. In this way they have come to dominate what I call 'the division of learning in society', which is now the central organising principle of the twenty-first-century social order, just as the divi-sion of labour was the key organising principle of society in the industrial age.

This power to shape behaviour for others' profit or power usurps decision rights and erodes the processes of individual autonomy that are essential to the function of a democratic society. The message here is simple: Once, I was mine. Now, I am theirs.

During the past two decades surveillance capitalists have had a pretty free run, with hardly any interference from laws and regulations. Democracy has slept while surveillance capitalists amassed unprecedented concentrations of knowledge and power. These dangerous asymmetries are institutionalised in their monopolies of data science, their dominance of machine intelligence, which is surveillance capital-ism's 'means of production', their ecosystems of suppliers and customers, their lucra-tive prediction markets, their ability to shape the behaviour of individuals and populations, their ownership and control of our channels for social participation, and their vast capital reserves. We enter the twenty-first century marked by this stark inequality in the division of learning: they know more about us than we know about ourselves, or than we know about them.

These new forms of social inequality are inherently anti-democratic. Moreover, surveillance capitalism depends upon undermining individual self-determination, autonomy and decision rights for the sake of an unobstructed flow of behavioural data to feed markets that are about us but not for us. This anti-democratic and anti-egalitar-ian juggernaut is best described as a market-driven coup from above: an overthrow of the people concealed as the technological Trojan horse of digital technology.

The tech leaders desperately want us to believe that technology is the inevitable force here, and their hands are tied. But there is a rich history of digital applications before surveillance capitalism that really were empowering and consistent with democratic values. Technology is the puppet, but surveillance capitalism is the puppet master.

Surveillance capitalism is a human-made phenomenon and it is in the realm of politics that it must be confronted. The resources of our democratic institutions must be mobilised, including our elected officials. GDPR (a recent EU law on data protection and privacy for all individuals within the EU) is a good start, and time will tell if we can build on that sufficiently to help found and enforce a new para-digm of information capitalism. Our societies have tamed the dangerous excesses of raw capitalism before, and we must do it again.

The first work begins with naming. Speaking for myself, this is why I've devoted the past seven years to this work . . . to move forward the project of naming as the first necessary step toward taming. My hope is that careful naming will give us all a better understanding of the true nature of this rogue mutation of capitalism and contribute to a sea change in public opinion, most of all among the young. **,,**

[*This quotation, with the author's permission, excerpts the interview between Shoshana Zuboff and John Naughton, technology correspondent for* The Observer.]

DIEM VOICE

QWERTYUIOP
ASDFGH JKL
ZXCVBNM?
CD

WHAT IS OUR WORK
ON LANGUAGE?
ARE WE ~~A~~
CAPABLE OF
TRANSLATING CONCEPTS?

DIEM
VOCE
DIEM VOZ
WHAT
IS
OUR
WORK
ON LANGUAGE ?
ARE WE CAPABLE OF
TRANSLATING CONCEPTS ?

An Open Europe by Daniel Erlacher

Emma Goldman once wrote she didn't believe in any revolution you can't dance to—and you proved her right.

Daniel "Danny" Schechter's feedback on his
Elevate Festival experience in Graz in 2007

The Free Space [is] the realm where all creative-response merges to establish a dynamic counterpoint to the bad ideologies that seek to push us backward.

Within the Free Space, creative response embraces the odd idea, the idiosyncratic thought, and the impractical strategy, twisting and bending our narrow ideas of what seems impossible into the possible. If we look back throughout the history of creative response and the Free Space, the most important ideas have been things that connect us and bring us together.

Antonino D'Ambrosio in *The Nation*

" What does it take to organise a festival? A healthy portion of madness, I suggested in an interview before the first Elevate Festival in 2005. Courage in risk-taking is vital since a festival always carries that scent of unpredictability.

Founders of festivals need to make an initial choice: are they working for profit or for the common good? At Elevate, since our team consisted of musicians, event organisers, technologists, and political activists, we chose to be a non-profit. The legal structure of an association for the common good made sense then. Fifteen years later, however, we miss certain advantages of the corporate legal structure, like limited liability.

Look at some alternative concepts: Free Festivals and Teknivals. Most of these festival strategies aim to create a Temporary Autonomous Zone (TAZ) and a transformational environment. Thanks to the underground, avant-garde, and DIY attitude, such festivals provide a very important and specific Autonomous Free Space. But over time it has proven hard to sustain such an experience while operating inside the boundaries of a state, which, naturally, does not accept TAZs.

As for the difference our festival could make, we took a risk: combining elements that rarely go together to create a unique programme of electronic music, art, and critical political discourse. Usually thought of as 'add-ons' to each other, combining these fields of interest on an equal platform had rarely been done before.

'Free Space' is a term coined by the Italian-American filmmaker Antonino D'Ambrosio. The tenth Elevate Festival in 2014 inspired Antonino and the Elevate team to feature the theme Creative Response in the eleventh edition.

Now, the Free Space is a core element of any festival, commercial or non-commercial. It is the space where the unpredictability of the event is embraced, a fertile ground for chance encounters with a potential to change the world. The more nutrients you add, the higher the chance for something to grow out of it. The more diversity and variety is presented at a festival, the more interesting is the outcome. An artist at a discussion panel using a set of turntables to explain, practically, how a remix works in the context of the creative commons? A filmmaker meeting an indigenous activist on a dance floor and plotting a new project together? There are countless Free Space stories to tell. The more you mix, the more you get!

The We Are Europe Festival cooperation project, coordinated by Lyon's ArtyFarty organisation, is a network of festivals that embraces the spirit of collaboration, exchange and, yes, friendship and inspiration. The participating festivals are very diverse, from Sónar in Barcelona (Spain) or Nuits Sonores in Lyon (France), both with audiences of 100,000 or more every year—to very small community-driven gems like Insomnia in Tromsø (Norway) that has an attendance of 2,500 a year. Also on the roster: c/o Pop in Cologne (Germany), Reworks in Thessaloniki (Greece), TodaysArt in The Hague (Netherlands), Unsound in Krakow (Poland), and Elevate in Graz (Austria).

We Are Europe is an attempt to unlock even more collaborative and creative potential by joining forces and sharing knowledge. Speakers, artists, musicians, a diverse audience, and enhanced mobility: the ingredients for new Free Spaces are already there. Big stages and great exposure for artists and speakers alike lay the ground for intense exchanges—on and off stage.

With unpredictable outcomes as standard, embraced to their fullest potential on the fertile ground of the Free Space, Europe's creative festival culture is overflowing with new ideas to challenge the status quo and build a more open, cooperative continent. 99

Previous spread: *What Is Our Work on Language? Are We Capable of Translating Concepts?*

PART NINE

Arts and Culture

The Politics of Creativity

Bobby Gillespie

"What are the politics of boredom?", asked former art student Malcolm McLaren in 1975 in a press release he wrote during his ill-fated tenure as manager of the glamorous but doomed New York Dolls. Nobody was listening at that point: the Dolls were falling apart, and the rock audience was not ready to question either themselves or the spectacle which had kept them passive spectators in a power play of a pampered, distant rock and roll aristocracy. McClaren couldn't test his theory on a mass audience until 1977, when he was manager of the Sex Pistols.

I was a teenage convert to the punk movement. The combination of the Pistols' high-energy rock and roll, the poetry of Johnny Rotten's lyrics, and the seditious sleeve art of Jamie Reid spoke to something deep inside me. Punk and the Pistols opened up my working-class Glasgow world. Punk gave me a frame of reference I would never have had otherwise. I left school at age sixteen with three O-Levels and became an apprentice lithographic printer. I hated it: the drudgery, the discipline, the hierarchy. Deference to the boss. The wages were good. It was a unionised factory and I was a paid-up member of the N.G.A. But still, 'the politics of boredom' prevailed: I felt a deep, unarticulated urge to express myself.

I was never taught about art or literature at school. I had to find that stuff for myself. I am still angry about this. I hungered to learn, but class and family circumstances demanded I work in the factory. I wish I had gone to art school. The system just wasn't set up that way. Education was set up so that the *clever* ones go to university and the rest of us into semi-skilled industrial work, unskilled labour, or unemployment. I found out I was creative not through school, but through punk. Rock and roll transformed and liberated me. I was lucky.

In the 1970s, further education was free in the UK. You could go to university or art school or technical college if you had the right grades, or if a teacher or parent saw potential in you. Due to forty years of neoliberalism, young people now must shackle themselves to tens of thousands of pounds of debt, which discriminates against students from poorer backgrounds and reinforces the class system in the arts. Professor Louise Wilson of Central St. Martins complained to me that she could no longer teach the modern equivalents of Alexander McQueen and John

Galliano (both working-class boys, both her former students) because "they couldn't afford to attend the school now".

This is deliberate. The culture war on the arts and education is part of a wider war on living conditions, wages, workers' rights, the privatisation of publicly owned utilities and spaces, and our freedoms. By financially blocking the right to further education for all who wish to pursue it, advancement has become the preserve of the privileged.

Art, culture, and education should be for everyone, regardless of their background. In the past, poets, artists, and writers all mostly came from the upper classes because their inherited wealth gave them so much free time. Halfway through the last century, that changed: art, literature, and pop culture thrived under the welfare state introduced by postwar social democracies. Suddenly, working-class people like Bryan Ferry, Brian Eno, Keith Richards, Ray Davies, David Hockney, Jake and Dinos Chapman, and Damien Hirst could attend art schools and widen their frame of reference and experiment and work with other students and dream their way out of their world and into one of their own making.

So I'd like to ask, what are the politics of creativity? How can we harness the potential of youthful creativity across not just our nation but our continent, free of the fear of debt exploitation and the need to slave away in low-paid, precarious jobs? I propose free education for all, funded by higher taxes on the wealthiest people in society and corporations, with more time devoted to the arts. Millions of young people do not know they are creative simply because they have never been properly introduced to art.

We need to increase funding for education, build more art schools and universities, train more teachers, and consider the future of Europe as an art project, because art connects people, transcending borders and all notions of identity and nationality. Art can be the strongest oppositional force to patriarchal, militaristic, fascist thinking, and rock and roll a revolutionary force for good.

Take the example of the fine artist Jim Lambie, my dear friend, who saw a painting by Andy Warhol in a book when he was a teenager in the working-class town of Airdrie in Scotland. This epiphanic moment made him start questioning his way of thinking, questioning the life mapped out for him. Jim attended the Glasgow School of Art, was nominated for the Turner Prize in 2005, and has shown his work across the world. Jim was a beneficiary of the British welfare state, has lived a successful creative life as a working artist, and now teaches at the art school.

Circling back to Malcolm McLaren and the Situationists, the lesson of punk was to be a participant, *not* a spectator: to get involved and tell your story. Consuming is passive; creating is active. Worship no one. Question authority. Question *yourself*. Read, learn, and create. Art and culture are bridges to empathy and solidarity, bridges that could span all of Europe and unite us in these turbulent times, and that is why they are currently under attack from the right. We on the progressive left must make people aware of this and use our work as an agent for change.

The politics of creativity are the politics of life. We don't make art alone. Art is a collaboration. Art is for everybody and everybody deserves access to it. We don't make art *for* ourselves. We make art for other people, to make a connection: a gesture of love to bring us together.

Here's to the future, and here's to art.

The Politics of Culture

Leila Jancovich in conversation with Rosemary Bechler

Rosemary Bechler: *Leila, you lead a Centre for cultural policy in the University of Leeds which brings together academics from a range of disciplines to look at two things: the politics of culture and the policing or management of it. Tell me more.*

Leila Jancovich: People often think too much about the technocratic management of cultural policy, forgetting about the politics implicit in the term. At the Centre, we are very consciously interdisciplinary and have a wide range of interests in cultural policy. We have people from arts and humanities backgrounds, but also from politics, history, and geography; people who are interested in how the arts or the media industries operate, and others interested in the role of culture in everyday life.

Within the Universal Declaration of Human Rights, the right of everyone to participate in *their culture* is explicitly stated, but this assumes a broad definition of what is at stake. Their definition includes tradition, religious beliefs, and, indeed, the anthropological study of everything that we do. But there is a real tendency in the western tradition on cultural policy, and in particular in Europe, to just be talking about the professional arts. That isn't at all the same in South America, for example, where there is a broader understanding of culture. So, I deliberately leave the definition of culture as open as possible, because I want as large a range of meanings as we can get.

This is intimately connected to one of my strongest convictions, that cultural policy should encourage people to define culture for themselves. The professional cultural sector can so easily become inward-looking and end up just talking to itself. Everything that I am writing about and thinking about seeks to break down those self-justifying logics and challenge that thinking. I think this is necessary if we want to create a progressive cultural policy.

RB: *You describe your specific area of interest as the power relationships within decision-making, and examining the extent to which policy can be changed by changing the voices who sit around the decision-making table. This sounds interesting.*

LJ: Take the Aarhus Capital of Culture in 2017. In applying to win this title, the Danish team decided to emphasise the regional rather than city character of their bid. All nineteen local authorities in the Central Denmark Region were involved in the process. They decided that the bid should be written collectively, and really asked themselves what would happen if they brought new people around the decision-making table. Eight thousand people got involved via roadshows, exhibitions, and all sorts of other initiatives and they wrote the bid on that basis; so it is full of phrases such as "Culture as a way of life", "Culture as local", "Culture in everything we do", and it is really interesting because that meant that it focused on what they defined as the DIY cultural 'growth layer', rather than around big, international events, with high-profile artists touring European art across the continent.

Now the interesting thing was in the implementation of that. 80 per cent of the budget did go out to the regions, and only 20 per cent remained with the professional delivery organisation in the city. But in terms of profile, the language changed to talking about world-class arts and culture. This was what 'Europe wanted', if you like, and from talking to people involved, many felt that this limited the participatory aspirations beyond the bidding stage. But, equally, others thought that the whole project had acted as a catalyst to inspire local activity in a way that just dispensing the funds would not have. So, it is interesting to see the possibilities but also the limitations of that kind of approach, when linked to a high-profile event.

The multiple criteria of success, which included increasing tourism and foregrounding the profile of European culture, meant that some of the minority cultures certainly felt left behind. It also became a bit of a political battleground, as the nationalists raised the stakes by using it to ask questions about what is European culture and what is Denmark's national culture as opposed to multiculturalism.

A second example must be Cultura Viva in Brazil, a cultural programme that built on the participatory budgeting projects of the 1990s, which grew out of the trade union and liberation movements in a very different Brazil from the one we see today. Those projects stemmed from the question: what will happen if we give communities the funding and they decide what public services *they* need and what *their* priorities are? Cultura Viva considered what might this mean for cultural policy by asking how the same communities define their culture. This was enormously successful in energising communities, and specifically in its redistributive effect of transferring funds from the cities and centres that usually soak up the majority of funding, to the far-and-out areas that are so often neglected and under-resourced.

The participatory budgeting model has been picked up by everyone, from the World Bank to European governments. But it is noticeable that, in a period of austerity in Europe, there is a much more cynical version of involving the community—what you might call a 'use it or lose it' approach, which relies on volunteerism instead of funding. This is the opposite of the participatory process in Brazil, which was used precisely to get more funding to the people who really needed it. So, it is important to recognise the risks in these processes which can be used in very different ways by both right-wing and left-wing governments.

Let me just mention one more example of transformation, and that is the Contact theatre in Manchester. It's a fantastic example of a DIY or activist approach that didn't wait for policymakers to catch up. Historically, the theatre had put on classical set texts for school audiences and traditional theatre audiences. When it had to close for renovation for a couple of years in the mid 1990s, there was a change of director and management, and the board decided that they would like to try and run a theatre where young people were at the heart of the decision-making and not just dragged along by their teachers. From 1999 to the current day, they have put young people under twenty-five on the board of directors. Every time a job is advertised, from the cleaners to the Artistic Director, they have to go through the Young People's Panel as well. They are involved in programming decisions, and volunteers for this are funded to go and see productions to build up their skills. That's very important: they aren't just expected to make their own expertise up from scratch.

What you get as a result is a theatre whose work has become more experimental and vibrant and they have the most culturally diverse theatre audiences in the country: 40 per cent are from black and minority ethnic audiences, 70 per cent are under thirty—the very demographic that more traditional theatres often say they cannot attract. They are now called just Contact, because they found that even the word 'theatre' was off-putting, and they are changing the very notion of what theatre means.

RB: *In your research you clearly have made a choice in favour of the need to celebrate everyday creativity for social change (as embodied in the work of William Morris) rather than the preoccupation with social control and preventing anarchy, which motivated Matthew Arnold when he first put 'culture' on the political map with his hugely influential work of 1869,* Culture and Anarchy.

LJ: Yes, for me this is central. Most cultural policy documents today focus on the value of arts and culture to society, its value in terms of social inclusion and cohesion, in terms of the individual benefits for health and wellbeing of those who take part— and there are many research projects with claims about the value of the arts in those terms. There has also been a big focus on the economic contribution that so-called 'cultural industries' make. But just as with any economic growth models throughout Europe, we can see that this benefits the few, rather than the many. I would argue that those very assumptions are still built on Matthew Arnold's belief that the role of culture is to prevent anarchy by making a healthy, socially included workforce happy to work within the current system. Although we often hear arguments about the role of the arts and culture in challenging the status quo, in many ways they reinforce dominant values, and we do forget, at our peril, that they can also be used to maintain it. Hitler supported the arts to prop up his idea of the super race; the CIA funded artists to promote the American dream; and around the world today, from the British Council in England to the Confucius Institute in China, governments use culture to increase their international prestige and to promote their own core values, exerting what is sometimes called 'soft power'—or social control—over people's minds.

RB: *Before we move on, I think it is worth lingering on this Arnoldian notion of culture as a civilising agent to lead the multitude at a time when, with the development of capitalism, as Arnold saw it, priesthoods and aristocracies were losing their hold over society.*

Culture and Anarchy, *written in the wake of the French Revolution, is a work haunted by the fear of large working-classes and civil strife, as you can hear in this account of the general populace: "Every time that we snatch up a vehement opinion in ignorance and passion, every time that we long to crush an adversary by sheer violence, every time that we are envious, every time that we are brutal . . . every time that we trample savagely on the fallen . . ." we find "the eternal spirit of the Populace". So, Arnold saw culture as an essential moral counterpart to the unifying function of the state. It connected every individual to the good of the whole through their 'best self', which involved rising above all petty partial interests and, quintessentially, rising above class interests. All discussions of capital and labour, he argued, "have small existence for a whole society that has resolved no longer to live by bread alone". What scared him was that there was a limit to the state using repression to curb dissent: and this is where culture, literature, and poetry came in, to bind society together.*

My interest in this began in university when I had a choice between studying politics or studying literature. I chose the latter, hoping that it would give me a deeper understanding of the world, which you could say made me a promising Arnoldian pupil. But I soon began to notice how, when you directly transferred Arnold's idea of culture to an institution like the BBC, as Lord Reith so expertly did, what happened instead of the production of the 'best self' was not only a repression of dissent and challenging new ideas in increasingly etiolated notions of editorial impartiality and balance, but that it left out vast swathes of our reality. In the political culture of Brexit Britain, for example, it is very difficult not to be reminded of Arnold's extraordinary recommendation to the students of Liverpool: "Don't think: try and be patient."

This repression of politics and of dissent seems to me to be coming home to roost now, in different ways in Brexit Britain and with the gilets jaunes in France, where the lack of a rich, diverse, and inclusive national debate is so stark; or in the United States, where Michael Sandel blames 'liberal neutrality' and its avoidance of substantive moral argument in politics, for a humiliating cultural estrangement that has turned many people into passionate Trump supporters.

Have you noticed a similar effect on your work of the continuing yet deadening impact of culture as "the best that has been thought and said"?

LJ: Yes, that quote—"the best that has been thought and said"—as you say, comes from a different era, and is riddled with class arrogance and fear, and yet it is probably still the most used quote in the arts and cultural sector. It was quoted as an aspiration in the UK Ofsted report on education at the start of this year, and my students come from all over the world to learn 'the English Model'.

There are some similarities in our starting points. I was brought up in a very political household, but chose to go to university to study the arts, theatre in particular. I had a working-class Yorkshire mother and an Egyptian father who met through politics. Our neighbours included South African ANC exiles. So, I could be listening to Arab poetry one minute, South African music or my Mum's favourite northern working-class dramas the next, and at school we studied Commonwealth literatures, rather than just English literature. This gave me an insight into another way of 'doing' culture. The shock for me came when I went to university to 'study' literature, and this continued when I moved into working in the cultural sector, because both seemed to represent a huge narrowing of my world. I felt that I was a foreigner in the monocultural National Us that you have written about so well.

It became increasingly important to me that, as a society, we don't just resource, nurture, and support access to a culture produced by one group and consumed by another, but one which provides us all with the cultural means of production. I'm talking about support for the library, the working mens' club, the community, or cultural centre, the basic local infrastructure that allows people to come together—something we are now losing at a great pace. I'm also talking about how to nurture public spaces that allow encounters between different types of people and, crucially, with the resources to secure a good collaborative outcome. Sadly, there are far too many so-called 'participatory processes' nowadays built around austerity, which ask what they can take money away from rather than what they can give funding to. They are deeply problematic.

A progressive cultural policy needs to ask how culture can be used to help change structural inequality, not be used as a sticking plaster to social ills. Rather than papering over the cracks to prevent 'anarchy' in society, it needs to go to the roots of injustice. So much cultural policy is about making our towns look better, not actually making them better, or making people feel happier, not actually improving their social conditions. Whilst I'm not saying that culture can 'save the world' on its own, at the moment I think culture is complicit in the neoliberal agendas which blame poverty or disenfranchisement on the individual, not the society.

Europe has not valued the culture, or cultural practices, of its diverse populations—not just in terms of cultural diversity, but also in terms of class. There is so much evidence internationally that the professional cultural sector is made up of a narrow range of people, both as workforce and audience. But that does not mean that people are not engaging in their own cultural practices—simply that these cultural practices are often overlooked. I would argue that this is committing an act of violence on working-class culture, contributing to the culture wars we see now, which the right is exploiting.

This is what the right is getting right, isn't it? Playing on people's sense of cultural disenfranchisement and the feeling that what gives meaning to people's social lives has been ignored, while centrists have shied away from this, battling for power over the economy and claiming we all have the same shared interests. The right has been quick to represent folk traditions, for example, which has a truly radical heritage, through the lens of nationalism looking to an imaginary past and a particular definition of who the 'real people' are. I believe that in order to challenge this, valuing everyday culture and creativity is not just desirable but essential.

It becomes, then, very important that we involve a wider range of voices in decision-making about establishing what any culture and cultural policy is made up of. This is not simply about community—because who is that community, and who decides? Neither is it a matter of representation, because people are people and don't necessarily 'represent' any type of community, whether racial, geographical, or communities of interest—but it is about having different voices around the table debating ideas.

Furthermore, it is important to say that it is also not about establishing consensus in a community or binding publics into a single view. Again this is something the right has used culture for, as another way to build a consensus around some Us versus Them. It is essential that the left creates a space where we can have dissenting voices and different perspectives.

RB: *I agree with you completely. I think in a many-too-many communications era, this coming together across differences is where the dignity and empowerment people are looking for actually resides.*

Nothing, however, could be more opposed to the culture wars instigated by the far right that are so rapidly gaining a purchase on the mainstream. It's a great irony for Arnoldian culture that the very characteristics that made Arnold so fearful of 'the Populace' are the ones assiduously cultivated by the new authoritarians in all our societies: the death of civility, the proliferation of enemy images, and the division of the world into Us and Them where we can only win or indeed belong, if we are willing to "trample savagely on the fallen". The hostile environment is not just about the unwelcoming treatment of refugees trying to reach Europe. Look at the speed at which 'Europeans' began to be sucked into the 'hostile environment' for migrants created by Theresa May when she was the UK's Home Secretary. It has become ubiquitous and widespread. We encounter the proliferation of enemy images in many aspects of daily life. This normalisation of hostile environments signals a worrying global shift in values of tolerance, empathy, compassion, hospitality, and responsibility for the vulnerable. It's a normalisation essential for the progress of the extreme right.

Some blame the success of this so-called 'populist revolt' on the 'strategy of avoidance' which is the liberal insistence that questions of personal meaning, identity, and purpose should be left outside when you enter the public square. And it is true that those leading the revolt have the humbling of the liberal order explicitly in their sights. The Hungarian Academy of Arts, for example, says that its goal is to "counter Liberal tendencies in contemporary fine arts".

But beyond this target there is another: the capture of the people themselves. Victor Orbán in a recent speech in Hungary said: "An era is determined by cultural trends, collective beliefs and social customs. This is now the task we are faced with: we must embed the political system in a cultural era". This is what Gáspár Miklós Tamás is warning us against when he says that Orbán is not just waging, but winning the culture war.

We should take careful note, shouldn't we, of the precise way in which the Nationalist International sets about filling this convenient liberal vacuum in addressing people's sense of identity and dignity, and its profoundly anti-democratic effect. Rather than creating a public square where we can come together constructively in all our differences and determine our futures built out of a rich coexistence, it instead divides people by reducing them to one identity, claiming to represent a fantasy monocultural National Us, and playing on people's insecurities and fears of the Other. Preventing the formation of a self-determining and multivalent public square, through violent division if necessary, is the far more important underlying task and historical mission of this extreme right-wing, I would argue.

DiEM25 makes a particularly important contribution to our understanding of culture precisely at this point in the argument, since it gets the intimate relationship of mutual dependency between the liberal elite and the Nationalist international—two sides of the same coin. Matteo Salvini, a key figure in this schema because in however a contradictory fashion he so clearly combines the two, has declared culture to be "the strategic asset of our country". Recently we learned about Steve Bannon's new "gladiator school for culture warriors" in Italy.

Hungary may be an extreme case, but none of our societies has yet found a way of empowering people to resist this fake set of identifications, because not a single political class is willing to trust the people with their own creative agency. So it sometimes seems that we need to reinvent the public square almost from scratch, and where do we start? It is an urgent matter, since powerlessness and humiliation make a ripe environment for that extreme right bacillus.

LJ: As you say, the right have a resonance because, at least superficially, they claim to be giving a voice to those who feel that they have been silenced. And this is a cultural question as much as it is an economic one and so one that cultural policy needs to address.

As much as the right are exploiting this situation, the third way politics of centrists is also to blame. The third way idea that we could ever find a simple accommodation between the needs of different interest groups, whether that is between business interests and workers' rights or between the values of different cultural groups was flawed. It aimed to replace ideological choices and conflicts with technocratic solutions. It aimed to govern by consensus rather than provide space for dissent and difference.

A key principle of the participatory decision-making that inspires me is that it is not about finding consensus, or replicating the failings of representative democracy, but about finding a space for dissenting voices to not only speak but be heard, reaching out to the people who aren't talking to you now. The right may claim that they are about giving new opportunities for voice, but the left has to actually give away power, otherwise we will perpetuate the violence done to working-class culture and cultural workers, and to the representation of women and ethnic minorities.

RB: *The liberal elites and the right have far too many starting assumptions in common. Take the biological determinist right-wing backlash against the fight for gender equality. Could the neoliberal state have done any more to pave the way for this than to use greater equality of access to the workplace since the 1970s as an opportunity to decimate unions, abandon any guarantee of a family wage, and introduce a period of unprecedented falling wages before slashing what remains of state assistance for care? How convenient to be able to channel the anger of men at how modern life prioritises waged work over the family into the culture wars.*

This is another reason why DiEM25 recognises its strong affinity with the movement that has emerged around Jeremy Corbyn in the UK and similar movements prioritising safe, interesting, and well-remunerated work to give people material support to make their own choices about children and care for the old and the sick. These are the people offering solutions to our profound societal problems. The neoliberal mindset celebrates individual autonomy while discrediting the kinds of collective and systemic action that would be necessary to realise such autonomy. This directly feeds not only into all the fairness questions of inequality and social mobility, but also into a dead-end competitive and scapegoating identity politics.

Many will respond to this sort of argument by saying, "Do we have to bring politics into culture?" But what we are saying is, yes, we do—and especially so if we want to save creative and democratic agency from that atomised personalisation of responsibility and blame.

LJ: Politics is there, whether or not you acknowledge it. Indeed, we shouldn't be surprised that cultural policy within a neoliberal state supports neoliberal policies and centres on the aspirational individual, stressing their personal self-improvement, individual responsibility, and well-being. Cultural policymakers throughout Europe have also taken on the neoliberal vocabulary about the economy promoting competition between cultures through the focus on national cultural institutions, and the creative cities discourse which is fundamentally about how to compete with our next-door neighbours to attract the creative class, and inward investment to us, rather than encouraging collaboration between places to build on and support what is already there.

Indeed, the whole process of the capital of culture, which I was talking about earlier, may have become about the regeneration of struggling cities reimagining themselves rather than already successful European cities—but it is still a competition. So, as in the Olympics and the World Cup, cities bid and spend a lot of money on bidding to win against the competition. Such strategies exacerbate inequality between places, and play into the economic growth model. Culturally, they also encourage what Institute for X from Denmark has described as the 'chain store version' of culture, where culture looks increasingly the same in every destination. It can also be all too short-term—a 'drug hit' rather than something that changes your life. I would contrast that spectacle or festivalisation approach with an embedded approach in which people come together locally in some way.

RB: *In that respect, the Fearless Cities network and its summit launched by Barcelona en Comú in 2017, provides a rather inspiring contrast. This launch of a global new municipalist movement is all about recognising the specificities of each city context, but mutual strengthening through sharing best practice, especially in exploring the new opportunities opened up by the collective co-organising of citizens.*

LJ: I'd like to know more about that. The Co-City project also offers an example. It is all about collaborative city-making and participatory governance. It sees the whole city as a commons and interestingly, although it started in Italy, it has been consciously shared and exported internationally.

The European Cultural Foundation has also been important in this area and in providing evidence that participatory processes can create progressive change in places that support diverse communities: projects like Pogon in Zagreb, which is a collaboration between the local authority who agrees to provide free space across the city and the young people who programme their own cultural activities in these spaces. Les Têtes des Arts in Marseille similarly has seen an arts organisation move from providing work for the diverse communities of its city to co-producing with them. Both focus on the long-term sustainability of their practice, rather than the short-termism of projects.

These schemes have been initiated by local authorities but there are also projects such as Teatro Valle in Rome and Asilo Filangieri in Naples, that have been led by activists taking over cultural buildings and relaunching them as a cultural commons, where people from all walks of life are invited in to redefine their cities' cultural spaces. In the former this has conflicted with the local authority, while the latter has at least achieved recognition as a legal organisation.

So, to conclude, I think it is really important that we remember that most people most of the time engage in culture within their neighbourhoods and their local community. They don't travel to European capitals of culture. The young don't even all go to popular music festivals despite the hype—in fact the average age at these is now people in their thirties. Cultural projects, which just bring in an artist who performs and goes away again, don't leave much behind.

However, when the same artists come to collabourate with local initiatives, rather than being the exotic Other or the remote 'star', that can be enormously rewarding. Interestingly, Coventry City of Culture in the UK, which on the surface is another creative cities project, is trying to define itself as a cultural movement, rather than just a cultural event. This will involve them working long-term with different groups across the city, and I look forward to seeing how this might change the model.

But, unless cultural policy acknowledges that culture is not autonomous but is contextual and political, it remains a puppet of the state and not its critic. A progressive cultural policy needs to recognise that as people experience culture locally, there needs to be equity between places, not competition. We need a distribution of resources that values different practices, not just professional or so-called 'great art'.

We need to stop just providing 'equal opportunities' to join the cultural elite. This means shifting the thinking in cultural policy from seeing culture as an industry to seeing it as a process, and it is through this collective process that the left can win the hearts and minds away from the right and work with, not separate from, the overall social project to change the bigger picture.

And, yes, this is about unleashing creative agency. We need to replace the means of consumption with the cultural means of production, giving people the opportunity to define their own culture for themselves.

The DiEM Voice Project:
Making Noise, Generating Voice

Xristina Penna & Danae Stratou

The DiEM Voice Project, initiated by artists and creatives within DiEM25, is a public engagement project that follows the events of DiEM25. During these events we reach out to participants and ask them to send us their thoughts in relation to the topics discussed, as well as any questions relating to the future of Europe and beyond that we should be raising.

These responses are passed on to artists and other creatives who wish to respond creatively to them. In this way, the resulting artworks and creative outputs (videos, installations, sound pieces, actions, spoken word, illustrations, etc.) enable a renewed exchange, both in content and in form between the thinking and questioning of the audience, the DiEM25 CC, the creatives, and a new audience that is exposed to these artworks.

For this book, we asked the artist Miltos Manetas to develop a number of drawings in response to some of our audiences' thoughts and questions. Manetas's original artistic response runs throughout this book as one of the manifestations of DiEM Voice, communicating with the reader using a constructively disruptive visual language.

Creativity Must Operate Across Borders

Rosemary Bechler

I want to talk not so much about the direct threat posed to our beleaguered democracies by what Yanis Varoufakis rightly calls the 'Nationalist—neo-fascistic—International', but about the challenge to a cultural politics of self and other that I believe is all around us.

Being able to operate across boundaries is at the heart of this challenge. As Inna Shevchenko, the exiled Ukrainian leader of FEMEN says, "Democracy is not only about counting silent hands . . . it is about allowing the confrontation of different opinions; many, many voices; about public debates, discussions, and disagreements too." These are 'discussions and disagreements' where people listen to each other, and may change their minds about what is the right or the winning position because, as Shevchenko says, "we all have multiple identities and we also have multiple answers."

She contrasts this with the way that right-wing populists and extreme nationalists aim instead to divide society "by reducing people to only one identity, only one adjective; by creating clashes between groups, groups that live in the same way, think in the same way, practise their religion in the same way. Then, they claim to represent these groups, manipulating societies by playing on the fear and insecurity of individuals."

The truth is that the Bannonite leaders of Europe cannot thrive in societies that are confident about crossing borders. If "Brexit means Brexit", it is because the 'people's will', this unitary sovereign will they are so fond of invoking, must be beyond question or change. The Bannonites only thrive in a profoundly unequal Us v. Them society, secured from its enemies without and within by the strong man who can act with impunity, breaking all the rules on behalf of the 'real people', people who are only readily convinced that they are winning if someone else is losing out.

Take a classic example from Italy. This August, using his loudspeaker, a train conductor ordered "gypsies and molesters" to get off the train on the grounds that they were "pissing off" the other passengers, presumably the 'real passengers'. As a public official, he was picking up on the wishes of Deputy Prime Minister Salvini, who had recently announced his intention of opening a file on the Roma people, regretting having 'to keep' ones holding Italian citizenship, as he put it. Matteo Salvini now promptly returns the compliment on his Facebook page, by publicly naming the passenger who had reported this discriminatory act. As a result, the passenger received *more than 50,000* messages—a familiar mixture of the sarcastic, the intimidating, and the menacing.

For DiEM25, the passenger operating across boundaries is the imaginary democrat here, a victory in itself against the Nationalist International. But what of the 50,000, a force proliferating enemy images and *en route* to violence? If we are to reinvent our democratic cultures, we need the skills to be able to reach out across those boundaries and change people's minds. And for that, my premise is that we need a culture of openness and generosity that acknowledges vulnerability as a strength.

This is why I am concerned at the shift in the meaning of the 'safe space' that has taken place in my lifetime. During the euphemistically-called 'Irish troubles', a 'safe space' was the place where brave Catholic and Protestant individuals, and the very brave people who brought them together, would meet to work out a better way forward than violent conflict. In these conflict resolution spaces, whatever the power imbalances between the parties, and regardless of the conflict raging outside, those present were equal. They were mutually vulnerable, face to face, and crossing boundaries to overcome the enemy images and change each others' minds. How different is the 'safe space of today'?—an identity politics that demands recognition and state protection for socioeconomic groups unjustly marginalised, by securing them *from the Other*, in a borderless space free from threatening conflict, criticism, or too unsettling debate.

Of course, inequality creates far too many victims in our societies today, but this culture of the victim worries me. The nationalists and the xenophobes are all too quick to capitalise on the worst aspects of a securitising relationship to the Other, with its repertoire of anger, authenticity, truth-speaking and public presence and its retreat to 'people like us'. Writ large, under their leadership, we can see in country after country the emergence of *aggrieved majorities*, encouraged by their political representatives to perceive themselves as the real people, the 'National Us', unfairly victimised by some Other—let us say a few thousand migrants destitute on European shores whose arrival has triggered a major political crisis throughout the European Union.

In renewing our democratic culture, our strength will never rely on force—whether the force of numbers or the strongman with his warlike qualities—but in sharing, time and again, the creativity and, yes, the pleasure and joy that is released in that moment when we are not frightened of the multiple identities and multiple answers in each of us. Theatre people surely feel this in their core, because theatre happens in those spaces between the different worlds that people are. "Even in political theatre", as Harold Pinter said in his famous Nobel lecture:

> The characters must be allowed to breathe their own air. The author cannot confine
> and constrict them to satisfy his own taste or disposition or prejudice. He must be

prepared to approach them from a variety of angles, from a full and uninhibited range of perspectives, take them by surprise, perhaps, occasionally, but nevertheless give them the freedom to go which way they will.

This is why I urge for us to freeze-frame the previous precious moment, which is the crossing of geographical borders, social borders, borders of all kinds—that openness to what is different when the outcome hangs in the balance for all, when whole new worlds can appear.

This is a pluralist democratic culture, one sorely needed back here in Brexit Britain, where two aggrieved majoritarian 'National Us's have been so busy tearing our political fabric apart.

There was an interesting moment at a Labour Party conference when a young delegate from Northumberland, confronting a sea of enthusiastic Remainer activists fresh from an impressive demonstration on the Liverpool seafront, was the first speaker to come out clearly against the People's Vote. He said:

> Delegates should remember what people feel about a 'people's vote' in places like my constituency in Blyth Valley *where we voted overwhelmingly to leave.* I am not against Europe. I myself am a European, from a third generation Polish refugee family expelled after the war. But now I believe the European Union to be a capitalist club that is for the few, not the many.
>
> I implore you all, come to Blyth Valley, go to Bowes Court where the buildings are crumbling behind St. Wilfrid's Catholic church. Go to Cowpen ward. Tell *them* why you want us to remain, and go to Kitty Brewster, where, for too long, they've felt marginalised *like they have not had their voices heard.* (my italics)

Here's my idea. Why don't we say: Yes, let us cross the boundaries between *us* and *them*—the geographical, the class, the age, and so many other borders. Let's bring the metropolitan Remainers to Bowes Court, St Wilfrid's Catholic church, Cowpen ward, so that we can all get to know each other better.

Let's ask ourselves why neither side in the Brexit debate and none of the main political parties have ever thought to propose and enable this—why they incite us, scare us, or maybe they just manage us—but never *invite* us onto the stage of history to meet each other and change each others' minds, confident that our differences can be mutually revealing and that we Leavers and Remainers can build a better future together?

It is my belief that we will never renew our democracies until we the people, in all our diversity, come onto that stage of history in our own right, once and for all. I'm hoping that you will agree that this is a job worthy of the best creative minds.

[*This is adapted from a speech delivered at Central Saint Martins in London on 13 October 2018, when DiEM Voice took to the stage to share its creative vision for Europe.*]

A Creative Europe by Jonas Staal

" Europe's crises are political, economic, humanitarian, ecological. But the overarching crisis is of the imagination. The Brexit vote is paradigmatic of this crisis: the Leave camp crafted by ultranationalists and racists, longing for a sovereignty that never was; the Remain camp ruled by the Eurocratic austerity elite, their policies of economic terrorism trialled and tested in Greece. Each camp strengthening the other, neither a genuine alternative.

The task of art is to challenge the taking-hostage of our imaginations by the Leave and Remain dichotomy, and to insist on a third, fourth, option: on a plurality of trans-democratic unions which are within our grasp, if only we can *imagine* them.

This is why the involvement of artists through DiEM Voice (the cultural wing of DiEM25) matters. Artists, designers, theatre makers, writers, and composers, are part of a greater imaginative endeavour. We will not democratise only politics, but the imagination as well!

So, what does that mean? First, that we recognise that art and culture are in common ownership, and that however different our local or national languages, symbols, and origin stories are, common threads run through them. This includes our capacity to think the world as we desire it to be, for if we cannot imagine another world, we will never be able to realise it. For DiEM25, art and culture take the form of a campaign for the imagination of all European citizens—and, ideally, well beyond the confines of Europe as well.

Pan-European education in art and culture, from the cities to the countryside, is crucial. But not just any education. To force pupils to marvel at the great masters of the past is to reinforce a class divide that manifold artworks have helped to maintain throughout the centuries. The message of a trans-democratic art and culture is that we have the imagination to contribute to the construction of our common reality.

Art and culture are not consumer objects or elite property: they are tools, propositions, and paradigm-altering mechanics that allow us to see our world as a human-made creation. Every encounter with an artwork triggers our own capacity to create it differently. So, it is crucial that a trans-democratic art and culture is not held captive in urban museums, but shapes our public sphere at large.

Those artists who have joined or worked in DiEM25 gatherings across Europe, reading poetry, performing theatre, creating new campaign assemblies or alternative symbols for the movement, are already shaping a trans-democratic cultural movement by refusing to separate it from other knowledge and specialisations, unionising instead our imagination across disciplines, and sharing our competence and crafts.

As an artist working within social movements, political parties, and stateless insurgencies, time and again I meet other artists and cultural workers hoping to liberate our squares, our public institutions, our imaginations from the prison of ultranationalists and the austerity elite. And to show the world: *this is what democracy looks like.*

Working for several months in the Kurdish Rojava region in North Syria, which has had to fight the forces of the Assad and Erdoğan regimes (as well as the Islamic State), I saw the profound importance of the involvement of artists in building a new democratic society together. Writers, filmmakers, sculptors, one encounter after another, made clear to me that a political transformation will not fly without a cultural transformation. Together with them, I developed an artwork for the region, *The People's Parliament of Rojava (2015–18)*: a public sculpture, a monument, but also a parliament, where the communes of the region gather to make their political project a reality.

Campaigning for the imagination does not mean turning art into a political tool. Art and politics are not the same. But they can mutually inspire to campaign for the imagination. That is how a parliament can also be an artwork, or an artwork can be a parliament. Our pan-European challenge is to make the new unions that we so desperately need a reality. **99**

Next spread: *Isn't This Room Full of "the Establishment" and Still Wondering How to Build an Alternative for the European Left?*

ISN'T

FULL OF "TH

AND STILL

HOW TO BUI

FOR THE EUR

ISN

AW

W

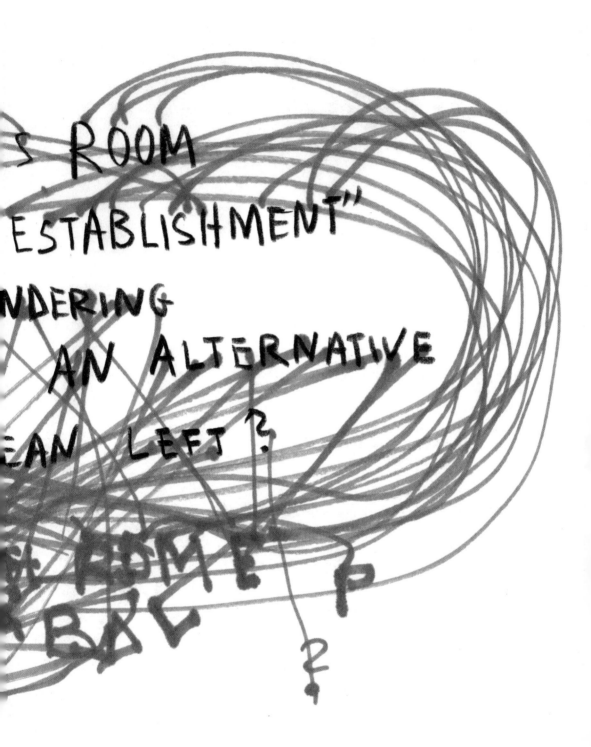

S ROOM

ESTABLISHMENT"

NDERING

AN ALTERNATIVE

EAN LEFT?

A Cultured Europe by Pamela Anderson

DiEM25 Is An Example of Pure Heart

It's almost impossible to reverse or try and convince people that maybe their image of me may be not as I am.

But
you may have some facts right.
I have done or am all the things you have mentioned over and over and over . . .
lucky me.
Yes
I have an unintentional sex tape or 2
I had a few internationally successful tv shows.
Playing 'CJ' on Baywatch
'Val' on VIP
Home Improvement's 'Lisa'
And Stacked, where I work in a book store. (I don't remember my character's
    name) this one didn't last long. I was talked into this TV show –
– but I was not ready –
my focus was not on TV it was on my young sons –
A film <u>Barb Wire</u> was
a big hit in Cannes film festival
before we shot a frame of film.
Which set expectations high –
Disappointing all at the box office.
Yes
I have been married 4x –
2x to the same man –
He was not sober/sober –
And
now the biggest risk of all.

A much younger professional *futballler* (am I crazy?—yes of course)

I've attempted a few 'dancing with the stars' which in Hollywood means you're
    desperate for attention
and/or money.

But if you give it to charity does it make it any better?

Nobody ever knows.
Reality shows are poisonous.
The only people who succeed are agents and managers.
Leeches – sucking your last drop of life's blood.
Exploitive and weird –

So
if you believe even most of that –
I might
catch you by pleasant surprise –

My ambition
was never to be an actress
– but fate had its way with me – like usual –
even though I was resistant.

If you believe that only an idiot
can play a dumb blonde –
you may have written me off as 'pneumatic' –
mysterious, misunderstood . . .
Oh.
That's 'enigmatic' –
sorry.

I still don't know what's next.

But
here we go –

The activism part of my life started very young.
My affinity with animals is authentic
and pure.
I'm an island girl.
A 'Vancouver Island' island girl.
I had a Finnish grandfather who read to me –

fairytales and mythology.
I grew to choose for myself authors I love like
Marie-Louise von Franz,
Carl Jung,
Robert A. Johnson, Joseph Campbell and Robert Bly.
The mischievous romantic in me related to Anaïs Nin,
While I blazed through
Anatole France,
and the rest.
I am an avid reader like my parents.
It's rare to see them or I without a book in hand.

Anyway
Purpose /
I felt I needed to share this attention or platform or notoriety
with something more important than I.
Like the planet.
Animals,
vulnerable people.
My foundation has grown
as I learn new things.
We are at a unique place in history right now and if you are not doing something.
    Personally (or publicly)
to make the world a better place.
We are all in trouble.
Collectively
we must face the truth.
Listen to the child protesters.
The yellow vests.
And open our doors and hearts to Refugees

DiEM25 is an example of pure heart.
Does anyone here really want to be a politician?
I'd be shocked.
Or suspicious.
Nobody should trust a self-inflicted politician
with a narcissistic agenda.

DiEM25 was created to stir the pot.
And offer real alternatives to the broken capitalistic system that doesn't care for the
    many, or the planet.

If I can understand it.
Anyone can.

I believe DiEM25ers are dreamers with solutions and substance

Not a utopian ideology.
They are a group of
Academics with
street smarts

I'm proud to support them.
As they support me on my path of wonder and mystery through
this sexy place called Europe.

A Historically-minded Europe

by Anthony Barnett

"We are seeing the emergence of a democratic Europe. Naturally, this is a rough and ready process driven by the vulgar, not the refined. Those with vested interests and lots of money are seeking to use its energy to divide us from each other, both within Europe and beyond. The causes of this democratic warming include massive frustration with austerity and inequality, fear of the rapid changes under way, the unruly transparency and connectedness of the digital world, and the evident corruptions of national and EU governments.

Our response should be to embrace it and enjoy democracy in its national forms, while expanding its European-wide expression and realities so that they positively reinforce each other. We must not oppose national and European-wide democracy, but forge them as two sides of the same coin. We should not be thinking about Europe in a linear, analogue fashion that goes from a singular past to a unified future. We will share an open, networked future with different pasts.

If we are to enjoy real democracy, it is essential that this is driven by a historical consciousness. We cannot take responsibility over outcomes and consequences, behave sustainably towards our environment, or remain committed to the education of our children and grandchildren if we do not understand ourselves as creatures of our history. The market—that is to say a capitalism that writes off sunk losses as yesterday and maximises them only for today with no concern for tomorrow—hates history, which is essential for any successful opposition to it.

The future of the planet, and by extension our future as Europeans, will not be decided within Europe. This is a hard fact to swallow for many Europeans. From Greece's claim as the originator of democracy to Portugal and Holland that shaped the early modern world (not to speak of the once major imperial powers), it might be in our culture to expect an influence that is universal and not confined.

Only by learning how to best share our own powers and differences with each other to mutual benefit, both material and democratic, can Europe provide a model the rest of the world might wish to borrow and adapt. Alas, other powers in the world may resist this as anathema, as does the current denizen of the White House. All the more reason to be committed to a democracy that holds all powers to account."

PART TEN

The Future

Challenges Ahead

Noam Chomsky

To describe the challenges we face as extremely severe would be an error. The phrase does not capture the enormity of what lies ahead. Any serious discussion of humanity's future must begin with recognising that this generation must answer a question that has never before arisen in human history: Will organised human society survive for long?

For over seventy years we have been living under the shadow of terminal nuclear war. Those who have troubled to review the record know that it is a near miracle that disaster has been averted. Miracles are not likely to persist. The threat is mounting. Three major arms control treaties offered some progress: the ABM, INF, and New Start treaties. The US pulled out of the first in 2002. The Trump administration has just withdrawn from the INF treaty, negotiated by Reagan and Gorbachev in 1987, greatly reducing imminent threats of destruction in Europe that could have quickly escalated. Both sides claim, with some plausibility, that the other has been violating the treaty. In a rational world, the dispute would lead to negotiations and analysis by independent experts, a course that has not been undertaken. Both sides are now enhancing their capacities to ensure that the worst will happen. Tensions are increasing at the Russian border, thanks to the expansion of NATO to the East in violation of verbal commitments to Gorbachev, which George Kennan and other senior statesmen warned would be a "fateful error" of historic proportions.

That leaves the New Start treaty, which went into effect in 2011, and is due to be renewed in 2021. The figure in charge—who modestly describes himself as "the greatest president in history"—has already accorded the treaty the routine designation of anything enacted by his predecessors: the worst agreement ever made, selling out the United States. Its fate is uncertain.

Global warming continues on its inexorable course. The new millennium has annually recorded the hottest year on record, with a single exception, and the pace of warming has been increasing since 1981. Recent scientific papers indicate that the pace might soon shift from linear to exponential, doubling every few decades. We are already approaching the conditions of 125,000 years ago, when sea levels were six to nine meters higher. The melting of the huge Antarctic ice sheet, now under way, might lead to major catastrophe.

Meanwhile, euphoric government and media reports regularly celebrate the good news that improved techniques of fossil fuel extraction have catapulted the US past Saudi Arabia as the world leader in oil production, and that new areas are being opened up for exploitation to carry forward the task of destroying the prospects for decent survival.

The Doomsday Clock of the *Bulletin of Atomic Scientists* was set in January 2019 at two minutes to midnight, as close as it has been to terminal disaster. The analysts once again cited the two existential threats, nuclear war and global warming, but for the first time added a third: the undermining of democracy, the sole hope for addressing significant challenges. Organised, militant popular action has been the critical factor in driving such progress as has been made in confronting the primary challenges to decent survival, and innumerable others. It remains the hope for today.

It is a commonplace these days to bemoan the erosion of the pillars of democracy under the onslaught of 'populist' forces. Sober analysts seek to penetrate beyond superficialities to seek the psychic disorders that provoke such irrational attacks on good order—in one respected version, impulses "deep in our psyches" such as "fear of the future, a sense of our own mortality."

It is, however, not really necessary to appeal to an epidemic of irrationality and emotional appeals that is mysteriously spreading over the domains subjected to the neoliberal assault of the past generation. It suffices, for example, to heed the words of Thomas Piketty and his colleagues: "An economy that fails to deliver growth for half of its people for an entire generation is bound to generate discontent with the status quo and a rejection of establishment politics." The effects are enhanced when economic growth has concentrated extraordinary wealth in a tiny fraction of the population and corporate profits skyrocket—including the largely predatory financial institutions that have enjoyed spectacular growth thanks in large measure to taxpayer largesse—while real wages stagnate and social benefits are undermined. The effects are enhanced still further by the deleterious impact on functioning democracy, a direct consequence of sharp concentration of wealth and corporate power, driven even further in Europe by transfer of essential decision-making to the unelected troika, with the northern banks looking over their shoulders.

In the US, there is a long-standing history of bought elections. With remarkable precision, electability for President and Congress is predictable by the single variable of campaign funding, persisting through the 2016 election, as Thomas Ferguson has shown in important work. Legislators spend many hours a day approaching donors in preparation for the next election, while swarms of lobbyists meet with staff to write legislation. These practices have rapidly escalated during the neoliberal years, with the help of the most reactionary Supreme Court in living memory. The result is that a large majority of the population is literally disenfranchised, in that their own representatives pay no attention to their preferences, as polls and voting records show. Rather, they are listening to the voices of the donor class.

People who are cast aside by social and economic policies and foresee a bleak future quite naturally feel resentment, anger, and fear, and it is all too easy for such feelings to be transmuted into a search for scapegoats, commonly those who are even more vulnerable. That is particularly true among populations that have been atomised by policies aimed at undermining the social order, guided by Margaret Thatcher's maxim that there is no society, only individuals—her unwitting paraphrase of Marx, who bitterly condemned the authoritarian rulers of Europe for seeking to turn society to a "sack of potatoes", an amorphous mass of isolated people who confront concentrated power alone. That a crisis of democracy should result comes as little surprise.

In election after election in Europe, centrist parties have been collapsing; there are similarities in the US, though the parties keep their names. Outcomes are often attributed to xenophobia, fear of immigrants, racism, and other social pathologies. A good bit of research shows that the basic problem is economic distress, stagnation, and insecurity, along with undermining of social policies, all of which open the door to pathological symptoms that can be exploited by demagogues for ugly ends.

The deterioration of functioning democracy is a positive feature of the neoliberal programmes from the perspective of the framers of this era of global capitalism. Their essential guiding principle was expressed well in 1969 by Austrian-American economist Fritz Machlup, a prominent figure in the neoliberal movement that took shape in Vienna after World War I and finally achieved hegemonic status under Thatcher and Reagan and their successors, and their counterparts elsewhere. Machlup urged that we should

> reflect on the proposition that full democracy may not be the most suitable system for government for such people [the 'politically and intellectually immature people']; that, for example, the unlimited right to vote and elect the men who will govern the country may lead to the destruction of many other freedoms and also of any real chance for economic development.

The 'other freedoms' are the sanctity of investor and property rights, including free movement of capital unhampered by sovereignty, unions, and other impediments to 'optimal use of economic resources'—a convenient euphemism which easily transmutes into what Adam Smith called "the vile maxim of the masters of mankind: All for ourselves and nothing for other people."

Machlup's proposition was not original. It is also useful to reflect on the proposition that distaste for democracy is deeply rooted in elite conceptions of a proper political order. In the first modern democratic revolution in England in the mid-seventeenth century, the 'men of best quality', as they called themselves, were appalled by the demands of the 'rascal multitude', who did not want to be ruled by either King or Parliament, but "by countrymen like ourselves, [who] know the people's sores". The rabble had become "so curious and so arrogant that they will never find humility enough to submit to a civil rule". They even raised outrageous demands for education, health, democratisation of law, and other crimes against good order.

Such ideas naturally appalled the men of best quality. They were willing to grant the people rights, but within reason. After the democrats had been defeated, John Locke commented that "day-labourers and tradesmen, the spinsters and dairy-maids" must be told what to believe; "The greatest part cannot know and therefore they must believe."

A century later, during the second great democratic revolution, the Framers of the American Constitution, drawn from the country's elites, expressed rather similar views. The leading figures were Alexander Hamilton and James Madison. Hamilton explained that the Constitution was designed to be a "defence against depredations which the democratic spirit is apt to make on property", which, as was generally agreed, "is certainly the principle object of society." Madison elaborated in rich detail. The Constitution was designed to secure "the permanent interests of the country against innovation", 'permanent interests' being property rights, and 'innovation' any threat to them. Effective power was to be placed in the hands of "the wealth of the nation", "the most responsible set of men", those who have sympathy for property and its rights and recognise that government must be "so constituted as to protect the minority of the opulent against the majority."

With justice, the major scholarly work on the establishment of the Constitution is entitled *The Framers' Coup* (Michael Klarman), a 'conservative counterrevolution' against the 'excessive democracy' demanded by the rascal multitude.

The same themes resonate through modern history. In the interwar period, while neoliberal principles were being developed in the Mises seminar in Vienna, then Geneva, American progressive intellectuals were warning that we should not be misled by the illusory idea that people are the best judges of their own interests. They are not. They are "ignorant and meddlesome outsiders" who must be "put in their place" as "spectators, not participants", while the intelligent minority of "responsible men" rule in the interests of all. To perform their duties properly they must be protected from "the trampling and the roar of a bewildered herd", deluded by their aspirations for excessive democracy. These are the thoughts of the most renowned US public intellectual of the twentieth century, Walter Lippmann, a Wilson-Roosevelt-Kennedy progressive and regular participant in the early neoliberal intellectual movement. It was at the Lippmann Colloquium in Paris in 1938 that the gathered thinkers settled on 'neoliberalism' as the term for the new ideology they were crafting, later carried forward by the Mont Pelerin society and implemented when the occasion arose after the financial turmoil of the early 1970s.

The neoliberal policy turn was adopted in the wake of another perceived 'crisis of democracy'. The phrase is the title of the first and most important 1975 publication of the Trilateral Commission, an organisation of distinguished liberal internationalists drawn from the three centres of capitalist democracy: the US, Europe, and Japan. Their political complexion is indicated by the fact that the Carter administration, which took the first steps in the neoliberal assault, was almost entirely drawn from the ranks of the Commission.

The crisis of democracy that they perceived was the upsurge of popular activism of the '60s, which was bringing too much democracy. Normally passive and obedient elements of the population were organising and entering the political arena to advance their demands: the young, the old, women, workers, farmers—in short the general population, the "bewildered herd", who do not comprehend the "optimal use of economic resources" and do not have "humility enough to submit to a civil rule".

A particular concern was the failures of what they called the institutions "responsible for the indoctrination of the young". Harsher discipline and other techniques of control were needed to restrain the rabble agitating for an end to a murderous war and too many rights.

The American rapporteur in the Trilateral study, Harvard political scientist Samuel Huntington, reminisced nostalgically about the days when President Truman "had been able to govern the country with the cooperation of a relatively small number of Wall Street lawyers and bankers", so that democracy flourished in its proper form. But that was before the activism of the 1960s threatened to shatter these civilised arrangements.

The remedy to the crisis of excessive democracy, the scholars quite naturally concluded, was "more moderation in democracy", a return to passivity and obedience so that the responsible men could undertake, unhindered, their task of securing the permanent interests of the country by protecting "the minority of the opulent against the majority".

On the right, at the other end of the mainstream consensus, similar concerns were voiced, though in more impassioned rhetoric, notably in the influential Powell memorandum delivered to the Chamber of Commerce warning that civilisation itself was under threat from the rascal multitude. Putting aside the hysteria, the business world was deeply concerned by declining rates of profit and militant labour actions, with young workers who were infected by the disorder of "the time of troubles" demanding not just benefits but a measure of dignity and even some control over the workplace.

Such concerns constituted a large part of the background for the abandonment of the regimented capitalism of the postwar period, the *trente glorieuses*—in the US, the 'Golden Age' of capitalism, with the most rapid sustained growth in history and relatively egalitarian growth, offering opportunities that were being exploited by the ignorant and meddlesome outsiders.

The reversal of these dangerous tendencies under neoliberal doctrine led to the widely hailed 'great moderation', under the guiding hand of Alan Greenspan, lauded as one of the greatest economists of history. Greenspan explained to Congress that his successful management of the economy relied on "atypical restraint on compensation increases [that] appears to be mainly the consequence of greater worker insecurity", the growing 'precariat' in current terms.

All was fine until the deep recession of 2008, with its catastrophic impact on the population at large while the perpetrators were amply cared for by taxpayer largesse. The crisis "peeled away the façade and revealed an anger that had been building for decades", the chief economist of one of the world's major financial firms observed: "The crisis was horrific, but its legacy pushed us over the edge in terms of the discontent" that had indeed been building since the onset of the neoliberal assault that reversed the crisis of democracy and restored a more "optimal use of economic resources".

The essentials are reviewed by Barry Eichengreen in his standard history of the international monetary system. In the nineteenth century, he observes, governments had not yet been "politicised by universal male suffrage and the rise of trade unionism and parliamentary labour parties". Therefore the severe costs imposed by favoured market doctrines of the masters of mankind could be transferred to the general population. But with the radicalisation of the general public during the Great Depression and the anti-fascist war, that luxury was no longer available to private power and wealth. Hence in the postwar Bretton Woods system, "limits on capital mobility substituted for limits on democracy as a source of insulation from market pressures". It is only necessary to add the obvious corollary: with the dismantling of the system from the 1970s, functioning democracy is sharply restricted and it becomes necessary to divert and control the rascal multitude by other means.

The challenges we face are formidable. They can be confronted and overcome. But in the light of their severity, delay is not an option.

Conclusion

Yanis Varoufakis in conversation with David McWilliams

David McWilliams: *I think it is fair to say that capitalism—in the course of this unprecedented crisis—has been suspended. We are not going back to where we were, to 'business as usual'. The state has come back in, and this episode will not be forgotten by the electorate. I don't know where we are going, but one thing seems clear: we are not going back.*

Yanis Varoufakis: I like this phrase: capitalism has been suspended. The last time capitalism was suspended in the West was during the Second World War, with the advent of the war economy: a command economy that fixed prices. As James Kenneth Galbraith noted then, prices were already fixed by the cartels. But nevertheless, the war economy marked the transcendence of the standard capitalist model.

But what we see now is not so much the suspension of capitalism. The rules of capitalism may have been suspended—all those sacrosanct policies are gone, the neat separation of fiscal and monetary policy is gone, the idea that public debt is a bad thing is gone.

But the institutions that are necessary to build 'the war economy without war', so to speak—to suspend and transcend capitalism—those have not been put in place. There is a profound difference between saying, "It's all going to shit, so we don't expect you to stick to the rules", and saying, "The rules themselves have changed, and we must make new ones to prevent an economic collapse". All this talk of quantitative easing by the European Central Bank suggests that we remain very far from a war economy mindset.

DMW: *This is a familiar category error in Europe. If you are basing your economic policy on the willingness of people who are traumatised and sick to borrow—which is the core logic of quantitative easing—then you have a very serious problem. A common image of quantitative easing is the hose: a huge monetary hose, with water gushing out to stop the fire of crisis. But the hose of monetary policy is limited by this little valve called the banks, a little valve called the credit committee, a little valve called the 'willingness of business to borrow money'. And, ultimately, that hose of*

money becomes a trickle—and even that trickle stands to benefit the wealthy much
more than the poor.

So I take your point that despite the suspension of the rules, the infrastructure
remains in place. But let's go back to your point about J. K. Galbraith. At his core,
Galbraith believed in markets as the way that economies do work. And so I think we
have to take the suspension of capitalism as an initial iteration, and the second phase
is the reconstitution of capitalism. People across Europe are now coming around to the
DiEM25 position and saying, "Hey, there is an alternative". This second phase will be
about how we move ahead in rethinking capitalism, in rethinking finance, rethinking
how economies work and for whom—potentially toward a new Bretton Woods-style
settlement for the entire global economy.

So that's where we are: in the first year of the third decade of the twenty-first
century. The third decade of the twentieth century was a particularly nasty one—
also kicked off by a pandemic. Looking out at the next decade, armed with history
as well as economics, what do you think the global and European economy will look
like?

YV: We live in a dynamic that has two possible limiting cases—and we are sitting on
a saddle point, prepared to tip in either direction. It is utterly indeterminate which
of the two directions we travel.

Let us start with the positive scenario. It builds from your earlier point about the
prospects for a new Bretton Woods—with its particular manifestation in the
European Union.

Here, the DiEM25 programme has always been built on an answer to this hypo-
thetical question: if we are going to have continental consolidation, what should it
look like? It would not be federation, because we can see that—even though federation is more necessary than ever—it is less likely than ever, because the centrifugal
forces of the coronavirus crisis, the migration crisis, and the euro crisis are pulling
us apart. But the alternative is to deploy the existing institutions in a way that can
simulate a federated Europe, and we can do this tomorrow, if we so choose: to
provide immediate cash to all those who are struggling in poverty, to invest in the
green transition—all the planks of the DiEM programme. This is a simulation of
federation, which would open up the discussion toward federation in a positive
sense.

There is a glimmer of hope here, because there is a profound difference between
2020 and 2010. Back then, when Ireland and Greece went belly up, there were
remarkable dissimilarities between what our countries were experiencing and what
Germany was experiencing, what Holland was experiencing. Today, Germany's
industrial machine is broken—and was broken long before the coronavirus hit. Two
main industries—auto and machine tooling—were already in serious trouble. So
the fact that Germany is now in the same predicament as the rest of us offers a glimmer of hope that they might say: "What should we do?" It's no longer, "Your problem. Here's the Troika".

DMW: *"And we will send you the bill as well!" So that's the positive scenario. The interruption of 'business as usual' gives way to new policies and new possibilities for Europe and beyond. What's the other option?*

YV: Well, we humans—and we Europeans, in particular—love to miss fantastic opportunities and end up with dystopic outcomes instead. It's very likely that we will encounter the same recalcitrance by the same set of European ordoliberals, who will keep putting roadblocks in the way of moves toward a genuine, democratic federalism.

DMW: *Obviously, such a roadblock will have a disproportionate impact on the Southern member-states of the European Union. What do you think the impact of this particular trauma will have on, say, Italy—a founding member of the European Union, and a crucial part of Europe's emotional hinterland?*

YV: Every time there is a crisis in Europe, Italian growth potential rates fall. Every time there is a problem, Italy sinks deeper into stagnation—with Salvini waiting in the wings. If Frankfurt, Berlin, and Brussels fail again to move toward the positive scenario, Italy—not just Italy, but all of Europe's most devastated regions—will move again toward the neo-fascist right. In that case, all bets are off.

This is the endpoint of the negative scenario: a giant domino effect, leading to the disintegration of the European Union. Not that the EU will cease to exist. Only that it will become irrelevant, like the Commonwealth of Independent States.

DMW: *Oh, I remember the Commonwealth of Independent States very well…*

YV: It still exists! It still has an office in Moscow. So the negative scenario is that: the European Union will become like the CIS. And that will be music to the ears of the Trumps, Bolsonaros, and Modis of the world. We would move into a transactional, Hobbesian global economy: nasty, brutish, and poor for the majority of people.

DMW: *When I was born in Ireland, the country was very poor. And then it became quite wealthy, on the back of the European project, on the back of Europe's position in the global supply chain, and with a tax policy that attracted lots and lots of capital. My sense is this model might be gone, and this style of globalisation along with it. I fear that the period when you could travel, engage, move—we might have reached the end of that open period. People will say, "This virus came from the cosmopolitan world, from the world of international movement". Whether it's right or not, we might begin to blame people. We know that the Black Death resulted in ferocious anti-Semitism in Europe. People asked, "Who can we blame for this?" And so they blamed the one community that was already in isolation in the ghetto.*

This is what terrifies me most, sitting here in the first year of the third decade of the twenty-first century. What we saw before may come again, and we turn back to Yeats:

"Turning and turning in the widening gyre / The falcon cannot hear the falconer; / Things fall apart; the centre cannot hold; / Mere anarchy is loosed upon the world". I fear now, unless we move quickly and in a new direction, the world that my kids will inherit is going to turn very nasty indeed. So it's a clarion call.

YV: The loudest call in a generation. I share all of your concern for the future, although I must challenge the analysis upon which it is based. The openness that you describe has always gone hand in hand with severe restriction: NAFTA and the US-Mexico border; Freedom of Movement in Europe and Frontex along the Mediterranean. This is not a contradiction; it is the logic of a system that prizes the movement of capital over the freedom of human beings.

If we fail now to stand together—to rally around a new Bretton Woods, to deliver the investments that humanity and the planet so desperately need—my fear is that this system will only deepen its cruel logic. Surfing on the hose of liquidity unleashed by policies like quantitative easing, the financial sector will increase its grip on the global economy; bankers are very good at getting rich from such volatility. So now is the time for us, here in Europe as around the world, to mobilise behind this shared vision of a global new deal. Because without it, the walls between us will only get taller and thicker: porous only to the money that flows through them.

Appendix

Authors' Biographies

Marko Anđelić graduated in Architecture at the Sapienza University of Rome and is now working in organic farming, sustainable agritourism, and tourism. He is taking part in local struggles against the neoliberal urban politics both in Belgrade and in Rome.

Pamela Anderson is an actress and an activist.

Kate Aronoff is a staff writer for the *New Republic*. She is the co-author of *A Planet To Win: Why We Need A Green New Deal*, the co-author of *We Own The Future: Democratic Socialism American Style*, and the author of *Overheated: How Capitalism Broke The Planet—and How We Fight Back*.

Renata Avila is an international human rights lawyer, specialising in the next wave of technological challenges to preserve and advance our rights, and to understand better the politics of data and their implications for trade, democracy, and society. She is a member of the Coordinating Collective of DiEM25, and a board member for Creative Commons.

Anthony Barnett is co-founder of openDemocracy, author of *The Lure of Greatness*, and an advisor to DiEM25.

Franco Berardi, aka Bifo, is a philosopher and writer. His latest book, *The Second Coming*, has been published by Polity Press.

Francesca Bria is currently the Commissioner of Digital Technology and Innovation for the City of Barcelona in Spain. She is an adviser for the European Commission on Future Internet and Innovation Policy and is leading the DECODE project on data sovereignty in Europe. She is Associate Professor at ESADE Business School and Visiting Professor at the Institute for Innovation and Public Purpose, UCL.

Noam Chomsky is a world-renowned linguist, philosopher, and political activist. He is regarded as the father of modern linguistics. He has authored over 100 books on topics in his field and on issues of dissent and US foreign policy. Chomsky is currently Institute Professor Emeritus at the Massachusetts Institute of Technology (MIT).

John Christensen is Chair of the Tax Justice Network.

Fabio De Masi is Vice Chairman and Financial Spokesperson for Die Linke and a Member of the German Bundestag.

Brian Eno is a musician, composer, producer, writer, and activist. He is best known for his pioneering work in ambient music and contributions to rock, pop, electronic, and generative music. Eno is a member of the Labour Party, President of the Stop the War Coalition, a trustee of the Institute for Innovation and Public Purpose, and a member of DiEM25's Coordinating Collective since its conception.

Daniel Erlacher is one of the founders of the Elevate Festival in Graz. He coordinates the discourse and activism team of the festival. Before working with Elevate he promoted music events in Graz and ran a record label including an international community website for a duration of more than fifteen years.

James K. Galbraith teaches at The University of Texas at Austin. He is the author of *Welcome to the Poisoned Chalice: The Destruction of Greece and the Future of Europe* (Yale UP, 2016) published in English, Greek, French, and Polish editions.

Ksenia Gerasimova is Affiliated Lecturer at the University of Cambridge and Professor in Public Policy in the Higher School of Economics, Russia. She has been involved in agricultural practices such as urban gardening since her childhood and sees her mission as promoting sustainable agriculture.

Bobby Gillespie is a singer and songwriter with the rock and roll band Primal Scream. Born in Glasgow, Scotland. A lifelong socialist and internationalist.

Alice-Mary Higgins is an Independent Senator and leader of the Civil Engagement Group in the Irish Seanad. She seeks to strengthen connections between politics and civil society and is not a representative of DiEM25 or any political party. This short piece is an updating of a contribution she made at a DiEM25 event in 2017.

Olivier Hoedeman is the coordinator at Corporate Europe Observatory (CEO), which he cofounded twenty years ago. He is also co-founder of the Alliance for Lobbying Transparency and Ethics Regulation (ALTER-EU) and several other civil society coalitions. He has co-authored books such as *Europe Inc.* (2000), *Reclaiming Public Water* (2005), and *Bursting the Brussels Bubble* (2010).

Srećko Horvat is a philosopher born in Croatia (then Yugoslavia) in 1983. Author of numerous books, most recently *Poetry from the Future* (Penguin, 2019), *Subversion!* (Zero, 2017), *The Radicality of Love* (Polity, 2015) and *What Does Europe Want?* (co-authored with Slavoj Žižek). He is one of the co-founders of DiEM25 and a member of its Coordinating Collective.

Sam Hufton is a student at King's College London and member of DiEM25 since February 2016, involved in the London DSC. Alongside his studies, he writes a blog on European politics and history: *Evropaïki Dimokratía*.

Tim Jackson is Director of the Centre for the Understanding of Sustainable Prosperity (CUSP) and the author of *Prosperity without Growth*.

Katrín Jakobsdóttir is the Prime Minister of Iceland and the Leader of the Left-Green Movement. She holds an MA degree in literature from the University of Iceland and a BA in Icelandic and French from the same university. Katrín was first elected to the Icelandic Parliament in 2007 and she served as Minister for Education, Culture and Science in the post-crash left-wing government from 2009 to 2013. She is the second female prime minister of Iceland.

Leila Jancovich is Associate Professor at the University of Leeds, where she leads an interdisciplinary research centre on cultural policy and a knowledge exchange network on cultural participation. Her research examines power and decision-making within cultural policy with a focus on the implications of participatory governance for the cultural sector.

Naomi Klein is an award-winning journalist, syndicated columnist and author of the *New York Times* and international bestsellers, *No is Not Enough: Resisting Trump's Shock Politics and Winning the World We Need* (2017), *This Changes Everything: Capitalism vs the Climate* (2014), *The Shock Doctrine: The Rise of Disaster Capitalism* (2007) and *No Logo* (2000).

Paul Laverty worked as a human rights lawyer in Central America before becoming a screenwriter. He has worked principally with directors Ken Loach (twelve films together, including Cannes Palme d'Or winners *The Wind that Shakes the Barley* and *I, Daniel Blake*) and Icíar Bollaín (three films together, including *Even the Rain*, Panorama winner at Berlin Festival).

Ken Loach was born in 1936 in Nuneaton. He attended King Edward VI Grammar School and went on to study law at St. Peter's Hall, Oxford. After a brief spell in the theatre, Loach was recruited by the BBC in 1963 as a television director. This launched a long career directing films for television and the cinema, from *Cathy Come Home* and *Kes* in the sixties to *Land And Freedom*, *Sweet Sixteen*, *The Wind*

That Shakes The Barley (Palme d'Or, Cannes Film Festival 2006), *Looking for Eric, The Angels' Share, I, Daniel Blake* (Palme d'Or, Cannes Film Festival 2016), and *Sorry We Missed You.*

Caroline Lucas is the Green Party's first MP, representing Brighton Pavilion. She has also served both as the Party Leader and Co-Leader. Caroline is an active campaigner on a range of issues and has consistently been voted the UK's most ethical politician. She has won awards for her work on tackling social exclusion, wildlife protection, women's rights and is in the Environment Agency's Top 100 Eco-Heroes of all time.

Miltos Manetas is a Greek painter, conceptual artist, and theorist, the founder of NEEN (a twenty-first-century art movement), a pioneer of art-after-videogames (MACHINIMA) and an instigator of Post-Internet. His artist's profile can be found at manetas.com while his social activism and ideas are at metamanetas.com.

Lorenzo Marsili is a philosopher, author, and political activist. He is the co-founder of the transnational NGO European Alternatives and was one of the initiators of the pan-European movement DiEM25. His latest book in English is *Citizens of Nowhere* (Zed Books, 2018). He is an active public speaker and media commentator and was the founding editor of cult independent journal *Naked Punch Review.*

Raoul Martinez is a philosopher, artist, filmmaker, and the author of *Creating Freedom.* He lives and works in London.

Bill McKibben is founder of the international climate campaign 350.org, a winner of the Right Livelihood Award, and author most recently of *Falter: Has the Human Game Begun to Play Itself Out?*

David McWilliams is an economist, author, journalist, documentary-maker, and broadcaster. He is Adjunct Professor of Global Economics at the School of Business Trinity College Dublin. He has written five bestsellers, one of which, *The Pope's Children*, is the best-selling nonfiction title published in Ireland this century.

Aleksandar Mirčov is VP of Operations for AdColony and holds a Master of Science in Business from San Francisco State University.

Vlassis Missos is a political economist and research fellow at the Centre of Planning and Economic Research in Athens, Greece. He has published on issues concerning social policy and income inequality, as well as on the history of economic thought.

Jakob Mohr is a member of DiEM25's National Collective in Germany. In recent years he helped build the movement's presence in Berlin and contributed to DiEM25's draft policy paper on forced migration.

Evgeny Morozov is a writer and thinker about the social and political implications of information technology. He is the author of *The Net Delusion* (2011) and *To Save Everything, Click Here* (2013) and writes regularly for international media. He holds a PhD in History of Science from Harvard University and has been a visiting scholar at Georgetown and Stanford Universities. He is also the founder of The Syllabus, a media project that seeks to make serious and academic knowledge more accessible to the general public, and is part of Unesco's high-level international commission on the future of education.

Preethi Nallu, writer, researcher and visual storyteller, has reported on displacement issues across the globe for news media, UN agencies, think tanks, and advocacy groups. After years of covering migration issues in the Mediterranean, she has started documenting returns of Afghan and Syrian refugees.

Rasmus Nordqvist is a member of the Danish Parliament representing Alternativet.

Xristina Penna is a performance practitioner, lecturer, and a co-founding member of DiEM Voice. In her performance work and research she investigates how participatory performance processes can be informed by neuroscience theories of human consciousness and cognition in order to facilitate collaborative thinking.

Ann Pettifor is best known for her prediction of the Great Financial Crisis in *The Coming First World Debt Crisis* (Palgrave, 2006). She edited the New Economics Foundation's *Real World Economic Outlook* (Palgrave, 2003) and, in 2008, co-authored The Green New Deal published by NEF. In 2017, Verso published *The Production of Money* on the nature of money, debt, and the finance sector.

Gerardo Pisarello is a professor in constitutional law, elected to the Spanish Congress of Deputies in April 2019 as part of the En Comú Podem coalition. From 2015 to 2019, he served as First Deputy Mayor of the city of Barcelona as part of the municipalist platform Barcelona en Comú, with responsibility for economy, work, and strategic planning.

Adam Ramsay is a writer, activist, journalist, and the co-editor of openDemocracyUK and (with Peter Geoghegan) heads up the Dark Money Investigation team looking into who is bankrolling UK and EU politics. He also works with Bright Green, and was a full-time campaigner with People & Planet.

Denis Jaromil Roio is an activist, hacker, artist, and co-founder of dyne.org. He has published several free and open-source software projects and his research focuses on decentralisation, algorithms, independent media practices, and community-based development.

Jerome Roos is a Fellow in International Political Economy at the London School of Economics, and author of *Why Not Default? The Political Economy of Sovereign Debt*. He is currently working on a history of global crises.

Bertie Russell is a Researcher at the University of Sheffield Urban Institute, and has written on Municipalism in *Antipode*, *Roar Magazine*, openDemocracy, and *Red Pepper*. Unreferenced quotes come from personal interviews conducted with municipalist activists.

Jeffrey Sachs is a world-renowned economics professor and global leader in sustainable development. He is Director of the UN Sustainable Development Solutions Network, a commissioner of the UN Broadband Commission for Development, and an SDG Advocate for UN Secretary General António Guterres. Professor Sachs is a University Professor at Columbia University and the Director of its Centre for Sustainable Development.

Saskia Sassen is the Robert S. Lynd Professor of Sociology and a member of The Committee on Global Thought, Columbia University, which she chaired until 2015. Together, her authored books are translated in over twenty languages. Her awards include election to the Royal Academy of Sciences of the Netherlands, and being made a Chevalier de l'Ordre des Arts et des Lettres by the French government. One recent book is *Expulsions: Brutality and Complexity in the Global Economy* (Harvard UP, 2014).

Vladimir Šestović graduated with a Masters in European Affairs at Paris III University. He is now working for a network of NGOs and citizens' movements, monitoring fundamental rights, and advocating for the general interest and common good in European institutions.

Elif Shafak is an award-winning British-Turkish novelist, the most widely read female author in Turkey, and has published seventeen books, eleven of which are novels, translated into fifty languages. An advocate for women's rights, LGBT rights, and freedom of speech, Shafak has judged numerous literary prizes..

Nicholas Shaxson is a journalist and writer. He is author of *Poisoned Wells*, a book about African oil; *Treasure Islands*, a book about tax havens, and *The Finance Curse*, a book about how oversized financial centres damage the countries that host them. He also writes for the Tax Justice Network.

Quinn Slobodian teaches history at Wellesley College. His most recent book is *Globalists: The End of Empire and the Birth of Neoliberalism*.

Jonas Staal is a visual artist whose work deals with the relation between art, propaganda, and democracy. He is the founder of the artistic and political organisation

New World Summit (2012–ongoing) and the campaign New Unions (2016–ongoing). His latest book is *Propaganda Art in the 21st Century* (The MIT Press, 2019).

Cole Stangler is a Paris-based journalist covering labour and politics. A writer and producer at France 24 English, Cole is also a contributor to *Jacobin*, *The Nation*, the *Washington Post* and *The Guardian*. He holds a Masters in Contemporary Social History from the University of Paris 1, Panthéon-Sorbonne.

Lyndsey Stonebridge is the author of *Placeless People: Writing, Rights, and Refugees*. She is Professor of Humanities and Human Rights at the University of Birmingham, UK.

Danae Stratou is an artist whose work consists of large-scale installations and audio-visual environments. She has shown her work internationally, including at the Venice Biennale (1999). She is founder of Vital Space, a global, interdisciplinary media platform addressing contemporary issues of art and politics, and initiator of DiEM Voice, the artistic platform of the pan-European political movement DiEM25.

Pawel Wargan is an activist and organiser based in Berlin. He co-founded and coordinates the Green New Deal for Europe campaign, sits on the Coordinating Collective of the Democracy in Europe Movement (DiEM25) and serves as the Coordinator of the Secretariat at the Progressive International. He publishes regularly in *Jacobin*, the *New Statesman*, *Tribune* and *Politico*.

Eyal Weizman is a British-Israeli architect, Professor of Spatial and Visual Cultures at Goldsmiths, University of London, and Director of Forensic Architecture. He is a founding member of the architectural collective DAAR in Beit Sahour/Palestine. His books include *Forensic Architecture: Violence at the Threshold of Detectability* (2017), *The Conflict Shoreline* (with Fazal Sheikh, 2015), *The Least of All Possible Evils* (2011), and *Hollow Land* (2007). In 2018, Forensic Architecture won the European Cultural Foundation Princess Margriet Award for Culture.

Slavoj Žižek is a Hegelian philosopher, Lacanian psychoanalyst, and Marxist social analyst. His recent work is focused on the possibilities of emancipation in today's global capitalism. His latest publications include *Like a Thief in Broad Daylight* (Penguin/Allen Lane, 2019) and *Incontinence in the Void* (MIT Press, 2018).

Shoshana Zuboff has devoted her career at the Berkman Centre for Internet and Society at Harvard Law School to the study of the rise of the digital, its individual, organisational, and social consequences, and its relationship to the history and future of capitalism. Her latest book is *The Age of Surveillance Capitalism: The Fight for a Human Future at the New Frontier of Power*, published in 2019 by PublicAffairs in the US and Campus Verlag in Germany.